A Bibliography
of the Works of
ROBERT
GRAVES

by

FRED H. HIGGINSON

LONDON
NICHOLAS VANE
1966

First published in 1966
by Nicholas Vane (Publishers) Ltd
London

Published in the United States by
The Shoe String Press, Inc.
60 Connolly Parkway, Hamden, Ct.

c

231845 Gen.

Printed in England by
Adlard and Son Limited
London and Dorking

CONTENTS

ILLUSTRATIONS

to

MY FRIENDS' CHILDREN

INTRODUCTION

THE ARRANGEMENT of works in this bibliography differs slightly from the customary plan, especially in Section A, because the career of Robert Graves differs from the customary literary career. Section A, therefore, includes not only books and pamphlets written by Graves alone, but also those written in collaboration with others and works edited, largely re-written or translated by him. About one-fourth of the material included in Section A falls into one or more of these latter categories:

1. Collaborations: the books written with Laura Riding, Alan Hodge, Joshua Podro and Raphael Patai.
2. 'Editions': the Skelton and nursery rhyme collections, both editions of the ballad books and the edition of letters from T. E. Lawrence.
3. Rewritings: *The Real David Copperfield*, the two books by Frank Richards and the Echard translation of Terence.
4. Translations: Apuleius, Galvan, Alarcon, Sand, Lucan, Suetonius, Hesiod, Homer and (with Laura Riding) Schwarz.

Section B consists of books and pamphlets containing contributions by Graves; but this otherwise unwieldy section has been restricted by the inclusion of first book printings only. Section C consists of contributions to press and periodicals, including a few translations. Section D consists of brief notes on manuscripts, phonograph records, music, ephemera and material which could not be included elsewhere. Section E is a highly selective bibliography of works about Graves. Introductory notes to each section explain the conventions.

The terminal date for Sections B–E is 31 December 1964; but it has been possible to include a few 1965 publications in A.

Finally, I should welcome the reproach of those who will be kind enough to inform me of additions or corrections which need to be made in the bibliography.

Cambridge
May 1965

ACKNOWLEDGEMENTS

WORK ON THIS BIBLIOGRAPHY was begun on a Faculty Fellowship from the Fund for the Advancement of Education. Support has been given at several times by the Faculty Research Fund of Kansas State University. And the Board of Regents of the State of Kansas granted the sabbatical leave during which final checking was possible.

A great many people have helped with the assembly of information. Professor Graves himself has replied graciously to such requests for information as I have had to make; so have his agents, A. P. Watt and Son and Willis Kingsley Wing. David Posner of the Lockwood Memorial Library made its extensive collection available to me at an early stage of work; in addition, their collection of manuscripts, arranged by him, is a model of how to order difficult material both usefully and elegantly; other scholars must be equally indebted to him. I should also like to thank Marguerite Bagshaw, Boys and Girls House, Toronto Public Libraries; V. C. Clinton-Baddeley, Jupiter Recordings; Blackwell's, Oxford; C. F. H. Evans, former Librarian of Charterhouse; George J. Firmage; Gotham Book Mart; Alan Hancox; Brian Haylett, who tracked down the 'FUZE' material; Selwyn Jepson; Mike Klug; Robert P. Mills; Anthony Newnham; Ed Quigley; F. W. Roberts and Mrs Ann Bowden of the Humanities Research Center of the University of Texas; Anthony Rota; Martha Shepard of the National Library of Canada, Ottawa; Violet Taylor of the University of Toronto Library; L. A. Wallrich; H. L. White of the National Library of Australia, Canberra; and G. Woledge of the British Library of Political and Economic Science.

I must also mention certain libraries of which I have made extensive use: the Lockwood Memorial Library of the State University of New York at Buffalo (Miss Anna Russell and David Posner); Yale University Library (John Ottemiller and Miss Barbara Simison); the Beinecke Library at Yale; the New York Public Library and the Henry W. and Albert A. Berg Collection of English and American Literature (John D. Gordan, Curator); the Kansas State University Library (Melvin Voigt, Joe Kraus, Elizabeth Davis, Edith M. Ridgeway, Thoburn Taggart, David May, Mrs Ellyn Taylor and James Mathews); the University of Kansas Library; the Library of Congress (Charles Goodrum, Roger J. Trienens, Frederick R. Goff, Alfred D. Hagle); the Cambridge University Library; and the British Museum and the Newspaper Library at Colindale. Less extensively, but quite as indispensably, the following libraries have lent books and answered requests for interlibrary loans: Antioch College Library; Arizona University Library; Brown University Library; Chicago

Public Library; Cleveland Public Library; Denver Public Library and the Rocky Mountain Bibliographical Center; Detroit Public Library; Harvard University Library; Haverford College Library; Newberry Library; New Mexico University Library; Oberlin College Library; University of Chicago Library; University of Cincinnati Library; University of Illinois Library; State University of Iowa Library; University of Michigan Library; University of Minnesota Library; University of Missouri Library; University of Utah Library; Western Reserve University Library and the Midwest Bibliographical Center; Wichita State University Library.

The following publishers and publications have responded patiently and helpfully to questions: Aldine Publishing Co.; George Allen & Unwin Ltd; W. H. Allen & Co. Ltd; The American Foundation for the Blind; *American Heritage*; The American Printing House for the Blind; Angus and Robertson Ltd; Arrow Books; Artemis Verlag; Avon Books; Arthur Barker Ltd; Beacon Press; Ernest Benn Ltd; Basil Blackwell; Books for Pleasure Ltd; British Broadcasting Corporation; Jonathan Cape Ltd; Cassell & Co. Ltd; William Collins Sons & Co. Ltd; William Collins Sons & Co. Canada, Ltd; Constable & Co. Ltd; *Daily Mail*; Dial Press; Doubleday & Co., Inc.; Drian Galleries; E. P. Dutton & Co. Inc.; *Evening News*; Eyre and Spottiswoode Ltd; Faber & Faber Ltd; Farrar Straus and Cudahy; Film Images, Inc.; Folio Society Ltd; Samuel French Inc.; *Gentleman's Quarterly*; *Georgia Review*; Victor Gollancz Ltd; Grosset & Dunlap Inc.; *The Guardian*; Hamish Hamilton Ltd; *Harper's Bazaar*; William Heinemann Ltd; Hogarth Press Ltd; Holt, Rinehart & Winston; *The Humanist*; Hutchinson Publishing Group; Indiana University Press; Michael Joseph Ltd; Alfred A. Knopf; Lawrence & Wishart; Literary Guild; Longmans Green & Co. Ltd; George J. McLeod Ltd; Macmillan Co.; May Fair Books; Mayflower Books Ltd; Methuen & Co. Ltd; National Library for the Blind; Thomas Nelson & Sons (Canada) Ltd; New English Library Ltd; *The Observer*; Oxford University Press; Penguin Books Ltd; Perpetua Ltd; Pocket Books Inc.; Poetry Book Society; Clarkson N. Potter Inc.; *Queen*; Random House Inc.; Readers Union Ltd; Routledge & Kegan Paul Ltd; S. J. Reginald Saunders and Co. Ltd; Martin Secker and Warburg Ltd; Sidgwick & Jackson Ltd; Stamperia del Santuccio; *Sunday Telegraph*; *Sunday Times*; Time Inc.; Vallentine, Mitchell & Co. Ltd; William H. Wise & Co. Inc.; *Woman*; Thomas Yoseloff.

BOOKS AND PAMPHLETS BY ROBERT GRAVES, ALONE OR IN COLLABORATION, AND WORKS EDITED, TRANSLATED OR REWRITTEN BY HIM

Graves has issued several books in revised versions. Each edition of his collected poems is listed separately; but revisions or abridgements of other books are listed under the earlier book.

Collations. Occasionally a notation such as $X/X^{\star 8/8}$ is used; this signifies an octavo in sixteens, signed on $X1$ and $X9 (=X^{\star}1)$. No notice has been taken of signings on second and/or third leaves of a regular gathering.

Bulk. For cloth-bound books the notation $2 \cdot 3/2 \cdot 8$ cm. means that the sheets and endpapers bulk $2 \cdot 3$ cm. and that with the binding included the bulk is $2 \cdot 8$ cm.

Number of copies. It has not always been possible to determine the number of copies. 'Unknown' means that the publisher no longer knows; 'undisclosed' means that he has not revealed the number; 'undetermined' means that the publisher no longer exists or has not responded to letters.

Contents. When not given, the contents of subsequent volumes with the same number may be assumed to be that of the first edition.

Dust-jackets. These are described where seen; others certainly exist.

Edition. Interest, notoriety or descriptive detail have sometimes necessitated separate listings for different impressions of the same edition; but generally subdivisions represent separate editions. Second and later editions are described in some detail. A certain light is thus thrown on Graves as a popular author, on modern publishing practice (see the extraordinary collations of the Belle Sauvage editions, the accommodation of the type of revision done in *The White Goddess* and the unusual succession of editions of *Old Soldiers Never Die*) and on the texts themselves.

a. First edition:

OVER THE BRAZIER | BY | ROBERT GRAVES | LON-
DON | THE POETRY BOOKSHOP | 35 DEVONSHIRE
STREET., THEOBALDS ROAD., W.C. | 1916

Collation: [1]⁴ 2–4⁴, 16 leaves.
p. [1] title-page; p. [2] blank; p. [3] CONTENTS; p. [4] THE POET IN THE
NURSERY; pp. [5] 6–17 [18] 19–32 text.

20·4 × 15·0 cm. Bulk: 0·5 cm. White wove paper; top edges unopened;
fore and lower edges untrimmed. Bound in grey paper covers; front
cover: OVER THE BRAZIER | [cut in black with blue background and soldiers
around red brazier] | BY | ROBERT GRAVES | THE POETRY BOOKSHOP 8ᴰ·
NET; inside front and back covers: publisher's advertisements; back cover:
blank.

Price: 8d. Number of copies unknown. Published 1 May 1916.

Contents: The Poet in the Nursery – [Charterhouse:] – The Dying
Knight and the Fauns – Willaree – The Face of the Heavens – Jolly Yellow
Moon – Youth and Folly – Ghost Music – Free Verse – In the Wilder-
ness – Oh, and Oh! – Cherry-Time – [La Bassée:] – On Finding Myself
a Soldier – The Shadow of Death – A Renascence – The Morning before
the Battle – Limbo – The Trenches – The First Funeral – The Adventure – I
Hate the Moon – Big Words – The Dead Fox Hunter – It's a Queer
Time – 1915 – Over the Brazier

Notes: Impressions: 2nd, 1917.
The design of Menin Gate on the cover is by Claud Lovat Fraser.

b. Second edition ([1920]):

OVER THE BRAZIER | BY ROBERT GRAVES | LON-
DON – THE POETRY | BOOKSHOP, 35 DEVONSHIRE |
ST., THEOBALDS RD. W.C.1

Collation: [1]–[2]⁸, 16 leaves.
p. [1] title-page; p. [2] list of books by Graves and edition notice; p. [3]
FOREWORD TO NEW EDITION; p. [4] THE POET IN THE NURSERY; p. [5] PART
I. – Poems Mostly Written | at Charterhouse – 1910–1914; pp. 6–18
text; p. [19] PART II. – Poems Written | Before La Bassée – 1915; p. [20]
blank; pp. 21 [22] 23–30 [31] 32 text.

21·4 × 13·8 cm. Bulk: 0·3/0·6 cm. White wove paper; all edges trimmed. White laid endpapers watermarked: [in double-rule rectangular box enclosing also clubs and balls:] Golf [and] J. R. Lockwood & Co. Bound in grey boards with narrow medium-blue cloth spine; back and spine blank; front, in blue: OVER THE BRAZIER | BY ROBERT GRAVES | [cut as cover of A1a, but blue only] | THE POETRY BOOKSHOP

Price: 3s. Number of copies: 1,000. Published in May 1920.

Contents: As A1a, but omitting 'On Finding Myself a Soldier' and 'A Renascence.'

A2 GOLIATH AND DAVID [1916]

First edition:

GOLIATH AND DAVID | BY | ROBERT GRAVES

Collation: 10 leaves, unsigned, sewn at centre.
p. [1] title-page; p. [2] blank; pp. 3–17 text; p. [18] printer's notice; pp. [19–20] blank.

18·2 × 13·7 cm. Bulk: 0·2 cm. White laid paper; all edges untrimmed. Bound in heavy dark red paper cover; all sides blank.

Not for sale. Number of copies: 200. Printed late in 1916.

Contents: The Bough of Nonsense – Goliath and David – A Pinch of Salt – Babylon – Careers – The Lady Visitor in the Pauper Ward – The Last Post – A Dead Boche – Escape – Not Dead

Notes: Printer: Chiswick Press: Charles Whittingham & Co., Tooks Court, Chancery Lane, London.

Boutell (E33, 1930), who consulted Graves, assigns the date 1916 to this book and says there were '150 copies, possibly less.' An unpublished letter from Siegfried Sassoon, dated 27 February 1917, says that 118 copies of the book had by that time been distributed by him according to Graves' instructions and that 82 copies remained at the printer's for his disposal. Graves himself now 'guesses' that the book was published in December 1916. Both versions of *Good-Bye to All That* speak of *Over the Brazier* as Graves' first book. The impression which exists in some quarters that *Goliath and David* is Graves' first book would therefore appear to be erroneous; and while the book is something of a rarity in catalogues, records of the Chiswick Press (British Museum Add. MS. 50927, f. 288b), dated 28 February 1917, state that 200 copies were printed.

a. First edition:

FAIRIES AND | FUSILIERS | BY | ROBERT GRAVES | [*publisher's emblem*] | LONDON | WILLIAM HEINEMANN

Collation: [A]⁴ χ² B–L⁴ M², 48 leaves.
2 pp. blank; p. [i] FAIRIES AND FUSILIERS; p. [ii] publisher's advertisements; p. [iii] title-page; p. iv publisher's notice; p. [v] TO THE ROYAL WELCH FUSILIERS; p. [vi] blank; p. vii acknowledgement; p. [viii] blank; pp. ix–x CONTENTS; pp. 1–83 text; p. [84] text and printer's notice.

18·0 × 11·9 cm. Bulk: 1·3/1·6 cm. Heavy white wove paper; all edges trimmed. Light white wove endpapers. Bound in wine-red cloth; front and back blank; spine stamped in gold: Fairies | and | Fusiliers | [*leaf and curlicue design*] | Robert | Graves | HEINEMANN

Price: 3s. 6d. Number of copies: 1,000. Published 8 November 1917.

Contents: To an Ungentle Critic – The Legion – To Lucasta on Going to the Wars-for the Fourth Time – Two Fusiliers – To Robert Nichols – Dead Cow Farm – Goliath and David – Babylon – Mr. Philosopher – The Cruel Moon – Finland – A Pinch of Salt – The Caterpillar – Sorley's Weather – The Cottage – The Last Post – When I'm Killed – Letter to S. S. from Mametz Wood – A Dead Boche – Faun – The Spoilsport – The Shivering Beggar – Jonah – John Skelton – I Wonder What It Feels Like to be Drowned? – Double Red Daisies – Careers – I'd Love to Be a Fairy's Child – The Next War – Strong Beer – Marigolds – The Lady Visitor in the Pauper's Ward – Love and Black Magic – Smoke-Rings – A Child's Nightmare – Escape – The Bough of Nonsense – Not Dead – A Boy in Church – Corporal Stare – The Assault Heroic – The Poet in the Nursery – In the Wilderness – Cherry-Time – 1915 – Free Verse

Notes: Impressions: 2nd, January 1919; it collates [A]⁴ B–L⁴ [M]⁴, 48 leaves; p. [iv] adds an edition notice; size: 18·0 × 12·0 cm.; bound in bright red cloth.

b. First American edition (1918):

Fairies | and Fusiliers | *By* | Robert Graves | [*publisher's emblem*] | New York | Alfred A. Knopf | MCMXVIII

Collation: [1]–[5]⁸ [6]⁴ [7]⁸, 52 leaves.
p. [i] [2 ll. at upper left:] Fairies | and Fusiliers | [at lower right:] [*pub-*

TREASURE BOX

BY

ROBERT GRAVES

GOLIATH AND DAVID

BY

ROBERT GRAVES

The title pages of *Treasure Box* (A4) and *Goliath and David* (A2)

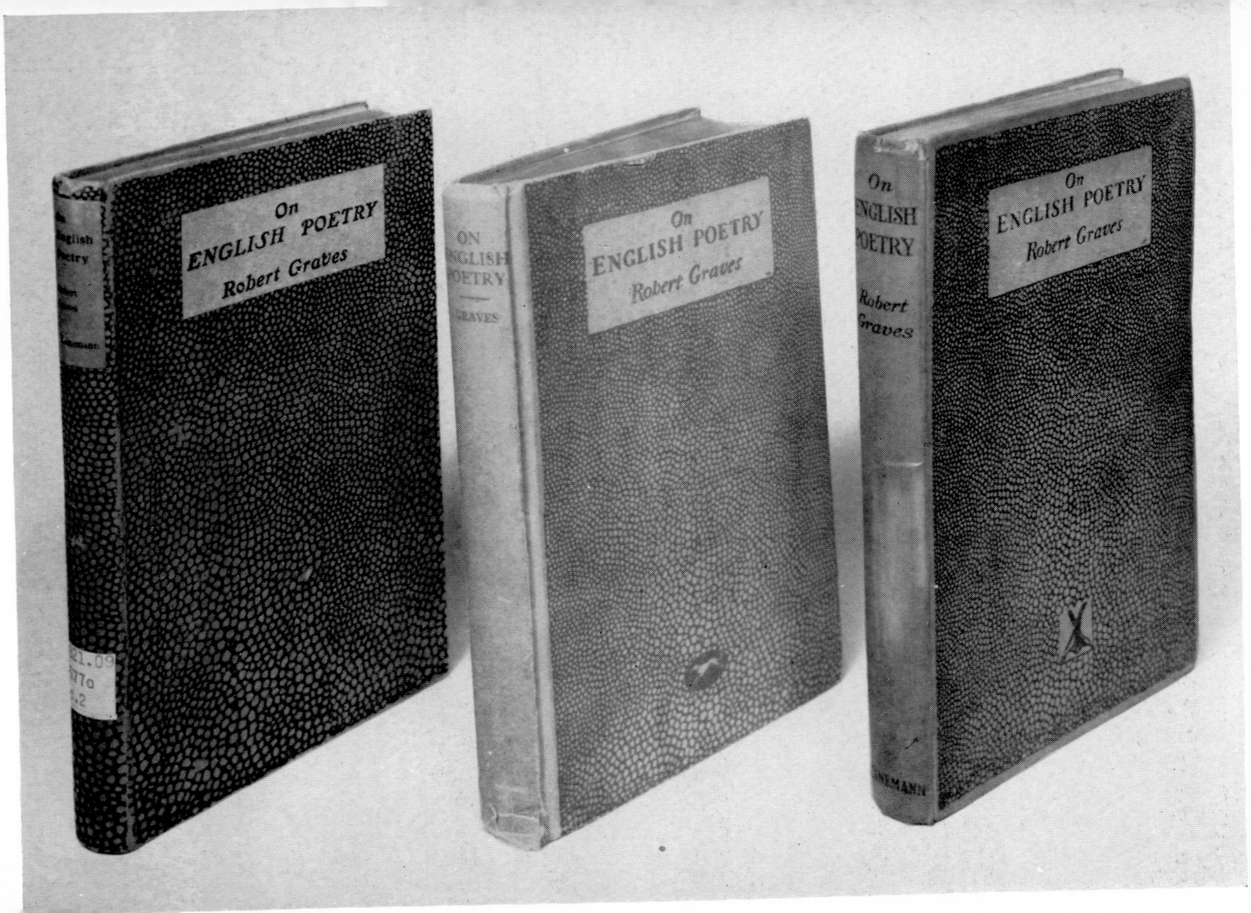

Three bindings of
On English Poetry
(A7b2, a, b1)

lisher's emblem]; p. [ii] publisher's advertisement; p. [iii] title-page; p. [iv] copyright and printing notices; p. [v] *TO | THE ROYAL WELCH FUSILIERS;* p. [vi] blank; p. [vii] acknowledgement; p. [viii] blank; pp. [ix–x] CONTENTS; pp. 1–94 text.

15·5 × 10·3 cm. Bulk: 1·0/1·4 cm. White wove paper watermarked with a D in a diamond and a script Regal Antique; top and fore-edges trimmed; top edge stained chartreuse. White wove endpapers. Bound in bright blue boards; chartreuse label pasted from front to back across spine; on front and back: [*rule*] | FAIRIES | *AND FUSILIERS* | *POEMS BY* | *ROBERT GRAVES* | [*rule*]; on spine: [*rule*] | *Fairies* | *and* | *Fusiliers* | *by* | *Robert* | *Graves* | *1918* | [*rule*].

Price: $1.00. Number of copies undisclosed. Published in November 1918.

c. *Second American edition* (*1919*):

FAIRIES | AND FUSILIERS | BY | ROBERT GRAVES | [*publisher's emblem*] | NEW YORK | ALFRED · A · KNOPF | MCMXIX

Collation: [1]–[6]⁸, 48 leaves.
p. [3] [2 ll. at right:] FAIRIES | AND FUSILIERS; p. [4] publisher's advertisements; p. [5] title-page; p. [6] copyright and printing notices; p. [7] *TO | THE ROYAL WELCH FUSILIERS;* p. [8] acknowledgement; pp. [9–10] CONTENTS; p. [11] [flush right:] FAIRIES AND FUSILIERS; p. [12] blank; pp. 13–97 text; p. [98] blank.

15·2 × 10·4 cm. Bulk: 0·9/1·1 cm. White wove paper watermarked OLDE STYLE; all edges trimmed. White wove endpapers watermarked OLDE STYLE. Bound in maroon cloth embossed with fine diagonal cross-hatching; chartreuse label as A3*b*, printed in blue; *1918* becomes *1919*.

Price: $1.25. Number of copies undisclosed. Published in May 1919.

A4   TREASURE BOX   [1919]

First edition:

TREASURE BOX | [*rule*] | [*cut of girl looking into box*] | BY | ROBERT GRAVES

Collation: 8 leaves, unsigned, stapled at centre.
p. [1] title-page; p. [2] blank; pp. 3–11 text; p. [12] illustration; pp. 13–14 text; p. [15] printer's notice; p. [16] blank.

17·8 × 13·5 cm. Bulk: 0·1 cm. White laid paper watermarked ALD-
WYCH; all edges trimmed. Bound in light blue paper covers; all sides
blank.

Not for sale. Number of copies: 200. Printed *c.* December 1919.

Contents: Morning Phoenix – Catherine Henry – The Kiss – Lost Love –
Fox's Dingle – Four Rhymes from *The Penny Fiddle:* The Dream – The
Fiddler – The Gifts – Mirror, Mirror

Note: Printer: Chiswick Press, Tooks Court, Chancery Lane, London.

Records of the Chiswick Press (British Museum Add. MS. 50928, f. 72b),
dated 20 January 1920, state that 200 copies were printed.

A5   COUNTRY SENTIMENT   [1920]

a. First edition:

COUNTRY SENTIMENT | BY ROBERT GRAVES | LONDON: MARTIN SECKER

Collation: [A]⁸⁻¹ B–D⁸ E⁸⁺¹, 40 leaves.
p. [3] COUNTRY SENTIMENT; p. [4] blank; p. [5] title-page; p. [6] edition
and printer's notice; p. [7] TO | NANCY NICHOLSON; p. [8] NOTE; pp. 9–10
CONTENTS; pp. 11–63 text; p. [64] blank; p. [65] RETROSPECT; p. [66]
blank; pp. 67–81 text; p. [82] blank.

18·7 × 12·6 cm. Bulk: 0·9/1·2 cm. White wove paper; top edges only
trimmed. White wove endpapers. Bound in light blue boards with
cobbled design; front and back blank; label pasted at top of spine: [*rule*] |
Country | *Sentiment* | [*diamond*] | *Robert* | *Graves* | [*rule*].

Price: 5s. Number of copies: 1,000. Published in March 1920.

Contents: A Frosty Night – Song for Two Children – Dicky – The Three
Drinkers – The Boy out of Church – After the Play – One Hard Look –
True Johnny – The Voice of Beauty Drowned – The God Called Poetry –
Rocky Acres – Advice to Lovers – Nebuchadnezzar's Fall – Give Us
Rain – Allie – Loving Henry – Brittle Bones – Apples and Water –
Manticor in Arabia – Outlaws – Balloo Loo for Jenny – Hawk and Buckle –
The *Alice Jean* – The Cupboard – The Beacon – Pot and Kettle – Ghost
Raddled – Neglectful Edward – The Well-Dressed Children – Thunder
at Night – To E.M.-A Ballad of Nursery Rhyme – Jane – Vain and Care-
less – Nine o'Clock – The Picture Book – The Promised Lullaby –
[RETROSPECT:] Haunted – Retrospect: The Jests of the Clock – Here They
Lie – Tom Taylor – Country at War – Sospan Fach – The Leveller – Hate
Not, Fear Not – A Rhyme of Friends – A First Review

Note: A2 is tipped to A1; E9 is tipped to E8.

b. First American edition (1920):

COUNTRY | SENTIMENT | BY | ROBERT GRAVES |
[*publisher's emblem*] | NEW YORK | ALFRED · A · KNOPF |
1920

Collation: [1]–[5]⁸ [6]⁴ [7]⁸, 52 leaves.
p. [1] [at top right:] COUNTRY SENTIMENT; p. [2] list of books by Graves;
p. [3] title-page; p. [4] copyright and printing notices; p. [5] TO | NANCY
NICHOLSON; p. [6] blank; p. [7] NOTE; p. [8] blank; pp. [9–10] CONTENTS;
p. [11] [at top right:] COUNTRY SENTIMENT; p. [12] blank; pp. 13–83 text;
p. [84] blank; p. [85] [at top right:] RETROSPECT; p. [86] blank; pp. 87–
104 text.

15·5 × 10·5 cm. Bulk: 0·9/1·3 cm. White wove paper watermarked
OLDE STYLE; top edges only trimmed and stained light green. White
wove endpapers. Bound in blue boards with green label running from
front to back across spine; on front and back of label in blue: [*rule*] |
COUNTRY SENTIMENT | *POEMS BY* | *ROBERT GRAVES* |
[*rule*]; on spine, in blue: [*rule*] | *Country* | *Senti-* | *ment* | *by* | *Robert* | *Graves* |
1920 | [*rule*].

Price: $1.25. Number of copies undisclosed. Published in March 1920.

A6   THE PIER-GLASS   [1921]

a. First edition:

THE PIER-GLASS | BY ROBERT GRAVES | LONDON:
MARTIN SECKER

Collation: [A]⁸ B–D⁸, 32 leaves.
p. [1] THE PIER-GLASS; p. [2] blank; [plate, facing title-page: portrait of
Graves by Ben Nicholson]; [protective tissue tipped to title-page]; p. [3]
title-page; p. [4] quotation (2 ll.) from Skelton and printer's notice;
p. [5] TO | NANCY NICHOLSON; p. [6] blank; p. [7] NOTE; p. [8] blank;
p. 9 CONTENTS; p. [10] blank; pp. 11–45 text; p. [46] blank; p. [47] THE
CORONATION MURDER and epigraph of 2 ll.; p. [48] blank; pp. 49–53
text; p. [54] blank; p. [55] author's advertisement; p. [56] blank; pp.
[57]–[64] publisher's advertisements.

18·8 × 12·5 cm. Bulk: 1·0/1·4 cm. White wove paper; top edges only trimmed. White wove endpapers. Bound in yellowish buff boards with black cobbled design; front and back blank; white label at top of spine: [rule] | The | Pierglass | [diamond] | Robert | Graves | [rule].

Price: 5s. Number of copies: 500. Published in February 1921.

Contents: The Stake – The Troll's Nosegay – The Pier-Glass – The Finding of Love – Reproach – The Magical Picture – Distant Smoke – Morning Phoenix – Catherine Drury – Raising the Stone – The Treasure Box – The Kiss – Lost Love – Fox's Dingle – The Gnat – The Patchwork Bonnet – Kit Logan and Lady Helen – Down – Saul of Tarsus – Storm: At the Farm Window – Black Horse Lane – Return – Incubus – The Hills of May – The Coronation Murder

b. First American edition (1921):

THE PIER-GLASS | BY | ROBERT GRAVES | [publisher's emblem] | NEW YORK | ALFRED · A · KNOPF | 1921

Collation: [1]–[4]⁸, 32 leaves.
p. [1] THE PIER-GLASS; p. [2] list of books by Graves; p. [3] title-page; p. [4] copyright and printing notices; p. [5] TO | NANCY NICHOLSON; p. [6] blank; p. [7] NOTE; p. [8] blank; p. [9] CONTENTS; p. [10] blank; pp. 11–63 text; p. [64] blank.

15·1 × 11·3 cm. Bulk: 0·6/1·0 cm. White wove paper; top edges only trimmed and stained green. White wove endpapers. Bound in orange boards with green label running from front to back across spine; on front and back: [rule] | THE PIER-GLASS | POEMS BY | ROBERT GRAVES | [rule]; on spine: [rule] | The | Pier- | Glass | by | Robert | Graves | 1921 | [rule].

Price: $1.25. Number of copies undisclosed. Published in September 1921.

A7   ON ENGLISH POETRY   1922

a. First edition:

ON ENGLISH POETRY | Being an Irregular Approach to the Psychology | of This Art, from Evidence Mainly Subjective | BY ROBERT GRAVES | [publisher's emblem] | NEW YORK ALFRED · A · KNOPF MCMXXII

Collation: [1]–[9]⁸ [10]⁴, 76 leaves.

p. [i] [at top right:] ON | ENGLISH POETRY; p. [ii] list of books by Graves; p. [iii] title-page; p. [iv] copyright, publishing, printer's, paper manufacturer's, binder's and manufacturing notices; p. [v] *To T. E. Lawrence of Arabia and | All Soul's College, Oxford, and to | W. H. R. Rivers of the Solomon Is- | lands and St. John's College, Cam- | bridge, my gratitude for valuable | critical help, and the dedication of | this book.*; p. [vi] quotations from Skelton (2 ll.) and Shelley (2 ll.); pp. vii–viii NOTE; pp. ix–xi CONTENTS; p. [xii] blank; pp. 13–149 text; pp. [150]–[152] blank.

19·3 × 13·3 cm. Bulk: 1·7/2·3 cm. White wove paper; all edges trimmed; top edges stained red. White wove endpapers. Bound in cream boards; back blank; front printed with cobbled design in red, with a rounded cream box near top, inside which, in red: *On* | ENGLISH POETRY | *Robert Graves*; near bottom is publisher's emblem; spine printed in red: ON | ENGLISH | POETRY | [*rule*] | GRAVES

Price $2.00. Number of copies undisclosed. Published in May 1922.

Contents: Note – I. Definitions – II. The Nine Muses – III. Poetry and Primitive Magic – IV. Conflict of Emotions – V. The Pattern Underneath – VI. Inspiration – VII. The Parable of Mr. Poeta and Mr. Lector – VIII. The Carpenter's Son – IX. The Gadding Vine – X. The Dead End and the Man of One Poem – XI. Spenser's Cuffs – XII. Connection of Poetry and Humour – XIII. Diction – XIV. The Daffodils – XV. Vers Libre – XVI. Moving Mountains – XVII. La Belle Dame Sans Merci – XVIII. The General Elliott – XIX. The God Called Poetry – XX. Logicalization – XXI. Limitations – XXII. The Naughty Boy – XXIII. The Classical and Romantic Ideas – XXIV. Colour – XXV. Putty – XXVI. Reading Aloud – XXVII. L'Arte della Pittura – XXVIII. On Writing Musically – XXIX. The Use of Poetry – XXX. Histories of Poetry – XXXI. The Bowl Marked Dog – XXXII. The Analytic Spirit – XXXIII. Rhyme and Alliteration – XXXIV. An Awkward Fellow Called Ariphrades – XXXV. Improvising New Conventions – XXXVI. When in Doubt. . . . – XXXVII. The Editor with the Muckrake – XXXVIII. The Moral Question – XXXIX. The Poet as Outsider – XL. A Polite Acknowledgement – XLI. Fake Poetry, Bad Poetry and Mere Verse – XLII. A Dialogue on Fake Poetry – XLIII. Asking Advice – XLIV. Surface Faults, An Illustration – XLV. Linked Sweetness Long Drawn Out – XLVI. The Fable of the Ideal Gadget – XLVII. Sequels Are Barred – XLVIII. Tom Fool – XLIX. Cross Rhythm and Resolution – L. My Name Is Legion, for We Are Many – LI. The Pig Baby – LII. Apology for Definitions – LIII. Time and Seasons – LIV. Two Heresies – LV. The Art of Expression – LVI. Ghosts in the Sheldonian – LVII. The Laying-On of Hands – LVIII. Ways and Means – LIX. Poetry as Labour – LX. The Necessity of Arrogance – LXI. In Procession – Appendix: The Dangers of Definition.

Note: Both A7a and A7b have the misprints 'that' for 'than that' on p. 33, IX, l. 2, and 'have' for 'how' on p. 145, l. 5. Both A7a and A7b were printed in the U.S.

b. English issue (1922):

ON ENGLISH POETRY | *Being an Irregular Approach to the Psychology* | *of This Art, from Evidence Mainly Subjective* | BY ROBERT GRAVES | 19 [*publisher's emblem*] 22 | LONDON: WILLIAM HEINEMANN

Collation as A7a, except p. [iv] printing notice.

20·2 × 13·0 cm. Bulk: 1·7/2·1 cm. White wove paper; all edges trimmed. White wove endpapers. Bound in bright yellow cloth printed in black; back blank; front printed with cobbled design; rounded box near top as A7a and publisher's emblem in rounded box near bottom; spine: *On* | ENGLISH | POETRY | *Robert* | *Graves* | HEINEMANN

Price: 8s. 6d. Number of copies: 1,560. Published 6 July 1922.

Notes: Impressions: 2nd, September 1922.

The first English issue exists in a variant binding. Neither William Nicholson (the designer) nor Graves liked the effect of the first state. The second state is buff boards with cobbled design in black; an off-white label on front reads: *On* | ENGLISH POETRY | *Robert Graves*; tan label on spine: [all flush left:] On | English | Poetry | Robert | Graves | Heinemann The half-title of the first impression is a cancel.

A8   WHIPPERGINNY   [1923]

a. First edition:

WHIPPERGINNY | BY | ROBERT GRAVES | [*publisher's emblem*] | LONDON | WILLIAM HEINEMANN, LTD.

Collation: [A]⁴ B–E⁸ F⁴, 40 leaves.
p. [i] WHIPPERGINNY; p. [ii] blank; p. [iii] title-page; p. [iv] TO | EDWARD MARSH and printing notice; pp. v–vi AUTHOR'S NOTE; pp. vii–viii CONTENTS; pp. 1–71 text; p. [72] text and printer's notice.

18·8 × 12·1 cm. Bulk: 0·9/1·4 cm. White wove paper; top and fore-edges trimmed. White wove endpapers. Bound in magenta boards printed with cobbled design; back blank; red label on front: *WHIPPERGINNY* | *Robert Graves;* red label on spine: [all flush left:] Whipper- | ginny | Robert | Graves | Heinemann

Price: 5s. Number of copies: 1,000. Published 15 March 1923 in magenta dust-jacket printed in black.

Contents: Author's Note – Whipperginny – The Bedpost – A Lover Since Childhood – Song of Contrariety – The Ridge Top – Song in Winter – Unicorn and the White Doe – Sullen Moods – A False Report – Children of Darkness – Richard Roe and John Doe – The Dialecticians – The Lands of Whipperginny – 'The General Elliott' – A Fight to the Death – Old Wives' Tales – Christmas Eve – The Snake and the Bull – The Red Ribbon Dream – In Procession – Henry and Mary – An English Wood – Mirror, Mirror! – What Did I Dream? – Interlude: On Preserving a Poetic Formula – A History of Peace – The Rock Below – An Idyll of Old Age – The Lord Chamberlain Tells of a Famous Meeting – The Sewing Basket – Against Clock and Compasses – The Avengers – On the Poet's Birth – The Technique of Perfection – The Sibyl – A Crusader – A New Portrait of Judith of Bethulia – A Reversal – The Martyred Decadents: A Sympathetic Satire – Epigrams: On Christopher Marlowe; A Village Conflict; Dedicatory; To R. Graves, Senior; 'A Vehicle, to wit, a Bicycle'; Motto to a Book of Emblems – The Bowl and Rim – A Forced Music – The Turn of a Page – The Manifestation in the Temple – To Any Saint – A Dewdrop – A Valentine.
Note: Both A8a and A8b were printed in Great Britain.

b. American issue (1923):

WHIPPERGINNY | BY | ROBERT GRAVES | [*publisher's emblem*] | NEW YORK | ALFRED A. KNOPF: MCMXXIII

Collation as A8a, except A2 is a cancel, recto as above, verso as A8a.

18·7 × 12·5 cm. Bulk: 0·9/1·4 cm. White wove paper; top edges only trimmed and stained pink. White wove endpapers. Bound in boards printed with flame-like design (13 × 11 designs) in blue, flesh, brown and green; pink label runs from front to back across spine with continuous decorative rule above and below legends; on front and back in green: [*decorative rule*] | *WHIPPERGINNY* | *POEMS BY* | *ROBERT GRAVES* | [*decorative rule*]; on spine: [*decorative rule*] | *Whip-* | *per-* | *ginny* | *by* | *Robert* | *Graves* | *1923* | [*decorative rule*].

Price: $2.00. Number of copies undisclosed. Published 29 June 1923.

First edition:

THE FEATHER BED | BY ROBERT GRAVES | *With a cover design by WILLIAM NICHOLSON* | PRINTED AND PUBLISHED BY | LEONARD & VIRGINIA WOOLF | AT THE HOGARTH PRESS | HOGARTH HOUSE RICHMOND | 1923

> *Collation:* [1]–[4]⁴, 16 leaves.
> p. [1] title-page; p. [2] blank; p. [3] *INTRODUCTORY LETTER*; p. [4] blank; pp. 5–8 text; p. [9] *THE FEATHER BED*; p. [10] blank; pp. 11–13 text; p. [14] blank; pp. 15–28 text; pp. [29–30] blank; pp. [31–32] blank, pasted to back cover.

> 21·9 × 17·0 cm. Bulk: 0·4/0·7 cm. White laid paper; all edges untrimmed; watermarked HAND MADE C C & CO and a circle with a cross. Front endpaper white laid; free recto blank; free verso has label: *This edition of THE FEATHER | BED is limited to 250 signed copies | of which this is Number [number written in] | [signature]*. Bound in pink boards printed in black, showing black spine and on front a repeated pattern (6 × 4) of feathers with rounded box containing: *The | Feather Bed | Robert Graves*

> *Price:* 5s. Number of copies: 254. Published 20 July 1923.

> *Contents:* Introductory letter (to John Crowe Ransom) – The Feather Bed: Prologue – The Feather Bed – Epilogue.

First edition:

MOCK BEGGAR HALL | BY ROBERT GRAVES | *With a cover design by WILLIAM NICHOLSON* | PUBLISHED BY | LEONARD & VIRGINIA WOOLF | AT THE HOGARTH PRESS | 52 TAVISTOCK SQUARE | LONDON, W.C.1 | 1924

> *Collation:* [A]⁴ B–F⁸, 44 leaves.
> p. [i] title-page; p. [ii] blank; p. [iii] CONTENTS; p. [iv] blank; pp. 1–79 text; p. [80] blank; pp. [81–84] publisher's advertisements.

25·1 × 18·7 cm. Bulk: 1·0/1·3 cm. Cream-white wove paper water-marked with crown and in Gothic: Abbey Mills | Greenfield; all edges untrimmed. White wove endpapers. Bound in grey boards; back and spine blank; front printed with design of hanging bat in upper foreground and house in lower background; at top left: Mockbeggar | Hall; at top right: by | Robert Graves

Price: 7s. 6d. Number of copies unknown. Published in May 1924.

Contents: Diplomatic Relations – Hemlock – Full Moon – Myrrhina – Twin Souls – The North Window – Attercop: The All-Wise Spider – Antinomies – Northward from Oxford – Witches – Antigonus: An Eclogue – Essay on Continuity – Interchange of Selves, by Basanta Mallik. The Editing and Prologue by Robert Graves – Knowledge of God – Mock Beggar Hall: A Progression – The Rainbow and the Sceptic.

A11   THE MEANING OF DREAMS   [1924]

a. First edition:

THE MEANING OF DREAMS | BY | ROBERT GRAVES | [*publisher's emblem*] | CECIL PALMER | FORTY-NINE | CHANDOS | STREET | W.C.2 | [*flush left, within square brackets:*] Printed in Great Britain

Collation: [A]⁶ B–L⁸ [M]⁴, 90 leaves.
p. [i] THE MEANING OF DREAMS; p. [ii] blank; p. [iii] title-page; p. [iv] copyright and printer's notices; p. [v] TO SUSAN | AND | JOHN BUCHAN; p. [vi] blank; pp. [vii] viii–xi TABLE OF CONTENTS; p. [xii] blank; p. [1] chapter title; p. [2] blank; pp. 3–167 text, with pp. [17, 31, 61, 77, 103, 113, 133] being chapter titles and [18, 32, 60, 62, 76, 78, 102, 104, 112, 114, 134] blank; p. [168] blank.

18·7 × 12·3 cm. Bulk: 2·1/2·5 cm. White wove paper; top edges only trimmed. White wove endpapers. Bound in dark blue cloth; front and back blank; white label pasted on spine: [*whole enclosed within rectangular decorative rule box:*] THE | MEANING | OF | DREAMS | Robert | Graves | Cecil | Palmer

Price: 6s. Number of copies undetermined. Published in September 1924.

Contents: Past Theories as Far as Freud – Theory of Double-Self – Primitive Thought – Varieties of Dreams – Survival of the Past and Other Problems – Value of Dreams on Their Own Account – Practical Benefits of Interpretation – Dreams and Poetry.

Note: A11*a* and A11*b* were both printed in England.

b. American issue (1925):

THE MEANING OF DREAMS | BY | ROBERT GRAVES |
[*publisher's emblem*] | NEW YORK | GREENBERG, PUB-
LISHER, INC. | 1925

> *Collation:* [A]⁶ B–K⁸ L¹², 90 leaves.
> Remainder as A11*a*.

> 17·8 × 11·9 cm. Bulk: 2·1 cm. (sheets). Paper as A11*a*. Binding not
> seen.

> *Price:* $2.00. Number of copies unknown. Published in May 1925.

A12   POETIC   UNREASON   [1925]

First edition:

POETIC | UNREASON | AND OTHER | STUDIES | BY |
ROBERT GRAVES | AUTHOR OF | 'THE MEANING OF
DREAMS', 'ON ENGLISH POETRY' | 'MOCK BEGGAR
HALL', ETC. | [*publisher's emblem*] | CECIL PALMER |
FORTY-NINE | CHANDOS | STREET | W.C. | 2

> *Collation:* [A]⁸ B–S⁸, 144 leaves.
> pp. [i–ii] blank; p. [iii] POETIC UNREASON; p. [iv] blank; p. [v] title-page;
> p. [vi] edition, copyright and printing notices; p. [vii] TO | HENRY HEAD;
> p. [viii] quotation from Skelton; pp. [ix–x] AUTHOR'S NOTE; p. [xi] CON-
> TENTS; p. [xii] blank; pp. 1–276 text, with printer's notice also at bottom
> of p. 276.

> 18·2 × 12·4 cm. Bulk: 2·8/3·3 cm. White wove paper; top edge only
> trimmed. White wove endpapers. Bound in dark blue cloth; front and
> back blank; white label pasted on spine: [*whole enclosed in rectangular
> decorative rule box:*] POETIC | UNREASON | Robert | Graves | Cecil | Palmer

> *Price:* 6s. Number of copies unknown. Published in February 1925.

> *Contents:* Author's Note – What is Bad Poetry? (An Address given at
> Leeds University, December, 1922) – A Theory of Consciousness –
> Jekyll and Hyde – Defence of Poetic Analysis – Secondary Elaboration –
> The Illogical Element in Poetry – Classical and Romantic – Problems
> for Classification – Naturally – The Tempest: An Analysis – Control by
> Spirits – Poetic Genius – Succession – Sensory Vehicles of Poetic Thought.

a. First edition:

John Kemp's Wager | A Ballad Opera | By ROBERT GRAVES | *Therefore roome! you moral precepts.* | *Give my legs leave to ende my Mor-* | *rice, or that being ended, my hands* | *leave to perfect this worthlesse poore* | *tattered volume.* | William Kemp's *Nine Daies Wonder* | Oxford: Basil Blackwell | *Publisher to the* Shakespeare Head Press | *of* Stratford-upon-Avon | 1925

Collation: [a]⁸ b–f⁸, 48 leaves.

p. [i] blank; p. [ii] British Drama League notice; p. [iii] [all flush left:] The British Drama | League Library | of Modern British | Drama No. 11 | John Kemp's | Wager | Robert Graves; p. [iv] British Drama League and British acting rights notices; p. [v] John Kemp's Wager; p. [vi] blank; p. [vii] title-page; p. [viii] printer's notice; p. [ix] To my friend | ERNEST NEALE | of Islip Post Office; p. [x] blank; pp. xi–xiii Author's Note; p. [xiv] Persons of the Play; p. xv Synopsis of Scenery; p. [xvi] blank; pp. 1–75 text; p. [76] blank; p. [77] colophon; pp. [78]–[80] blank.

18·5 × 12·4 cm. Bulk: 0·6/1·0 cm. White wove paper; all edges trimmed. No endpapers; pp. [i–ii] and [79–80] pasted down to covers. Bound in white boards; front and back have green borders and overall interlocked ring design; back without legend; front has green-bordered box with: THE BRITISH DRAMA LEAGUE LIBRARY | OF MODERN BRITISH DRAMA. NO. 11. | JOHN KEMP'S WAGER | BY ROBERT GRAVES.; at lower left, in green-bordered box, in green: OXFORD. BASIL BLACKWELL. | AT THE SHAKESPEARE HEAD; spine, from bottom to top: BRITISH DRAMA LEAGUE LIBRARY. NO. 11 JOHN KEMP'S WAGER.

Price: 3s. 6d. Number of copies: 750. Published 12 May 1925.

Note: A13a–c were all printed in Great Britain.

b. Limited issue (1925):

Title-page as A13a.

Collation as A13a.

Remainder differs as follows: p. [iv] adds: ONE HUNDRED COPIES OF THIS PLAY | HAVE BEEN PRINTED ON KELMSCOTT | HAND-MADE PAPER, OF WHICH THIS | IS NUMBER [*number*] | [*signature of Graves*].

19·3 × 12·3 cm. White laid paper; top edges unopened; all edges untrimmed. White laid endpapers. Bound in white boards with parchment spine; front and back have paper labels as A13a; spine stamped in gold, from top to bottom, same legend as A13a.

Price: 10s. 6d. Number of copies: 100. Published in June 1925.

c. American issue (1925):

John Kemp's Wager | A Ballad Opera | By ROBERT GRAVES | [6 ll. quotation as A13*a*] | COPYRIGHT, 1925, BY ROBERT GRAVES | SAMUEL FRENCH (*Incorporated* 1898) | T. R. Edwards, *Managing Director* | 25 West 45th Street, NEW YORK CITY | 1925

Collation as A13*a*.
Remainder differs as follows: p. [iv] has a paper label pasted below the League notice assigning American and Canadian acting rights to French; pp. [vii–viii] is a cancel, pasted to the stub of a4.

18·5 × 12·4 cm. Bulk: 0·8/1·2 cm. Paper and binding as A13*a*.

Price: $1.25. Number of copies: 250. Date of publication unknown.

A14   MY HEAD! MY HEAD!   1925

a. First edition:

My Head! My Head! | Being the History of Elisha and the | Shunamite Woman; with the History | of Moses as Elisha related it, and | her Questions put to him. | *by* | Robert Graves | 1925 | [*rule*] | *London:* Martin Secker

Collation: [A]⁸ B–I⁸, 72 leaves.
p. [1] My Head! My Head!; p. [2] quotation (4 ll.) from Skelton; p. [3] title-page; p. [4] printing and publisher's notices; p. [5] *To* | *T. E LAWRENCE* [no point after initial E]; p. [6] blank; p. [7] CONTENTS; p. [8] blank; pp. 9–27 ARGUMENT; p. [28] blank; p. [29] MY HEAD! MY HEAD!; p. [30] blank; pp. 31–141 text; p. [142] printer's notice; pp. [143–144] publisher's advertisements.

19·0 × 11·5 cm. Bulk: 1·6/2·1 cm. White laid paper; top and fore-edges trimmed. Bound in red cloth with black veining design; spine black cloth stamped in gold: MY | HEAD! | MY | HEAD! | [*circle*] | GRAVES | SECKER

Price: 5s. Number of copies: 1,000. Published in June 1925.

Note: A second issue was made up from 500 sheets of the earlier edition in March 1928; it differs as follows: title-page: [*whole enclosed within rectangular heavy-rule box:*] | [*whole enclosed within rectangular light-rule box:*] | My Head! My Head! | *by* | Robert Graves | 1 9 2 8 | [*rule*] | *London:* Martin Secker; p. [2] series notice; p. [4] publication and publisher's notices; pp. [143–144] publisher's advertisements; 17·2 × 11·0 cm.; binding not seen; price: 3s. 6d.

Both A14a and A14b were printed in Great Britain.

b. American issue (1925):

My Head! My Head! | Being the History of Elisha and the | Shunamite Woman; with the History | of Moses as Elisha related it, and | her Questions put to him. | by | Robert Graves | [publisher's emblem] | 1925 | [rule] | New York: Alfred A. Knopf

Collation: [A]⁸ B–H⁸ I⁷, 71 leaves.
Remainder differs as follows: p. [4] printing notice; pp. [143–144] missing.

18·7 × 12·0 cm. Bulk: 1·8/2·2 cm. White laid paper; top edges only trimmed and stained yellow. White wove endpapers. Bound in cream boards printed with large angular design in black and irregular ink-blots of red, blue, yellow, orange and green; back blank; front has orange label: [*rectangular decorative rule box enclosing all:*] My Head! My Head! | ROBERT GRAVES; spine has orange label: [*rectangular decorative rule box enclosing all:*] My | Head! | My | Head! | ROBERT | GRAVES

Price: $2.00. Number of copies: 500. Published 5 June 1925 in light purple dust-jacket printed in black.

A15   CONTEMPORARY TECHNIQUES   1925
OF POETRY

First edition:

Contemporary Techniques | of Poetry | A POLITICAL ANALOGY | By | Robert Graves | [publisher's emblem] | Published by | Leonard & Virginia Woolf at The Hogarth Press | 52 Tavistock Square, London, W.C.1 | 1925

Collation: [1]⁸ 2–3⁸, 24 leaves.
p. [1] *Contemporary Techniques* | *of Poetry*; p. [2] publisher's advertisements; p. [3] title-page; p. [4] TO | EDITH SITWELL | IN ALL FRIENDSHIP and printer's notice; pp. 5–46 [47] text; p. [48] printer's notice.

21·7 × 13·8 cm. Bulk: 0·4 cm. White wove paper; all edges trimmed. White wove endpapers. Bound in light blue boards; back blank; front printed: THE HOGARTH ESSAYS | *Contemporary Techniques* | *of Poetry* | ROBERT GRAVES | [*design of vase with columns at sides and grid beneath*] | THE HOGARTH PRESS

Price: 3s. 6d. Number of copies unknown. Published in July 1925.

Contents: The State of the Parties – Diction – Metre – Texture – Rhyme – Structure.

Notes: Issued as Hogarth Essays, Series 1, No. VIII. The design is by Vanessa Bell.

A16 WELCHMAN'S HOSE 1925

First edition:

WELCHMAN'S HOSE | BY | ROBERT GRAVES | [*engraving of bird on lectern*] | WOOD ENGRAVINGS BY PAUL NASH | LONDON | THE FLEURON | 1925

Collation: [A]/A2⁴/⁴ B/B2–D/D2⁴/⁴ E⁴, 36 leaves.
p. [i] WELCHMAN'S HOSE; p. [ii] *This edition is limited to 525 copies* | *of which 500 copies are for sale*; p. [iii] title-page; p. [iv] printer's notice; p. [v] TO EDITH AND WILLIAM NICHOLSON; p. [vi] blank; p. vii CONTENTS; p. [viii] blank; p. ix quotations from Skelton (7 ll.) and Jewel (3 ll.); p. [x] illustration; pp. 1–13 text; p. 14 illustration; pp. 15–61 text with engraving of head on pp. 21 and 44 and engraving of form on pp. 38 and 61; p. [62] blank.

20·6 × 15·0 cm. Bulk: 0·5/0·9 cm. White wove paper watermarked P. M. P; top edges only trimmed. Bound in boards with repeated (6 × 4 designs) floral design; black cloth spine stamped in gold from bottom to top in upper half: WELCHMAN'S HOSE: ROBERT GRAVES

Price: 12s. 6d. Number of copies: 525. Published in September 1925 in transparent parchment wrapper.

Contents: Alice – Burrs and Brambles – From Our Ghostly Enemy – The Figure-Head – Ovid in Defeat – Diversions: I. To an Editor – II. The Kingfisher's Return – III. Love Without Hope – IV. The Traveller's Curse after Misdirection (from the Welsh) – V. Tilly Kettle – The College Debate – Sergeant-Major Money – A Letter from Wales – The Presence – The Clipped Stater – The Poetic State – Essay on Knowledge – At the Games

A17 ROBERT GRAVES [1925]

First edition:

[*rectangular heavy rule box enclosing all:*] | [*rectangular light rule box enclosing all:*] | [*rectangular broad decorative rule box enclosing all:*] |

[*rectangular light rule box enclosing all:*] | *THE AUGUSTAN
BOOKS OF* | *MODERN POETRY* | [*rule*] | *ROBERT* |
GRAVES | [*rule*] | *LONDON: ERNEST BENN LTD.* | *8,
BOUVERIE STREET, E.C.4*

Collation: 16 leaves, unsigned, stapled twice at centre.
p. [i] title-page; p. [ii] publisher's advertisement and printer's notice;
p. iii ROBERT GRAVES; p. iv CONTENTS; pp. 5–30 text; p. 31 BIBLIOGRAPHY;
p. [32] publisher's advertisements.

22·1 × 14·0 cm. Bulk: 0·2 cm. White wove paper; top and fore-edges
trimmed. Pp. [i–ii] and 31–[32] serve as covers.

Price: 6d. Number of copies unknown. Published in November 1925.

Contents: In the Wilderness – A Boy in Church – Escape – Vain and Care-
less – Pot and Kettle – Song: One Hard Look – Dicky – Ghost Raddled –
Allie – A Frosty Night – Rocky Acres – A Lover Since Childhood – A
Crusader – The Ridge-Top – Song of Contrariety – A Forced Music –
I Am the Star of Morning – The North Window – The Rainbow and
the Sceptic – Diplomatic Relations – Alice – The Presence – From Our
Ghostly Enemy

Note: A second impression (not seen) was issued in 1933.

A18   THE MARMOSITE'S MISCELLANY   1925

First edition:

The Marmosite's | Miscellany. | JOHN DOYLE. | *Published by
Leonard and Virginia Woolf at* | *The Hogarth Press, 52, Tavistock
Square, W.C.1.* | 1925.

Collation: 1/2⁴ᐟ⁸, 12 leaves.
p. [1] THE | MARMOSITE'S MISCELLANY.; p. [2] blank; p. [3] title-page;
p. [4] NOTE; pp. 5–23 text; p. [24] blank.

22·5 × 14·7 cm. Bulk: 0·5 cm. White wove paper; all edges trimmed.
White wove endpapers. Bound in mauve and yellow floral boards; back
and spine blank; front has label: [*rectangular double rule box enclosing all:*]
THE | MARMOSITE'S MISCELLANY | JOHN DOYLE

Price: 3s. Number of copies unknown. Published in December 1925.

Contents: To M. in India; with the Poem that Follows – The Marmosite's Miscellany – Tail Piece – Notes – The Moment of Weakness

Note: Acknowledged by Graves by republication in A23.

First edition:

ANOTHER FUTURE | OF POETRY | BY | ROBERT
GRAVES | [*publisher's emblem*] | Published by | Leonard &
Virginia Woolf at The Hogarth Press | 52 Tavistock Square,
London, W.C.1 | 1926

> *Collation:* [A]⁸ B⁸ C², 18 leaves.
> p. [1] ANOTHER FUTURE OF POETRY; p. [2] publisher's advertisement; p. [3]
> title-page; p. [4] TO | L. R. G. and printer's notice; pp. 5–33 text; p. [34]
> printer's notice; pp. [35–36] blank.

> 21·7 × 13·8 cm. Bulk: 0·6 cm. White wove paper; all edges trimmed.
> White wove endpapers. Bound in light blue boards; back and spine
> blank; on front: THE HOGARTH ESSAYS | *Another Future of* | *Poetry* | ROBERT
> GRAVES | [*design of vase and flowers, two line crook at left and right, hatching
> below*] | THE HOGARTH PRESS

> *Price:* 2s. 6d. Number of copies unknown. Published in July 1926.

> *Notes:* Issued as Hogarth Essays, Series 1, Number XVIII. Cover design by
> Vanessa Bell.

A20   THE ENGLISH BALLAD   1927

a. First edition:

[*light-light-heavy rectangular rule box enclosing all:*] The | *English*
Ballad | ★ | *A Short Critical Survey* | *by* | ROBERT GRAVES |
★ | LONDON | *Ernest Benn Ltd.* | *Bouverie House, Fleet Street* | 1927

> *Collation:* [A]⁸ B–H⁸ I⁶, 70 leaves.
> p. [1] [at top right:] The | English Ballad; p. [2] blank; p. [3] title-page;
> p. [4] TO | MY FATHER and printing notice; p. [5] INDEX OF BALLADS; p. 6
> completion of index and acknowledgements; pp. 7–36 INTRODUCTION;
> p. [37] [at top right:] BALLADS; p. [38] blank; pp. 39–138 text; p. 139 text
> and printer's notice; p. [140] blank.

> 18·8 × 12·7 cm. Bulk: 1·7/2·1 cm. White wove paper; top edges only
> trimmed. Bound in red cloth; front and back blank; white label on spine
> THE | ENGLISH | BALLAD | ★ | GRAVES | ★

> *Price:* 6s. Number of copies unknown. Published in January 1927.

Contents: Introduction – The Maid Freed from the Gallows: or, The Briary Bush – The Cleveland Lyke Wake Dirge – The False Knight on the Road – The Twa Corbies – Kemp Owyne – Sir Patrick Spens – The Wife of Usher's Well – Graeme and Bewick – The Demon Lover – The Battle of Otterbourne – Johnny Cock – The Cherry Tree Carol – Hugh of Lincoln – Bruton Town – Robin Hood and the Three Squires – The Old Cloak – Wednesbury Cocking – The Night before Larry Was Stretched – The Unquiet Grave – Waly, Waly – The Holy Land of Walsinghame – Loving Mad Tom – The Children in the Wood – The Welsh Buccaneers – The Death of King Edward VII – The Compleat History of Bob of Lyn – The Peeler and the Goat – Boney – Blow the Man Down – Jack o' Diamonds – Jesse James – 'I Want to go Home' – The Top of the Dixie Lid – Two Red Roses across the Moon

Note: Some copies have an extra spine label tipped in at p. [140].

b. Second English edition (revised) ([1957]):

ENGLISH | AND SCOTTISH | BALLADS | *Edited with an Introduction* | *and Critical Notes* | *by* | ROBERT GRAVES | [*publisher's emblem*] | WILLIAM HEINEMANN LTD | MELBOURNE :: LONDON :: TORONTO

Collation: [A]⁸ B–M⁸, 96 leaves.
p. [i] ENGLISH AND SCOTTISH | BALLADS; p. [ii] publisher's advertisements; [frontispiece, back blank]; p. [iii] title-page; p. [iv] publication, publisher's and printer's notices; pp. v–vi CONTENTS; pp. vii–xxvi INTRODUCTION; p. [xxvii] BALLADS; p. [xxviii] blank; pp. 1–143 text; p. [144] blank; pp. 145–160 NOTES TO THE BALLADS; pp. 161–163 INDEX OF TITLES AND FIRST LINES; p. [164] blank.

18·4 × 12·2 cm. Bulk: 0·9/1·3 cm. White wove paper; all edges trimmed. White wove endpapers. Bound in medium-blue simulated cloth boards; front and back blank; spine stamped in gold, top to bottom: *Robert Graves* [*ornament*] English and Scottish Ballads [*ornament*] Heinemann

Price: 9s. 6d. Number of copies undetermined. Published 6 May 1957 in white dust-jacket printed in black and magenta.

Contents: Introduction – Ballads: 1. The False Knight on the Road – 2. The Twa Sisters of Binnorie – 3. Lord Rendal – 4. Clerk Colvill – 5. Kemp Owyne – 6. Thomas the Rimer – 7. Sir Patrick Spens – 8. The Twa Corbies – 9. Hugh of Lincoln – 10. The Cherry Tree Carol – 11. The Demon Lover – 12. Robin and Gandelyn – 13. The Cleveland Lyke Wake Dirge – 14. The Golden Vanitie – 15. Young Beichan – 16. Johnny of Cockley's Well – 17. The Unquiet Grave – 18. Graeme and Bewick – 19. The Wife of Usher's Well – 20. The Heron – 21. Johnny Faa, the

Lord of Little Egypt – 22. King John and the Abbot – 23. Get Up and Bar the Door – 24. Loving Mad Tom – 25. The Dead Brother – 26. Chevy Chase – 27. Waly, Waly – 28. Barbara Allan – 29. Robin Hood and the Three Squires – 30. The Holy Land of Walsinghame – 31. Sir Andrew Barton – 32. Bruton Town – 33. The Death of Robin Hood – 34. The Gaberlunzie Man – 35. Admiral Benbow – 36. Wednesbury Cocking – 37. The Children in the Wood – 38. The Banished Duke of Grantham – Notes to the Ballads – Index of Titles and First Lines

Note: The introduction is greatly revised from that of A20*a*.

Both A20*b* and A20*c* were printed in Great Britain.

c. First American edition (revised text) ([1957]):

ENGLISH | AND SCOTTISH | BALLADS | *Edited with an Introduction | and Critical Notes | by | ROBERT GRAVES |* THE MACMILLAN COMPANY | NEW YORK

Collation as A20*b*.
Remainder as A20*b*, except p. [ii] blank, p. [iv] printing notice.

Size, bulk, paper, endpapers and binding as A20*b*, except '*Macmillan*' for '*Heinemann*' on spine.

Price: $2.00. Number of copies undetermined. Published in July 1957 in dust-jacket as A20*b*.

A21   LARS PORSENA   [1927]

a. First edition:

LARS PORSENA | OR | THE FUTURE OF SWEARING | AND IMPROPER LANGUAGE | BY | ROBERT GRAVES | LONDON: | KEGAN PAUL, TRENCH, TRUBNER AND CO., LTD. | NEW YORK: E. P. DUTTON & CO.

Collation: [A]⁸ B–F⁸, 48 leaves, plus 16 pp. publisher's advertisements.
p. [1] LARS PORSENA; p. [2] series advertisement; p. [3] title-page; p. [4] printer's notice; pp. 5–94 text; pp. [95–96] blank; 16 pp. publisher's advertisements.

15·3 × 10·4 cm. Bulk: 1·1/1·4 cm. White laid paper; all edges trimmed. White wove endpapers. Bound in plum boards; back blank; front has white label: [*rectangular heavy rule box enclosing all:*] | [*rectangular light rule box enclosing all:*] | LARS PORSENA | OR | THE FUTURE OF SWEARING | *ROBERT GRAVES;* spine has white label: [*heavy rule*] | [*light rule*] | LARS | PORSENA | GRAVES | [*light rule*] | *Kegan Paul* | [*heavy rule*]

Price: 2s. 6d. Number of copies undetermined. Published in February 1927.

Notes: There are many impressions of this work: 2nd, April 1927; 3rd, July 1927; 4th, March 1928; 5th, October 1929; 6th, November 1931. In the 5th and later impressions, a note by Graves occupies p. [2], a list of impressions is added on p. [4], and the text occupies pp. 5–96 (the extensions are at the end).

Issued in the To-Day and To-Morrow Series.

b. First American edition: ([1927]):

LARS PORSENA | *or* | THE FUTURE OF SWEARING | AND IMPROPER LANGUAGE | BY | ROBERT GRAVES | New York | E. P. DUTTON & COMPANY | 681 Fifth Avenue

Collation: [1]–[6]⁸, 48 leaves.
pp. [i–ii] blank, pasted down to front cover; pp. [iii–iv] blank; p. [v] LARS PORSENA; p. [vi] blank; p. [vii] title-page; p. [viii] copyright and printing notices; p. [1] LARS PORSENA; p. [2] blank; pp. 3–77 text; pp. [78]–[86] blank; pp. [87–88] blank, pasted down to back cover.

14·4 × 10·4 cm. Bulk: 1·0/1·6 cm. White wove paper; all edges trimmed. Bound in blue cloth; back blank; front has white label: Lars Porsena | or | THE FUTURE OF SWEARING | AND IMPROPER LANGUAGE | By | ROBERT GRAVES; spine has white label: LARS | PORSENA | [*rule*] | GRAVES

Price: $1.00. Number of copies unknown. Published in 1927 in white dust-jacket printed in red and black.

Note: Some copies are bound in light olive-green cloth with buff labels.

c. Second edition (revised) (1936):

THE FUTURE | OF SWEARING | AND | IMPROPER LANGUAGE | By | ROBERT GRAVES | [*publisher's emblem*] | LONDON | KEGAN PAUL, TRENCH, TRUBNER & CO., LTD | BROADWAY HOUSE: 68–74 CARTER LANE, E.C. | 1936

Collation: [A]⁸ B–G⁸, 56 leaves.
2 pp., blank; p. [i] THE FUTURE | OF SWEARING; p. [ii] publisher's advertisements; p. [iii] title-page; p. [iv] printer's and edition notices; pp. v–vi PREFACE TO | NEW EDITION; pp. 1–100 text; pp. [101]–[104] blank.

18·5 × 12·0 cm. Bulk: 1·4/1·8 cm. White wove paper; all edges trimmed. White wove endpapers. Bound in sea-green cloth; front and back blank; spine stamped in gold: [*heavy rule*] | [toward back:] THE FUTURE | [toward front, parallel to previous:] OF SWEARING | [*heavy rule*] | ROBERT GRAVES | [*heavy rule*].

Price: 3s. 6d. Number of copies undetermined. Published in March 1936 in white dust-jacket printed in blue-green and black.

Notes: Issued in the Today, Tomorrow and After Series. Some copies have 4 pp. publisher's advertisements following p. [104].

A22   IMPENETRABILITY   1926

First edition:

IMPENETRABILITY | OR | THE PROPER HABIT OF ENGLISH | ROBERT GRAVES | [*publisher's emblem*] | *Published by Leonard & Virginia Woolf at The | Hogarth Press, 52 Tavistock Square, London, W.C.1 | 1926*

Collation: [1]⁸ 2–4⁸, 32 leaves.
p. [1] IMPENETRABILITY | OR | THE PROPER HABIT OF ENGLISH; p. [2] publisher's advertisements; p. [3] title-page; p. [4] printer's notice; pp. 5–61 text; p. [62] text and printer's notice; pp. [63–64] publisher's advertisements.

16·6 × 10·4 cm. Bulk: 0·7/1·0 cm. White wove paper; all edges trimmed. White wove endpapers. Bound in light blue boards; front and back have ovals containing: Hogarth Essays *and* Second Series plus additional oval and circular designs; spine printed from bottom to top: IMPENETRABILITY. BY ROBERT GRAVES

Price: 2s. 6d. Number of copies unknown. Published in March 1927.

Notes: Issued as Hogarth Essays, Second Series, Number III. Cover design by Vanessa Bell. Reprinted in part in Chapter I of A55.

A23   POEMS (1914–1926)   1927

a. First edition:

POEMS | (1914–1926) | By | ROBERT GRAVES | LONDON | WILLIAM HEINEMANN, LTD. | MCMXXVII

Collation: $a^2 b^4$ B–O^8 P^4 Q^1, 115 leaves.

p. [i] POEMS (1914–1926); p. [ii] blank; p. [iii] title-page; p. [iv] printer's notice; p. V NOTE; p. [vi] TO | N. AND L.; pp. vii–xi CONTENTS; p. xii quotation (7 ll.) from Skelton; p. [1] 1 | 1914–20; p. [2] blank; pp. 3–43 text; p. [44] blank; p. [45] II | WAR | 1915–19; p. [46] blank; pp. 47–64 text; p. [65] III | MAINLY 1920–23; p. [66] blank; pp. 67–118 text; p. [119] IV | MAINLY 1923–25; p. [120] blank; pp. 121–78 text; p. [179] V | RECENT POEMS: 1925–26; p. [180] blank; pp. 181–216 text; p. 217 BIBLIO-GRAPHY; p. [218] printer's notice.

19·1 × 12·8 cm. Bulk: 1·8 × 2·3 cm. White laid paper watermarked ADELPHI; top edges only trimmed; fore-edges unopened. White wove endpapers. Bound in slick white cloth with black cobbled design; front has blue paper label: POEMS (1914-1926) | *Robert Graves*; back has blue paper label with publisher's emblem; spine has blue paper label: POEMS | 1914 | *to* | 1926 | *Robert* | *Graves* | [*rule*] | Heinemann

Price: 7s. 6d. Number of copies: 1,000. Published 2 June 1927 in light blue dust-jacket printed in black.

Contents: Note – 1: The Poet in the Nursery – In the Wilderness – In Spite – John Skelton – Strong Beer – A Frosty Night – The Troll's Nose-gay – A Song for Two Children – Dicky – Song: One Hard Look – True Johnny – Allie – Loving Henry – Brittle Bones – An English Wood – Henry and Mary – The Country Dance – The Rose and the Lily – Love without Hope – The Traveller's Curse after Misdirection – Mirror, Mirror – What Did I Dream? – The Cupboard – The Beacon – Pot and Kettle – Neglectful Edward – Thunder at Night – Wild Strawberries – Vain and Careless – The Sewing Basket – 'The General Elliott' – A Lover Since Childhood – The Bedpost – Black Horse Lane – Apples and Water – The Finding of Love – II: 1919 – Over the Brazier – The Dead Fox Hunter – Dead Cow Farm – Corporal Stare – Goliath and David – Not Dead – The Last Post – Familiar Letter to Siegfried Sassoon – The Leveller – Escape – The Bough of Nonsense – The Legion – Two Fusiliers – To R. N. – An Occasion – A Dedication of Three Hats – III: Ghost Rad-dled – The Stake – The Pier-Glass – Reproach – The Gnat – Down – Incubus – The Hills of May – The Coronation Murder: 1 and II – Lost Love – Return – Ancestors – Richard Roe and John Doe – Burrs and Brambles – Song of Contrariety – The Ridge-Top – Unicorn and White Doe – Sullen Moods – Children of Darkness – The Dialecticians – Old Wives' Tales – Christmas Eve – The Lands of Whipperginny – The Witches' Cauldron – The Snake and the Bull – A Fight to the Death – In Procession – A Crusader – The Turn of a Page – An Idyll of Old Age – A Valentine – The Poet's Birth – The Lord Chamberlain Tells of a Famous Meeting – I am the Star of Morning – A Forced Music – Full Moon – IV: The Bowl and Rim – The Avengers – A History of Peace – Hemlock – Myrrhina – Twin Souls – Diplomatic Relations – The North

Window – Attercop: the All-Wise Spider – Witches – Essay on Contin-
uity – Knowledge of God – The Rainbow and the Sceptic – Alice – From
Our Ghostly Enemy – The Figure-Head – Ovid in Defeat – To an Editor –
The College Debate – A Letter from Wales – The Presence – The Clipped
Stater – The Poetic State – Essay on Knowledge – The Corner Knot –
Virgil the Sorcerer – To M. in India – v: The Marmosite's Miscellany:
with Notes – The Moment of Weakness – Pygmalion to Galatea – In
Committee – A Letter to a Friend – This is Noon – The Time of Day –
Blonde or Dark? – Boots and Bed – The Taint – Dumpling's Address to
Gourmets – Sorrow – The Nape of the Neck – A Visit to Stratford –
Pure Death – The Cool Web – Bibliography

b. Second English impression (1928):

POEMS | (1914–1926) | By | ROBERT GRAVES | LONDON |
WILLIAM HEINEMANN, LTD. | MCMXXVIII

Collation: a^2 b^4 B–O^8 P^4 Q^2, 116 leaves.

Remainder differs from A23a as follows: p. [iv] has impression and printer's notices; pp. [219–220] blank.

18·7 × 12·6 cm. Bulk: 1·9/2·4 cm. Paper and binding as A23a; labels
are grey-blue with legends as A23a.

Price: 7s. 6d. Number of copies unknown. Published in June 1928.

c. American issue (1929):

POEMS | (1914–1926) | By | ROBERT GRAVES | GARDEN
CITY NEW YORK | DOUBLEDAY, DORAN & COM-
PANY | 1929

Collation: [a]^2 b^4 B–O^8 P^4 Q^2, 116 leaves.

Remainder differs from A23b as follows: p. [iv] has printing notice only.

18·0 × 11·6 cm. Bulk: 2·4/2·9 cm. Cream-white unwatermarked laid
paper; all edges trimmed. White wove endpapers. Bound in brown cloth;
back blank; tan label on front: [*rectangular light rule box enclosing all:*]
Collected Poems | 1914–1926 | [*rule*] | ROBERT GRAVES; tan label on spine:
[*rectangular single rule box enclosing all:*] *Collected* | *Poems* | 1914 | 1926 |
[*rule*] | ROBERT | GRAVES

Price: $2.50. Number of copies unknown. Published 13 September 1929.

Note: A23a–c were all printed by The Westminster Press, London; but
A23a and A24 have 'all', A23b–c have 'All' at p. v, l. 14; and pp. v/[vi],
xi/xii and 217/[218] register differently in A23b and A23c, though the
material is the same. These differences all occur in preliminary or final
matter.

First edition:

POEMS | (1914–1927) | By | ROBERT GRAVES | LONDON |
WILLIAM HEINEMANN, LTD. | MCMXXVII

Collation: $a^2 b^4$ B–P^8 Q^4, 122 leaves.
p. [i] POEMS (1914–1927); p. [ii] *This edition is limited to One Hundred | and Fifteen copies of which One Hun- | dred are for sale. | This is No. [number] | [signature of Graves]*; p. [iii] title-page; p. [iv] printer's notice; p. v NOTE; p. [vi] TO | N. AND L.; pp. vii–xi CONTENTS; p. xii quotation (7 ll.) from Skelton; p. [1] I | 1914–20; p. [2] blank; pp. 3–43 text; p. [44] blank; p. [45] II | WAR | 1915–19; p. [46] blank; pp. 47–64 text; p. [65] III | MAINLY 1920–23; p. [66] blank; pp. 67–118 text; p. [119] IV | MAINLY 1923–25; p. [120] blank; pp. 121–178 text; p. [179] V | RECENT POEMS: 1925–26; p. [180] blank; pp. 181–216 text; p. [217] VI | NINE ADDITIONAL POEMS: 1927; p. [218] blank; pp. 219–227 [228] text; p. 229 BIBLIOGRAPHY; p. [230] printer's notice; pp. [231–232] blank.

22·2 × 14·5 cm. Bulk: 1·8/2·3 cm. White laid paper; top edges only trimmed and gilt; watermarked with a unicorn and: ELLERSLIE. White laid endpapers watermarked with a crown and: Abbey Mills | Greenfield. Bound in white boards with parchment spine stamped in gold: POEMS | 1914–27 | ROBERT | GRAVES | HEINEMANN

Price: 30s. Number of copies: 115. Published in June 1927.

Contents: In addition to the contents of A23, the following: The Progress – Hell – The Dead Ship – O Jorrocks, I have promised – The Lost Acres – The Awkward Gardener – To a Charge of Didacticism – The Philatelist Royal – To be Less Philosophical

A25 JOHN SKELTON (LAUREATE) [1927]

First edition:

[*rectangular heavy rule box enclosing all:*] | [*rectangular light rule box enclosing all:*] | [*rectangular broad decorative rule box enclosing all:*] | [*rectangular light rule box enclosing all:*] | *THE AUGUSTAN BOOKS OF | ENGLISH POETRY | SECOND SERIES NUMBER TWELVE | [rule] | JOHN SKELTON | (LAURE-ATE) | 1460(?)–1529 | [rule] | LONDON: ERNEST BENN, LTD. | BOUVERIE HOUSE, FLEET STREET*

Collation: 16 leaves, unsigned, stapled twice at centre.

p. [i] title-page; p. [ii] publisher's advertisement; p. iii NOTE; p. [iv] blank; p. v CONTENTS; p. [vi] blank; [errata slip tipped between [vi] and 7]; pp. 7–31 text; p. [32] publisher's advertisements.

22·1 × 14·0 cm. Bulk: 0·2 cm. White wove paper; all edges trimmed. Pp. [i–ii] and 31–[32] serve as covers.

Price: 6d. Number of copies unknown. Published in October 1927.

Contents: Note – Jane Scroop's Lament for Philip Sparrow – Skelton's Address to Philip Sparrow – From 'On the Death of King Edward the Fourth' – To Mistress Isabel Pennell – From 'The Manner of the World Nowadays' – Prayer to the Father of Heaven – From 'Speak, Parrot' – Lullay, Lullay, Like a Child – From 'The Tunning of Elinour Rumming' – To His Wife – Woefully Arrayed

Note: Graves wrote the note (p. iii) and selected and modernized the poems.

A26   LAWRENCE AND THE ARABS   [1927]

a. First edition:

LAWRENCE AND THE | ARABS | *By* | ROBERT GRAVES | [*publisher's emblem*] | ILLUSTRATIONS EDITED BY | ERIC KENNINGTON | MAPS BY | HERRY PERRY | LONDON | JONATHAN CAPE 30 BEDFORD SQUARE

Collation: [A]⁸ B–Z⁸ AA–EE⁸ FF⁴, 228 leaves.

p. [i] LAWRENCE AND THE ARABS; p. [ii] quotation (2 ll.) from Jeremiah; p. [1] title-page; p. [2] publication and printer's notices; pp. 3–4 LIST OF ILLUSTRATIONS; pp. 5–7 INTRODUCTION; p. [8] blank; p. [9] LAWRENCE AND THE ARABS; p. [10] blank; pp. 11–437 text; pp. 438–448 appendices; pp. 449–454 INDEX. Illustrations face pp. [1], 48, 60, 72, 92, 118, 142, 156, 164, 178, 196, 212, 226, 254, 260, 274, 278, 298, 308, 326, 336, 342, 346, 358, 370, 386, 402 and 428.

20·0 × 13·6 cm. Bulk: 3·0/3·5 cm. White wove paper; all edges trimmed. White wove endpapers. Bound in mustard-orange cloth; front blank; back blind-stamped with publisher's emblem; spine stamped in gold: LAWRENCE | AND THE | ARABS | [*four diamonds in diamond shape*] | ROBERT | GRAVES | JONATHAN CAPE

Price: 7s. 6d. Number of copies undisclosed. Published early in November 1927 in white dust-jacket printed in black and blue-green.

Notes: Many copies have an order blank for Doughty's *Arabia Deserta* tipped in between pp. 448 and 449.

Impressions: 2nd, November 1927; 3rd, November 1927 (in slick brown cloth); 4th, November 1927.

This book has been translated into French and German.

b. First American edition (1928):

LAWRENCE | AND THE ARABIAN | ADVENTURE | By | ROBERT GRAVES | ILLUSTRATIONS EDITED BY ERIC KENNINGTON | [*rule*] | DOUBLEDAY, DORAN & COMPANY, INC. | GARDEN CITY, NEW YORK, 1928

Collation: [1]–[26]⁸, 208 leaves.

pp. [i–ii] blank; p. [iii] LAWRENCE AND THE ARABIAN ADVENTURE | [*publisher's emblem*]; p. [iv] quotation (2 ll.) from Jeremiah; [frontispiece, back blank, photograph of Kennington bust]; p. [v] title-page; p. [vi] copyright and printer's notices; pp. [vii–viii] LIST OF ILLUSTRATIONS; pp. [ix]–[xi] INTRODUCTION; p. [xii] blank; pp. 1–400 text; pp. [401]–[404] blank. Illustrations are tipped in facing pp. 32, 56, 76, 96, 116, 132, 148, 164, 176, 184, 196, 216, 224, 236, 268, 284, 296, 300, 312, 324, 336, 352, 376.

21·8 × 14·7 cm. Bulk: 3·2/3·6 cm. White wove paper; top edge only trimmed and stained red. White wove endpapers; backs blank; inner sides contain maps in red and blue; front: THE ARAB AREA *and* THE RIDE TO AKABA; back: LAWRENCE'S RIDES *and* THE CAMPAIGN IN THE NORTH. Bound in medium brown cloth; front and back blank; spine stamped in gold: LAWRENCE | & *THE* | ARABIAN | ADVENTURE | [*man with lance on camel*] | ROBERT | GRAVES | DOUBLEDAY | DORAN

Price: $3.00. Number of copies: 20,000. Published 30 March 1928.

c. Concise edition, Florin impression ([1934]):

LAWRENCE AND THE | ARABS | *By* | ROBERT GRAVES | Author of | Good-Bye to All That | [*publisher's emblem*] | [*square bracket*] CONCISE EDITION [*square bracket*] | LONDON | JONATHAN CAPE 30 BEDFORD SQUARE | AND AT TORONTO

Collation: [A]¹⁶ B–H¹⁶ I/I*⁸/⁸, 144 leaves.

p. [1] LAWRENCE AND THE ARABS | [at lower right:] *Florin Books*; p. [2] publisher's advertisement; p. [3] title-page; p. [4] publication, publisher's and printer's notices; p. [5] Note; p. [6] blank; p. [7] map; p. [8] blank;

p. [9] LAWRENCE AND THE ARABS; p. [10] blank; pp. 11–94 text; p. [95] map; pp. 96–146 text; p. [147] map; pp. 148–232 text; p. [233] map; pp. 234–288 text. A 16 pp. gathering of publisher's advertisements, on cheaper paper than the text, is sewn in at the end.

17·8 × 11·6 cm. Bulk: 1·8/2·2 cm. White wove paper; all edges trimmed. White wove endpapers. Bound in beige cloth; back blank; front stamped in brownish grey: LAWRENCE | AND THE ARABS | ROBERT GRAVES; spine stamped in brownish grey: LAW- | RENCE | AND THE | ARABS | ROBERT | GRAVES | JONATHAN | CAPE

Price: 2s. Number of copies undisclosed. Published in March 1934.

Note: There is a second impression in April 1934; 3rd, February 1935; 4th, May 1935; 5th, June 1935; 6th, August 1935; 7th, September 1935; 8th, March 1936. A Life and Letters impression was published in June 1935 at 4s. 6d.; it was reissued in 1937; this impression (not seen) contained 4 maps and 8 illustrations.

d. Concise edition, children's impression ([1935]):

LAWRENCE | AND THE | ARABS | By | ROBERT GRAVES | [*publisher's emblem*] | ILLUSTRATIONS EDITED BY | ERIC KENNINGTON | JONATHAN CAPE | THIRTY BEDFORD SQUARE | LONDON

Collation: [A]⁸ B–S⁸, 144 leaves.

p. [1] LAWRENCE AND THE ARABS; p. [2] blank; p. [3] title-page; p. [4] publication, publisher's and printer's notices; p. [5] Note; p. [6] blank; p. 7 LIST OF ILLUSTRATIONS; p. 8 MAPS; p. [9] LAWRENCE AND THE ARABS; p. [10] map; pp. 11–94 text; p. [95] map; pp. 96–146 text; p. [147] map; pp. 148–232 text; p. [233] map; pp. 234–288 text. Illustrations face pp. [3], 28, 36, 80, 92, 122, 134, 170, 186, 206, 228, 236, 242, 250, 278, 284.

19·0 × 12·5 cm. Bulk undetermined. White wove paper; all edges trimmed. Binding not seen.

Price: 3s. 6d. Number of copies undisclosed. Published in November 1935.

Note: Impressions: 2nd, November 1935; 3rd, October 1936.

e. English school edition ([1940]):

[*rectangular decorative rule box enclosing all:*] | LAWRENCE AND THE | ARABS | By | ROBERT GRAVES | CONCISE

EDITION PREPARED BY | W. T. Hutchins, M. A. |
LONGMANS, GREEN AND CO. | LONDON · NEW
YORK · TORONTO

Collation: [A]/A★⁸/⁸ B/B★–F/F★⁸/⁸, 96 leaves.

p. [i] [5 ll. flush right:] [lamp with shade on table with book open under-
neath] | *The Heritage of* | *Literature Series* | [*rule*] | SECTION A, NO. 36 |
LAWRENCE AND THE ARABS; p. [ii] series advertisement; p. [iii] blank; p.
[iv] cut of Lawrence; p. [v] title-page; p. [vi] publisher's notices and
printer's notice; p. [vii] permission notice; p. [viii] map; pp. ix–xi PRO-
LOGUE; p. [xii] blank; pp. 1–8 text; p. [9] portrait of Feisal; p. [10] blank;
pp. 11–46 text; p. [47] blank; p. [48] portrait of Auda; pp. 49–178 text; p.
179 EPILOGUE; p. [180] blank.

16·3 × 10·9 cm. Bulk: 1·1/1·4 cm. White wove paper; all edges trimmed. White wove endpapers. Bound in dark yellow-olive cloth; front
and back blank; spine stamped in gold: *Lawrence* | *and the* | *Arabs* | [*series
emblem, as p.* (i)] | *Longmans*

Price: 1s. 6d. Number of copies unknown. Published 3 June 1940.

A27   THE LESS FAMILIAR NURSERY RHYMES [1927]

First edition:

[*rectangular heavy rule box enclosing all:*] | [*rectangular light rule
box enclosing all:*] | [*rectangular broad decorative rule box enclosing
all:*] | [*rectangular light rule box enclosing all:*] | *THE AUGUSTAN
BOOKS OF* | *ENGLISH POETRY* | *SECOND SERIES
NUMBER FOURTEEN* | [*rule*] | THE LESS FAMILIAR |
NURSERY | RHYMES | [*rule*] | *LONDON: ERNEST BENN
LTD.* | *BOUVERIE HOUSE, FLEET STREET*

Collation: 16 leaves, unsigned, stapled twice at centre.

p. [i] title-page; p. [ii] publisher's advertisements; pp. iii–iv FOREWORD;
pp. v–vi INDEX; pp. 7–31 text; p. [32] publisher's advertisements.

22·1 × 13·9 cm. Bulk: 0·3 cm. White wove paper; all edges trimmed.
Pp. [i–ii] and 31–[32] serve as covers.

Price: 6d. Number of copies unknown. Published in November 1927.

Note: Graves wrote the foreword (pp. iii–iv) and selected the poems.

a. First edition:

A SURVEY OF | MODERNIST POETRY | BY | LAURA RIDING AND ROBERT GRAVES | [*publisher's emblem*] | LONDON | WILLIAM HEINEMANN LTD. | 1927

> *Collation:* [A]⁸ B–S⁸ T⁴, 148 leaves.
> p. [1] A SURVEY OF | MODERNIST POETRY; p. [2] blank; p. [3] title-page; p. [4] printer's notice; p. [5] NOTE; p. [6] blank; p. [7] CONTENTS; p. [8] blank; pp. 9–291 text; p. [292] blank; pp. 293–295 INDEX OF | PRINCIPAL PROPER NAMES; p. [296] blank.
>
> 19·0 × 12·4 cm. Bulk: 2·5/2·9 cm. White laid paper; top and fore-edges trimmed. White laid endpapers. Bound in cream boards printed with a red design in columns; black cloth spine stamped in gold: A SURVEY | OF MODERNIST | POETRY | LAURA RIDING | AND | ROBERT GRAVES | HEINEMANN
>
> *Price:* 7s. 6d. Number of copies: 1,000. Published 3 November 1927.
>
> *Contents:* I. Modernist Poetry and the Plain Reader's Rights – II. The Problem of Form and Subject-Matter in Modernist Poetry – III. William Shakespeare and E. E. Cummings: A Study in Original Punctuation and Spelling – IV. The Unpopularity of Modernist Poetry with the Plain Reader – V. Modernist Poetry and Dead Movements – VI. The Making of the Poem – VII. Modernist Poetry and Civilization – VIII. Variety in Modernist Poetry – IX. The Humorous Element in Modernist Poetry – X. Conclusion – Index
>
> *Note:* Both A28a and A28b were printed in Great Britain.

b. American issue (1928):

A SURVEY OF | MODERNIST POETRY | BY | LAURA RIDING AND ROBERT GRAVES | Garden City, New York | DOUBLEDAY, DORAN & COMPANY, INC. | 1928

> Collation as A28a.
>
> 18·7 × 12·5 cm. Bulk: 2·3/2·9 cm. White laid paper; all edges trimmed. White laid endpapers. Bound in grey boards; front and back blank; red cloth spine with grey paper label printed in orange: [*decorative rule*] | A SURVEY | OF MODERNIST | POETRY | [*decorative rule*] | LAURA RIDING | and | ROBERT GRAVES | [*decorative rule*]
>
> *Price:* $2.00. Number of copies: 500. Published 28 September 1928.
>
> *Note:* The title-page is a cancel.

c. Second English impression (1929):

A SURVEY OF | MODERNIST POETRY | BY | LAURA
RIDING AND ROBERT GRAVES | [*publisher's emblem*] |
LONDON | WILLIAM HEINEMANN LTD. | 1929

Collation as A28*a*, except p. [4] has impression and printer's notices.

18·9 × 12·3 cm. Bulk: 2·4/2·9 cm. Cream-white laid paper; top and
fore-edges trimmed. Bound in black cloth; front and back blank; spine
stamped in gold: A SURVEY | OF MODERNIST | POETRY | LAURA RIDING | AND |
ROBERT GRAVES | HEINEMANN

Price: 7s. 6d. Number of copies unknown. Published in September 1929
in cream dust-jacket printed in red.

A29   A PAMPHLET AGAINST ANTHOLOGIES   [1928]

a. First edition:

A Pamphlet | AGAINST ANTHOLOGIES | by | LAURA
RIDING | AND ROBERT GRAVES | [*publisher's emblem*] |
JONATHAN CAPE | THIRTY BEDFORD SQUARE |
LONDON

Collation: [A]⁸ B–M⁸, 96 leaves.
p. [1] A PAMPHLET AGAINST ANTHOLOGIES; p. [2] blank; p. [3] title-page;
p. [4] publication and printer's notices; p. 5 CONTENTS; p. [6] blank;
pp. 7–8 FOREWORD; p. [9] A PAMPHLET AGAINST ANTHOLOGIES; p. [10]
blank; pp. 11–192 text.

19·1 × 12·8 cm. Bulk: 1·5/2·0 cm. White wove paper; all edges trimmed. White wove endpapers. Bound in mustard-brown cloth; front
blank; back blind-stamped with publisher's emblem; spine stamped in
gold: PAMPHLET | AGAINST | ANTHOLOGIES | [*leaf device*] | RIDING | & GRAVES |
JONATHAN CAPE

Price: 7s. 6d. Number of copies undisclosed. Published in July 1928 in
cream dust-jacket printed in red and black.

Contents: Foreword – The True Anthology and the Trade Anthology –
Anthologies and the Book Market – The Anthologist in Our Midst –
The Popular Poem and the Popular Reader – The Perfect Modern Lyric –
'Best Poems' – Poetry and Anthology Labels – Anthologies and the Living
Poet – Conclusion

Note: Both A29*a* and A29*b* were printed in Great Britain.

45

b. American issue (1928):

A Pamphlet | AGAINST ANTHOLOGIES | by | LAURA RIDING | AND ROBERT GRAVES | GARDEN CITY, NEW YORK | DOUBLEDAY, DORAN & COMPANY, INC. | 1928

Collation as A29*a*, except p. [4] has printer's notice only.

Size, bulk, paper as A29*a*. Bound in buff boards with wine cloth spine; front and back blank; white label on spine printed in red: [*decorative rule*] | A | PAMPHLET | AGAINST | ANTHOLOGIES | [*decorative rule*] | RIDING | *and* | GRAVES | [*decorative rule*]

Price: $2.00. Number of copies unknown. Published in January 1929.

A30   MRS FISHER   1928

First edition:

MRS FISHER | OR | THE FUTURE OF HUMOUR | BY | ROBERT GRAVES | *Author of 'Lars Porsena, or the Future of* | *Swearing'*, etc. | LONDON | KEGAN PAUL, TRENCH, TRUBNER & CO., LTD. | NEW YORK: E. P. DUTTON & CO. | 1928

Collation: [B]⁸ C–G⁸, 48 leaves, plus 12 leaves publisher's advertisements. p. [1] MRS FISHER | OR | THE FUTURE OF HUMOUR; p. [2] series advertisement; p. [3] title-page; p. [4] quotation (6 ll.) from Skelton and printer's notice; pp. 5–95 text; p. [96] blank; pp. [1] 2–24 publisher's advertisements.

15·8 × 10·8 cm. Bulk: 1·1/1·5 cm. White laid paper; all edges trimmed. White wove endpapers. Bound in plum boards; back blank; front has white paper label: [*rectangular heavy rule box enclosing all:*] | [*rectangular light rule box enclosing all:*] | MRS FISHER | OR | THE FUTURE OF HUMOUR | *ROBERT GRAVES*; spine has white label: [*heavy rule*] | [*light rule*] | MRS | FISHER | GRAVES | [*light rule*] | *Kegan Paul* | [*heavy rule*]

Price: 2s. 6d. Number of copies undetermined. Published in November 1928.

Notes: A second impression (November 1928) differs in that the quotation from Skelton appears on the title-page between ll. 7 and 8 of the above; p. [4] has publication data and printer's notice.

First edition:

[*rectangular heavy rule box enclosing all:*] | [*rectangular light rule box enclosing all:*] | THE SHOUT | by | ROBERT GRAVES | *being Number Sixteen of* | *The Woburn Books* | [*publisher's emblem*] | *Published at London in 1929 by* | ELKIN MATHEWS & MAR-ROT

Collation: [A]⁴ B–D⁴, 16 leaves.

p. [1] title-page; p. [2] Five hundred and thirty numbered | copies of this story have been set in | Monotype Pica Bodoni, and printed | by Robert MacLehose & Co. Ltd., at the University Press, Glasgow; | Nos. 1–500 only are for sale and | Nos. 501–530 for presentation. | This is copy No. [*number written in by hand*] | [*signature of Graves*]; pp. 3–31 [32] text.

19·1 × 13·8 cm. Bulk: 0·5/0·8 cm. Cream wove paper; all edges untrimmed. Grey laid endpapers printed with repeated plume design in purple; inner sides of free endpapers blank. Bound in grey boards printed with wave design in purple; on front cover: THE | SHOUT | By | ROBERT | GRAVES; on back: THE WOBURN BOOKS | JGP '28

Price: 6s. Number of copies: 530. Published in November 1929, in grey laid dust-jacket printed in purple as cover.

A32 GOOD-BYE TO ALL THAT [1929]

a. First edition:

GOOD-BYE TO ALL THAT | An Autobiography | BY | ROBERT GRAVES | [*publisher's emblem*] | JONATHAN CAPE | THIRTY BEDFORD SQUARE | LONDON

Collation: [A]⁸ B–Z⁸ 2A–2E⁸, 224 leaves.

p. [1] GOOD-BYE TO ALL THAT; p. [2] list of works by Graves; [portrait plate, facing title-page, back blank]; p. [3] title-page; p. [4] publication and printer's notices; p. [5] MY DEDICATION IS | AN EPILOGUE; p. [6] blank; pp. 7–9 LIST OF ILLUSTRATIONS; p. [10] WORLD'S END; p. [11] GOOD-BYE TO ALL THAT; p. [12] blank; pp. 13–437 text, with illustrations facing pp. 152, 190, 246, 262, 296 and 364, all backs blank, and double fold-out plate between pp. 322/323, back blank; p. [438] blank; pp. 439–443 text; p. [444] blank; pp. 445–448 DEDICATORY EPILOGUE | TO | LAURA RIDING

20·9 × 13·2 cm. Bulk: 3·0/3·5 cm. White wove paper; top and fore-edges trimmed. White wove endpapers. Bound in salmon cloth; front blank; back blind-stamped with publisher's emblem; spine stamped in gold: GOOD-BYE | TO | ALL THAT | [*four diamonds in diamond shape*] | ROBERT | GRAVES | JONATHAN CAPE

Price: 10s. 6d. Number of copies undisclosed. Published on 18 November 1929 in white photographic dust-jacket printed in black; the photography is by Alfred Cracknell; the design is by Len Lye.

Notes: Expurgations in later states consist of a short passage on p. 290 and a poem by Siegfried Sassoon consisting of the last 4 ll. of p. 341 and all of pp. 342–343. Faber and Foyle, *Modern First Editions: Points and Values (Second Series)* (London: Foyle, 1931) suggest that less than 100 copies of the first state exist. This book has been translated into German and Swedish.

The nature of the changes between A32a and A32b seem to indicate that A32a is merely a pre-publication state, rather than a true first edition; nevertheless, A32a is generally considered the collector's impression.

b. *Second state (expurgated)* ([*1929*]):

Title-page as A32a.

Collation as A32a.
Remainder as A32a, except that p. 290 has a deletion marked by 3 asterisks in a V-shape; p. 341 has 3 asterisks in a V-shape at the bottom; pp. 342–343 have 4 asterisks in a diamond shape; and there is an erratum slip tipped in between pp. 398/399.

Otherwise as A32a.

c. *Second impression* ([*1929*]):

Title-page as A32a.

Collation as A32a.
Remainder as A32a except: pp. 290–295 reset; as A32a to p. 341; then: pp. 341–435 text; p. [436] blank; pp. 437–441 text; p. [442] blank; pp. 443–446 DEDICATORY EPILOGUE | TO | LAURA RIDING; pp. [447–448] blank.

Size, bulk and paper as A32a. Binding: red cloth; otherwise as A32a.

Price: 10s. 6d. Number of copies: *c.* 30,000. Published in November 1929 with dust-jacket as A32a.

Notes: Impressions: 3rd, November 1929; 4th, November 1929; 5th December 1929.
An erratum slip (as A32b) is tipped between pp. 396/397.
Illustrations face as in A32a.
This book sold 20,000 copies in the first week and 30,000 by December

d. First American edition ([1930]):

GOOD-BYE TO ALL THAT | An Autobiography | BY |
ROBERT GRAVES | [*publisher's emblem*] | NEW YORK |
JONATHAN CAPE & HARRISON SMITH

Collation: [1]–[27]⁸ [28]⁴, 220 leaves.
p. [i] GOOD-BYE TO ALL THAT; p. [ii] publisher's notice and list of books by
Graves; [portrait plate, facing title-page, back blank]; p. [iii] title-page;
p. [iv] copyright, printing, printer's and binder's notices; p. [v] MY DEDICA-
TION IS | AN EPILOGUE; p. [vi] blank; pp. [vii–viii] LIST OF ILLUSTRATIONS;
p. [ix] WORLD'S END; p. [x] blank; pp. 1–426 text; pp. 427–430 DEDICATORY
EPILOGUE | TO | LAURA RIDING; illustrations face pp. 141, 179, 235, 251,
284, 308 (foldout) and 350.

21·0 × 15·0 cm. Bulk: 3·0/3·7 cm. White wove paper; top edges only
trimmed and stained black. White laid endpapers. Bound in maroon cloth;
front and back blind-stamped with double-rule rectangular box with
double-rule diagonals with publisher's emblem in centre in double-rule
circle; spine stamped: [*heavy rule*] | [*dashed rule*] | GOOD-BYE | TO ALL THAT |
[*dash*] | ROBERT GRAVES | [*dashed rule*] | [*heavy rule*] | JONATHAN CAPE |
HARRISON SMITH

Price: $3.00. Number of copies undetermined. Published in January 1930
in white dust-jacket as A32a; printed in December 1929.

Notes: Impressions: 2nd, December 1929; 3rd, December 1929.
No American edition I have seen contains the passages expurgated from
A32a.
Printed by the Vail-Ballou Press.

e. Life and Letters impression ([1931]):

THE LIFE AND LETTERS SERIES NO. 22 | [*swelled rule*] |
ROBERT GRAVES | GOOD-BYE | TO ALL THAT | An
Autobiography | With eight illustrations | London – JONA-
THAN CAPE – Toronto

Collation as A32c.
p. [1] [entire at right:] THE LIFE & LETTERS | SERIES, VOLUME 22 | GOOD-BYE |
TO ALL THAT | [*series emblem*]; p. [2] series notice; [frontispiece]; p. [3]
title-page; p. [4] publication, publisher's, printer's and papermaker's
notices; pp. [7] 8–9 LIST OF ILLUSTRATIONS; then as A32c.

19·9 × 13·5 cm. Bulk: 3·0/3·6 cm. White wove paper; all edges trimmed. White wove endpapers. Bound in green cloth; front stamped in
gold: [*double angular wavy rule*] GOOD-BYE [*double angular wavy rule*]

[*rule as before*] TO ALL THAT [*rule as before*] | [at left: *series emblem*]; back blind-stamped with publisher's emblem; spine stamped in gold: GOOD-BYE | TO ALL | THAT | [*series emblem*] | ROBERT | GRAVES | JONATHAN CAPE

Price: 4s. 6d. Number of copies undisclosed. Published in July 1931 in a white dust-jacket printed in green.

Note: Up to 36 pp. of publisher's advertisements are bound in at the end.

f. Blue Ribbon impression ([*1931*]):

GOOD-BYE TO ALL THAT | An Autobiography | BY | ROBERT GRAVES | [*publisher's emblem*] | BLUE RIBBON BOOKS | NEW YORK

Collation as A32*d*.
p. [i] GOOD-BYE TO ALL THAT; p. [ii] publisher's notice and list of books by Graves; p. [iii] blank; p. [iv] portrait; p. [v] title-page; p. [vi] copyright, impression and printer's notices; p. [vii] MY DEDICATION IS | AN EPILOGUE; p. [viii] blank; then as A32*d*; no plates.

20·2 × 13·9 cm. Bulk: 2·7/3·4 cm. White wove paper; all edges trimmed. White wove endpapers. Bound in dark blue cloth; front and back blank; spine stamped: [*heavy rule*] | [*dashed rule*] | GOOD-BYE | TO ALL THAT | [*dash*] | ROBERT GRAVES | [*dashed rule*] | [*heavy rule* | BLUE RIBBON BOOKS

Price: $1.00. Number of copies unknown. Published in 1931.

Note: Printed by the Cornwall Press.

g. Second edition (revised) (*1957*):

Good-bye | to All That | NEW EDITION, REVISED, | WITH A PROLOGUE | AND AN EPILOGUE | Robert Graves | DOUBLEDAY ANCHOR BOOKS | DOUBLE-DAY & COMPANY, INC. | GARDEN CITY, NEW YORK, 1957

Collation: 180 leaves, glued at spine.
p. [i] Good-bye to All That; p. [ii] blank; pp. [iii–iv] list of books by Graves; p. [v] title-page; p. [vi] designer's, photographer's, typographer's, Library of Congress card, copyright and printing notices; p. [vii] Prologue; p. [viii] blank; p. [ix] Good-bye to All That; p. [x] blank; pp. [1] 2–243 text, with pp. [12, 17, 22, 29, 36, 41, 47, 61, 67, 82, 91, 106, 119,

141, 166, 181, 192, 199, 209, 226, 238, 245, 255, 265, 279, 291, 297, 312, 320, 324, 334] unnumbered; pp. [344] 345–347 Epilogue; pp. [348]–[350] blank.

18·1 × 10·5 cm. Bulk: 2·0 cm. White wove paper; all edges trimmed. Bound in white paper covers printed in red, black and blue-grey; front has solid red box upper left, at upper left of which is: A123; below the box is the photo of Graves used on the A32a jacket; below this is a solid blue-grey box reading: *An autobiography* | [*publisher's emblem*] *A Doubleday Anchor Book*; right-hand side of cover appears as a white column, inside which: 95c | *Good-* | *bye* | *to* | *All* | *That* | *by Robert Graves* | *A Revised Second Edition*; the last two lines are continuous with the last two lines of the left-hand column. The back has a white column at left, inside which: *Good-bye* | [blurb of 28 ll.] | *An autobiography*; the right side has a solid blue-grey box at top, inside which: *to All That* continuous with rest of title; below is a photograph of Graves *c.* 1957 in a pose similar to that on front; below this is a solid red box inside which: *by Robert Graves* | [*publisher's emblem*] *A Doubleday Anchor Book*. The spine has a red band at top, inside which: *Robert Graves*; below is white band, inside which: *Good-bye to All That* [from top to bottom]; below is a blue-grey band, inside which, upright: *Anchor* | *A123*

Price: $0.95. Number of copies: 25,000. Published 7 November 1957.

Notes: A second impression of 10,000 copies has been published. The jacket design is by George Giusti; the later photograph is by Susan Greenberg. The 'revisions' make substantially a new book.

h. Second English edition (revised) ([*1957*]):

ROBERT GRAVES | *GOODBYE* | *TO ALL THAT* | *New edition, revised,* | *with a prologue and epilogue* | [*publisher's emblem*] | CASSELL & COMPANY LTD | LONDON

Collation: [A]⁸ B–T⁸ U⁶, 152 leaves.
p. [i] GOODBYE TO ALL THAT; p. [ii] list of books by Graves; p. [iii] title-page; p. [iv] publisher's, copyright and printer's notices; p. v LIST OF ILLUSTRATIONS; p. [vi] blank; p. vii PROLOGUE; p. [viii] blank; pp. 1–303 text; pp. 304–306 EPILOGUE; pp. [307–308] blank; plates, printed on both sides, appear between pp. 88/89, 104/105, 216/217 and 232/233.

21·6 × 13·5 cm. Bulk: 2·5/3·1 cm. White wove paper; all edges trimmed. White wove endpapers. Bound in black cloth; front and back blank; spine stamped in gold: ROBERT | GRAVES | Goodbye | to All That | CASSELL

Price: 21s. Number of copies: 6,027. Published 14 November 1957 in white dust-jacket printed in black and yellow.

Note: Impressions: 2nd, May 1958. Number of copies: 2,001. 3rd, November 1961. Number of copies: 1,512.

i. Third English edition (revised) ([1960]):

ROBERT GRAVES | [swelled rule] | Goodbye to All That | PENGUIN BOOKS

Collation: [A]¹⁶ B–I¹⁶, 144 leaves.

p. [1] PENGUIN BOOKS | 1443 | GOODBYE TO ALL THAT | ROBERT GRAVES | [*publisher's emblem*]; p. [2] blank; p. [3] title-page; p. [4] publisher's, copyright and printer's notices; p. [5] LIST OF ILLUSTRATIONS; p. [6] blank; p. [7] PROLOGUE; p. [8] blank; pp. 9–144 text; [8 pp. illustrations]; pp. 145–278 [279] text; pp. 280–281 [282] EPILOGUE; pp. [283]–[288] publisher's advertisements.

17·9 × 11·0 cm. Bulk: 1·4 cm. White wove paper; all edges trimmed. Bound in white paper covers printed in pink, grey and black.

Price: 3s. 6d. Number of copies: 40,000. Published 24 March 1960.

A33   POEMS 1929   1929

First edition:

POEMS 1929 | BY | ROBERT GRAVES | [publisher's emblem] | Printed and published at The Seizin Press | 35a St. Peter's Square Hammersmith | London 1929

Collation: [1]–[3]⁸, 24 leaves.

pp. [i–ii] pasted down as front endpaper; pp. [iii–iv] blank; p. [v] POEMS 1929; p. [vi] 225 numbered copies of SEIZIN THREE have been printed | and this is number [*number written in by hand*] | [*signature of Graves*]; p. [vii] title-page; p. [viii] blank; pp. 1–31 text; p. [32] blank; p. 33 CONTENTS; p. [34] blank; p. [35] publisher's advertisements; pp. [36]–[38] blank; pp. [39–40] pasted down as rear endpaper.

20·3 × 13·4 cm. Bulk: 0·4/0·9 cm. White laid paper; all edges trimmed; watermarked with a hammer and anvil, BS *and* seal: BRITISH HAND MADE enclosing four clasped hands. Bound in yellow-green cloth; front and back blank; spine stamped in gold, from bottom to top: POEMS 1929: ROBERT GRAVES

Price: 12s. 6d. Number of copies: 225. Published in December 1929.

Contents: Between Dark and Dark – In No Direction – In Broken Images – To the Galleys – Warning to Children – A Dismissal – Guessing Black or White – Hector – Against Kind – Midway – Green Cabbage Wit – Castle – Railway Carriage – Back Door – Front Door – The Tow-Path – Repair Shop – Landscape – Sandhills – Pavement – Return Fare – Single Fare – It Was All Very Tidy – A Sheet of Paper – Contents

First edition:

[3 ll. flush left:] TEN | POEMS | MORE | ROBERT | [flush right:] GRAVES | HOURS PRESS | 15, Rue Guénégaud, PARIS | 1930

Collation: [1]² [2]⁸ [3]², 12 leaves.
p. [i] TEN POEMS MORE | by | Robert Graves | Covers | by | LEN LYE;
p. [ii] blank; p. [iii] title-page; p. [iv] CONTENTS; pp. [1] 2–17 text;
p. [18] blank; p. [19] 200 COPIES OF THIS BOOK | SET BY HAND AND PRI-
VATELY | PRINTED ON HAND-PRESS | EACH COPY HAS BEEN | SIGNED BY THE
AUTHOR | THIS IS No [*number written in*] | [*signature of Graves*]; p. [20] blank.

28·2 × 19·3 cm. Bulk: 0·3/0·7 cm. White Vidalon Haut wove paper
watermarked VIDALON HAUT and a cross and IHSV in a circle; all edges
untrimmed. White Vidalon Haut wove endpapers. Bound in boards
covered with reproductions of photographs by Len Lye; front rocks and
chicken-wire; back pebbles, rocks and basin; spine is green morocco
stamped in gold from bottom to top: ROBERT GRAVES 1930 TEN POEMS
MORE

Price: 30s. Number of copies: 200. Published in June 1930 in transparent
paper wrapper.

Contents: To the Reader over My Shoulder – History of the Word –
Interruption – Survival of Love – The Age of Certainty – The Beast –
Cracking the Nut against the Hammer – The Terraced Valley – Oak,
Poplar, Pine – Act V Scene 5 – Tail Piece: A Song to Make You and
Me Laugh

Notes: p. 7, ult., has 'Rep' for 'Red'; p. 7, l. 3 has 'witheld' for 'withheld';
p. 10, l. 5 has 'impraticable' for 'impracticable'; p. 15, l. 9 has 'futher'
for 'further'.

A35   BUT IT STILL GOES ON   [1930]

a. First edition:

BUT IT STILL GOES ON | An Accumulation | BY | ROBERT
GRAVES | [*publisher's emblem*] | JONATHAN CAPE | LON-
DON & TORONTO

Collation: [A]⁸ B–U⁸, 160 leaves.
2 pp. blank; p. [1] BUT IT STILL GOES ON; p. [2] list of books by Graves;
p. [3] title-page; p. [4] publication, publisher's and printer's notices;
p. [5] CONTENTS; p. [6] blank; p. [7] FOREWORD; p. [8] blank; p. [9] epi-

graph (6 ll.) by Laura Riding; p. [10] blank; p. [11] PART ONE; p. [12] blank; pp. 13–104 text; p. [105] PART TWO; p. [106] blank; pp. 107–207 text; p. [208] blank; p. [209] PART THREE; p. [210] blank; pp. 211–315 text; pp. [316]–[318] blank.

19·9 × 13·2 cm. Bulk: 2·4/2·9 cm. White wove paper; all edges trimmed. White wove endpapers. Bound in bright green cloth; front blank; back has blind-stamped publisher's emblem; spine stamped in gold: BUT IT | STILL | GOES ON |[*four diamonds in diamond shape*] | ROBERT | GRAVES | JONATHAN CAPE

Price: 10s. 6d. Number of copies undisclosed. Published in November 1930 in blue-green dust-jacket printed in purple.

Contents: I: Postscript to 'Good-Bye to All That' – Old Papa Johnson – Avocado Pears – The Shout – II: A Journal of Curiosities, with the First and Last Chapters of 'The Autobiography of Baal' – III: But It Still Goes On: A Play

Note: As with A32, the nature of the changes between A35a and A35b seem to indicate that A35a is merely a pre-publication state, rather than a true first edition; nevertheless, as with A32a, A35a is generally considered the collector's impression.

b. *Second state* ([*1930*]):

Title-page, collation, paper and binding as A35a; but p. 157 has no reference to *The Child She Bare* in the first paragraph and pp. 157/158 is a cancel pasted to the stub of K7.

c. *Second impression* ([*1930*]):

As A35b but with no cancel. Some copies of both A35a and A35c are 19·7 × 13·4 cm., the binding correspondingly smaller; but the type-page of both is the same size.

d. *First American edition* ([*1931*]):

[*rectangular single rule box enclosing all:*] | [*rectangular decorative rule box enclosing all:*] | But It Still Goes On | *An Accumulation* | By | ROBERT GRAVES | [*publisher's emblem*] | New York | Jonathan Cape & Harrison Smith

Collation: [1]–[21]⁸, 168 leaves.
pp. [i–ii] blank; p. [iii] BUT IT STILL GOES ON; p. [iv] list of books by Graves and publisher's notices; p. [v] title-page; p. [vi] copyright, publishing and printing notices; p. [vii] epigraph (6 ll.) by Laura Riding; p. [viii] blank; p. [ix] FOREWORD; p. [x] blank; p. [xi] CONTENTS; p. [xii] blank; p. [1] PART ONE; p. [2] blank; pp. [3] 4–98 text with pp. [49, 64, 72] unnumbered; p. [99] PART TWO; p. [100] blank; pp. [101] 102–203 text with pp. [170, 192] unnumbered; p. [204] blank; p. [205] PART THREE; p. [206] blank; pp. [207] 208–319 text with pp. [209, 249, 288] unnumbered; pp. [320]–[324] blank, fore-edges unopened.

20·4 × 13·9 cm. Bulk: 2·9/3·5 cm. White wove paper; top and bottom edges trimmed; top edges stained black. White wove endpapers. Bound in dark green cloth; back blank; front blind-stamped with publisher's emblem and circular curlicues above and below; spine stamped in gold: BUT IT | STILL | GOES ON | [*swirl*] | ROBERT GRAVES | JONATHAN CAPE | HAR-RISON SMITH

Price: $2.50. Number of copies undetermined. Published 26 January 1931.

Note: p. 152 of this edition contains the reference to *The Child She Bare.*

A36 POEMS 1926–1930 1931

First edition:

POEMS | 1926–1930 | BY | ROBERT GRAVES | LON-DON | WILLIAM HEINEMANN LTD | MCMXXXI

Collation: [A]⁸ B–F⁸ G⁴, 52 leaves.
p. [i] POEMS 1926–1930; p. [ii] blank; p. [iii] title-page; p. [iv] publication and printer's notices; p. [v] NOTE; p. [vi] blank; p. [vii] quotation (2 ll.) from Laura Riding; p. [viii] blank; pp. [ix]–[xi] CONTENTS; p. [xii] blank; p. [1] I; p. [2] blank; pp. 3–14 text; pp. [15–16] blank; p. [17] II; p. [18] blank; pp. 19–34 text; pp. [35–36] blank; p. [37] III; p. [38] blank; pp. 39–48 text; pp. [49–50] blank; p. [51] IV; p. [52] blank; pp. 53–74 text; pp. [75–76] blank; p. [77] V; p. [78] blank; pp. 79–89 text; pp. [90]–[92] blank.

20·2 × 13·4 cm. Bulk: 1·1/1·6 cm. White laid paper; top edge only trimmed. White wove endpapers. Bound in maroon cloth with white cobbled design; back blank; front has maroon label: POEMS (1926–1930) | *Robert Graves*; spine has maroon label: POEMS | 1926 | to | 1930 | *Robert Graves* | [*rule*] | Heinemann

Price: 3s. 6d. Number of copies: 1,000. Published 9 February 1931 in mauve dust-jacket printed in white and black.

Contents: Note – I: Thief – Saint – Gardener – Ship Master – Philatel-ist-Royal – Lift-Boy – Brother – II: Castle – Cabbage Patch – Railway Carriage – Front Door – Repair Shop – Landscape – Bay of Naples – Tap Room – Sandhills – Pavement – Quayside – III: To the Reader over My Shoulder – In Broken Images – Flying Crooked – Hector – Interruption - Act v, Scene 5 – Dismissal – Reassurance to a Satyr – IV: Hell – To be Less Philosophical – Synthetic Such – Anagrammagic – Midway – Lost Acres – In No Direction – Guessing Black or White – Warning to Child-ren – Dragons – History of the Word – Against Kind – V: O Love in Me – Return Fare – Single Fare – It was All Very Tidy – The Terraced Valley – The Age of Certainty – The Next Time

Note: An extra spine label is tipped to p. [92] in some copies.

A37   TO WHOM ELSE?   1931

First edition:

TO WHOM ELSE? | BY | ROBERT GRAVES | The Seizin Press | Deyá, Majorca | 1931

Collation: [1]–[4]⁴, 16 leaves.
pp. [i–ii] blank, pasted down to front cover; pp. [iii–iv] blank; p. [v] A SEIZIN; p. [vi] blank; p. [vii] title-page; p. [viii] blank; pp. 1–19 text; p. [20] There are 200 numbered and signed copies of | Seizin 6 hand-set and hand-printed by ourselves | on hand-made paper. The cover is by Len Lye. | [*number written in*] | [*signature of Graves*]; pp. [21–22] blank; pp. [23–24] blank, pasted down to back cover.

27·1 × 19·4 cm. Bulk: 0·3/0·8 cm. White laid paper; top edges only trimmed; watermarked: GUA [*design of diamond with bars and crosses*] RRO. | . Bound quarter cloth; front and back covered with paper printed in silver, black and dark blue; design on front suggests peacock's tail; design on back is circles and rectangles in rows; spine stamped in silver, from bottom to top: SEIZIN 6 TO WHOM ELSE? ROBERT GRAVES

Price: 25s. Number of copies: 200. Published in July 1931.

Contents: Largesse to the Poor – The Felloe'd Year – On Time – On Rising Early – On Dwelling – Of Necessity – The Foolish Senses – Devilishly Disturbed – The Legs – Ogres and Pygmies – To Whom Else? – As It Were Poems: I: 'In the legend of Reynard the Fox ...' – II: 'A sick girl went from house to house ...' – III: 'Dear Name, how shall I call you?' – On Portents

First edition:

NO DECENCY LEFT | BY | BARBARA RICH | [*publisher's emblem*] | JONATHAN CAPE | THIRTY BEDFORD SQUARE | LONDON

Collation: [A]⁸ B–S⁸, 144 leaves.
p. [1] NO DECENCY LEFT; p. [2] blank; p. [3] title-page; p. [4] edition, publisher's, printer's, paper supplier's and binder's notices; p. [5] TO | MY PUBLISHER; p. [6] blank; p. [7] NO DECENCY LEFT; p. [8] blank; pp. 9–287 [288] text.

19·3 × 12·5 cm. Bulk: 2·3/2·8 cm. White wove paper; top and fore-edges trimmed. White wove endpapers. Bound in flesh cloth; front stamped in blue with a crown; back blind-stamped with publisher's emblem; spine stamped in blue: NO | DECENCY | LEFT | [*star*] | BARBARA | RICH | JONATHAN CAPE

Price: 7s. 6d. Number of copies undisclosed. Published in February 1932 in white dust-jacket printed in blue, flesh, brown and black.

Notes: Impressions: 2nd, March 1932; 3rd, April 1932; 4th, March 1935, at 2s. 6d. Written in collaboration with Laura Riding. Variant binding: The Library of Congress copy is bound in orange cloth; front and back blank.

A39   THE REAL DAVID COPPERFIELD   [1933]

a. First edition:

THE REAL | DAVID COPPERFIELD | BY | ROBERT GRAVES | LONDON | ARTHUR BARKER, LTD. | 21 GARRICK STREET, COVENT GARDEN

Collation: [1]⁸ 2–26⁸ 27⁴, 212 leaves.
p. [1] THE REAL | DAVID COPPERFIELD; p. [2] blank; p. [3] title-page; p. [4] printing, copyright and printer's notices; pp. 5–9 FOREWORD; p. [10] blank; pp. 11–418 text; pp. 419–424 APPENDIX.

20·4 × 13·8 cm. Bulk: 3·6/4·1 cm. White wove paper; all edges trimmed. White wove endpapers. Bound in bright medium-blue cloth; front and back blank; spine stamped in gold: The Real | David | Copperfield | ROBERT | GRAVES | BARKER

Price: 9s. Number of copies unknown. Published in March 1933 in light blue dust-jacket printed in black and pink.

Note: The appendix reprints Dickens' Chapter LXII, 'A Light Shines on My Way.' Though the texts of A39a and A39b are for the most part identical, the two books are not identical in purpose. A39a is a rewriting to produce the 'real' book, while A39b abandons some of the plot changes made in A39a to make merely an abridged version of the novel for school use. Compare particularly the beginnings of the two Chapters XXIII, the scene with Emily at the end of Chapter XXX, the end of Chapter XXXII, Chapters LIII and LIV of the two versions and the epilogue.

b. *First American edition* (*1934*):

David Copperfield | BY CHARLES DICKENS | *Condensed by Robert Graves* | *Edited by Merrill P. Paine* | DIRECTOR OF ENGLISH, | ELIZABETH, NEW JERSEY | [*publisher's emblem*] | NEW YORK · CHICAGO | HARCOURT, BRACE AND COMPANY | 1934

Collation: [1]⁸ [2]⁹ [3]–[4]⁸ [5]–[17]¹⁶ [18]–[20]⁸, 265 leaves.
p. [i] David Copperfield; p. [ii] map of David Copperfield's England; p. [iii] title-page; p. [iv] copyright and printing notices; p. [v] CONTENTS; p. [vi] blank; pp. [vii] viii–xxxi INTRODUCTION; p. [xxxii] blank; p. [xxxiii] David Copperfield; p. [xxxiv] blank; pp. [1] 2–474 text; pp. [475] 476–486 STUDY QUESTIONS; pp. [487]–488 GENERAL TOPICS FOR STUDY; pp. [489]–490 SUGGESTIONS FOR ADDITIONAL READING; pp [491]–[496] blank.

18·6 × 12·5 cm. Bulk: 2·6/3·3 cm. White wove paper; all edges trimmed. White wove endpapers. Bound in blue cloth, printed in orange; on front: David | Copperfield | [*decorative swirl*]; back blank; on spine: David | Copperfield | BY | CHARLES DICKENS | GRAVES | [*decorative dash*] | PAINE | HARCOURT, BRACE | AND COMPANY

Price: $1.00. Number of copies undetermined. Published in 1934.

Note: The book was being reprinted as late as 1940. See note to A39a.

The title-page is a cancel, tipped in.

A40   POEMS 1930–1933   1933

First edition:

POEMS | 1930–1933 | BY | ROBERT GRAVES | London: | ARTHUR BARKER LTD. | 21 Garrick St,W.C.2 | 1933

Collation: [1]–[3]⁸, 24 leaves.

p. [i] POEMS | 1930–1933; p. [ii] blank; p. [iii] title-page; p. [iv] publishing and printer's notices; p. [v] CONTENTS; p. [vi] blank; p. [vii] NOTE; p. [viii] blank; pp. 1–38 text; pp. [39–40] blank.

21·4 × 13·6 cm. Bulk: 0·6/1·2 cm. White laid paper; all edges trimmed. White wove endpapers. Bound in grey boards with black cloth spine; back blank; front stamped: POEMS | [*swelled rule*] | BY ROBERT GRAVES | [*swelled rule*] | *Nineteen Thirty to* | *Nineteen Thirty Three;* spine stamped in gold, near top, running up: POEMS *by* Robert Graves

Price: 5s. Number of copies unknown. Published in May 1933.

Contents: Note – The Bards – Time – Ulysses – Down, Wanton, Down! – The Cell – The Succubus – Nobody – Danegeld – Trudge, Body – On Rising Early – On Necessity – Ogres and Pygmies – Music at Night – The Legs –Without Pause – Devilishly Disturbed – The Clock Men – The Commons of Sleep – The Foolish Senses –What Times are These? – The Felloe'd Year – Largesse to the Poor – On Dwelling – To Whom Else? – On Portents – As It Were Poems I, II, III.

Note: Impressions: 2nd, September 1933.

A41   OLD SOLDIERS NEVER DIE   [1933]

a. First edition:

OLD SOLDIERS | NEVER DIE | BY | PRIVATE | FRANK RICHARDS | D.C.M., M.M. | *Late of the Second Battalion* | *Royal Welch Fusiliers* | LONDON | FABER & FABER LIMITED | 24 RUSSELL SQUARE

Collation: [A]⁸ B–T⁸ u/u★²/⁸, 162 leaves.

pp. [1–2] blank; p. [3] OLD SOLDIERS NEVER DIE; p. [4] blank; p. [5] title-page; p. [6] publisher's, printer's and rights reservation notices; pp. 7–8 CONTENTS; pp. 9–324 text.

18·8 × 12·0 cm. Bulk: 2·6/3·1 cm. White wove paper; all edges trimmed. White wove endpapers. Bound in orange cloth; front and back blank; spine stamped in gold: Old | Soldiers | Never | Die | Frank | Richards | Faber | and Faber

Price: 7s. 6d. Number of copies: 2,000. Published in August 1933.

Notes: This book was rewritten by Graves.
Impressions: 2nd, September 1933 (2,000 copies); 3rd, October 1933 (2,000 copies); 4th, July 1936 (3,000 copies) at 3s. 6d.

b. First Australian edition (1933):

OLD SOLDIERS | NEVER DIE | By | FRANK RICHARDS, D.C.M., M.M. | Late of the Second Battalion | Royal Welch Fusiliers | AUSTRALIA | ANGUS & ROBERTSON LIMITED | 89 CASTLEREAGH STREET, SYDNEY | 1933

Collation: [A]⁸ B–T⁸, 152 leaves.

p. [i] OLD SOLDIERS NEVER DIE; p. [ii] blank; p. [iii] title-page; p. iv printing and copyright notices; pp. [v]–vi CONTENTS; p. [vii] OLD SOLDIERS NEVER DIE; p. [viii] blank; pp. [1]2–295 text with pp. [6, 14, 22, 41, 53, 58, 88, 97, 116, 125, 134, 146, 160, 172, 181, 192, 201, 208, 217, 235, 242, 250, 260, 269, 276, 285, 290] unnumbered; p. 296 text and printer's notice.

18·2 × 12·2 cm. Bulk: 2·7/3·2 cm. White wove paper; all edges trimmed. White wove endpapers. Bound in bright orange cloth; back blank; front stamped in black: [*heavy rule*] | [*light rule*] | [*light rule*] | Old Soldiers | Never Die | Frank Richards | [*light rule*] | [*light rule*] | [*heavy rule*]; spine stamped in black: [*heavy rule*] | [*light rule*] | [*light rule*] | Old | Soldiers | Never | Die | Frank | Richards | Angus & | Robertson | [*light rule*] | [*light rule*] | [*heavy rule*]

Price: 6s. Australian. Number of copies: 1,998. Published 17 November 1933.

c. Second English edition ([1942]):

Private FRANK RICHARDS | D.C.M., M.M. | *Late of the Second Battalion Royal Welch Fusiliers* | [*rule*] | OLD SOLDIERS | NEVER DIE | FABER AND FABER LIMITED | 24 Russell Square | London

Collation: [A]¹⁶ B–H¹⁶, 128 leaves.

p. [1] OLD SOLDIERS NEVER DIE; p. [2] author's advertisement; p. [3] title-page; p. [4] publication, printer's, rights reservation and war economy notices; pp. v–vi CONTENTS; pp. 7–256 text, with p. [128] being unnumbered.

18·3 × 12·5 cm. Bulk: 1·5 cm. White wove paper; all edges trimmed. Bound in white paper covers printed in light blue and black.

Price: 2s. Number of copies: 25,000. Published in May 1943 in white dust jacket printed in light blue and black as cover.

d. First edition, fourth English impression ([1964]):

OLD SOLDIERS | NEVER DIE | BY | PRIVATE | FRANK RICHARDS | D.C.M., M.M. | *Late of the Second Battalion* | *Royal Welch Fusiliers* | *With an introduction by* | ROBERT GRAVES | LONDON | FABER & FABER LIMITED | 24 RUSSELL SQUARE

Collation: π^2 [A]^8 B–T^8 u/u$\star^{2/8}$, 164 leaves.
p. [i] OLD SOLDIERS NEVER DIE; p. [ii] blank; p. [iii] title-page; p. [iv] publication and copyright notices; pp. 1–7 INTRODUCTION; p. [8] blank; pp. 9–324 text.

18·4 × 12·0 cm. Bulk: 1·6 cm. White wove paper; all edges trimmed. Bound in white paper covers printed in black, pink and olive-gold.

Price: 7s. 6d. Number of copies: 10,068. Published 26 November 1964.

Note: The first impression with an introduction by Graves.

A42   I, CLAUDIUS   1934

a. First edition:

ROBERT GRAVES | [*heavy rule*] | [*light rule*] | I, CLAUDIUS | *From the Autobiography of* | TIBERIUS CLAUDIUS | [*facsimile signature of Tiberius Claudius*] | *Emperor of the Romans* | born B.C. 10 | murdered and deified | A.D. 54 | [*publisher's emblem*] | 1934 | [*light rule*] | [*heavy rule*] | ARTHUR BARKER : LONDON

Collation: [A]^8 B–Z^8 2A–2H^8, 248 leaves.
pp. [1–2] blank; p. [3] I, CLAUDIUS; p. [4] blank; p. [5] title-page; p. [6] printer's and publication notices; p. [7] quotation (7 ll.) from Tacitus; p. [8] blank; pp. 9–10 AUTHOR'S NOTE; p. [11] I, CLAUDIUS; p. [12] blank; pp. 13–494 text; [genealogical table tipped to p. [495]]; pp. [495–496] blank.

21·8 × 13·8 cm. Bulk: 3·5/4·1 cm. White laid paper; top and fore-edges trimmed. White wove endpapers. Bound in black cloth; front and back blank; spine stamped in gold: ROBERT GRAVES | [*light rule*] | [*heavy rule*] | I, | CLAUDIUS | BARKER

Price: 8s. Number of copies unknown. Published in May 1934 in white dust-jacket printed in blue, brown, flesh and black.

Notes: The jacket design is by John Aldridge.
The book has been translated into Czech, Danish, Dutch, Finnish, French,

German, Hebrew, Italian, Magyar, Norwegian, Polish, Portuguese, Slovenian, Spanish, Swedish and Ukranian.

Impressions: 2nd, 3rd, May 1934; 4th, June 1934; 5th, September 1934; 6th, December 1934; 7th, January 1935; 8th, May 1935; 9th, October 1935.

See *Notes* to A43*a*.

Printed in Great Britain.

b. American issue (1934):

I, CLAUDIUS | FROM THE AUTOBIOGRAPHY OF TIBERIUS CLAUDIUS | BORN B.C. 10 · MURDERED AND DEIFIED A.D. 54 | [*facsimile signature of Tiberius Claudius*] | [*medallion of Claudius*] | BY ROBERT GRAVES | [*rule*] | NEW YORK · MCMXXXIV | HARRISON SMITH AND ROBERT HAAS

Collation: [1]–[12]¹⁶ [13]⁸ [14]–[16]¹⁶, 248 leaves.
Remainder as A42*a*.

21·4 × 14·1 cm. Bulk: 3·1/3·7 cm. White wove paper; all edges trimmed. White wove endpapers. Bound in dark slate-blue cloth; back blank; front stamped in gold with medallion of Claudius; spine stamped in gold: I, | CLAUDIUS | [*double rule*] | Graves | [*publisher's emblem*]

Price: $2.00. Number of copies undetermined. Published 4 June 1934 in dust-jacket as A42*a*.

Note: Impressions: 2nd, 3rd, 4th, June 1934; 5th, July 1934; 6th, 7th, August 1934.

Printed in the U.S.

c. Second American edition ([1935]):

I, CLAUDIUS | FROM THE AUTOBIOGRAPHY OF TIBERIUS CLAUDIUS | BORN B.C. 10 · MURDERED AND DEIFIED A.D. 54 | [*facsimile signature*] | [*medallion*] | BY ROBERT GRAVES | [*swelled rule*] | GROSSET & DUNLAP | *Publishers* New York

Collation: [1]–[12]¹⁶ [13]¹² [14]¹⁶, 220 leaves.
p. [i], I, CLAUDIUS; p. [ii] blank; p. [iii] title-page; p. [iv] copyright notice; p. [v] biographical note; p. [vi] blank; p. [vii] quotation (6 ll.) from Tacitus; p. [viii] blank; pp. ix–x AUTHOR'S NOTE; p. [1] I, CLAUDIUS; p. [2] blank; pp. 3–427 text; pp. [428]–[430] blank.

21·1 × 14·0 cm. Bulk: 2·9/3·6 cm. White wove paper; all edges trimmed; top edges stained blue-green. White wove endpapers. Bound in dark blue cloth; back blank; front blind-stamped with medallion; spine stamped in gold: I, | CLAUDIUS | [*double rule*] | Graves | GROSSET | & DUNLAP

Price: $1.00. Number of copies unknown. Published on 10 June 1935.

d. Cheap English issue (1936):

Title-page as A42a, except for date.

Collation: [A]/A*8/8 B/B*–P/P*8/8Q8, 248 leaves.
Remainder as A42a.

19·7 × 13·2 cm. Bulk: 2·1/2·6 cm. White wove paper; all edges trimmed. White wove endpapers. Bound in grey cloth; front and back blank; spine printed in brown: ROBERT GRAVES | [*rule*] | [*solid brown rectangular box, grey cloth showing through to read 2 ll.:*] I, | CLAUDIUS | [*rule*] | BARKER

Price: 5s. Number of copies unknown. Published in May 1936.

Notes: Impressions: 2nd, November 1936; 3rd, May 1937; 4th, July 1938. In August 1939 the Barker rights were taken over by Methuen, who received 275 copies and 1,000 sheets. Methuen published an impression of 3,000 copies (the '14th edition') in 1940; 2,000 of these were destroyed by enemy action. See also note to A42i.

e. Second American edition, Modern Library issue ([1937]):

I, CLAUDIUS | FROM THE AUTOBIOGRAPHY OF | TIBERIUS CLAUDIUS | BORN B.C. 10 | MURDERED AND DEIFIED A.D. 54 | BY | ROBERT GRAVES | [*publisher's emblem*] | [*rule*] | THE MODERN LIBRARY · NEW YORK | [*rule*]

Collation: [1]16 [2]–[7]32 [8]16, 224 leaves.
p. [i] THE MODERN LIBRARY | *OF THE WORLD'S BEST BOOKS* | [*swelled rule*] | I, CLAUDIUS | [*swelled rule*] | [6 ll. publisher's advertisement]; p. [ii] blank; p. [iii] title-page; p. [iv] copyright, publisher's and manufacturer's notices; p. [v] biographical note; p. [vi] blank; 'p. [vii] quotation (6 ll.) from Tacitus; p. [viii] blank; pp. ix–x AUTHOR'S NOTE; p. [1] I, CLAUDIUS; p. [2] blank; pp. 3–427 text; p. [428] blank; pp. [429]–[438] publisher's advertisements.

17·8 × 12·0 cm. Bulk: 1·7/2·2 cm. White wove paper; all edges trimmed; top edges stained black. White wove endpapers; first and fourth sides blank; second and third sides printed with grey overall design of books and: ml;

publisher's emblem in centre. Bound in red cloth; back blank; front stamped in gold: [*rectangular single-rule box enclosing all:*] | [*rectangular single-rule box enclosing solid black box, inside which 3 ll.:*] I, CLAUDIUS | [*wedge*] | GRAVES | [*between two gold-rule boxes:*] [*publisher's emblem*]; spine stamped in gold: [*publisher's emblem*] | [*rectangular gold-rule box enclosing black solid box, enclosing remainder:*] I, | CLAUDIUS | BY | Robert | Graves | [*wedge*] | MODERN | LIBRARY

Price: $0.95; later $1.25. Number of copies: 89,000 to June 1964. Published 25 February 1937.

f. Second English edition (1941):

ROBERT GRAVES | [*swelled rule*] | I, CLAUDIUS | From the Autobiography of | TIBERIUS CLAUDIUS | [*facsimile signature*] | Emperor of the Romans | born B.C. '10 | murdered and deified | A.D. 54 | VOLUME I [II] | [*publisher's emblem*] | ALLEN LANE | PENGUIN BOOKS | HARMONDSWORTH MIDDLE-SEX ENGLAND | 41 EAST 28TH STREET NEW YORK U.S.A.

Collation: [both volumes:] [A]/A★8/8 B–G16, 112 leaves.
Vol. I: p. [1] blurb; p. [2] portrait of Graves and biographical note; p. [3] title-page; p. [4] publication notice, list of books by Graves and printer's notice; p. [5] quotation (6 ll.) from Tacitus; p. [6] the Sibylline verses; pp. [7–8] AUTHOR'S NOTE; pp. [9] 10–222 text, with pp. [19, 33, 45, 53, 71, 89, 105, 111, 123, 131, 151, 165, 177, 189, 199, 211] unnumbered and pp. [52, 70, 88, 104, 110, 122, 150, 164, 176, 188] blank; pp. [223–224] advertisements.

Vol. II: p. [i] blurb; p. [ii] portrait of Graves and biographical note; p. [iii] title-page; p. [iv] publication notice, list of books by Graves and printer's notice; p. [v] quotation (6 ll.) from Tacitus; p. [vi] blank; pp. [vii–viii] AUTHOR'S NOTE; pp. [223]224–433 text, with pp. [229, 245, 261, 271, 289, 299, 311, 319, 329, 345, 355, 369, 385, 403, 417, 429] unnumbered and pp. [260, 270, 298, 310, 328, 344, 368, 384, 416, 428] blank; pp. [434]–[438] advertisements.

18·0 × 10·6 cm. Bulk: 0·8 cm. White wove paper; all edges trimmed. Bound in paper covers printed in black and orange; inside covers and back covers have advertisements.

Price: 9d. per volume. Number of copies: 55,000. Published in July 1941 in white dust-jacket printed in orange and black.

Almost Forgotten Germany (A45)

(Photo: British Museum)

MAMMON

ORATION DELIVERED AT THE
LONDON SCHOOL OF ECONOMICS
AND POLITICAL SCIENCE
ON FRIDAY, 6 DECEMBER 1963

BY

ROBERT GRAVES

THE LONDON SCHOOL OF ECONOMICS
AND POLITICAL SCIENCE
1964

The title page of *Mammon* (A104)

Old Soldiers Never Die

Frank Richards

Old
Soldiers
Never
Die

Frank
Richards

Angus &
Robertson

Notes: These books are Penguins 318 and 319.

Volume I, p. [4], l. 6 has *'Decdmber'* for *'December'*; volume II has not this misprint. Both volumes, same page, have *'Perany'* for *'Penny'* in the list of Graves' titles.

g. *Third English edition* ([*1944*]):

ROBERT GRAVES | [*swelled rule*] | I, CLAUDIUS | *From the Autobiography of* | TIBERIUS CLAUDIUS | [*facsimile signature*] | *Emperor of the Romans* | born B.C. 10 | murdered and deified | A.D. 54 | VOLUME II | [*publisher's emblem*] | PENGUIN BOOKS | HARMONDSWORTH MIDDLESEX ENGLAND | 245 FIFTH AVENUE NEW YORK U.S.A.

Collation: Vol. 1: unknown; Vol. II [1]^{16}2–6^{16}, 96 leaves.

Vol. 1: unknown.

Vol. II: p. [i] I, CLAUDIUS | VOLUME II | [blurb, 7 ll.]; p. [ii] portrait of Graves and biographical note; p. [iii] title-page; p. [iv] publication data and author's advertisement; p. [v] quotation (8 ll.) from Tacitus; p. [vi] blank; pp. [vii–viii] AUTHOR'S NOTE; pp. 201–379 text; p. [380] text and printer's notice; pp. [381–382] advertisements; pp. [383–384] publisher's advertisements.

18·0 × 10·9 cm. Bulk: (I) unknown; (II) 0·8 cm. White wove paper; all edges trimmed. Bound in white paper covers printed in orange and black; inside front and back covers: advertisements.

Price: unknown. Number of copies: unknown. Published in 1944.

Note: p. [iv] indicates that this edition is merely a reprinting of the 1941 Penguin edition (A42*f*), but it obviously is not.

h. *Third American edition* ([*1944*]):

[*whole enclosed within double-rule rectangular box:*] [4 ll. in left half of page:]PUBLISHED BY ARRANGEMENT WITH|RANDOM HOUSE, INC., NEW YORK | COPYRIGHT, 1934 | BY HARRISON SMITH AND ROBERT HAAS, INC. | [*rule, dividing left from right half of page*] | [6 ll. in right half of page:] I, CLAUDIUS | by | Robert Graves | *Editions for the Armed Services, Inc.* | A NON-PROFIT ORGANIZATION ESTAB-LISHED BY | THE COUNCIL ON BOOKS IN WARTIME, NEW YORK | [*outside of double-rule box, at lower left:*] L–27

Collation: [1]–[12]^{16} [13]–18^8, 240 leaves.

p. [1] title page; p. [2] quotation (6 ll.) from Tacitus; pp. [3–4] AUTHOR'S NOTE; pp. [5] 6–477 text; p. [478] blank; pp. [479–480] ABOUT THE AUTHOR.

16·7 × 11·6 cm. Bulk: 1·8 cm. White wove paper; all edges trimmed. Bound in white paper covers with multicolour printing; front has title, author and rights notice; inside front and back covers are publisher's announcements; back cover is blurb.

Note: This edition was never for sale, but only for distribution to members of the U.S. Armed Forces overseas. It is printed in double columns throughout, with the exception of p. [2]; the gatherings are stabbed together with a single staple at the centre of the gutter. The Library of Congress copy was received on 24 October 1944.

i. Fourth English edition ([1949?]):

ROBERT GRAVES | [*double rule*] | I, CLAUDIUS | *From the Autobiography of* | TIBERIUS CLAUDIUS | [*facsimile signature*] | *Emperor of the Romans* | born B.C. 10 | murdered and deified | A.D. 54 | [*publisher's emblem*] | [*double rule*] | METHUEN & CO. LTD. LONDON

Collation: [1]⁸ 2/2★–15/15★⁸/⁸, 232 leaves.
p. [i] I, CLAUDIUS; p. [ii] list of books by Graves; p. [iii] title-page; p. [iv] quotation (7 ll.) from Tacitus, edition and printer's notices; pp. v–vi AUTHOR'S NOTE; pp. 1–454 text; [fold-out genealogical table tipped to p. [455]]; pp. [455]–[458] blank.

18·4 × 12·2 cm. Bulk: 2·0/2·4 cm. White wove paper; all edges trimmed. White wove endpapers. Bound in grey cloth; front and back blank; spine printed in brown: ROBERT GRAVES | [*rule*] | [solid rectangular box with cloth showing through for 2 ll.:] | I, | CLAUDIUS | [*rule*] | METHUEN

Price: 8s. 6d. Number of copies: 3,000. Published in 1949 in dust-jacket as A42a.

Notes: Impressions: 2nd, 1952 (3,250 copies); 3rd, 1956 (3,000 copies); 4th, 1962 (3,000 copies). There remain unaccounted for an impression in 1941 (3,000 copies), 1943 (3,000 copies) and 1946 (2,500 copies); but I have been unable to ascertain whether these belong to A42a/d or to A42i.

j. Fifth English edition ([1953]):

ROBERT GRAVES | [*swelled rule*] | I, CLAUDIUS | FROM THE AUTOBIOGRAPHY OF | TIBERIUS CLAUDIUS | [*facsimile signature*] | EMPEROR OF THE ROMANS | BORN 10 B.C. | MURDERED AND DEIFIED | A.D. 54 | PENGUIN BOOKS

Collation: [A]¹⁶ B–L¹⁶ M⁸ N¹⁶, 200 leaves.
p. [1] PENGUIN BOOKS | 318 | I, CLAUDIUS | ROBERT GRAVES | [*publisher's emblem*]; p. [2] blank; p. [3] title-page; p. [4] publisher's notice, printing history and printer's notice; p. [5] the Sibylline verses; p. [6] quotation (10 ll.) from Tacitus; pp. 7–[8] *Author's Note;* pp. 9–395 [396] text; p. [397] TREE OF THE | IMPERIAL FAMILY AND CONNEXIONS | TO THE YEAR A.D. 41 | GIVING NAMES AS ABBREVIATED | IN THIS BOOK; pp. [398–399] genealogical table; p. [400] blank.

18·0 × 11·0 cm. Bulk: 1·9 cm. White wove paper; all edges trimmed. Bound in paper covers printed in black and orange.

Price: 3s. 6d. Number of copies unknown. Published in 1953.

Note: Impressions: 2nd, 1955.

k. *Fourth American edition* ([1957]):

I, CLAUDIUS | ROBERT GRAVES | COMPLETE AND UNABRIDGED | [*publisher's emblem*] | AVON PUBLICATIONS, INC. | 575 MADISON AVENUE · NEW YORK 22, N.Y.

Collation: 224 leaves, glued at spine.
pp. [3–4] blurbs; p. [5] title-page; p. [6] copyright, acknowledgement and printing notices; p. [7] I, CLAUDIUS; p. [8] blank; pp. 9–445 [446] text; pp. [447–448] AUTHOR'S NOTE; pp. [449–450] publisher's advertisements.

16·0 × 10·7 cm. Bulk: 2·3 cm. White wove paper; all edges trimmed; all edges stained yellow. Bound in pictorial paper covers.

Price: $0.35. Number of copies: 250,000. Published in October 1953.

Note: This book is Avon Red and Gold Library No. AT–68.

l. *Fifth American edition* ([1961]):

[*elaborate 10-line rule and decorative rule device*] | I, CLAUDIUS | FROM THE AUTOBIOGRAPHY OF | TIBERIUS CLAUDIUS | BORN B.C. X | MURDERED AND DEIFIED A.D. LIV | BY | ROBERT GRAVES | [*publisher's emblem*] | VINTAGE BOOKS | A DIVISION OF RANDOM HOUSE | NEW YORK

Collation: 224 leaves, glued at spine.

p. [i] [*decorative rule*] | [*rule*] | I, CLAUDIUS | [*rule*]; p. [ii] blank; p. [iii] title-page; p. [iv] copyright, rights reservation, publisher's and manufacturing notices; p. [v] quotation (10 ll.) from Tacitus; p. [vi] blank; pp. [vii]–viii AUTHOR'S NOTE; p. [1] [*decorative rule*] | [*rule*] | I, CLAUDIUS | [*rule*]; p. [2] blank; pp. [3]4–432 text; p. [433] biographical and typographical notices; pp. [434]–[440] publisher's advertisements.

18·4 × 11·1 cm. Bulk: 2·1 cm. White wove paper; all edges trimmed. Bound in white paper covers printed in red, blue and black.

Price: $1.45. Number of copies undisclosed. Published 13 February 1961.

Note: This book is Vintage Book V–182.

m. Sixth American edition ([*1965*]):

[*7 ll. in magenta:*] FROM THE | AUTOBIOGRAPHY | OF TIBERIUS CLAUDIUS | BORN B.C. 10 | MURDERED | AND DEIFIED | A.D. 54 | I, CLAUDIUS | [*in magenta:*] BY ROBERT GRAVES | WITH A NEW INTRODUCTION | BY THE AUTHOR | [*in magenta: publisher's emblem*] | TIME READING PROGRAM | SPECIAL EDITION | TIME INCOR-PORATED, NEW YORK

Collation: 228 leaves, glued at spine.

p. [i] [*in magenta:*] I, CLAUDIUS; p. [ii] blank; p. [iii] title-page; p. [iv] publisher's emblem, staff credits, copyright, rights reservation and printing notices; pp. [v–vi] solid magenta, otherwise blank; pp. vii–xi EDITORS' | PREFACE; p. [xii] solid magenta, otherwise blank; pp. xiii–xvii INTRODUCTION; p. [xviii] blank; pp. xix–xx AUTHOR'S | NOTE; p. [xxi] quotation (11 ll.) from Tacitus; p. [xxii] blank; p. [xxiii] [*in magenta:*] I, CLAUDIUS; p. [xxiv] solid magenta, otherwise blank; pp. 1–429 text; p. [430] blank; p. [431] colophon; p. [432] blank.

20·3 × 13·2 cm. Bulk: 2·7 cm. White wove paper; all edges trimmed. Bound in paper covers; inner sides scarlet; outer sides white printed with pictorial design in orange, green, blue, yellow and black.

Price: $3.95. Number of copies undisclosed. Published in February 1965.

Note: The introduction (pp. xiii–xvii) has not appeared elsewhere.

a. First edition:

ROBERT GRAVES | [*heavy rule*] | [*light rule*] | CLAUDIUS | THE GOD | *and his wife* | MESSALINA | *The troublesome reign of Tiberius Claudius* | *Caesar, Emperor of the Romans (born* | *B.C. 10, died A.D. 54), as described by* | *himself; also his murder at the hands* | *of the notorious Agrippina (mother of* | *the Emperor Nero) and his subsequent* | *deification, as described by others* | [*publisher's emblem*] | 1934 | [*light rule*] | [*heavy rule*] | ARTHUR BARKER: LONDON

Collation: [A]⁸ B–Z⁸ 2A–2N⁸, 288 leaves.

p. [1] CLAUDIUS THE GOD | *and his wife* | MESSALINA; p. [2] *By the same Author* | I, CLAUDIUS; p. [3] title-page; p. [4] printer's, publisher's and edition notices; pp. 5–6 AUTHOR'S NOTE; p. [7] CLAUDIUS THE GOD; p. [8] blank; pp. 9–76 text; [genealogical table of the Herods pasted to p. 77]; pp. 77–302 text; p. 303 map; pp. 304–353 text; pp. 554–559 THREE ACCOUNTS OF CLAUDIUS'S DEATH; pp. 560–575 THE PUMPKINIFICATION OF CLAUDIUS; p. [576] blank; [genealogical table of the Roman Imperial Family tipped to p. [576]].

21·4 × 13·8 cm. Bulk: 3·7/4·3 cm. White laid paper; top and fore-edges trimmed. White wove endpapers. Bound in black cloth; front and back blank; spine stamped in gold: ROBERT GRAVES | [*double rule*] | CLAUDIUS | THE GOD | *and his wife* | MESSALINA | BARKER

Price: 10s. 6d. Number of copies unknown. Published in November 1934 in white dust-jacket printed in light and dark blue, pink and red-brown.

Notes: Impressions: 2nd, November 1934; 3rd, December 1934; 4th, January 1935; 5th, December 1935; 6th, May 1936 ('cheap' edition). Translated into Danish, Finnish, German, Greek, Hebrew, Italian, Magyar, Norwegian, Polish, Portuguese, Russian, Slovenian and Swedish.

There are two combined issues of A42 and A43. The first is bound in red morocco, top edges gilt, sheets of A42*a* and A43*a*, issued in December 1935 at 25s. the set. The second is bound in three-quarter green leather, top edges gilt, sheets of A42*c* and the cheap issue of A43*a*, boxed, issued in November 1936 at 21s. the set; mottled pink and grey endpapers, inside which, front and back, is a heavy binder's sheet of two leaves; spines stamped in gold: [*heavy rule*] | [*light rule*] | I, CLAUDIUS | ROBERT GRAVES | [*light rule*] | [*heavy rule*] and [*heavy rule*] | [*light rule*] | CLAUDIUS | THE GOD | ROBERT GRAVES | [*light rule*] | [*heavy rule*].

In August 1939 the Barker rights were taken over by Methuen, who received 1,100 copies; of their impression in 1940 (3,000 copies), 1,500 copies were destroyed by enemy action.

b. First American edition (1935):

BY ROBERT GRAVES | CLAUDIUS the GOD | and his
wife Messalina | [medallion of Claudius] | The troublesome reign of
Tiberius Claudius | Caesar, Emperor of the Romans (born B.C. 10, |
died A.D. 54), as described by himself; also | his murder at the hands
of the notorious | Agrippina (mother of the Emperor Nero) | and his
subsequent deification, as described | by others | NEW YORK ·
MCMXXXV | HARRISON SMITH AND ROBERT HAAS

Collation: [1]–[17]¹⁶ [18]⁴ [19]¹⁶, 292 leaves.

p. [1] CLAUDIUS THE GOD; p. [2] *By the same author* | 1, CLAUDIUS; p. [3] title-
page; p. [4] copyright, publisher's and printing notices; pp. 5–6 *Author's
Note;* p. [7] CLAUDIUS THE GOD | *and his wife* | *Messalina;* p. [8] blank; pp.
9–64 text; [genealogical table tipped in facing p. 64]; pp. 65–559 text;
pp. 560–565 THREE ACCOUNTS OF CLAUDIUS'S DEATH; pp. 566–583 THE
PUMPKINIFICATION OF CLAUDIUS; p. [584] blank; [genealogical table, foldout, tipped to rear end paper].

21·3 × 14·3 cm. Bulk: 3·5/4·3 cm.White wove paper; all edges trimmed.
White wove endpapers. Bound in black cloth; back blank; front stamped in
gold with medallion; spine stamped in gold: CLAUDIUS | THE GOD | [*double
rule*] | Graves | [*publisher's emblem*]

Price: $3.00. Number of copies undetermined. Published 4 March 1935 in
dust-jacket as A43a.

Note: Grosset and Dunlap issued an impression of this edition in 1939 at
$1.00. The Book of the Month Club issued this book as its selection for
March 1935.

c. Second English edition ([1943]):

CLAUDIUS THE GOD | and his wife | MESSALINA | BY |
ROBERT GRAVES | The troublesome reign of Tiberius
Claudius Caesar, | Emperor of the Romans (born 10 B.C., died
A.D. 54), | as described by himself; also his murder at the hands |
of the notorious Agrippina (mother of the Emperor | Nero) and
his subsequent deification, as described by | others | VOLUME
[II] | [*publisher's emblem*] | PENGUIN BOOKS | HARMONDS-
WORTH MIDDLESEX ENGLAND | 300 FOURTH
AVENUE NEW YORK U.S.A.

Collation: [both volumes:] [A]¹⁶ B–G¹⁶, 112 leaves.

Vol. 1: p. [1] CLAUDIUS THE GOD | *and his wife* | MESSALINA | VOLUME I; p. [2
list of books by Graves; p. [3] title-page; p. [4] publication history an

printer's notices; p. [5] CONTENTS; p. [6] blank; pp. [7–8] AUTHOR'S NOTE; pp. 9–223 text; p. [224] portrait and biographical note.

Vol. II: p. [i] CLAUDIUS THE GOD | *and his wife* | MESSALINA | VOLUME II; pp. [ii]–[viii], as pp. [2]–[8] in Vol. I; pp. 225–243 text; p. 244 map; pp. 245–424 text; pp. 425–428 THREE ACCOUNTS OF CLAUDIUS'S DEATH; pp. 429–439 THE PUMPKINIFICATION OF CLAUDIUS; p. [440] portrait and biographical note.

I: 17·2 × 10·7 cm.; II: 18·2 × 10·7 cm. Bulk [each volume]: 0·8 cm. White wove paper; all edges trimmed. Bound in paper covers printed in black and red-orange; inside front and back covers and back cover: advertisements.

Price: 9d. per volume. Number of copies unknown. Published in March 1943.

Note: These are Penguin Books Nos. 421–422.

d. Third English edition ([1949]):

ROBERT GRAVES | [*heavy rule*] | [*light rule*] | CLAUDIUS | THE GOD | *and his wife* | MESSALINA | *The troublesome reign of Tiberius Claudius* | *Caesar, Emperor of the Romans (born* | *1 0 B.C., died A.D. 54), as described by* | *himself; also his murder at the hands* | *of the notorious Agrippina (mother of* | *the Emperor Nero) and his subsequent* | *deification, as described by others* | [*publisher's emblem*] | [*light rule*] | [*heavy rule*] | METHUEN & CO. LTD. LONDON

Collation: [1]/1★8/8 2/2★–16/16★8/8 17⁸, 264 leaves.

p. [i] CLAUDIUS THE GOD | *and his wife* | MESSALINA; p. [ii] list of books by Graves; p. [iii] title-page; p. [iv] publication, catalogue number and printing notices; pp. v–vi AUTHOR'S NOTE; pp. 1–64; [genealogical table tipped to p. 65]; pp. 65–272 text; p. 273 map; pp. 274–499 text; pp. 500–504 THREE ACCOUNTS OF CLAUDIUS'S DEATH; pp. 505–520 THE PUMPKINIFICATION OF CLAUDIUS; [genealogical table tipped to p. [521]]; p. [521] blank; p. [522] printer's notice [blank in later impressions].

18·4 × 12·2 cm. Bulk: 2·7/3·3 cm. White wove paper; all edges trimmed. White wove endpapers. Bound in grey cloth; front and back blank; spine stamped in blue: ROBERT GRAVES | [*rule*] | [solid rectangular box with cloth showing through to read 2 ll.:] | CLAUDIUS | THE GOD | [*rule*] | *Methuen*

Price: 10s. 6d. Number of copies: 3,000. Published in 1949 in dust-jacket as A43*a*.

Notes: Impressions: 2nd, 1951 (3,250 copies); 3rd, 1957 (3,000 copies); 4th, 1962 (3,000 copies). There remain unaccounted for an impression in 1944 (2,500 copies) and 1946 (2,500 copies); but I have been unable to ascertain whether these belong to A43*a* or A43*d*.

e. Fourth English edition ([1954]):

ROBERT GRAVES | CLAUDIUS THE GOD | AND HIS
WIFE MESSALINA | [*swelled rule*] | THE TROUBLESOME
REIGN OF TIBERIUS CLAUDIUS | CAESAR, EMPEROR
OF THE ROMANS | (BORN 10 B.C., DIED A.D. 54), |
AS DESCRIBED BY HIMSELF; | ALSO HIS MURDER AT
THE HANDS OF THE | NOTORIOUS AGRIPPINA |
(MOTHER OF THE EMPEROR NERO) | AND HIS SUB-
SEQUENT DEIFICATION, | AS DESCRIBED BY | OTHERS
| PENGUIN BOOKS

Collation: [A]^{16} B–O^{16}, 224 leaves.

p. [1–2] blank; p. [3] PENGUIN BOOKS | 421 | CLAUDIUS THE GOD | ROBERT
GRAVES | [*publisher's emblem*]; p. [4] blank; p. [5] title-page; p. [6] publisher's,
publication and printer's notices; pp. 7–8 *Author's Note*; pp. 9–418 text;
p. 419 map; p. [420] blank; pp. 421–425 *Three Accounts* | *of Claudius's
Death;* p. [426] blank; pp. 427–439 *The Pumpkinification of Claudius;* p.
[440] blank; p. [441] THE | ROYAL FAMILY | OF THE | HERODS; pp. 442–443
genealogical table; p. [444] blank; p. [445] publisher's advertisement; p.
[446] blank; pp. [447–448] publisher's advertisements.

18·0 × 11·0 cm. Bulk: 1·2 cm. (later 1·6 cm.). White wove paper; all
edges trimmed. Bound in paper covers printed in black and orange.

Price: 3s. 6d. Number of copies unknown. Published in 1954.

Note: Impressions: 2nd, 31 May 1956; 3rd, 1957; 4th, 1959.

A44   OLD-SOLDIER SAHIB   [1936]

a. First edition:

OLD-SOLDIER SAHIB | *by* | Private | FRANK RICHARDS |
D.C.M., M.M. | *Late of the Second Battalion* | *Royal Welch Fusiliers* |
London | FABER & FABER LIMITED | 24 Russell Square

Collation: [A]^8 B–X^{8}Y^4, 172 leaves.

p. [1] OLD-SOLDIER SAHIB; p. [2] author's advertisement; p. [3] title-page;
p. [4] publisher's and printer's notices; p. [5] To | THE PRAYER-WALLAH | in
the hope | that this meets his eye; p. [6] blank; p. 7 CONTENTS; p. [8] blank;
pp. 9–341 text; pp. [342]–[344] blank.

18·5 × 12·2 cm. Bulk: 2·6/3·1 cm. White wove paper; all edges trimmed.
White wove endpapers. Bound in bright blue cloth; front and back blank;
spine stamped in gold: Old– | Soldier | Sahib | Frank | Richards | Faber
and Faber

Price: 7s. 6d. Number of copies: 5,000. Published in April 1936.

Notes: Impressions: 2nd, September 1938 at 3s. 6d (5,000 copies). Graves rewrote this book.

b. *First American edition ([1936]):*

Old Soldier Sahib | By Private Frank Richards | D.C.M., M.M., LATE OF THE SECOND BATTALION | ROYAL WELCH FUSILIERS | [*cut of soldier with rifle; fort with Union Jack at right; native village at left; signed 'Floethe'*] | WITH AN INTRODUC-TION BY ROBERT GRAVES | [*rule*] | HARRISON SMITH AND ROBERT HAAS | [*rule*]

> *Collation:* [1]–[18]⁸ [19]⁴ [20]⁸, 156 leaves.
> p. [1] OLD SOLDIER SAHIB; p. [2] blank; p. [3] title-page; p. [4] copyright and printing notices; p. [5] To | THE PRAYER WALLAH | in the hope | that this meets his eye; p. [6] blank; p. [7] Contents; p. [8] blank; pp. 9–18 Introduction; p. [19] OLD SOLDIER SAHIB; p. [20] blank; pp. 21–310 text with pp. [62, 76, 106, 124, 168, 178, 190, 206, 220, 235, 246, 260, 298] blank; pp. [311–312] blank.

> 21·2 × 14·0 cm. Bulk: 2·7/3·3 cm. White wove paper; all edges trimmed; top edges stained red. White wove endpapers. Bound in buff cloth; front stamped in red with helmet, beneath which is a bayonet and below which is a grenade; back blank; spine stamped in red: RICHARDS | OLD | SOLDIER | SAHIB | [*publisher's emblem*]

> *Price:* $2.50. Number of copies undetermined. Published 6 April 1936.

A45   ALMOST FORGOTTEN GERMANY   [1936]

First edition:

ALMOST FORGOTTEN | GERMANY | by | GEORG SCHWARZ | Translated by | LAURA RIDING and ROBERT GRAVES | [*publisher's emblem*] | THE SEIZIN PRESS · DEYÁ MAJORCA | AND | CONSTABLE & CO., LTD. | London

> *Collation:* [A]¹⁶ B–I¹⁶, 144 leaves.
> p. [i] ALMOST FORGOTTEN GERMANY; p. [ii] publisher's advertisements; [plate, back blank, facing title-page, portrait of Schwarz]; p. [iii] title-page; p. [iv] publication and printer's notices; p. v CONTENTS; p. [vi] blank; pp. vii–viii FOREWORD; pp. 1–278 text; pp. [279–280] blank.

18·5 × 12·3 cm. Bulk 3·0/3·5 cm.White wove paper; all edges trimmed. White wove endpapers. Bound in medium brown cloth; front and back blank; spine stamped in black: ALMOST | FORGOTTEN | GERMANY | GEORG SCHWARZ | Translated by | LAURA RIDING | and | ROBERT GRAVES | [*publisher's emblem*] | SEIZIN PRESS | AND | CONSTABLE

Price: 7s. 6d. Number of copies unknown. Published in April 1936.

Note: This book was issued in the U.S. by Random House at $2.50.

A46   ANTIGUA, PENNY, PUCE   [1936]

a. First edition:

'ANTIGUA, PENNY, PUCE' | by | ROBERT GRAVES | [*publisher's emblem*] | THE SEIZIN PRESS – DEYÁ MAJORCA | AND | CONSTABLE & COMPANY LTD | LONDON

Collation: [A]⁸ B–U⁸, 160 leaves.
p. [i] 'ANTIGUA, PENNY, PUCE'; p. [ii] list of books by Graves; p. [iii] title-page; p. [iv] publication and printer's notices; p. [v] TO | WILLIAM FULLER | IN GRATITUDE; p. [vi] blank; p. vii CONTENTS; p. [viii] blank; pp. 1–311 text; p. [312] blank.

18·4 × 12·2 cm. Bulk: 2·8/3·2 cm.White wove paper; all edges trimmed. White wove endpapers. Bound in dull maroon cloth; front and back blank; spine stamped in white: ANTIGUA | PENNY | PUCE | a novel by | ROBERT | GRAVES | SEIZIN– | CONSTABLE

Price: 10s. 6d. Number of copies unknown. Published in October 1936 in white dust-jacket printed in black and purplish-brown.

Notes: Impressions: 2nd, April 1938 at 3s. 6d. The first impression, p. 100, l. 11, has 'ytyle' for 'style'; p. 103, l. 15, has 'being' for 'been'; p. 293 ult. has lowered 'l' as last letter; in some copies these misprints have been corrected by hand. Translated into German, Magyar, Polish, Spanish and Swedish.

b. First American edition ([1937]):

[*whole enclosed in wavy-rule rectangular box:*] | [*whole enclosed in single-rule rectangular box:*] | THE | ANTIGUA | STAMP | by | Robert Graves | [*publisher's emblem*] | Random House · New York

Collation: [1]–[21]⁸, 168 leaves.

p. [i] [*whole enclosed in wavy-rule rectangular box:*] The | *Antigua* | *Stamp*; p. [ii] list of books by Graves; p. [iii] title-page; p. [iv] edition, copyright and manufacturing notices; p. [v] TO | WILLIAM FULLER, | in gratitude; p. [vi] blank; p. [vii] *Contents*; p. [viii] blank; p. [1] [*whole enclosed in wavy-rule rectangular box:*] The | *Antigua* | *Stamp;* p. [2] blank; pp. 3–326 text; pp. [327–328] blank.

20·4 × 13·8 cm. Bulk: 2·8/3·4 cm. White wove paper; top edges only trimmed and stained salmon. Buff wove endpapers. Bound in rust-brown cloth; back blank; front has label facsimile of stamp; spine stamped in gold: [*double wavy rule*] | THE | ANTIGUA | STAMP | [*double wavy rule*] | ROBERT | GRAVES | RANDOM HOUSE

Price: $2.50. Number of copies undisclosed. Published 8 March 1937.

c. *Second English edition* ([*1948*]):

'ANTIGUA, PENNY, PUCE' | BY | ROBERT GRAVES | [*publisher's emblem*] | PENGUIN BOOKS | WEST DRAYTON MIDDLESEX ENGLAND | 245 FIFTH AVENUE NEW YORK U.S.A.

Collation: [A]¹⁶ B–K¹⁶, 160 leaves.

p. [1] 'ANTIGUA, PENNY, PUCE' | BY ROBERT GRAVES | (605); p. [2] publisher's note; p. [3] title-page; p. [4] publication, publisher's and printer's notices; p. [5] CONTENTS; p. [6] blank; p. [7] TO | WILLIAM FULLER | IN GRATITUDE; p. [8] blank; pp. 9–314 text; pp. [315]–[320] publisher's advertisements.

18·0 × 11·0 cm. Bulk: 1·4 cm. White wove paper; all edges trimmed. Bound in white paper covers printed in orange and black.

Price: 2s. Number of copies: 60,000. Published in January 1948.

A47   COUNT BELISARIUS   [1938]

a. *First edition:*

[*double rule rectangular box enclosing all:*] | *COUNT BELISARIUS* | *By* | ROBERT GRAVES | *Author of* | '*I, Claudius*' *and* '*Claudius the God*' | [*publisher's emblem*] | CASSELL | *and Company Limited* | *London Toronto Melbourne* | *and Sydney*

Collation: [A]⁸ B–Z⁸ 2A–2L⁸, 272 leaves.

p. [i] COUNT BELISARIUS; pp. [ii–iii] blank; p. [iv] map; p. [v] title-page; p. [vi] arrangement, publication and printer's notices; pp. vii–ix FOREWORD;

p. [x] CONTENTS; pp. 1–526 [527] text; p. [528] publisher's advertisement; p. [529] map; p. [530] blank; p. [531] map; p. [532] blank; pp. [533–534] maps.

21·2 × 13·8 cm. Bulk: 2·9/3·6 cm. White wove paper; all edges trimmed; top edge stained reddish brown. White wove endpapers. Bound in dark blue-green cloth; front and back blank; spine stamped in gold: COUNT | BELISARIUS | [medallion] | ROBERT GRAVES | [medallion] | CASSELL

Price: 8s. 6d. Number of copies: 16,000. Issued in April 1938 in white dust-jacket printed in blue, red-brown, purple, green and black.

Notes: Impressions: 2nd, October 1939 (5s.); 3rd, May 1948 (2,813 copies). The first impression also exists in a brown cloth' Colonial' binding, of which there were 4,000 copies, making a total of 20,000 copies of the first impression.

The jacket design is by John Aldridge.

Translated into Czech, Finnish, German, Greek, Magyar, Polish, Serbo-Croatian and Swedish.

b. First American edition ([*1938*]):

[*whole enclosed within rectangular single-rule box:*] | [*in brown decorative scallop-and-dot box:*] Robert Graves | COUNT | BELISARIUS | [*in brown: medallion*] | RANDOM HOUSE · NEW YORK

Collation: [1]–[36]⁸, 288 leaves.

p. [i] [*in decorative box:*] COUNT BELISARIUS; p. [ii] list of works by Graves; p. [iii] title-page; p. [iv] printing and publisher's notices; pp. v–viii FOREWORD; p. [ix] CONTENTS; p. [x] blank; p. [xi] LIST OF MAPS; p. [xii] blank; p. [1] [*in decorative box:*] COUNT BELISARIUS; p. [2] map; pp. 3–92 text; p. [93] map; pp. 94–114 text; p. [115] map; pp. 116–228 text; p. [229] map; pp. 230–312 text; p. [313] map; pp. 314–564 text.

21·9 × 14·1 cm. Bulk: 3·4/4·0 cm. White wove paper; all edges trimmed; top edges stained green. White wove endpapers. Bound in dark green cloth; front and back blank; spine stamped in gold: [*rule*] | [*5 ll. on solid rectangular black box:*] COUNT | BELISARIUS | [*medallion*] | ROBERT GRAVES | [*medallion*] | [*rule*] | RANDOM HOUSE

Price: $3.00. Number of copies undisclosed. Issued on 21 November 1938.

c. Literary Guild impression ([*1938*]):

Robert Graves | COUNT BELISARIUS | [*medallion*] | LITERARY GUILD · NEW YORK

Collation: [1]–[18]¹⁶, 288 leaves.
Remainder as A47*b*, except p. [ii] is blank.

21·3 × 14·1 cm. Bulk: 3·5/4·2 cm.White wove paper; all edges trimmed;
top edges stained rust.White wove endpapers. Bound in rust cloth; front
and back blank; spine stamped in gold as A47*b*, except solid black box is
solid cream.

Price: $2.00. Number of copies undisclosed. Published in December 1938.

d. Second English edition ([1955]*):*

COUNT | BELISARIUS | BY ROBERT GRAVES | [*star*] |
PENGUIN BOOKS

Collation: [A]¹⁶ B–F¹⁶ G²⁴ H–N¹⁶, 216 leaves.
p. [1] PENGUIN BOOKS | 1025 | COUNT BELISARIUS | ROBERT GRAVES | [*pub-
lisher's emblem*]; p. [2] blank; p. [3] title-page; p. [4] publisher's, publication
and printer's notices; p. [5] CONTENTS; p. [6] blank; pp. [7]–8 FOREWORD;
pp. [9]10–421 text, with pp. [29, 46, 61, 76, 92, 108, 124, 142, 161, 179, 197,
215, 229, 245, 265, 284, 304, 318, 340, 356, 371, 388, 406] unnumbered;
pp. [422]–[426] maps; p. [427] publisher's announcement; p. [428] blank;
pp. [429]–[432] publisher's advertisements.

18·0 × 11·0 cm. Bulk: 2·1 cm.White wove paper; all edges trimmed.
Bound in white paper covers printed in black and orange; inside front
cover: blurb; inside back cover: publisher's advertisements.

Price: 3s. 6d. Number of copies: 40,000. Published 24 March 1955.

e. Third English edition ([1962]*):*

Count Belisarius | ROBERT GRAVES | [*publisher's emblem*] |
CASSELL · LONDON

Collation: [1]–[33]⁸ [34]⁶, 270 leaves.
p. [i] COUNT BELISARIUS and blurb; p. [ii] list of novels by Graves; p.
[iii] blank; p. [iv] map; p. [v] title-page; p. [vi] publisher's, rights reservation, edition and printing notices; pp. 1–[534] as A47*a*.

19·9 × 13·2 cm. Bulk: 3·6/4·3 cm. White wove paper; all edges
trimmed; top edges stained brown. Bound in orange-brown cloth: front
and back blank; spine stamped in gold: COUNT | BELISARIUS | [*heavy rule*] |
ROBERT | GRAVES | CASSELL

Price: 18s. Number of copies: 4,000. Published 11 January 1962 in dust-
jacket as A47*a*.

Note: This book is a line-for-line, page-for-page resetting of A47*a*; printed
in Czechoslovakia.

a. First edition:

COLLECTED POEMS | [*swelled rule*] | ROBERT GRAVES |
[*publisher's emblem*] | CASSELL | AND COMPANY LIMITED |
LONDON, TORONTO, MELBOURNE AND SYDNEY

Collation: [*a*] /*a*1⁴/⁸ A–M⁸, 108 leaves.

p. [i] COLLECTED POEMS; p. [ii] blank; p. [iii] title-page; p. [iv] copyright,
printing and printer's notices; p. v list of works by Graves; p. vi quotations
from Riding (3 ll.) and Skelton (7 ll.); pp. vii–xi CONTENTS; p. [xii]
blank; pp. xiii–xxiv FOREWORD; pp. [1]–190 text, with pp. [1, 35, 75, 107,
171] being section headings and pp. [2, 36, 74, 76, 106, 108, 170, 172] blank;
pp. [191–192] blank.

21·6 × 13·9 cm. Bulk: 1·7/2·3 cm. White wove paper; all edges trimmed.
White wove endpapers. Bound in medium green cloth; front and back
blank; spine stamped in gold: [*first five lines enclosed in oval wreath:*] |
COLLECTED | POEMS | · | Robert | Graves | CASSELL

Price: 10s. 6d. Number of copies unknown. Published in November 1938
in buff dust-jacket printed in black and red.

Contents: Foreword – 1: The Haunted House – Reproach – The Finding of
Love – 'The General Elliott' – Outlaws – One Hard Look – A Frosty Night
– Allie – Unicorn and the White Doe – Henry and Mary – Love without
Hope –What Did I Dream? – The Country Dance – The Hills of May – Lost
Love – Vain and Careless – An English Wood – The Bedpost – The Pier-
Glass – Apples and Water –Wanderings of Christmas – Pygmalion and
Galatea – Down – Mermaid, Dragon, Fiend – II: In Procession – Angry
Samson –Warning to Children – Song: To Be Less Philosophical – Alice –
Blonde or Dark? – Richard Roe and John Doe – The Witches' Cauldron –
Ancestors – Children of Darkness – The Cool Web – Certain Mercies –
The Cuirassiers of the Frontier – Love in Barrenness – The Presence – The
Land of Whipperginny – In No Direction – The Castle – Return – Lust in
Song – Nobody –Without Pause – Full Moon – Vanity – Pure Death –
Sick Love – It Was All Very Tidy – III: Callow Captain – Thief – Saint – The
Furious Voyage – Song: Lift-Boy – The Next Time – Ulysses – The
Succubus – The Stranger – Trudge, Body – The Clock Man – The Reader
over My Shoulder – The Smoky House – Green Loving – The Legs –
Gardener – Front Door Soliloquy – In Broken Images – On Rising Early –
Flying Crooked – The Foolish Senses – Largesse to the Poor – The Goblet
Fiend, Dragon, Mermaid – Fragment of a Lost Poem – IV: Galatea and
Pygmalion – The Devil's Advice to Story-Tellers – Sea Side – Lunch-Hour
Blues –Wm. Brazier –Welsh Incident – Vision in the Repair-Shop – Hot
Bed – Progressive Housing – Interruption – Act V, Scene 5 – Midway

Hell – Leda – Synthetic Such – The Florist Rose – Being Tall – Lost Acres –
At First Sight – RecallingWar – Down,Wanton, Down! – X – A Former
Attachment – Nature's Lineaments – Time – The Philosopher – On
Dwelling – Parent to Children – Ogres and Pygmies – History of the
Word – Single Fare – To Challenge Delight – ToWalk on Hills – To Bring
the Dead to Life – To Evoke Posterity – The Poets – Defeat of the Rebels –
The Grudge – Never Such Love – The Halfpenny – The Fallen Signpost –
The China Plate – Idle Hands – The Laureate – A Jealous Man – The
Cloak – The Halls of Bedlam – Or to Perish before Day – A Country
Mansion – The Eremites – The Advocates – Self-Praise – v: On Portents –
The Terraced Valley – The Challenge – ToWhom Else? – To the Sovereign
Muse – The Ages of Oath – New Legends – Like Snow – The Climate of
Thought – End of Play – The Fallen Tower of Siloam – The Great-
Grandmother – No More Ghosts – Leaving the Rest Unsaid

Note: Both A48*a* and A48*b* were printed in Great Britain.

b. *American issue* ([*1939*]):

COLLECTED POEMS | [*swelled rule*] | ROBERT GRAVES |
[*publisher's emblem*] | RANDOM HOUSE | NEW YORK

Collation as A48*a*.

21·6 × 13·9 cm. Bulk: 1·7/2·2 cm. White wove paper; all edges trimmed;
top edges stained black.White wove endpapers. Bound in dark brick-red
cloth; front and back blank; spine stamped in gold: [*publisher's emblem in
black and gold*] | [*solid rectangular black box, inside which next 7 ll.:*] [*rectangular
broad rule box, inside which:*] | [*rectangular light rule box, inside which the next
5 ll.:*] | COLLECTED | POEMS | [*wedge*] | ROBERT | GRAVES | [next 2 ll. at bottom
of spine:] RANDOM | HOUSE

Price: $2.50. Number of copies undisclosed. Published 16 March 1939.

A49   T. E. LAWRENCE TO HIS BIOGRAPHER   1938

a. First edition:

[*in brown:*] T. E. Lawrence | TO HIS BIOGRAPHER, | Robert
Graves | INFORMATION ABOUT HIMSELF, IN THE
FORM | OF LETTERS, NOTES AND ANSWERS TO
QUESTIONS, | EDITED WITH A CRITICAL COMMEN-
TARY. | [*in brown: cut of crossed rifles, flags, swords, scimitar and
sabre, with leaves*] | NEW YORK | Doubleday, Doran & Com-
pany, Inc. | MCMXXXVIII

Collation: [1]⁸⁺² [2]–[10]⁸ [11]¹⁰ [12]⁸, 100 leaves.

one leaf, verso blank, on the recto of which: *This edition* | *is limited to 1,000 numbered and* | *signed copies for sale, of which 500 copies* | *are printed for the United States.* | *This is number* —— *[number written in by hand]* | *[signature of Graves]*; p. [i] T. E. Lawrence | TO HIS BIOGRAPHER, | ROBERT GRAVES; p. [ii] blank; [*frontispiece, back blank*]; p. [iii] title-page tipped in; p. [iv] printer's, designer's, copyright, rights reservation and edition notices; p. [v] PUBLISHER's NOTE; p. [vi] blank; pp. vii–viii FOREWORD; p. ix CONTENTS; p. [x] blank; p. [1] PART I | *1920–1926;* p. [2] blank; pp. 3–39 text; p. [40] blank; p. [41] PART II | *1927;* p. [42] blank; pp. 43–144 text; p. [145] PART III | *1928–1935;* p. [146] blank; pp. 147–187 text; p. [188] blank.

22·7 × 15·2 cm. Bulk: 1·7/2·3 cm. Cream laid paper; top edge only trimmed and gilt. Cream laid endpapers. Bound in buff cloth; back blank; front blind-stamped: T. E. LAWRENCE | TO HIS BIOGRAPHER | ROBERT GRAVES; spine stamped: [*triple light-heavy-light rule of brown, gold, brown*] | [*triple rule as above*] | [*triple rule as above*] | [*brown light rule*] | [*double heavy gold rule*] | [*solid brown rectangular box, inside which next 8 ll.:*] T. E. | LAWRENCE | TO HIS | BIOGRAPHER | ROBERT | GRAVES | DOUBLEDAY | DORAN | [*two heavy gold rules*] | [*brown light rule*] | [*eleven triple rules as at top*]

Price: $20.00. Number of copies: 500. Published on 2 December 1938.

Note: Issued with Liddell Hart's book of the same title. The book was designed by A. P. Tedesco.

b. First English issue ([1939]):

[*in brown:*] T. E. Lawrence | TO HIS BIOGRAPHER, | Robert Graves | INFORMATION ABOUT HIMSELF, IN THE FORM | OF LETTERS, NOTES AND ANSWERS TO QUESTIONS. | EDITED WITH A CRITICAL COMMENTARY. | [*in brown: cut of crossed rifles, flags, swords, scimitar and sabre, with leaves*] | FABER AND FABER LIMITED | 24 Russell Square London

Collation as A49a.
one leaf, recto blank, on the verso of which: *This edition* | *is limited to 1,00 numbered and* | *signed copies for sale, of which 500 copies* | *are printed for Gre Britain.* | *This is number* —— *[number written in by hand]* | *[signature of Graves]* pp. [i]–[ii] as A49a; p. [iii] title-page tipped in; p. [iv] *First published December Mcmxxxviii* | *by Faber and Faber Limited* | *24 Russell Squar London,W.C.* | *Printed in the United States of America* | *All Rights Reserved* DESIGNED BY A. P. TEDESCO | CL | The Publishers are grateful to Messrs. Jonathan Cape, Ltd., for permission to | include copyright material remainder as A49a.

7

the Dipper can get off free. Why not I? Waterford

I remonstrated with Harlowe, pointing out the manifest dangers of such a course but he persisted. The vessels that put into Waterford were frequently short-handed and he could no doubt stow himself aboard one of them and work his passage to America which was his objective indirectly, by way of the love of Cork or some other port. The name of America struck sympathetically in my ears, and, desperate as I was myself, I began to think that his project was not so rash as I had judged. That evening, after a particularly warm day under Portal Harry, I was fully determined to ally myself with Harlowe. There was a manner of breaking out of barracks known to two or three of us which presented no difficulties to a pair of active men. ... would stere mounting on the other's shoulder, in order to climb a ten foot wall, and pull up his comrade after him a short stretch of walk along this wall brought the ... to a holly tree into the branches of which one must leap, and so descend. A sentry had his walk along the outer wall of the barracks. ... to choose the moment when the sentry had turned the corner of the wall ... into the tree, and waiting

Marginal notes:

"... is a harbour of good omen: it was from here that King James II escaped from his enemies and sailed to his kingdom in France."

in the Newfoundland trade

with cargoes of pork, butter, and potatoes

The harbour extended about eight miles in length ... depth a straggling line ... was wide and ... so that the navigation ... the many small ... in lonely parts which would facilitate his escape

The route began with the necessary house. One man

even on moonlit nights by but he could be eluded by making the passage in three stages. The first stage was

What I have suffered is enough to turn a man rank Jacobite

he would stow himself aboard a coasting vessel which would be less likely to be searched by the guard ... and make America

Part of a page of the MS of *Sergeant Lamb of the Ninth* (A51)

A Country Mood

Take now a country mood,
  Resolve, distil it :—
Nine acre swaying alive,
  June flowers that fill it,

Spicy sweet-briar bush,
  The uneasy wren
Fluttering from ash to birch
  And back again,

Milkwort on its low stem,
  Spread hawthorn tree,
Sun light patching the wood,
  A hive bound bee,

Girls riding nim-nim-nim,
  Ladies, trot-trot,
Gentlemen hard at gallop,
  Shouting, steam hot.

Now over the rough turf
  Bridles go jingle
And there's a well-loved pool
  By Fox's Dingle

Where Sweetheart my brown mare
  Old Glory's daughter
May loll her leathern tongue
  In snow-cold water.

MS of 'A Country Mood' (C76)

Size, bulk and paper as A49a. Bound in red cloth; back blank; front stamped with solid grey rectangular box stamped in gold: [*three successively smaller rectangular light rule boxes, inside which:*] T. E. LAWRENCE | to his biographer | ROBERT GRAVES; spine stamped with solid grey rectangular box inside which: [*three light rules*] | T. E. | LAWRENCE | to his | biographer | ROBERT | GRAVES | [*light rule*] | Faber and | Faber | [*three light rules*]

Price: 5 gns. Number of copies: 500. Published in January 1939 in glassine wrapper and included in a light grey-green box with Liddell Hart's book.

c. Second English edition ([1963]):

T. E. Lawrence | TO HIS BIOGRAPHERS | Robert Graves | AND | Liddell Hart | [*publisher's emblem*] | CASSELL · LONDON

Collation: [A]⁸ B–P¹⁶, 232 leaves.

p. [i] T. E. Lawrence | TO HIS BIOGRAPHERS | ROBERT GRAVES | AND | LIDDELL HART; p. [ii] blank; [*frontispiece, back blank*]; p. [iii] title-page; p. [iv] publisher's, copyright, acknowledgement and printer's notices; p. [v] T. E. Lawrence | TO HIS BIOGRAPHER | ROBERT GRAVES | *Information about himself, in the form of letters, notes and answers to* | *questions, edited with a critical commentary.*; p. [vi] PUBLISHER'S NOTE; pp. vii–viii FOREWORD; p. ix CONTENTS; p. [x] blank; p. [1] PART I | *1920–1926;* p. [2] blank; pp. 3–39 text; p. [40] blank; p. [41] PART II | *1927;* p. [42] blank; pp. 43–144 text; p. [145] PART III | *1928–1935;* p. [146] blank; pp. 147–187 text; p. [188] blank; p. [i] T. E. Lawrence | TO HIS BIOGRAPHER | LIDDELL HART | *Information about himself, in the form of letters, notes, answers to* | *questions and conversations.*; p. [ii] PUBLISHER'S NOTE; pp. iii–iv FOREWORD; pp. [1]2–233 text; p. [234] blank; pp. 235–260 INDEX; pp. [261–262] blank.

21·5 × 13·8 cm. Bulk: 3·1/3·7 cm.White wove paper; all edges trimmed. White wove endpapers. Bound in dark beige cloth; front and back blank; spine stamped in gold: [at top of spine, facing front:] T. E. LAWRENCE | [remainder across spine:] TO HIS | BIOGRAPHERS | ROBERT | GRAVES | & | LIDDELL | HART | CASSELL

Price: 42s. Number of copies: 2,062. Published 7 March 1963 in white dust-jacket printed in black and yellowish grey-green.

Note: Impressions: 2nd, May 1963 (1,000 copies).
Printed in Great Britain.

d. Second edition, American issue (1963):

T. E. Lawrence | TO HIS BIOGRAPHERS | Robert Graves | AND | Liddell Hart | [*Cassell publisher's emblem*] | DOUBLE-DAY & COMPANY, INC. | GARDEN CITY, NEW YORK, 1963

Collation as A49c.
Remainder as A49c, except lacks frontispiece and p. [iv] has acknowledgement, Library of Congress card, copyright, rights reservation and printing notices.

20·8 × 14·1 cm. Bulk: 3·1/3·7 cm. White wove paper; top and fore-edges trimmed. White wove endpapers. Bound in rust cloth; front and back blank; quarter cloth spine in buff, printed in two rows, top to bottom: [*in black:*] T. E. LAWRENCE [*in rose buff:*] TO HIS BIOGRAPHERS | [*in black:*] *Robert Graves & B. H. Liddell Hart* [*in rose buff:*] DOUBLEDAY

Price: $6.50. Number of copies: 3,500. Published 16 August 1963 in white dust-jacket printed in black, orange and green.

Note: Impressions: 2nd (2,500 copies), 1963; p. [iv] has *'Johnathan'* for *'Jonathan'* in first impression.
Printed in the U.S.

A50   NO MORE GHOSTS   [1940]

First edition:

NO MORE GHOSTS | Selected Poems | by | ROBERT GRAVES | Faber and Faber | 24 Russell Square | London

Collation: [A]⁸ B–E⁸, 40 leaves.
p. [1] NO MORE GHOSTS; p. [2] blank; p. [3] title-page; p. [4] publication, printer's and rights reservation notices; p. 5 SELECT BIBLIOGRAPHY; p. [6] blank; pp. 7–8 CONTENTS; pp. 9–79 text; p. [80] blank.

18·7 × 12·4 cm. Bulk: 0·7/1·0 cm. White wove paper; all edges trimmed; watermarked with a crown and Abbey Mills | Greenfield. White wove end-papers. Bound in grey-tan boards; back blank; front printed in blue: *No More* | *Ghosts* | [*star*] | *Robert* | *Graves;* spine printed in blue from top to bottom: NO MORE GHOSTS BY ROBERT GRAVES FABER

Price: 2s. 6d. Number of copies: 2,000. Published in September 1940 in bright blue dust-jacket printed in black.

Contents: 1. The Haunted House – 2. Apples and Water – 3. Time – 4. On Dwelling – 5. Love in Barrenness – 6. Vain and Careless – 7. In Procession – 8. Angry Samson – 9. Ogres and Pygmies – 10. The Bards – 11. The Cool Web – 12. The Cuirassiers of the Frontier – 13. The Castle – 14. Full Moon – 15. Vanity – 16. Pure Death – 17. Sick Love – 18. The Presence – 19. Nature's Lineaments – 20. The Furious Voyage – 21. Callow Captain – 22. The Beast – 23. A Love Story – 24. The Legs – 25. Flying Crooked – 26.

Warning to Children – 27. The Laureate – 28. The Terraced Valley – 29. Recalling War – 30. Certain Mercies – 31. Ulysses – 32. Down, Wanton, Down! – 33. The Florist Rose – 34. The Thieves – 35. Sea Side – 36. The Devil's Advice to Story-Tellers – 37. The Cloak – 38. To Bring the Dead to Life – 39. Defeat of the Rebels – 40. Never Such Love – 41. The Poets – 42. A Jealous Man – 43. The Advocates – 44. On Portents – 45. Like Snow – 46. End of Play – 47. The Fallen Tower of Siloam – 48. The Great-Grandmother – 49. To Sleep – 50. No More Ghosts

Notes: Impressions: 2nd, March 1941 (2,000 copies); 3rd, June 1945 (2,000 copies); 4th, January 1947 (2,000 copies). The cover legend on the second and third reads: *No More Ghosts | selected poems | [star] | Robert | Graves;* the second impression has black printing on the covers; the third blue.

A51   SERGEANT LAMB OF THE NINTH   [1940]

a. First edition:

SERGEANT LAMB | OF THE NINTH | *by* | ROBERT GRAVES | AUTHOR OF | 'I, CLAUDIUS', 'CLAUDIUS THE GOD' | 'COUNT BELISARIUS' ETC. | [*publisher's emblem*] | METHUEN & CO. LTD. LONDON | *36 Essex Street, Strand, W.C.2*

Collation: π^6 1–23^8 24^4, 194 leaves.
p. [i] SERGEANT LAMB | OF THE NINTH; p. [ii] list of regiments; [*frontispiece, letter from Lamb, back blank*]; p. [iii] title-page; p. [iv] publication and printing notices; pp. v–vi *FOREWORD;* pp. vii–xi ROGER LAMB'S NOTE OF EXPLANATION; p. [xii] blank; pp. 1–376 text; [foldout map tipped to p. 376 and rear endpaper].

18·5 × 12·3 cm. Bulk: 3·0/3·4 cm. White wove paper; all edges trimmed. White wove endpapers. Bound in plum-red cloth; front and back blank; spine stamped in white: *SERGEANT | LAMB | OF | THE NINTH | ROBERT | GRAVES | METHUEN*

Price: 8s. 6d. Number of copies: 10,000. Published 12 September 1940 in white dust-jacket printed in red, black, brown, green and blue.

Notes: Impressions: 2nd, July 1945 (2,500 copies).
The dust-jacket was designed by John Aldridge.
This book has been translated into German and Spanish.
The second impression is called 'SECOND EDITION' between ll. 7/8 on the title-page; it collates [1]^{16} 2–11^{16} 11/13$^{2/16}$ [*sic:* 11 *for* 12]; 18·2 × 12·3 cm.

b. First American edition ([1940]):

[*rectangular double-rule box enclosing all:*] | *Sergeant* LAMB'S | [*in red:*] AMERICA | [*rule*] | by Robert Graves | [*rule*] | [*in red: publisher's emblem*] | RANDOM HOUSE | *New York*

Collation: [1]–[25]^{8}, 200 leaves.
2 pp., blank; p. [i] SERGEANT LAMB'S | AMERICA; p. [ii] list of books by Graves; p. [iii] title-page; p. [iv] acknowledgement, printing and copyright notices; p. [v] facsimile of letter by Lamb; p. [vi] transcript of letter facing; pp. vii–viii Foreword; pp. ix–xiii Roger Lamb's Note of *Explanation;* p. [xiv] list of regiments; p. [1] SERGEANT LAMB'S | AMERICA; p. [2] blank; pp. 3–380 text; pp. [381]–[384] blank.

21·2 × 14·2 cm. Bulk: 3·4/4·1 cm. White wove paper; all edges trimmed. Rear endpapers blank white wove paper; front endpapers white wove, inner sides printed with map of Lamb's travels. Bound in red cloth; back blank; front has blue paper label with white legend: [*double-rule rectangular box enclosing all:*] *Sergeant* LAMB'S | AMERICA | [*rule*] | Robert Graves; spine has blue label with white legend: [*double-rule rectangular box enclosing all:*] | *Sergeant* LAMB'S | AMERICA | [*rule*] | ROBERT | GRAVES | Random House

Price: $2.50. Number of copies undisclosed. Published 1 November 1940.

c. Second English edition ([1950]):

SERGEANT LAMB | OF THE NINTH | [*swelled rule with elliptical asterisk in centre*] | ROBERT GRAVES | [*star*] | PENGUIN BOOKS | HARMONDSWORTH · MIDDLESEX

Collation: [A]^{16} B–L^{16}, 176 leaves.
p. [1] PENGUIN BOOKS | 725 | SERGEANT LAMB OF THE NINTH | ROBERT GRAVES | [*publisher's emblem*]; p. [2] publication, publisher's and printer's notices; p. [3] title-page; p. 4 list of regiments; p. 5 *Foreword;* pp. 6–7[8] ROGER LAMB'S NOTE OF EXPLANATION; pp. 9–15 text; pp. [16–17] map; pp. 18–352 text.

18·1 × 11·1 cm. Bulk: 1·6 cm. White wove paper; all edges trimmed. Bound in white paper covers printed in orange and black.

Price: 1s. 6d. Number of copies: 45,000. Published in February 1950.

d. Third English edition ([1961]):

ROBERT GRAVES | [*rule*] | SERGEANT LAMB | OF THE NINTH | MAY FAIR BOOKS

Collation: [A]^{16} B–I^{16} [K]^{16}, 160 leaves.

p. [1] blurb; p. [2] publisher's notice, list of books by Graves, copyright and publication notices; p. [3] title-page; pp. [4–5] map; p. 6 list of regiments; pp. 7–316 text; p. 317 *Postscript;* pp. 318–320 *Roger Lamb's Note of Explanation*

17·4 × 10·8 cm. Bulk: 1·8 cm. White wove paper; all edges trimmed. Bound in white paper covers printed in green, blue, red, magenta and black; inside of front and back covers blank.

Price: 3s. 6d. Number of copies: 25,000. Published on 15 July 1961.

Note: This is May Fair Book no. 12.

e. Second American edition ([1962]):

ROBERT GRAVES | [*decorative divider*] | Sergeant Lamb's | AMERICA | [*publisher's emblem*] | VINTAGE BOOKS | *A Division of Random House* | New York

Collation: 176 leaves, glued at spine.

p. [i] Sergeant Lamb's | AMERICA; p. [ii] blank; p. [iii] title-page; p. [iv] edition, publisher's, copyright and manufacturing notices; pp. [v]–vi Foreword; pp. [vii]viii–xi Roger Lamb's | Note of Explanation; p. [xii] list of regiments; p. [1] Sergeant Lamb's | AMERICA; p. [2] blank; pp. [3]4–339 text, pp. [92, 105, 119, 147, 241] being unnumbered; p. [340] biographical, typographical, printer's and designer's notices.

18·4 × 11·1 cm. Bulk: 1·6 cm. White wove paper; all edges trimmed. Bound in white paper covers printed in blue, red and black.

Price: $1.45. Number of copies undisclosed. Published on 30 April 1962.

A52   THE LONG WEEK-END   [1940]

a. First edition:

THE LONG WEEK-END | A Social History of Great Britain | 1918–1939 | *by* | ROBERT GRAVES | *and* | ALAN HODGE | FABER AND FABER LIMITED | 24 *Russell Square* | London

Collation: [A]^8 B–Z^8 2A–2F^8 2G^4, 236 leaves.

p. [1] THE LONG WEEK-END | A Social History of Great Britain | 1918–1939; p. [2] blank; p. [3] title-page; p. [4] publication, publisher's and printer's notices; p. [5] To | K. G. | in gratitude for much | hard work; p. [6] blank; p. 7 Authors' Note; p. [8] blank; pp. 9–10 Contents; pp. 11–455 text; pp. 456–472 Index.

21·6 × 13·9 cm. Bulk: 2·7/3·2 cm.White wove paper; top and fore-edges trimmed.White wove endpapers. Bound in brown cloth; front and back blank; spine stamped in gold: THE | LONG | WEEK-END | [double-rule] | Robert Graves | and | Alan Hodge | [double rule] | FABER AND | FABER

Price: 12s. 6d. Number of copies: 4,000. Published in November 1940 in canary dust-jacket printed in red and black.

Contents: Authors' Note – 1. Armistice, 1918 – 2. Revolution Averted, 1919 – 3.Women – 4. Reading Matter – 5. Post-War Politics – 6. Various Conquests – 7. Sex – 8. Amusements – 9. Screen and Stage – 10. Revolution Again Averted – 11. Domestic Life – 12. Art, Literature and Religion – 13. Education and Ethics – 14. Sport and Controversy – 15. The Depression, 1930 – 16. Pacifism, Nudism, Hiking – 17. The Days of the Loch Ness Monster – 18. Recovery, 1935 – 19. The Days of Non-Intervention – 20. 'The Deepening Twilight of Barbarism' – 21. Three Kings in One Year – 22. Keeping Fit and Doing the LambethWalk – 23. Social Consciences – 24. 'Markets Close Firmer' – 25. Still at Peace – 26. Rain Stops Play, 1939 – Index

Notes: The 'second edition' is a photographic reprint of this edition with minor rearrangements in [A]; the dedication has been moved to p. [4]; p. [5] Note to First Edition; pp. 6–8 Note to Second Edition; 4,050 copies were published in May 1950 at 16s.
This book has been translated into Danish and Swedish.

b. First American edition (1941):

THE LONG WEEK END | A Social History of Great Britain | 1918–1939 | *by* | ROBERT GRAVES | *and* | ALAN HODGE | *New York* | THE MACMILLAN COMPANY | 1941

Collation: [1]–[13]¹⁶ [14]¹² [15]¹⁶, 236 leaves.
p. [i–ii] blank; p. [iii] THE LONG WEEK END | A Social History of Great Britain | 1918–1939; p. [iv] publisher's emblem and notice; p. [v] title-page; p. [vi] copyright and printer's notices; p. [vii] To | K. G. | in gratitude for much | hard work; p. [viii] blank; p. [ix] Authors' Note; p. [x] blank; pp. [xi–xii] Contents; p. [xiii] THE LONG WEEK END | A Social History of Great Britain | 1918–1939; p. [xiv] blank; pp. 1–439 text; p. [440] blank; pp. 441–455 Index; pp. [456]–[458] blank.

23·4 × 15·5 cm. Bulk: 3·0/3·5 cm.White wove paper; all edges trimmed. Heavy white wove endpapers. Bound in dark blue cloth; front and back blank; spine stamped in gold: THE | LONG | WEEK END | [double rule] | Robert Graves | and | Alan Hodge | [double rule] | MACMILLAN | [long-short-long dashes]

Price: $3.00. Number of copies unknown. Published 27 May 1941.

Note: Impressions: 2nd, 1941.

c. *Readers' Union impression (1941):*

THE LONG WEEK-END | A Social History of Great Britain |
1918–1939 | *by* | ROBERT GRAVES | *and* | ALAN HODGE |
READERS' UNION LIMITED | *by arrangement with* | FABER
AND FABER LIMITED | *London 1941*

Collation: [A]/A*⁸/⁸ B/B*–O/O*⁸/⁸ P⁸ Q⁴, 236 leaves.
pp. [1–2] front pastedown endpaper; pp. [3–4] blank; p. [5] THE LONG WEEK-
END | A Social History of Great Britain | 1918–1939; p. [6] blank; p.
[7] title-page; p. [8] printer's, publisher's and dedication notices; p. 9
Contents; p. 10 Authors' Note; pp. 11–472 as A52*a*.

19·7 × 12·9 cm. Bulk: 2·4/2·8 cm. White wove paper; all edges trimmed.
Rear endpapers white wove. Bound in wine-red cloth; front and back
blank; spine stamped in silver: *Graves* | [*rule*] | [*rectangular rule box enclosing
2 ll.:*] THE LONG | WEEK-END | [*rule*] | *Hodge* | [*remainder blind stamped:*]
[*rule*] | [*Readers' Union emblem*]

Price: 2s. 9d. Number of copies: 19,000. Published in November 1941.

d. *Second English edition ([1961]):*

[7 ll. flush left:] The Long | Week-End | A Social History of
Great Britain, | 1918–1939 | ROBERT GRAVES and | ALAN
HODGE | [*publisher's emblem*] | [centred:] FOUR SQUARE
BOOKS LTD BARNARD'S INN HOLBORN LONDON
EC1

Collation: [A]¹⁶ B–N¹⁶ [O]¹⁶, 224 leaves.
p. [1] [title and publisher flush left:] The Long | Week-End | [centred 3-ll.
blurb] | A FOUR SQUARE BOOK; p. [2] publisher's advertisement; p. [3] title-
page; p. [4] publication notice, dedication, and publisher's and printer's
notices; p. [5] CONTENTS; p. [6] AUTHORS' NOTE and NOTE TO THIS EDITION;
pp. 7–448 text.

17·8 × 10·8 cm. Bulk: 2·0 cm. White wove paper; all edges trimmed.
Bound in white paper covers printed in magenta, red, blue, gold and
black; inner sides blank.

Price: 5s. Number of copies undetermined. Published in 1961.

e. Second American 'edition' ([1963]):

THE LONG WEEK-END | A Social History of Great Britain |
1918–1939 | *by* | ROBERT GRAVES | *and* | ALAN HODGE |
[*publisher's emblem*] | The Norton Library | W · W · NORTON
& COMPANY · INC · | NEW YORK

Collation: 240 leaves, unsigned, glued at spine.

p. [i] THE LONG WEEK-END | A Social History of Great Britain | 1918–1939;
p. [ii] blank; p. [1] biographical notices; p. [2] blank; p. [3] title-page;
p. [4] copyright, publication, dedication and printing notices; p. 5 Note to
First Edition; pp. 6–8 Note to Second Edition; pp. 9–472, as A52a; p. [473]
blank; pp. [474]–[477] publisher's advertisements; p. [478] blank.

19·6 × 12·9 cm. Bulk: 2·2 cm. White wove paper; all edges trimmed.
Bound in white paper covers printed in red, blue and black.

Price: $1.95. Number of copies undetermined. Published in 1963.

Note: This book would appear to be a photographic reprint of the second
'edition' of A52a.

A53   PROCEED, SERGEANT LAMB   [1941]

a. First edition:

PROCEED, SERGEANT LAMB | *by* | ROBERT GRAVES |
AUTHOR OF | 'SERGEANT LAMB OF THE NINTH'
| [*publisher's emblem*] | METHUEN & CO. LTD. LONDON |
36 Essex Street, Strand, W.C.2

Collation: π^6 1–19^8 20^6, 164 leaves.

2 pp., blank, as front pastedown endpaper; p. [i] PROCEED, | SERGEANT
LAMB; p. [ii] list of regiments; [*frontispiece, back blank*]; p. [iii] title-page;
p. [iv] publication and printing notices; pp. v–vii *FOREWARD;* p. [viii]
blank; p. [ix] PROCEED, | SERGEANT LAMB; p. [x] blank; pp. 1–314 text;
p. [315] blank; p. [316] printer's notice; [map tipped to rear endpaper].

18·6 × 12·3 cm. Bulk: 2·3/2·6 cm. White wove paper; all edges trimmed.
White wove rear endpaper. Bound in sea-green cloth; front and back blank;
spine stamped in white: PROCEED, | SERGEANT | LAMB | ROBERT
| GRAVES | METHUEN

Price: 8s. 6d. Number of copies: 10,000. Published 13 February 1941 in
white dust-jacket printed in black, red, blue and brown.

Notes: This book has been translated into Spanish.

The dust-jacket was designed by John Aldridge.

According to Methuen, 4,000 copies of signatures 1–16 'were destroyed by enemy action during 1942' and were reprinted.

b. First American edition ([1941]):

[*whole enclosed within double-rule rectangular box:*] PROCEED, | [*in red:*] SERGEANT LAMB | [*rule*] | by Robert Graves | *Author of* | SERGEANT LAMB'S AMERICA | [*rule*] | [*in red: publisher's emblem*] | RANDOM HOUSE | *New York*

Collation: [1]–[21]⁸, 168 leaves.

p. [i] PROCEED, | SERGEANT LAMB; p. [ii] list of regiments; p. [iii] title-page; p. [iv] publication, printer's and copyright notices; p. [v] facsimile of letter; p. [vi] transcript of letter; pp. vii–xi Foreword; p. [xii] blank; p. [1] PROCEED, | SERGEANT LAMB; p. [2] map; pp. 3–322 text; pp. [323–324] blank.

21·3 × 14·3 cm. Bulk: 3·0/3·6 cm. White wove paper; all edges trimmed; top edges stained blue. Cream wove endpapers. Bound in red cloth; back blank; blue label on front printed in white: [*whole enclosed in double-rule rectangular box:*] PROCEED, | SERGEANT | LAMB | [*rule*] | by Robert Graves; blue label on spine, printed in white: [*whole enclosed in double-rule rectangular box:*] PROCEED, | SERGEANT | LAMB | [*rule*] | ROBERT | GRAVES | Random House

Price: $2.50. Number of copies undisclosed. Published 15 October 1941.

c. Second English edition ([1947]):

PROCEED, | SERGEANT LAMB | *by* | ROBERT GRAVES | AUTHOR OF | 'SERGEANT LAMB OF THE NINTH' | SECOND EDITION | [*publisher's emblem*] | METHUEN & CO. LTD. LONDON | *36 Essex Street, Strand, W.C.2*

Collation: [A]⁸ B–L¹⁶, 168 leaves.

p. [i] PROCEED, | SERGEANT LAMB; p. [ii] list of regiments; [*frontispiece, back blank*]; p. [iii] title-page; p. [iv] publication and printing notices; pp. v–vii *FOREWORD;* pp. vii–ix *NOTE TO SECOND EDITION;* p.[x] blank; pp. 1–321 text; p. [322] printer's notice; [map tipped to following page]; pp. [323–324] blank; pp. [325–326] pasted down to back cover.

18·2 × 12·3 cm. Bulk: 2·1/2·4 cm. White wove paper; all edges trimmed. White wove front endpapers. Bound in sea-green cloth; front and back blank; spine stamped in white: *PROCEED,* | *SERGEANT* | *LAMB* | *ROBERT* | *GRAVES* | *METHUEN*

Price: 8s. 6d. Number of copies: 5,000. Published in February 1947.

Note: The last 1,750 sheets of this edition were issued 10 September 1953 at 6s.; the book went out of print in December 1959.

d. Third English edition ([1961]):

ROBERT GRAVES | [*rule*] | PROCEED, SERGEANT | LAMB | MAY FAIR BOOKS

Collation: [A]¹⁶ B–H¹⁶ [I]¹⁶, 144 leaves.
p. [1] publisher's advertisements; p. [2] list of books by Graves and copyright and printing notices; p. [3] title-page; pp. [4–5] map; p. [6] list of regiments; pp. [7–8] *FOREWORD;* pp. 9–288 text.

17·4 × 10·6 cm. Bulk: 1·6 cm. White wove paper; all edges trimmed. Bound in white paper covers printed in blue, magenta and black.

Price: 3s. 6d. Number of copies: 25,000. Published 15 July 1961.

A54   WIFE TO MR. MILTON   [1943]

a. First edition:

THE STORY OF MARIE POWELL, | WIFE TO MR. MILTON | by | ROBERT GRAVES | *With two half-tone plates* | [*publisher's emblem*] | CASSELL AND COMPANY LTD. | London, Toronto, Melbourne | and Sydney

Collation: [A]¹⁶ B–M¹⁶, 192 leaves.
p. [i] WIFE TO MR. MILTON; p. [ii] list of novels by Graves; [*frontispiece, back blank*]; p. [iii] title-page; p. [iv] economy, publication and printer's notices; p. v CONTENTS; p. vi ILLUSTRATIONS; pp. vii–viii FOREWORD; pp. 1–112 text; [plate, facing p. 112, back blank]; pp. 113–346 text; pp. 347–357 EPILOGUE; pp. 358–363 APPENDIX; pp. 364–372 GLOSSARY; pp. [373–374] blank, as rear free endpaper; pp. [375–376] blank, as rear pastedown endpaper.

18·4 × 12·0 cm. Bulk: 1·6/1·9 cm. White wove paper; all edges trimmed. Front endpapers white wove. Bound in tan cloth; front and back blank; spine printed in black: *Wife to* | *Mr. Milton* | ROBERT | GRAVES | CASSELL

Price: 10s. 6d. Number of copies: 9,420. Published in January 1943 in white dust-jacket printed in orange and black.

Notes: Impressions: 2nd, January 1943. Number of copies: 2,950; 3rd, June 1949. Number of copies: 3,471.

This book has been translated into French and Polish.

The page numbers appear in brackets; on p. 33 the right bracket is reversed; on p. 283 the left bracket is missing.

b. *First American edition* ([1944]):

[*in red-brown:*] WIFE | [*in red-brown:*] TO MR. MILTON | The Story of | MARIE POWELL | by | ROBERT GRAVES | [*in red-brown:*] [*publisher's emblem*] | *NEW YORK* | CREATIVE AGE PRESS, INC.

Collation: [1]⁸ [2]–[12]¹⁶ [13]⁸, 192 leaves.

p. [iii] title-page; p. [iv] economy, copyright, designer's and printer's notices; pp. v–vi *Contents;* pp. vii–viii *Foreword;* pp. 3–356 text; pp. 357–366 *Epilogue;* pp. 367–372 *Appendix;* pp. 373–380 *Glossary.*

20·2 × 13·6 cm. Bulk: 2·3/3·0 cm. White wove paper; all edges trimmed; top edges stained blue. White wove endpapers; inner sides maps. Bound in blue cloth; back blank; front stamped in gold with facsimile signature of Graves; spine stamped in gold: ROBERT GRAVES | [*five lines in solid black rectangular box:*] | [*rule*] | WIFE | *to* | MR. MILTON | [*rule*] | CREATIVE AGE | PRESS

Price: $2.75. Number of copies unknown. Published in November 1944 in white dust-jacket printed in pink and blue.

c. *Second English edition* ([1954]):

ROBERT GRAVES | WIFE TO MR MILTON | *The Story of Marie Powell* | PENGUIN BOOKS

Collation: [A]¹⁶ B–O¹⁶, 208 leaves.

p. [1] PENGUIN BOOKS | 1024 | WIFE TO MR MILTON | ROBERT GRAVES | [*publisher's emblem*]; p. [2] map; p. [3] title-page; p. [4] publisher's, printing and printer's notices; p. [5] CONTENTS; p. [6] blank; pp. [7–8] FOREWORD; pp. [9]10–387 text, with pp. [58, 72, 114, 141, 166, 201, 283, 302, 331, 368] being unnumbered; p. [388] blank; pp. [389]390–399 EPILOGUE; p. [400] blank; pp. [401]402–407 APPENDIX; p. [408] blank; pp. [409] 410–415 GLOSSARY; p. [416] blank.

18·0 × 11·0 cm. Bulk: 1·9 cm. White wove paper; all edges trimmed. Bound in white paper covers printed in orange and black.

Price: 3s. 6d. Number of copies: 40,000. Published on August 27 1954.

d. Second American issue ([1962]):

WIFE | TO MR. MILTON | The Story of | MARIE POWELL |
by | ROBERT GRAVES | [*publisher's emblem*] | The Noonday
Press, a division of | Farrar, Straus & Cudahy New York

> *Collation:* [1]–[12]¹⁶, 192 leaves.
> p. [i] *WIFE TO MR. MILTON;* p. [ii] blank; p. [iii] title-page; p. [iv]
> copyright, publication, designer's and manufacturing notices; pp. v–vi
> *Contents;* pp. vii–viii *Foreword;* pp. 3–356 text; pp. 357–366 *Epilogue;*
> pp. 367–372 *Appendix;* pp. 373–378 *Glossary.*
>
> 20·3 × 13·6 cm. Bulk: 3·0 cm. White wove paper; all edges trimmed.
> Bound in white paper covers printed in purple, black and red.
>
> *Price:* $1.95. Number of copies unknown. Published 20 April 1962.

A55 THE READER OVER YOUR SHOULDER [1943]

a. First edition:

The | READER | OVER YOUR SHOULDER | *A Handbook*
for Writers | *of English Prose* | *by* | ROBERT GRAVES | *B. Litt.,*
Oxon, once Professor of English Literature | *at the Royal Egyptian*
University | & | ALAN HODGE | *B.A., Oxon* | *Authors of* The
Long Week End | [*publisher's emblem*] | JONATHAN CAPE |
THIRTY BEDFORD SQUARE | LONDON

> *Collation:* [A]⁸ B–Z⁸ AA–DD⁸ EE⁷, 223 leaves.
> p. [1] THE READER OVER YOUR SHOULDER; p. [2] blank; p. [3] title-page;
> p. [4] publication, publisher's, war economy, printer's, papermaker's and
> binder's notices; pp. 5–6 CONTENTS; p. 7 ACKNOWLEDGEMENTS; p. [8] *To* |
> *JENNY NICHOLSON;* pp. 9–446 text.
>
> 21·8 × 14·4 cm. Bulk: 2·3/2·6 cm. White wove paper; top and fore-edges
> trimmed; top edges stained blue. White wove endpapers. Bound in blue
> cloth; front and back blank; spine stamped in gold: THE READER | OVER
> YOUR | SHOULDER | [*decorative swirl*] | ROBERT | GRAVES | & | ALAN | HODGE |
> [*publisher's emblem*].
>
> *Price:* 18s. Number of copies undisclosed. Published in May 1943.
>
> *Contents:* Part 1: The Reader over Your Shoulder: 1. The Peculiar
> Qualities of English – 11. The Present Confusion of English Prose – 111.
> Where is Good English to be Found? – 1v. The Use and Abuse of Official
> English – v. The Beginnings of English Prose – v1. The Ornate and

Plain Styles – VII. Classical Prose – VIII. Romantic Prose – IX. Recent Prose – X. The Principles of Clear Statement I – XI. The Principles of Clear Statement II – XII. The Principles of Clear Statement III – XIII. The Graces of Prose – Part II: Examinations and Fair Copies: Sir Norman Angell – Irving Babbitt – Earl Baldwin of Bewdley – Clive Bell – Viscount Castlerosse (now the Earl of Kenmare) – Bishop of Chichester – G. D. H. Cole – Marquess of Crewe – Dr. Hugh Dalton, M.P. – Daphne du Maurier – Sir Arthur Eddington – T. S. Eliot – Lord Esher – Admiral C. J. Eyres – Negley Farson – Major-Gen. J. F. C. Fuller – Major-Gen. Sir Charles Gwynn – Viscount Halifax – Cicely Hamilton – 'Ian Hay' – Ernest Hemingway – Aldous Huxley – Prof. Julian Huxley – Paul Irwin – Sir James Jeans – Prof. C. E. M. Joad – Senator Hiram Johnson – J. M. Keynes (now Lord Keynes) – Com. Stephen King-Hall – Dr. F. R. Leavis – Cecil Day Lewis – Desmond MacCarthy – Brig.-Gen. J. H. Morgan, K.C. – J. Middleton Murry – Sir Cyril Norwood – 'Observator' – An Editor of The Oxford English Dictionary – Eric Partridge – 'Peterborough' – Ezra Pound – J. B. Priestley – D. N. Pritt, K. C., M. P. – Herbert Read – I. A. Richards – Bertrand Russell – Viscount Samuel – G. B. Shaw – Stephen Spender – J. W. N. Sullivan – Helen Waddell – Sir Hugh Walpole – H. G. Wells – Prof. A. N. Whitehead – Sir Leonard Woolley
Note: Printed in Great Britain.

b. *American issue (1944):*

The | READER | OVER YOUR SHOULDER | *A Handbook for Writers* | *of English Prose* | *by* | ROBERT GRAVES | *B. Litt., Oxon, once Professor of English Literature* | *at the Royal Egyptian University* | *&* | ALAN HODGE | *B.A., Oxon* | *Authors of* The Long Week End | NEW YORK | THE MACMILLAN COM-PANY | 1944

Collation: [1]–[28]⁸, 224 leaves.

p. [1] THE READER OVER YOUR SHOULDER; p. [2] publisher's device and notice; p. [3] title-page; p. [4] publisher's device and copyright and printing notices; pp. 5–[6] CONTENTS; p. 7 ACKNOWLEDGEMENTS; p. [8] *To* | *JENNY NICHOLSON;* pp. 9–446 text; pp. [447–448] blank.

21·3 × 14·1 cm. Bulk: 2·7/3·1 cm. White wove paper; all edges trimmed. White wove endpapers. Bound in grey-green cloth; front and back blank; spine stamped in blue: THE READER | OVER YOUR | SHOULDER | [*decorative swirl*] | ROBERT | GRAVES | & | ALAN | HODGE | MACMILLAN | [*long-short-long dashes*]

Price: $3.00. Number of copies unknown. Published 16 November 1943. *Note:* Printed in the U.S.

c. Readers Union impression (1944):

The | READER | OVER YOUR SHOULDER | *A Handbook for Writers* | *of English Prose* | *by* | ROBERT GRAVES | *B. Litt., Oxon, once Professor of English Literature* | *at the Royal Egyptian University* | & | ALAN HODGE | *B.A., Oxon* | *Authors of* The Long Week End | [*Readers Union emblem*[| *LONDON:* 1944 | READERS UNION/JONATHAN CAPE

Collation: [A]/A★⁸/⁸ B/B★–O/O★⁸/⁸, 224 leaves.
Remainder as A55a, except p. [4] has war economy, printer's and Readers Union notices and pp. [447–448] blank.

21·4 × 13·7 cm. Bulk: 1·5/1·9 cm. White wove paper; all edges trimmed; top edges stained purple. White wove endpapers. Bound in maroon cloth; front and back blank; spine printed in white: *GRAVES* | *and* | *HODGE* | THE | READER | OVER | YOUR | SHOULDER | [*in red:* Readers Union emblem].

Price: 7s. 6d. Number of copies unknown. Published in July 1944.

d. Abridged impression ([1947]):

Title-page as A55a.

Collation: [A]⁸ B–O⁸, 112 leaves.
Remainder as A55a, except that p. [4] has publication, printer's and binder's notices, p. [6] is blank, pp. 9–221 are text and pp. [222]–[224] are blank.

22·2 × 14·4 cm. Bulk: 1·7/2·4 cm. White wove paper; top and fore-edges trimmed; top edge stained green. White wove endpapers. Bound in green cloth; front and back blank; spine stamped in gold: THE | READER | OVER | YOUR | SHOULDER | [*decorative swirl*] | GRAVES | & | HODGE | [*publisher' emblem*].

Price: 10s. 6d. Number of copies undisclosed. Published 19 May 1947.

Notes: Impressions: 2nd, February 1948; 3rd, December 1949; 4th, Octobe 1952; 5th, 1955; 6th, September 1963; 7th (paperbound), January 196

Contents: Part I: The Reader over Your Shoulder: I. The Peculiar Qualitie of English – II. The Present Confusion of English Prose – III. Where is Goo English to be Found? – IV. The Use and Abuse of Official English – ' The Principles of Clear Statement, I – VI. The Principles of Clear Stat ment, II – VII. The Principles of Clear Statement, III – VIII. The Graces Prose – Part II: Examinations and Fair Copies: Sir Norman Angell

Viscount Castlerosse (later the Earl of Kenmare) – Bishop of Chichester –
T. S. Eliot – Major-Gen. J. F. C. Fuller – Earl Halifax – Sir James Jeans –
J. M. Keynes (later Lord Keynes) – Sir Cyril Norwood – J. B. Priestley –
D. N. Pritt, K.C., M.P. – I. A. Richards – Bertrand Russell – G. B. Shaw –
H. G. Wells – Prof. A. N. Whitehead – Sir Leonard Woolley

e. Second American impression (1961):

Title-page as A55b, except date is 1961.

Collation as A55b.
Remainder as A55b except p. [2] is blank, p. [4] lacks the publisher's emblem and adds a statement of edition and pp. [5] and [7] are unnumbered.

21·0 × 13·7 cm. Bulk: 2·6 cm. White wove paper; all edges trimmed.
Bound in white paper covers printed in black, yellow and dull mustard
gold.

Price: $2.25. Number of copies unknown. Published on 27 March 1961.

f. Second English edition ([1962]):

[bar] | THE READER OVER | YOUR SHOULDER | [rule] |
[flush right:] by | [rule] | [flush right:] Robert Graves & | [flush
right:] Alan Hodge | [bar] | [flush right:] [publisher's emblem] A
MAYFLOWER BOOK

Collation: [A]^{16} B–G^{16} [H]^{16}, 128 leaves.
p. [i] title and blurbs; p. [2] title and publication, copyright, permission,
publisher's and printer's notices; p. [3] title-page; p. [4] blank; pp. 5–256
text.

18·0 × 11·3 cm. Bulk: 1·6 cm. White wove paper; all edges trimmed.
Bound in paper covers.

Price: 3s. 6d. Number of copies unknown. Published 4 May 1962.

Contents: As A55d.

56   ROBERT GRAVES   [1943]

irst edition:

hole enclosed within green-filled double-rule with scallops:] | [whole
closed in rectangular single-rule box:] | [green-filled:] THE AUGUS-
AN POETS | [green shaded tent with hangings] | [green-shaded

fancy design with next two lines inside:] ROBERT | GRAVES | [*green-shaded:*] 9ᴰ | [*double branch*] | EYRE & SPOTTISWOODE

Collation: 16 leaves, stapled in centre.

p. [i] biographical note; p. ii TO | EDWARD THOMPSON | in happy memory of the Islip village football | team, canoeing on the Ray, and the children | who have now grown up.; p. iii CONTENTS; p. [iv] blank; pp. 2–30[31] text; p. [32] blank.

18·5 × 12·5 cm. Bulk: 0·3 cm. White wove paper; all edges trimmed. Bound in wine-red cloth-effect paper; outside front cover transcribed as title-page; inside front and back covers blank; outside back cover cloth-effect print only.

Price: 9d. Number of copies: 5,000. Published in November 1943.

Contents: Rocky Acres – In the Wilderness – Outlaws – Reproach – Allie – The Haunted House – Love without Hope – The Troll's Nosegay – Song of Contrariety – Sullen Moods – A Crusader – An English Wood – Henry and Mary – A Frosty Night – One Hard Look – Lost Love – The Return – Ancestors – The Presence –What Did I Dream? – The Country Dance – The Hills of May – Unicorn and the White Doe – The Land of Whipperginny – The 'General Elliott' –The Bedpost – Love in Barrenness – Vain and Careless – In Procession – Apples and Water – Vanity

Note: This is Augustan Poets Series, no. 2.

A57   THE GOLDEN FLEECE   [1944

a. First edition:

THE GOLDEN FLEECE | *By* | ROBERT GRAVES [*publisher's emblem*] | CASSELL AND COMPANY LTD. London, Toronto, Melbourne and Sydney

Collation: [A]/A★⁸/⁸ B/B★–L/L★⁸/⁸ M/M★²/⁸, 186 leaves.

p. [1] THE GOLDEN FLEECE; p. [2] list of novels by Graves; p. [3] title-page; p. [4] economy, publication and printer's notices; p. 5 quotation (9 l) from Diodorus Siculus; p. 6 list of maps, table and illustrations; pp. 7– CONTENTS; pp. 9–27 INTRODUCTION, with pp. [16–17] being a genealogic table; p. 28 INVOCATION; pp. 29–44 text; p. 45 map; pp. 46–116 text; p. 1 illustrations; pp. 118–260 text; p. [261] illustrations; pp. 262–370[371] te p. [372] blank.

21·7 × 13·3 cm. Bulk: 2·1/2·4 cm. White wove paper; all edges trimme White wove endpapers; outer sides of free endpapers blank; inner sides maps, front of the outward voyage, back of the return voyage, of the *Argo*. Bound in medium blue cloth; front and back blank; spine stamped in orange: THE | GOLDEN | FLEECE | ROBERT | GRAVES | CASSELL

Price: 12s. 6d. Number of copies: 11,073. Published in October 1944 in white dust-jacket printed in black and brown.

Notes: Impressions: 2nd, January 1948 (1,966 copies).
This book has been translated into Croatian, Czech, Danish, Dutch, French, German, Hebrew, Polish, Russian and Swedish.

b. First American edition ([1945]):

[*two lines in blue:*] HERCULES, | MY SHIPMATE | *A Novel By* | ROBERT GRAVES | [*in blue: publisher's emblem*] | *NEW YORK* | CREATIVE AGE PRESS, INC

Collation: [1]⁸ [2]–[15]¹⁶ [16]⁸, 240 leaves.
p. [i] *HERCULES, MY SHIPMATE;* p. [ii] blank; p. [iii] list of novels by Graves; p. [iv] map in blue; p. [v] title-page; p. [vi] economy, copyright and printer's notices; p. [vii] quotation (8 ll.) from Diodorus Siculus; p. [viii] blank; pp. ix–x *Contents;* p. [1] *HERCULES, MY SHIPMATE;* p. [2] *Invocation;* pp. 3–445 text; p. [446] blank; pp. 447–464 *Historical Appendix,* with pp. [456–457] being a genealogical table; pp. [465]–[470] blank.

20·2 × 13·6 cm. Bulk: 3·0/3·6 cm. White wove paper; all edges trimmed and sprinkled with blue. White wove endpapers are maps; first and fourth sides of endpapers blank; second and third sides of front show outward, of rear return, voyage of the *Argo.* Bound in buff cloth; back blank; front printed with solid blue rectangular box around which is stamped a gold rule border and inside which is stamped a facsimile signature of Graves; spine has gold stamping and blue printing: [*five-rule crossbar design of two gold rules, blue decorative rule and two gold rules*] | [*solid blue rectangular box, in which:*] ROBERT GRAVES | [*three gold rules*] | [*solid blue rectangular box, inside which three lines:*] HERCULES, | *my* | SHIPMATE | [*three gold rules*] | [*solid blue rectangular box, inside which two lines:*] CREATIVE AGE | PRESS | [*a series of three five-rule devices, as at top*] | [*solid blue rectangular box, in which: publisher's emblem*] | [*five-rule device, as at top*].

Price: $3.00. Number of copies unknown. Published 7 September 1945 in white dust-jacket printed in black, red and gold-brown.

c. Second American impression ([1957]):

[at right, facing spine, from top to bottom:] ROBERT GRAVES | [3 ll. flush left:] HERCULES | MY SHIPMATE | GROSSET & DUNLAP · NEW YORK | [at right, facing spine, from top to bottom:] Grosset's UNIVERSAL Library

Collation: 240 leaves, glued at spine.
Remainder as A57*b*, except p. [I] publisher's advertisement, pp. [ii–iii] are front endpaper maps of A57*b*, p. [iv] map in black, p. [vi] has copyright and printing notices, pp. [466–467] are rear endpaper maps of A57*b*.

20·2 × 13·4 cm. Bulk: 2·2 cm. White wove paper; all edges trimmed. Bound in white paper covers printed in red, blue and black.

Price: $1.25. Number of copies undisclosed. Published 22 April 1957.

Note: This book is Grosset's Universal Library no. UL–19.

d. Third American impression ([1957]):

HERCULES, | MY SHIPMATE | *A Novel By* | ROBERT GRAVES | *NEW YORK* | FARRAR, STRAUS AND CUDAHY

Collation: [1]–[15]¹⁶, 240 leaves.
Remainder as A57*c*, except p. [i] 25 A57*b*, p. [vi] copyright and printing notices.

20·2 × 13·7 cm. Bulk: 2·3/2·9 cm. White wove paper; all edges trimmed. Bound in cloth-simulating orange and grey paper; front and back blank; spine stamped: ROBERT | GRAVES | Hercules, | My | Shipmate | FARRAR | STRAUS | CUDAHY

Price: $4.50. Number of copies unknown. Published in August 1957 in white dust-jacket printed in black, brown and orange.

a. First edition:

ROBERT GRAVES | POEMS | [*elaborate red circular design, inside which:*] 1938–1945 | CASSELL & COMPANY LTD. | [*heavy rule*] | [*light rule*] | LONDON, TORONTO, MEL-BOURNE | AND SYDNEY

Collation: [A]–[B]⁴ C–F⁴, 24 leaves.

p. [i] ROBERT GRAVES | POEMS (1938–1945); p. [ii] blank; p. [iii] title-page; p. [iv] publication and printer's notices; pp. [v–vi] CONTENTS; p. [vii] FOREWORD; p. [viii] blank; pp. 1–40 text.

18·4 × 11·9 cm. Bulk: 0·4/0·7 cm. Cream laid paper; all edges trimmed; watermarked with a crown and Abbey Mills | Greenfield. White wove endpapers. Bound in blue-green cloth; front and back blank; spine stamped in gold, bottom to top: [*light-heavy-light rules*] CASSELL [*four-pointed star*] POEMS (1938–1945) [*four-pointed star*] ROBERT GRAVES [*light-heavy-light rules*]

Price: 5s. Number of copies: 3,000. Published November 1945 in a sea-green dust-jacket printed in black.

Contents: Foreword – POEMS: 1. A Love Story – 2. Dawn Bombardment – 3. The Worms of History – 4. The Beast – 5. A Withering Herb – 6. The Shot – 7. The Thieves – 8. Lollocks – 9. To Sleep – 10. Despite and Still – 11. The Suicide in the Copse – 12. Frightened Men – 13. A Stranger at the Party – 14. The Oath – 15. Language of the Seasons – 16. Mid-Winter Waking – 17. The Rock at the Corner – 18. The Beach – 19. The Villagers and Death – 20. The Door – 21. Under the Pot – 22. Through Nightmare – 23. To Lucia – 24. Death by Drums – 25. She Tells Her Love while Half Asleep – 26. Instructions to the Orphic Adept – 27. Theseus and Ariadne – 28. Lament for Pasiphaë – 29. The Twelve Days of Christmas – 30. Cold Weather Proverb – 31. To Juan at the Winter Solstice – SATIRES AND GROTESQUES: 32. Dream of a Climber – 33. The Persian Version – 34. The Weather of Olympus – 35. Apollo of the Physiologists – 36. The Oldest Soldier – 37. Grotesques i–v – 38. The Eugenist – 39. 1805 – 40. At the Savoy Chapel

Note: Impression: 2nd, April 1946. Number of copies: 4,387.

b. First American edition ([1946]):

POEMS | 1938–1945 | [*double rule*] | By | ROBERT GRAVES | [*double rule*] | NEW YORK | CREATIVE AGE PRESS

Collation: [1]–[2]⁸ [3]¹⁰ [4]⁸, 34 leaves.

p. [i] POEMS | 1938–1945 | [*double rule*]; p. [ii] blank; p. [iii] title-page; p. [iv] copyright, designer's and printer's notices; p. [v] FOREWORD; p. [vi] blank; pp. [vii]–[ix] CONTENTS; p. [x] blank; p. [1] POEMS; p. [2] blank; pp. 3–42 text; p. [43] SATIRES AND GROTESQUES; p. [44] blank; pp. 45–58 text.

21·4 × 13·8 cm. Bulk: 0·5/1·1 cm.White wove paper; all edges trimmed. Cream wove endpapers. Bound in red cloth; front and back blank; spine stamped in silver, top to bottom: POEMS 1938–1945 [*floral decoration*] Robert Graves [*floral decoration*] CREATIVE AGE PRESS [*floral decoration*]

Price: $2.00. Number of copies unknown. Published in June 1946 in white dust-jacket printed in black, grey and blue.

A59   KING JESUS   [1946]

a. First edition:

KING | JESUS | *By* | *Robert Graves* | *New York* | CREATIVE AGE PRESS, INC.

Collation: [1]⁸ [2]–[13]¹⁶ [14]–[15]⁸, 216 leaves.
p. [*i*] KING | JESUS; p. [*ii*] blank; p. [*iii*] list of books by Graves; p. [*iv*] map of Palestine; p. [*v*] title-page; p. [*vi*] copyright and printing notices; pp. *vii–viii* CONTENTS; p. [1] KING | JESUS; p. [2] quotations from Clement of Alexandria (11 ll.) and Lexicon Talmudicum (8 ll.); pp. 3–32 text; p. [33] illustration; pp. 34–155 text; p. [156] blank; pp. 157–267 text; p. [268] blank; pp. 269–418 text; pp. 419–424 HISTORICAL COMMENTARY.

20·2 × 13·4 cm. Bulk: 2·3/2·9 cm.White wove paper; all edges trimmed. White wove endpapers. Bound in buff cloth; back blank; front stamped with octagonal green box inside which are various animals, a wall, a seven-branched candelabrum, etc.; spine stamped with three solid green rectangular boxes printed in gold: [ten lines in first box:] | [*heavy rule*] | [*light rule*] | [*decorative rule*] | [*light rule*] | King | Jesus | [*light rule*] | [*decorative rule*] | [*light rule*] | [*heavy rule*] | [four lines in second box:] | [*heavy-rule rectangular border*] | [*light-rule rectangular border*] | ROBERT | GRAVES | [remainder in third box:] | [*heavy-rule rectangular border*] | [*light-rule rectangular border*] | CREATIVE | AGE | PRESS

Price: $3.00. Number of copies unknown. Published on 30 September 194. in white dust-jacket printed in flesh and green.

Note: This book has been translated into German and Swedish.

b. First English edition ([1946]):

KING JESUS | ROBERT GRAVES | [*publisher's emblem*] | CASSELL | AND COMPANY LIMITED | LONDON · TORONTO · MELBOURNE · SYDNEY

Collation: [A]/A*8/8 B/B*–K/K*8/8 L/L*/L**2/8/8, 178 leaves.
p. [1] KING JESUS; p. [2] list of novels by Graves; p. [3] title-page; p. [4] economy, publication and printer's notices; p. 5 CONTENTS; p. 6 quotations from Clement of Alexandria (10 ll.) and Lexicon Talmudicum (7 ll.); pp. 7–31 text; p. [32] description of facing plate; [plate, back blank]; pp. 33–351 text; pp. 352–355[356] HISTORICAL COMMENTARY; [map, tipped to rear endpaper].

21·6 × 13·3 cm. Bulk: 2·0/2·6 cm. White wove paper; all edges trimmed. White wove endpapers. Bound in ochre cloth; front and back blank; spine stamped in gold: [*double rule*] | [*solid rectangular box*] | [*double rule*] | CASSELL; box contains, in relief, in ochre: KING | JESUS | ROBERT | GRAVES

Price: 12s. 6d. Number of copies: 10,152. Published on 28 November 1946 in buff dust-jacket printed in black and brown.

Note: Impressions: 2nd and 3rd published February 1960 (6,042 copies); 4th, 28 April 1960 (2,780 copies); 5th, September 1960 (1,492 copies); 6th, June 1962 (2,000 copies). The publisher confirms the discrepancies between these dates and those on versos of title-pages.

c. Second American impression ([1955]):

KING | JESUS | By | Robert Graves | New York | FARRAR, STRAUS & CUDAHY, INC.

Collation: [1]–[12]¹⁶ [13]⁸ [14]¹⁶, 216 leaves.
Remainder as A59a.

20·2 × 13·5 cm. Bulk: 3·0/3·7 cm. Paper and endpapers as A59a. Bound in tan cloth stamped in blue; back and front as A59a; spine stamped with rules and legend as A59a without solid boxes; at bottom: FARRAR, | STRAUS AND | CUDAHY

Price undetermined. Number of copies unknown. Published in 1955.

First edition:

COLLECTED POEMS | (1914–1947) | [*swelled rule*] | ROBERT
GRAVES | [*publisher's emblem*] | CASSELL | AND COM-
PANY LIMITED | LONDON, TORONTO, MELBOURNE
AND SYDNEY

Collation: π⁸ A/A★– G/G★⁸/⁸ H⁸, 128 leaves.
4 pp., blank, as front endpapers; p. [i] COLLECTED POEMS; p. [ii] blank;
p. [iii] title-page; p. [iv] publication and printer's notices; pp. v–x CON-
TENTS; pp. xi–xii FOREWORD; pp. [1]–[240] text, with pp. [1, 37, 71, 95, 151,
169, 207] being section headings and pp. [2, 36, 38, 72, 96, 152, 170, 208]
being blank and p. [240] being unnumbered.

21·6 × 13·7 cm. Bulk: 1·5/2·0 cm. Cream wove paper; all edges trimmed.
Rear endpapers white wove. Bound in dark olive-green cloth; front and
back blank; spine stamped in gold: [5 ll. enclosed within gold wreath:]
COLLECTED | POEMS | · | 1914– | 1947 | Robert | Graves | CASSELL

Price: 12s. 6d. Number of copies: 2,962. Published in April 1948 in cream
dust-jacket printed in red and black.

Contents: Foreword – I: In the the Wilderness – The Haunted House –
Reproach – The Finding of Love – 'The General Elliott' – Rocky
Acres – Outlaws – One Hard Look – A Frosty Night – Allie – Unicorn and
the White Doe – Henry and Mary – Love Without Hope –What Did I
Dream? – The Country Dance – The Troll's Nosegay – The Hills of May –
Lost Love – Vain and Careless – An English Wood – The Bedpost – The
Pier-Glass – Apples and Water – Angry Samson – Down – Mermaid,
Dragon, Fiend – II: In Procession –Warning to Children – Alice – Richard
Roe and John Doe – The Witches' Cauldron – Ancestors – Children of
Darkness – The Cool Web – Love in Barrenness – Song of Contrariety –
The Presence – The Land of Whipperginny – In No Direction – The Castle
– Return – Lust in Song – Nobody –Without Pause – Full Moon – Vanity –
Pure Death – Sick Love – It Was All Very Tidy – III: Callow Captain –
Thief – Saint – The Furious Voyage – Song: Lift-Boy – The Next Time –
Ulysses – The Succubus – Trudge, Body – The Clock Man – The Reader
over My Shoulder – Green Loving – The Legs – Gardener – Front Door
Soliloquy – In Broken Images – On Rising Early – Flying Crooked –
Largesse to the Poor – Fragment of a Lost Poem – IV: Galatea and Pyg-
malion – The Devil's Advice to Story-Tellers – Sea Side –Wm. Brazier –
Welsh Incident – Vision in the Repair-Shop – Interruption – Act V,
Scene 5 – Midway – Hell – Leda – Synthetic Such – The Florist Rose – Lost
Acres – At First Sight – Recalling War – Down, Wanton, Down! – A
Former Attachment – Nature's Lineaments – Time – The Philosopher – Or

Dwelling – Parent to Children – Ogres and Pygmies – History of the Word
– Single Fare – To Walk on Hills – To Bring the Dead to Life – To Evoke
Posterity – The Poets – Defeat of the Rebels – Never Such Love – The
Fallen Signpost – The China Plate – Certain Mercies – The Cuirassiers of
the Frontier – The Laureate – A Jealous Man – The Cloak – The Halls of
Bedlam – Or to Perish before Day – A Country Mansion – The Eremites –
The Advocates – Self-Praise – v: On Portents – The Terraced Valley –
The Challenge – To the Sovereign Muse – The Ages of Oath – New
Legends – Like Snow – The Climate of Thought – End of Play – The
Fallen Tower of Siloam – The Great-Grandmother – No More Ghosts –
vi: A Love Story – Dawn Bombardment – The Worms of History – The
Beast – A Withering Herb – The Shot – The Thieves – Lollocks – To Sleep –
Despite and Still – The Suicide in the Copse – Frightened Men – A Stranger
at the Party – The Oath – Language of the Seasons – Mid-Winter Waking–
The Rock at the Corner – The Beach – The Villagers and Death – The
Door – Under the Pot – Through Nightmare – To Lucia at Birth – Death
by Drums – She Tells Her Love while Half Asleep – Theseus and Ariadne –
The Twelve Days of Christmas – Three Short Poems: Cold Weather
Proverb – To Poets under Pisces – June – 1805 – At the Savoy Chapel – The
Last Day of Leave (1916) – To be Named a Bear – vii: Satires and Grotes-
ques: Dream of a Climber – The Persian Version – The Weather of
Olympus – Apollo of the Physiologists – The Oldest Soldier – Grotesques
i, ii, iii, iv, v – The Eugenist – A Civil Servant – Gulls and Men – Magical
Poems: To Juan at the Winter Solstice – The Allansford Pursuit – The
Alphabet Calendar of Amergin – The Siren's Welcome to Cronos – Diche-
tal do Chennaib – The Battle of the Trees – The Song of Blodeuwedd –
Intercession in Late October – Instructions to the Orphic Adept – Lament
for Pasiphaë – The Tetragrammaton – Nuns and Fish – The Destroyer –
Return of the Goddess. [The final three poems are separated in the table of
contents from the 'Magical Poems.']

A61　　THE WHITE GODDESS　　[1948]

a. First edition:

THE | WHITE GODDESS | *A historical grammar* | *of poetic myth* |
by | ROBERT GRAVES | FABER AND FABER LIMITED |
24 Russell Square | London

Collation: π^8 A–Z^8 2A–2C^8 2D^4, 216 leaves.
　p. [1] THE WHITE GODDESS; p. [2] list of books by Graves; p. [3] title-page;
　p. [4] publication, publisher's and printer's notices; p. [5] IN DEDICATION;
　p. [6] blank; pp. 7–[8] CONTENTS; pp. 9–12 FOREWORD; pp. 13–412 text;
　pp. 413–430 INDEX; pp. [431–432] blank.

21·8 × 13·6 cm. Bulk: 2·4/2·8 cm.White wove paper; all edges trimmed; top edges stained brown; watermarked with a crown and in Gothic: Abbey Mills | Greenfield.White wove endpapers. Bound in medium blue cloth; front and back blank; spine stamped in gold: [*triple rule*] | THE | WHITE | GODDESS | [*triple rule*] | ROBERT | GRAVES | FABER

Price: 30s. Number of copies: 2,340. Published in May 1948 in canary dust-jacket printed in black and red.

Contents: 'In Dedication' – Foreword – I. Poets and Gleemen – II. The Battle of the Trees – III. Dog, Roebuck and Lapwing – IV. The White Goddess – V. Gwion's Riddle – VI. A Visit to Spiral Castle – VII. Gwion's Riddle Solved – VIII. Hercules on the Lotus – IX. Gwion's Heresy – X. The Tree-Alphabet (1) – XI. The Tree-Alphabet (2) – XII. The Song of Amergin – XIII. Palamedes and the Cranes – XIV. The Roebuck in the Thicket – XV. The Seven Pillars – XVI. The Holy Unspeakable Name of God – XVII. The Lion with the Steady Hand – XVIII. The Bull-Footed God – XIX. The Number of the Beast – XX. A Conversation at Paphos–A.D.43 – XXI. The Waters of the Styx – XXII. The Triple Muse – XXIII. Fabulous Beasts – XXIV. The Single Poetic Theme – XXV. War in Heaven – Index

Note: 'In Dedication' is 10 lines long.
Impressions: 2nd, October 1948 (1,500 copies).

b. *First American edition* (*1948*):

The WHITE | GODDESS | *A historical grammar of poetic myth* | Robert Graves | [*design of star and three cranes*] | Creative Age Press, New York, 1948

Collation: [1]⁸ [2]–[13]¹⁶ [14]⁴ [15]⁸, 212 leaves.
p. [i] THE WHITE GODDESS; p. [ii] list of books by Graves; p. [iii] title-page; p. [iv] copyright, edition and printer's notices; p. [v] IN DEDICATION; p. [vi] blank; pp. vii–viii CONTENTS; pp. ix–xii FOREWORD; p. [1] THE WHITE GODDESS; p. [2] blank; pp. 3–392 text; pp. 393–412 SUBJECT INDEX.

21·5 × 14·8 cm. Bulk: 2·7/3·3 cm. White laid paper; top edges only trimmed. White wove endpapers. Bound in brown cloth; back blank; front stamped with three-quarter box, open toward spine, containing three cranes and star below, the edges of the box aligning with rules on spine; spine stamped in black: [*rule*] | GRAVES | THE | WHITE | GODDESS | CREATIVE AGE | [*rule*]

Price: $4.50. Number of copies unknown. Published 26 August 1948 in white dust-jacket printed in brown and black.

c. Second English edition ([1952]):

THE | WHITE GODDESS | *A historical grammar | of poetic myth |
by* | ROBERT GRAVES | *amended and enlarged edition* | FABER
AND FABER LIMITED | 24 Russell Square | London

Collation: [A]⁸ B–Z⁸ 2A–2H⁸, 248 leaves.
p. [1] THE WHITE GODDESS; p. [2] list of books by Graves; p. [4] publication,
publisher's and printer's notices; p. [5] IN DEDICATION; p. [6] blank;
pp. 7–[8] CONTENTS; pp. 9–15 FOREWORD; p. [16] blank; pp. 17–478 text;
pp. 479–496 INDEX.

Measurements and paper as A61*a*, except top edges not stained.

Price: 35s. Number of copies: 2,000. Published in October 1952.

Contents: As A61*a*, but the foreword has been revised and Chapter XXVI
(The Return of the Goddess) is new; 'In Dedication' has 22 lines.

Note: Impressions: 2nd, February 1959 (2,000 copies).

d. Second American impression ([1958]):

The WHITE | GODDESS | *A historical grammar of poetic myth* |
Robert Graves | *[design as A61b]* | Farrar Straus and Cudahy,
Inc.

Collation as A61*b*.
Remainder as A61*b*, except p. [iv] has copyright and printing notices only.

20·3 × 13·5 cm. Bulk: 2·1/2·7 cm. White wove paper; all edges trimmed.
White wove endpapers. Binding as A61*b*, except spine reads: *[rule]* |
GRAVES | THE | WHITE | GODDESS | *[rule]* | FARRAR, | STRAUS | and | CUDAHY

Price: $5.00. Number of copies unknown. Published in 1958.

Note: This impression is a photographic reproduction of A61*b*.

e. Second American edition (1958):

A historical grammar of poetic myth | THE | WHITE | GODDESS |
Amended and enlarged edition | BY | ROBERT | GRAVES |
Vintage Books: New York: 1958

Collation: 288 leaves, glued at spine.

p. [i] *The White Goddess;* p. [ii] blank; p. [iii] title-page; p. [iv] publisher's, arrangement, copyright and manufacturing notices; pp. [v]vi–xi *Foreword;* p. [xii] *Contents;* p. [1] *The White Goddess;* p. [2] *In Dedication;* pp. [3]4–541 text, with pp. [15, 35, 50, 66, 91, 110, 121, 140, 168, 196, 215, 236, 262, 278, 294, 329, 342, 375, 384, 402, 424, 455, 471, 495, 526] unnumbered; p. [542] blank; pp. [i]ii–xix *Index;* p. [xx] biographical note and printer's, paper-maker's and designer's notices; pp. [xxi–xxii] publisher's advertisements.

18·4 × 11·0 cm. Bulk: 2·6 cm. White wove paper; all edges trimmed. Bound in white paper covers printed in black, light blue, medium blue and brown.

Price: $1.25. Number of copies undisclosed. Published on 10 February 1958.

Notes: This edition is Vintage Book K–56. The text is that of A61c.

f. Third English edition: ([1961]):

THE | WHITE GODDESS | *A historical grammar* | *of poetic myth* | *by* | ROBERT GRAVES | *amended and enlarged edition* | FABER AND FABER LIMITED | 24 Russell Square | London

Collation: [A]¹⁶ B–Q¹⁶, 256 leaves.
Remainder differs from A61d as follows: pp. 17–492 text; pp. 493–511 INDEX; p. [512] blank.

21·0 × 13·4 cm. Bulk: 1·9 cm. White wove paper; all edges trimmed. Bound in paper covers printed in blue and brown.

Price: 12s. 6d. Number of copies: 10,000. Published in March 1961.

Contents: As A61d, with the addition of Chapter XXVII (Postscript 1960); 'In Dedication' has 22 lines.

Note: There are omissions as well as additions throughout the text; the revisions of A61d are retained. Impressions: 2nd, March 1963 (8,000 copies).

A62   WATCH THE NORTH WIND RISE   1949

a. First edition:

Robert Graves | [*three lines within rectangular box of decorative band:*] WATCH THE | NORTH WIND RISE | A NOVEL | Creative Age Press | NEW YORK · 1949

Collation: [1]–[16]⁸ [17]⁴ [18]–[19]⁸, 148 leaves.

p. [i] *[decorative band]* | WATCH THE NORTH WIND RISE; p. [ii] list of books by Graves; p. [iii] title-page; p. [iv] copyright, printer's and designer's notices; pp. v–vi *Contents;* pp. 1–290 text.

20·0 × 13·4 cm. Bulk: 2·3/2·8 cm.White wove paper; all edges trimmed. White wove endpapers. Bound in cloth-textured grey paper; front and back blank; spine black cloth stamped in gold in solid blue rectangular box: *[decorative band]* | *Graves* | WATCH THE | NORTH WIND | RISE | *Creative Age* | *[decorative band]*

Price: $3.00. Number of copies unknown. Published 18 March 1949 in white dust-jacket printed in olive, yellow, red, blue and black.

Note: This book has been translated into Italian and Swedish.

b. First English edition ([1949]):

SEVEN DAYS IN | NEW CRETE | *A Novel* | by | ROBERT GRAVES | *[publisher's emblem]* | CASSELL & COMPANY LIMITED | LONDON . TORONTO . MELBOURNE | SYDNEY . WELLINGTON

Collation: [1]/1★⁸/⁸ 2/2★–9/9★⁸/⁸, 144 leaves.

p. [i] SEVEN DAYS IN NEW CRETE; p. [ii] list of books by Graves; p. [iii] title-page; p. [iv] publication and printer's notices; p. [v] CONTENTS; p. [vi] blank; pp. 1–281 text; p. [282] blank.

18·3 × 12·3 cm. Bulk: 1·9/2·3 cm.White wove paper; all edges trimmed. White wove endpapers. Bound in black cloth; front and back blank; spine stamped in gold: SEVEN | DAYS | IN | NEW | CRETE | *[nine rules in downward-pointing triangle, plus dot]* | ROBERT | GRAVES | CASSELL

Price: 9s. 6d. Number of copies: 12,257. Published on 29 September 1949 in white dust-jacket printed in blue, red, yellow, grey and green.

c. Second American edition ([1963]):

entire flush left:] WATCH | THE | NORTHWIND | RISE | ROBERT | GRAVES

Collation: 128 leaves, glued at spine.

p. [1] summary and blurbs; p. [2] blank; p. [3] title-page; p. [4] copyright, publication and publisher's notices; pp. [5–6] CONTENTS; pp. 7–254 text; pp. [255–256] publisher's advertisements.

16·3 × 10·9 cm. Bulk: 1·7 cm. White wove paper; all edges trimmed and stained green. Bound in white paper covers printed in yellow, green, blue, pink and black.

Price: \$0.75. Number of copies undisclosed. Published 18 July 1963.

Note: This edition is Avon Book V–2075.

A63   THE COMMON ASPHODEL   [1949]

First edition:

THE | COMMON | ASPHODEL | *COLLECTED ESSAYS ON POETRY* | 1922–1949 | by | ROBERT GRAVES | [*publisher's emblem*] | HAMISH HAMILTON | LONDON

Collation: [A]⁸ B–X⁸ Y⁶, 174 leaves.
p. [i] THE COMMON ASPHODEL; p. [ii] blank; [frontispiece, back blank]; p. [iii] title-page; p. [iv] publication and printer's notices; pp. v–vi CONTENTS; pp. vii–xi INTRODUCTION; p. [xii] blank; pp. 1–329 text, with pp. [50, 60, 168, 196, 224, 326] blank; p. [330] blank; pp. 331–335 INDEX; p. [336] blank.

21·3 × 13·6 cm. Bulk: 2·4/2·9 cm. White wove paper; all edges trimmed. White wove endpapers. Bound in orange-red cloth; front and back blank; spine stamped in gold: [*six lines enclosed in rectangular decorative rule box:*] THE | COMMON | ASPHODEL | ★ | ROBERT | GRAVES | [*publisher's emblem*]

Price: 15s. Number of copies undisclosed. Published in September 1949 in white dust-jacket printed in black and powder blue.

Contents: Introduction – Observations on Poetry (1922–1925): I. The Poetic Trance – II. Prose and Poetry – III. Fake Poetry and Bad Poetry – IV. Schools – V. Rhyme – VI. Ariphrades – VII. *Vers Libre* – VIII. The Hounds of Spring – IX. The Outward and Inward Ears – X. Secondary Elaboration – XI. The Arrogance of Poets – XII. Scientific English – XIII. Texture – XIV. Fashions in Poetry – XV. 'Bread I Dip in the River' – XVI. *Hélas, C'est Victor Hugo* – XVII. Shakespeare's Fair Copies – XVIII The Grosser Senses – XIX. Centenaries – XX. *Hamlet* – The Sources of *The Tempest* (1925) – The Future of Poetry (1926) – Modernist Poetry (with Laura Riding, 1926): I. Modernist Poetry and the Plain Reader' Rights – II. The Problem of Form and Subject-Matter – III. A Study in Original Punctuation and Spelling – IV. The Unpopularity of Modernist Poetry – V. Dead Movements – VI. The Making of the Poem – VII Modernist Poetry and Civilization – VIII. Variety in Modernist Poetry IX. The Humorous Element – Anthologies (with Laura Riding, 1927) I. True Anthologies and Popular Anthologies – II. The Perfect Modern Lyric – Loving Mad Tom (1927) – Rudyard Kipling (1928) – Essays from

Epilogue (1935–1937): I. Nietzsche – II. Coleridge and Wordsworth – III. Keats and Shelley – IV. The Pastoral – V. Official and Unofficial Literature – VI. Lucretius and Jeans – VII. Poetry and Politics (with Laura Riding) – VIII. Poetic Drama (with Laura Riding) – How Poets See (1939) – The Poets of World War II (1942) – 'Mad Mr. Swinburne' (1945) – The Ghost of Milton (1947) – The Common Asphodel (1949) – Index.

A64   THE ISLANDS OF UNWISDOM   1949

a. First edition:

The Islands of Unwisdom | BY ROBERT GRAVES | [*publisher's emblem*] | DOUBLEDAY & COMPANY, INC. | *Garden City, New York,* 1949

Collation: [1]–[11]¹⁶, 176 leaves.
2 pp., blank; p. [i] The Islands of Unwisdom; p. [ii] list of novels by Graves; p. [iii] title-page; p. [iv] copyright and printer's notices; p. [v] epigraphs (3 ll. and 5 ll.); p. [vi] blank; pp. vii–viii Contents; pp. ix–xi MEMBERS OF THE EXPEDITION | MENTIONED BY NAME; p. [xii] blank; pp. xiii–xv Introduction; p. [xviii] blank; pp. [1]2–328 text, with pp. [10, 23, 35, 51, 62, 76, 91, 102, 113, 128, 141, 153, 167, 179, 192, 205, 218, 230, 245, 258, 274, 287, 299, 311, 320, 327] unnumbered; pp. [329]–[332] blank.

21·1 × 14·3 cm. Bulk: 2·3/2·9 cm. White wove paper; top edges only trimmed and stained brown gold. White wove endpapers with identical maps back and front; inner free sides blank. Bound in wine-red cloth; front and back blank; spine stamped in gold: ROBERT | GRAVES | [*decorative rule*] | The | Islands | of | Un- | wisdom | [*decorative rule*] | DOUBLEDAY

Price: $3.50. Number of copies: 12,000 (in two printings). Published on 3 November 1949 in white dust-jacket printed in black and multi-colour, browns predominating.

Note: This book has been translated into Finnish, German, Italian and Swedish.

b. First English edition ([1950]):

THE | ISLES OF UNWISDOM | *by* | ROBERT GRAVES | [*publisher's emblem*] | CASSELL AND COMPANY LIMITED | LONDON . TORONTO . MELBOURNE | SYDNEY AND WELLINGTON

Collation: [1]¹⁶ 2–13¹⁶ 14⁸, 216 leaves.
p. [i] THE ISLES OF UNWISDOM; p. [ii] list of books by Graves; p. [iii] title-page; p. [iv] publication, printing and printer's notices; p. v CONTENTS;

pp. vi–vii MEMBERS OF THE EXPEDITION; pp. [viii–ix] map; p. [x] epigraph (7 ll.); pp. xi–xiv INTRODUCTION; pp. 1–415 text; pp. 416–417 HISTORICAL EPILOGUE; p. [418] blank.

18·4 × 12·3 cm. Bulk: 2·5/2·9 cm. White wove paper; all edges trimmed. White wove endpapers. Bound in black cloth; front and back blank; spine stamped in gold: [heavy rule] | [light rule] | THE ISLES | of | UNWISDOM | ROBERT | GRAVES | [light rule] | [heavy rule] | CASSELL

Price: 10s. 6d. Number of copies: 14,988. Published on 20 April 1950 in white dust-jacket printed in red, blue, yellow and black.

c. Readers Union impression (1952):

Robert Graves | [decorative swirl] | THE ISLES | OF UNWIS-DOM | London [Readers Union emblem] 1952 | READERS UNION · CASSELL

Collation: [1]⁸ [2]¹⁶ 3/3*–14/14*⁸/⁸, 216 leaves.
p. [i] THE ISLES OF UNWISDOM; p. [ii] list of novels by Graves; p. [iii] title-page; p. [iv] edition notice, colophon, and acknowledgement; remainder as A64b.

17·2 × 11·1 cm. Bulk: 1·5/1·9 cm. White wove paper; all edges trimmed. White wove endpapers. Bound in light blue cloth; front and back blank; spine stamped in yellow: [heavy rule] | [light rule] | ROBERT | GRAVES | The | Isles of | Unwisdom | [light rule] | [two heavy rules] | [light rule] | [Readers Union emblem] | [light rule] | [heavy rule]

Price: 4s. 6d. Number of copies: more than 25,000. Published in May 1952.

Note: At least one copy collates 2/2*⁸/⁸.

d. Second American edition ([1962]):

[entire text flush right; first word above floral design:] THE ISLANDS OF | UNWISDOM | ROBERT GRAVES | [rule]

Collation: 160 leaves, glued at spine.
p. [1] publisher's advertisements; p. [2] publisher's notices; p. [3] title-page; p. [4] epigraph, copyright and arrangement notices; p. [5] CONTENTS; pp. [6–7] map; pp. [8–9] list of characters; p. [10] blank; pp. [11]–[13] Introduction; p. [14] blank; pp. 15–317 text; pp. 318–319 HISTORICAL EPILOGUE; p. [320] blank.

18·1 × 10·7 cm. Bulk: 1·6 cm.White wove paper; all edges trimmed and stained green. Bound in paper covers, inner sides blank.

Price: $0.75. Number of copies undisclosed. Published in 1962.

Note: This edition is Avon Book V–2062.

A65   OCCUPATION: WRITER   1950

a. First edition:

ROBERT GRAVES | [*decorative rule*] | *Occupation: Writer* | [*decorative rule*] | CREATIVE AGE PRESS | NEW YORK: 1950

Collation: [1]–[9]¹⁶ [10]⁸ [11]¹⁶, 168 leaves.

p. [i] [*decorative rule*] | *Occupation: Writer* | [*decorative rule*]; p. [ii] list of books by Graves; p. [iii] title-page; p. [iv] copyright notice; pp. v–viii *Intro-duction;* p. ix *Contents;* p. [x] blank; p. [xi] [*decorative rule*] | *Occupation: Writer* | [*decorative rule*]; p. [xii] blank; pp. 1–320 text; pp. [321]–[324] blank.

20·3 × 13·2 cm. Bulk: 2·5/3·2 cm.White wove paper; all edges trimmed. White wove endpapers. Bound in buff cloth; front and back blank; brown quarter cloth spine stamped in gold: ROBERT | GRAVES | [facing back:] *OCCUPATION: WRITER* | CREATIVE | AGE

Price: $4.00. Number of copies unknown. Published 23 February 1950 in white dust-jacket printed in brown and black.

Contents: Introduction – Lars Porsena – Mrs. Fisher – The Shout – Avocado Pears – Old Papa Johnson – Interview with a Dead Man – Thames-Side Reverie – -Ess – Charity Appeals – But It Still Goes On: a Play – The Cult of Tolerance – Horses: a Play – Colonel Blimp's Ancestors – The Search for Thomas Atkins – It Was a Stable World – Caenis on Incest – 'Esta En Su Casa' – How Mad are Hatters? – Pharaoh's Chariot Wheels – Dead Man's Bottles – Occupation: Writer.

First English edition (1951):

ccupation: | WRITER | [*centred decorative rule with sunburst*] | OBERT GRAVES | [*publisher's emblem*] | MCMLI | CASSELL CO. LTD | LONDON

Collation: [A]⁶ B–Q⁸ R/R★²/⁸ S⁸, 144 leaves.

pp. [i–ii] blank; p. [iii] OCCUPATION: WRITER; p. [iv] list of books by Graves; p. [v] title-page; p. [vi] publisher's, publication and printer's notices; p. vii CONTENTS; p. [viii] blank; pp. ix–xi INTRODUCTION; p. [xii] blank; pp. 1–276 text, with pp. [102, 174] being blank and p. [221] being a genealogical table.

21·5 × 13·8 cm. Bulk: 2·1/2·7 cm. White wove paper; all edges trimmed; top edges stained grey. Bound in wine-brown cloth; front and back blank; spine stamped in gold: [*five lines in a rectangular decorative rule box:*] Occupation: | WRITER | ★ | ROBERT | GRAVES | CASSELL

Price: 12s. 6d. Number of copies: 7,500. Published on 27 September 1951 in cream dust-jacket printed in maroon and purple-grey.

Note: 'Dead Man's Bottles' of the American edition is here called 'Bins K to T.'

c. Second American impression ([1951]):

ROBERT GRAVES | *Occupation: Writer* | *The Universal Library* | GROSSET & DUNLAP | NEW YORK [*publisher's emblem faces last three lines*]

Collation as A65a.

p. [i] biographical note; p. [ii] blank; p. [iii] title-page; pp. [iv]–[x] as A65a; p. [xi] OCCUPATION: WRITER; p. [xii] blank; pp. 1–320 text; p. [321] publisher's advertisements; pp. [322]–[324] blank.

20·3 × 13·7 cm. Bulk: 2·1 cm. White wove paper; all edges trimmed. Bound in paper covers; inner sides blank.

Price: $1.25. Number of copies undisclosed. Published in 1951.

Note: This impression is Universal Library U–53.

A66   THE GOLDEN ASS   [1950

a. First edition:

THE | TRANSFORMATIONS OF LUCIUS | OTHERWIS KNOWN AS | THE GOLDEN ASS | BY LUCIUS APULE IUS | TRANSLATED BY | ROBERT GRAVES | [*star*] PENGUIN BOOKS | HARMONDSWORTH · MIDDLE SEX

Collation: [A]⁸ B–K¹⁶ L⁸, 152 leaves.

pp. [1–2] blank; p. [3] THE PENGUIN CLASSICS | EDITED BY E. V. RIEU | LI | [*publisher's emblem*]; p. [4] blank; p. [5] title-page; p. [6] publication, publisher's and printer's notices; p. [7] CONTENTS; p. [8] blank; pp. [9]10–21 INTRODUCTION; p. [22] blank; p. [23] THE | TRANSFORMATIONS OF LUCIUS | OTHERWISE KNOWN AS | THE GOLDEN ASS | [*star*]; p. [24] blank; p. [25] *Apuleius's Address to the Reader;* p. [26] blank; pp. [27]28–293 text with pp. [42, 61, 73, 88, 99, 114, 124, 138, 158, 175, 193, 212, 228, 239, 249, 262, 274, 288] being unnumbered; p. [294] blank; pp. [295]296–298 APPENDIX; pp. [299]–[302] publisher's advertisements; pp. [303–304] blank.

18·0 × 11·1 cm. Bulk: 1·2 cm. White wove paper; all edges trimmed. Bound in paper covers; front cover: [*solid rectangular purple border, inside which:*] | [*rectangular decorative rule border, inside which:*] APULEIUS | THE | GOLDEN ASS | [*roundel of Cupid and Psyche*] | A NEW TRANSLATION BY | ROBERT GRAVES | [*swelled purple rule*] | THE PENGUIN | CLASSICS | [*over-printed in lower left corner of border:*] 1/6; back cover: solid and decorative borders as front, inside which are publisher's advertisements; spine: [*purple band*] | [*decorative band*] | [up spine:] THE GOLDEN ASS | [*publisher's emblem*] | [up spine:] APULEIUS | [*decorative band*] | [*purple band, inside which:*] LI; inner sides of both covers blank.

Price: 1s. 6d. Number of copies unknown. Published in April 1950.

Notes: Impressions: 2nd, 1956.
This book was also issued hardbound (two printings in 1950); it differs as follows: 18·0 × 10·8 cm.; bulk: 1·4/1·9 cm.; white wove endpapers; bound in bright red cloth; front and back blank; spine stamped in gold: [*rule*] | [*design of decorative rule, 14 rules forming an oval with a star inside and decorative rule*] | APULEIUS | [*dash*] | *The Golden* | Ass | [*series of 3 designs (4 decorative rules only) as above*] | [*publisher's emblem*] | [*design as at top*] | [*rule*]; price: 7s. 6d.; number of copies unknown; published in 1950 in cream dust-jacket printed in red and grey. The hardbound edition was also reissued in 1956.

b. *Limited issue (1951):*

THE | TRANSFORMATIONS OF LUCIUS | OTHER-WISE KNOWN AS | THE GOLDEN ASS | BY LUCIUS APULEIUS | TRANSLATED | BY ROBERT GRAVES | [*star*] | 1950 | PENGUIN BOOKS | HARMONDSWORTH · MIDDLESEX

Collation: [A]⁸ B–S⁸ T⁷, 151 leaves.

pp. [1–2] blank; p. [3] publisher's emblem in red; p. [4] blank; p. [5] title-page; p. [6] blank; p. [7] CONTENTS; p. [8] blank; pp. [9]–298 as A66*b;* p. [299] [*signature of Graves*] | The edition of Apuleius' | GOLDEN ASS, |

translated by Robert Graves, | was first published in 1951. | The typography and the binding were | designed by Jan Tschichold. | It is set in Monotype Lutetia, | and printed by Silk & Terry Ltd, | London and Birmingham, | on Blue-White Wove paper | made by Wiggins, Teape & Co, Ltd. | The binding, with a marbled paper | supplied by Douglas Cockerell & Son, | is by James Burn & Co, London. | The edition is limited to | 2,000 copies numbered and signed | by the translator | of which this is No. [*number*]; pp. [300]–[302] blank.

19·2 × 11·3 cm. Bulk: 1·5/1·9 cm. White wove paper; all edges trimmed; top edges gilt. Heavy grey laid endpapers watermarked: Charles I. Bound in marbled boards with parchment spine stamped in gold: The | Golden | Ass | [*heavy rule*] | [*light rule*].

Price: 30s. Number of copies: 2,000. Published in December 1951 in buff dust-jacket printed in black; boxed; box printed in red and black.

c. First American edition ([1951]):

THE TRANSFORMATIONS OF | LUCIUS OTHERWISE KNOWN AS | THE GOLDEN ASS | A NEW TRANSLATION BY | ROBERT GRAVES *from* APULEIUS | FARRAR, STRAUS & YOUNG · NEW YORK

Collation: [1]–[10]^{16}, 160 leaves.
2 pp., blank; p. [i] [flush right:] THE GOLDEN ASS; p. [ii] [flush left:] list of books by Graves; p. [iii] title-page; p. [iv] copyright, manufacturer's and designer's notices and publisher's emblem; p. [v] [flush right:] CONTENTS; p. [vi] blank; p. [vii] [flush right:] APULEIUS'S ADDRESS TO THE READER; p. [viii] blank; pp. ix–xxii [flush right:] INTRODUCTION; p. [1] [flush right:] THE GOLDEN ASS; p. [2] blank; pp. 3–288 text; pp. 289–293 APPENDIX; pp. [294]–[296] blank.

20·2 × 13·4 cm. Bulk: 1·9/2·5 cm. White wove paper; all edges trimmed. White wove endpapers. Bound in yellow cloth; front and back blank; spine stamped in brown: [*decorative rule*] | [*solid box, inside which 8 lines:*] GRAVES | THE | GOLDEN | ASS | FARRAR | STRAUS | AND | YOUNG | [*decorative rule*]

Price: $3.50. Number of copies unknown. Published 11 September 1951

Note: This book was designed by Stefan Salter.

d. Second American edition ([1952]):

CARDINAL [cardinal] EDITION | [decorative rule] | THE
GOLDEN ASS | OF APULEIUS | [decorative rule] | A NEW
TRANSLATION BY | ROBERT GRAVES | [decorative
rule] | POCKET BOOKS, INC. · NEW YORK

Collation: 144 leaves, glued at spine.
p. [i] quotations from reviews; p. [ii] list of books by Graves; p. [iii] title-
page; p. [iv] publication, publisher's, copyright and acknowledgement
notices; p. [v] CONTENTS; p. [vi] APULEIUS'S ADDRESS TO THE READER;
pp. vii–xix INTRODUCTION; p. [xx] blank; p. [1] [decorative rule] THE
GOLDEN ASS; p. [2] blank; pp. 3–259 text; p. [260] blank; pp. 261–264
APPENDIX; pp. [265]–[267] publisher's advertisements; p. [268] blank.

16·3 × 10·6 cm. Bulk: 1·5 cm. White wove paper; all edges trimmed.
Bound in white paper covers with multicolour printing.

Price: $0.35. Number of copies: 150,753. Published in September 1952.
Notes: Impressions: 2nd, 48,715 copies.

This book was also issued in a Pocket Library impression, which differs
as follows: lacks first line of title-page; final line: THE POCKET LIBRARY |
[publisher's emblem]; covers printed in grey, blue, gold and black; all
edges stained gold. Published in May 1954, with four printings sub-
sequently, for a total in five printings of 126,129 copies.

e. Second English edition (1960):

THE | TRANSFORMATIONS OF LUCIUS | OTHER-
WISE KNOWN AS | THE GOLDEN ASS | BY LUCIUS
APULEIUS | TRANSLATED BY ROBERT GRAVES |
LITHOGRAPHS BY MICHAEL AYRTON | LONDON |
THE FOLIO SOCIETY | 1960

Collation: [A]⁸ B–N⁸, 154 leaves.
[plate, back blank, facing title-page]; p. [1] title-page; p. [2] acknowledgement, printer's and binder's notices; p. [3] CONTENTS; p. [4] ILLUSTRATIONS;
pp. 5–13 INTRODUCTION; p. [14] blank; p. [15] THE | TRANSFORMATIONS OF
LUCIUS | OTHERWISE KNOWN AS | THE GOLDEN ASS; p. [16] blank; p. [17]
APULEIUS'S ADDRESS TO | THE READER; p. [18] blank; pp. 19–208 text, with
plates facing pp. 49, 64, 76, 97, 112, 141, 180, 195.

24·6 × 15·3 cm. Bulk: 1·5/2·1 cm. White wove paper; all edges trimmed;
top edge stained brown. White wove illustrated endpapers, inner sides
blank. Bound in parchment with front and back stamped at top and bottom
with brown illustrative bands; spine stamped in gold: APULEIUS | The |
Golden | Ass | GRAVES | [elongated figure of ass] | The | Folio | Society

Price: 22s. 6d. Number of copies undisclosed. Published in January 1960 without dust-jacket in blank marbled-effect grey-green box.

A67   POEMS AND SATIRES   1951

First edition:

ROBERT GRAVES | ★ | [in red:] POEMS | AND | [in red:] SATIRES | 1951 | CASSELL & COMPANY LTD | [*heavy rule*] | [*light rule*] | LONDON

Collation: [A]⁶ B–F⁴, 26 leaves.

p. [i] POEMS AND SATIRES; p. [ii] blank; p. [iii] title-page; p. [iv] publisher's, publication and printer's notices; pp. [v–vi] CONTENTS; pp. vii–x FOREWORD; p. [xi] POEMS; p. [xii] blank; pp. 1–21 text; p. [22] blank; p. [23] SATIRES; p. [24] blank; pp. 25–33 text; p. [34] blank; p. [35] REVISIONS; p. [36] blank; pp. 37–40 text.

18·3 × 11·7 cm. Bulk: 0·4/0·7 cm. Cream wove paper; all edges trimmed; watermarked: Basingwerk Parchment. White wove endpapers. Bound in green cloth; front and back blank; spine stamped in gold, bottom to top: [*light rule*] [*heavy rule*] [*light rule*] CASSELL [*four-pointed star*] POEMS AND SATIRES 1951 [*four-pointed star*] ROBERT GRAVES [*light rule*] [*heavy rule*] [*light rule*]

Price: 7s. 6d. Number of copies: 3,100 (1,100 wasted). Published on 30 November 1951 in cream dust-jacket printed in light maroon.

Contents: Foreword – POEMS: 1. The White Goddess – 2. The Chink – 3. Counting the Beats – 4. The Jackals' Address to Isis – 5. The Death Room – 6. The Young Cordwainer – 7. Your Private Way – 8. My Name and I – 9. Conversation Piece – 10. The Ghost and the Clock – 11. Advice on May Day – 12. For the Rain It Raineth Every Day – 13. Questions in a Wood – 14. The Portrait – 15. Darien – 16. The Survivor – 17. Prometheus – SATIRES: 18. Queen Mother to New Queen – 19. Secession of the Drones – 20. Damocles – 21. Homage to Texas – 22. The Dilemma – 23. General Bloodstock's Lament for England – 24. « ¡Welcome, to the Caves of Arta! » 25. To a Poet in Trouble – REVISIONS: 26. The Progress – 27. Traveller's Curse after Misdirection – 28. Sergeant-Major Money – 29. Brother

A68   POEMS 1953   195?

a. First edition:

ROBERT GRAVES | POEMS | 1953 | CASSELL & COM-PANY LTD | [*heavy rule*] | [*light rule*] | LONDON

Collation: [1]–[5]⁴, 20 leaves.

p. [i] POEMS 1953; p. [ii] list of books by Graves; p. [iii] title-page; p. [iv] publisher's, publication and printer's notices; pp. v–vi CONTENTS; p. vii FOREWORD; p. [viii] blank; pp. 1–30 text; pp. [31–32] blank.

18·4 × 12·0 cm. Bulk: 0·3/0·7 cm. White wove paper; all edges trimmed. White wove endpapers. Bound in sea-green cloth; front and back blank; spine stamped in gold, bottom to top: [*light rule*] [*heavy rule*] [*light rule*] CASSELL [*four-pointed star*] POEMS 1953 [*four-pointed star*] ROBERT GRAVES [*light rule*] [*heavy rule*] [*light rule*]

Price: 7s. 6d. Number of copies: 1,777. Published 24 September 1953.

Contents: Foreword – To Calliope – The Straw – The Foreboding – Cry Faugh! – Hercules at Nemea – Dialogue on the Headland – Lovers in Winter – Esau and Judith – The Mark – With the Gift of a Ring – Liadan and Curithir – The Sea Horse – The Devil at Berry Pomeroy – Reproach to Julia – Dethronement – Cat-Goddesses – The Blue-Fly – Rhea – The Hero – Marginal Warning – The Encounter – I'm Through with You for Ever – With Her Lips Only – The Blotted Copy-book – The Sacred Mission – From the Embassy – Sirocco at Deyá – Leaving the Rest Unsaid

b. Limited issue (1953):

Title-page as A68*a*.

Collation as A68*a*.
Remainder as A68*a* through p. 30; p. [31] THIS EDITION ON HAND-MADE PAPER | IS LIMITED TO 250 COPIES FOR SALE, | NUMBERED 1 to 250, AND SIGNED BY | THE AUTHOR | This is Number [*number*] | [*signature of Graves*]; p. [32] blank.

Size, bulk and paper as A68*a*. Bound in bright green boards with white cloth spine stamped in gold, from middle to top, up spine: ROBERT GRAVES: POEMS 1953

Price: 15s. Number of copies: 260. Published 24 September 1953 in transparent parchment dust-jacket.

A69   THE NAZARENE GOSPEL RESTORED   1953

a. First edition:

THE | NAZARENE GOSPEL | RESTORED | *By* | ROBERT GRAVES | AND | JOSHUA PODRO | [*publisher's emblem*] | CASSELL AND COMPANY LIMITED | LONDON | MCMLIII

Collation: [1]/1★8/8 2/2★–32/32★8/8 33/33★4/8, 524 leaves.

p. [i] THE NAZARENE GOSPEL RESTORED; p. [ii] list of books by Graves; p. [iii] title-page; p. [iv] publisher's, publication and printer's notices; pp. v–ix CONTENTS; p. [x] blank; pp. xi–xxiii FOREWORD; p. [xxiv] blank; p. [1] PART ONE; p. [2] blank; pp. 3–41 text; p. [42] blank; p. [43] PART TWO; p. [44] blank; pp. 45–827 text; p. [828] blank; p. [829] PART THREE; p. [830] blank; pp. 831–833 SUMMARY OF CRITICAL PRINCIPLES; p. [834] blank; p. [835] THE NAZARENE GOSPEL; pp. 836–1011 text; p. [1012] blank; p. [1013] CHAPTER INDEX; p. [1014] blank; pp. 1015–1021 CHAPTER INDEX; pp. [1022]–[1024] blank.

24·2 × 15·4 cm. Bulk: 3·4/4·0 cm. White wove paper; all edges trimmed. White wove endpapers. Bound in black cloth; front and back blank; spine stamped in gold: [*heavy rule*] | [*light rule*] | [*decorative rule*] | THE | NAZARENE | GOSPEL | RESTORED | [*decorative rule*] | [*light rule*] | [*heavy rule*] | ROBERT GRAVES | AND | JOSHUA PODRO | CASSELL

Price: 63s. Number of copies: 2,981. Published on 22 October 1953 in white dust-jacket printed in grey, red and black.

Contents: Foreword – Part One: I. Curiosities of New Testament Criticism – II. The Pauline Heresy – III. The Hand of Simon Magus – IV. The Process of Gospel-Making – Part Two: [parallel texts of the Gospels, commentary and reconstruction] – Part Three: Summary of Critical Principles – Prolegomena to the Nazarene Gospel – The Nazarene Gospel [in 53 chapters] – Epilegomena by James the Just unto the Faithful – Chapter Index

b. First American edition (1954):

THE | NAZARENE GOSPEL | RESTORED | *by* | ROBERT GRAVES | *and* | JOSHUA PODRO | [*publisher's emblem*] | *Garden City, New York* | DOUBLEDAY & COMPANY, INC. | 1954

Collation: [1]–[30]¹⁶ [31]⁸ [32]¹⁶, 504 leaves.

p. [i] THE | NAZARENE GOSPEL | RESTORED; p. [ii] blank; p. [iii] title-page; p. [iv] copyright, printer's and publication notices; pp. v–xvii FOREWORD; p. [xviii] blank; pp. xix–xxiv CONTENTS; p. [1] *Part One;* p. [2] blank; pp. [3]4–42 text; p. [43] *Part Two;* p. [44] blank; pp. [45]46–790 text with p. [118] genealogical table; p. [791] *Part Three;* p. [792] blank; pp. [793] 794–795 text; p. [796] blank; pp. [797–798]799–975 text; p. [976] blank; pp. [977]978–982 CHAPTER INDEX; pp. [983–984] blank; unnumbered page throughout at each chapter.

23·2 × 15·4 cm. Bulk: 4·7/5·3 cm. White wove paper; all edges trimmed; top edges stained red. White wove endpapers. Bound in grey cloth; front and back blank; spine stamped in gold: [ten lines stamped in solid blac rectangular box:] [*light rule*] | [*heavy rule*] | [*light rule*] | THE | NAZARENE | GOSPEL | RESTORED | [*light rule*] | [*heavy rule*] | [*light rule*] | ROBERT GRAVES | AND | JOSHUA PODRO | DOUBLEDAY

Price: $10.00. Number of copies: 5,000. Published 15 July 1954.

c. Partial edition (1955):

THE | NAZARENE GOSPEL | *by* | ROBERT GRAVES and JOSHUA PODRO | Being PART III (text only) | of their | NAZARENE GOSPEL RESTORED | [*publisher's emblem*] | CASSELL AND COMPANY LIMITED | LONDON |MCMLV

Collation: [1]⁸ 2–12⁸, 96 leaves.
p. [i] THE NAZARENE GOSPEL; p. [ii] list of books by Graves; p. [iii] title-page; p. [iv] publisher's printer's and copyright notices; pp. v–vi CONTENTS; pp. vii–ix SUMMARY OF CRITICAL PRINCIPLES; p. x NOTE; p. xi PROLEGOMENA; p. [xii] blank; pp. 1–175 text; pp. [176]–[178] blank.

24·6 × 15·4 cm. Bulk: 1·4/2·0 cm. White wove paper; all edges trimmed. White wove endpapers. Bound in black cloth; front and back blank; spine stamped in gold: [*heavy rule*] | [*light rule*] | THE | NAZARENE | GOSPEL | [*light rule*] | [*heavy rule*] | ROBERT | GRAVES | AND | JOSHUA | PODRO | CASSELL

Price: 15s. Number of copies: 756. Published 24 February 1955 in cream dust-jacket printed in black and red.

Contents: Part III only of A69a.

A70   THE CROSS AND THE SWORD   [1955]

a. First edition:

[p. *ii:*] *Manuel de Jesús Galván's* | *"Enriquillo"* | THE CROSS | UNESCO COLLECTION OF REPRESENTATIVE WORKS: | LATIN AMERICAN SERIES. PUBLISHED WITH | THE COOPERATION OF THE ORGANIZATION OF | AMERI- CAN STATES.

[p. *iii:*] AND THE SWORD | *translated by Robert Graves* | INDIANA UNIVERSITY PRESS | BLOOMINGTON

Collation: [1]⁸ [2]–[12]¹⁶ [13]⁸, 192 leaves.
p. [i] THE CROSS AND THE SWORD; p. [*ii–iii*] title-page; p. [*iv*] copyright, UNESCO and permission notices; pp. [*v*]–*vi* CONTENTS; pp. [*vii*]*viii–xi* FOREWORD; p. [*xii*] blank; pp. [*xiii*]*xiv–xvii* TRANSLATOR'S NOTE; p. [*xviii*]

PREFACE TO 1894 EDITION; p. [1] *Part One;* p. [2] map; pp. [3]4–80 text; p. [81] *Part Two;* p. [82] blank; pp. [83]84–189 text; p. [190] blank; p. [191] *Part Three;* p. [192] blank; pp. [193]194–352 text; pp. [353]354–364 *Notes;* pp. [365]–366 CAST OF CHARACTERS.

20·7 × 13·6 cm. Bulk: 2·7/3·3 cm. White wove paper; top and fore-edges only trimmed; top edge stained black. White wove endpapers. Bound in green cloth; back blank; front blind-stamped in lower left with arrow overlaid with compass; spine stamped in bronze, top to bottom: THE CROSS AND THE SWORD [upright:] *Galván* [as title:] INDIANA

Price: $3.75. Number of copies: 2,000. Published 29 October 1954.

Note: Printed in the U.S.

b. First English issue (1956):

THE CROSS | AND THE SWORD | by | MANUEL DE JESUS GALVAN | *Translated by* | ROBERT GRAVES | LONDON | VICTOR GOLLANCZ LTD | 1956

Collation: [A]/A*8/8 B/B*–M/M*8/8, 192 leaves.
p. [i] THE CROSS AND THE SWORD; p. [ii] *The original title | of this book is |* ENRIQUILLO; p. [iii] title-page; p. [iv] acknowledgements and printer's and publisher's notices; remainder as A70a, except page-numbers in preliminaries are not italics.

19·4 × 12·6 cm. Bulk: 1·8/2·1 cm. White wove paper; all edges trimmed. White wove endpapers. Bound in wine-red cloth; front and back blank; spine stamped in gold: THE | CROSS | AND | THE | SWORD | BY | MANUEL | DE JESUS | GALVAN | GOLLANCZ

Price: 15s. Number of copies undisclosed. Published 11 June 1956 in cream dust-jacket printed in red, blue, yellow, green, brown and black.

Note: This issue appears to be largely a photographic reproduction of the American edition. The type-page of the American text is 16·8 × 10·1 cm., that of the English 16·2 × 9·7 cm.

Printed in Great Britain.

A71   HOMER'S DAUGHTER   [1955]

a. First edition:

HOMER'S DAUGHTER | by | ROBERT GRAVES | [*publisher's emblem*] | CASSELL & COMPANY LTD | LONDON

Collation: [A]⁸ B–O⁸, 112 leaves.

p. [i] HOMER'S DAUGHTER; p. [ii] list of novels by Graves; p. [iii] title-page; p. [iv] publisher's, publication and copyright notices; p. [v] To Selwyn Jepson, of course; p. [vi] blank; p. vii CONTENTS; p. [viii] blank; pp. ix–xvii PROLOGUE; p. [xviii] blank; pp. 1–204 text; pp. [204–205] blank.

18·4 × 12·3 cm. Bulk: 1·9/2·3 cm. White wove paper; all edges trimmed. White wove endpapers. Bound in black cloth; front and back blank; spine stamped in gold: Homer's | Daughter | ROBERT | GRAVES | CASSELL

Price: 10s. 6d. Number of copies: 15,000. Published 24 February 1955 in eggshell dust-jacket printed in black, yellow and matt olive.

Note: This book has been translated into Croatian, German, Italian, Polish, Russian and Swedish.

b. First American edition (1955):

[entire flush left:] HOMER'S | DAUGHTER | by Robert Graves | DOUBLEDAY & COMPANY, INC., GARDEN CITY, NEW YORK, 1955

Collation: [1]–[9]¹⁶, 144 leaves.

p. [i] HOMER'S | DAUGHTER; p. [ii] blank; p. [1] list of novels by Graves; p. [2] blank; p. [3] title-page; p. [4] copyright, printer's, designer's and edition notices; p. [5] *To Selwyn Jepson, of course*; p. [6] blank; pp. [7]8–9 HISTORICAL NOTE; p. [10] blank; pp. [11]–12 CONTENTS; p. [13] HOMER'S | DAUGHTER; p. [14] blank; pp. [15]16–283 text, with pp. [27, 34, 48, 71, 89, 104, 119, 137, 154, 168, 186, 199, 214, 231, 246, 267] being unnumbered; pp. [284]–[286] blank.

20·8 × 13·9 cm. Bulk: 2·3/2·8 cm. White wove paper; all edges trimmed. White wove endpapers. Bound in black cloth; back blank; front stamped in orange at middle near spine with figure of Greek warrior and horse; spine stamped in orange, top to bottom: by Robert Graves [in second row, toward back:] HOMER'S [in centre: figure of Greek warrior and horse] DAUGHTER [in second row, toward front:] DOUBLEDAY

Price: $3.95. Number of copies: 12,500 (in three printings). Published on 24 February 1955.

A72   THE GREEK MYTHS   [1955]

a. First edition:

ROBERT GRAVES | THE GREEK MYTHS | VOLUME ONE [TWO] | PENGUIN BOOKS

Collation: I: [A]¹⁶ B–M¹⁶, 192 leaves; II: [A]¹⁶ B–N¹⁶, 208 leaves.

2 pp., blank; p. [1] PENGUIN BOOKS | 1026 | THE GREEK MYTHS | VOLUME ONE | ROBERT GRAVES | [*publisher's emblem*]; p. [2] blank; p. [3] title-page; p. [4] publisher's, edition and printer's notices; pp. [5]6–7 CONTENTS OF VOLUME ONE; p. [8] frontispiece; pp. [9]10–13[14–15]16–23 INTRODUCTION, with pp. [14–15] being a map; p. [24] blank; p. [25] THE GREEK MYTHS | VOLUME ONE; p. [26] blank; pp. [27]28–370 text, with pp. [48, 83, 89, 101, 131, 151, 281, 319, 349, 356] being unnumbered; pp. [371]–[382] publisher's advertisements, with p. [372] being blank.

II: p. [1] PENGUIN BOOKS | 1027 | THE GREEK MYTHS | VOLUME TWO | ROBERT GRAVES | [*publisher's emblem*]; p. [2] blank; p. [3] title-page; p. [4] publisher's and printer's notices; pp. [5]–6 CONTENTS OF VOLUME TWO; p. [7] THE GREEK MYTHS | VOLUME TWO; p. [8] blank; pp. [9]10–376 text, with pp. [25, 40, 80, 113, 145, 207, 241, 290, 313, 346] being unnumbered; pp. 377–412 INDEX; pp. [413]–[416] publisher's advertisements; [folding map tipped to outside edge of inner back cover].

18·1 × 11·2 cm. Bulk: I: 1·8 cm.; II: 2·0 cm. White wove paper; all edges trimmed. Bound in paper covers; front has brown columns down each side with publisher's emblem half-way down in right-hand column; middle white space reads: [*in brown:*] PENGUIN BOOKS | [*heavy rule across whole cover*] | ROBERT GRAVES | [*brown rule*] | The Greek Myths | VOLUME ONE [TWO] | [*brown rule*] | [summary of 9 ll.] | [*heavy rule across whole cover* | [*in brown:*] 3/6; back has same arrangement of brown columns, the publisher's emblem being in the left-hand column; middle white space reads: [*in brown:*] PENGUIN BOOKS] [*heavy rule*] | [*photo of Graves*] | [biographical note of 25 ll.] | [*heavy rule*] | *Not for sale 3/6 in the U.S.A.* [*price only in brown*]; spine has brown bands top and bottom, inside which the heavy rule; at bottom, upright: 1026 [1027]; spine reads from bottom to top: Robert Graves [*publisher's emblem upright in brown*] The Greek Myths · Volume 1 [2]; inside front covers is blurb; inside back cover has ad for *Count Belisarius.*

Price: 3s. 6d. per volume. Number of copies unknown. Published 24 February 1955 in white dust-jacket printed in brown and black like cover.

Note: Impressions: 2nd, November 1955; 3rd, 1957.
This book has been translated into German.

b. *First American issue* ([*1955*]):

ROBERT GRAVES | THE GREEK MYTHS | VOLUME ONE [TWO] | PENGUIN BOOKS | BALTIMORE · MARYLAND

Collation: I: [1]–[12]¹⁶, 192 leaves; II: [1]–[13]¹⁶, 208 leaves.
Remainder as A72a, except pp. I.[4] and II.[4] have publication, publisher's copyright and printing notices and pp. I.[382] and II.[416] are blank.

Measurements and paper as A72a. Covers as A72a.

Price: $0.85 per volume. Number of copies: 35,000. Published 17 June 1955.

Note: Impressions: 2nd, January 1957; 3rd, June 1959; 4th, May 1961.

There is also an American issue bound in red cloth; back blank; front stamped in gold with facsimile signature of Graves; spine stamped in gold: ROBERT | GRAVES | [*rule*] | THE | GREEK | MYTHS | I [II]; top edges stained black; white wove endpapers; price: $6.50 per volume; 3,000 copies published in 1955.

c. Second American 'edition' (1957):

ROBERT GRAVES | THE GREEK MYTHS | VOLUME ONE [TWO] | GEORGE BRAZILLER, INC. | NEW YORK | 1957

Collation: I: [1]–[9]¹⁶ [10]¹² [11]–[12]¹⁶, 188 leaves, but retaining also the signing of the English issue A72a; II: [A]¹⁶ B–N¹⁶, 208 leaves.

2 pp., blank; p. [1] THE GREEK MYTHS | VOLUME ONE | ROBERT GRAVES; p. [2] blank; p. [3] title-page; p. [4] publication, copyright, Library of Congress card and printing notices; pp. [5]6–7 CONTENTS OF VOLUME ONE; p. [8] blank; p. [8a] illustration; p. [8b] blank; pp. [9]–370 as A72a; pp. [371–372] blank.

II: p. [1] THE GREEK MYTHS | VOLUME TWO | ROBERT GRAVES; p. [2] blank; p. [3] title-page; p. [4] publication, copyright, Library of Congress card and printing notices; pp. [5]–412 as A72a; pp. [413]–[416] blank; [map pasted to inside back cover].

18·0 × 11·2 cm. Bulk: I: 1·7/2·2 cm.; II: 1·8/2·3 cm. White wove paper; all edges trimmed; top edges stained green. White wove endpapers. Bound in black cloth; front and back blank; spine stamped in gold: ROBERT | GRAVES | [*rule*] | THE | GREEK | MYTHS | [*rule*] | I [II]

Price: $6.50 for two volumes. Number of copies undetermined. Published in 1957.

Note: There is also a one-volume issue, which differs as follows: no map; top edges stained blue; grey cloth spine stamped: *Robert Graves* | [*rectangular single-rule box enclosing 3 ll.:*] | THE | GREEK | MYTHS | *George Braziller;* front and back covers simulated black leather; price: $4.75; published 28 October 1957.

d. Second English 'edition' ([1958]):

GREEK MYTHS | [*rule*] | ROBERT GRAVES | [*publisher's emblem*] | CASSELL & COMPANY LTD | LONDON

Collation: [A]/A2⁸/⁸ B/B2–Z/Z2⁸/⁸ 2A/2A2⁸/⁸ 2B⁶, 390 leaves.
p. [1] GREEK MYTHS; p. [2] blank; p. [3] title-page; p. [4] publisher's, publication, copyright and printer's notices; pp. [5]6–9 CONTENTS; p. [10] illustration; pp. [11]12–24 INTRODUCTION; p. [24a] blank; pp. [24b–24c] map; p. [24d] blank; p. [25] GREEK MYTHS; p. [26] blank; pp. [27]28–738 text, with pp. [48, 83, 89, 101, 131, 151, 281, 319, 349, 356, 371, 387, 402, 442, 475, 507, 569, 603, 652, 675, 708] being unnumbered; [map pasted to p. [739]]; pp. [739]740–774 NAME INDEX; pp. [775–776] blank.

20·3 × 13·0 cm. Bulk: 3·1/3·7 cm. White wove paper; all edges trimmed. White wove endpapers. Bound in rust cloth; front and back blank; spine stamped in gold: [*double-rule rectangular box enclosing 2 ll.:*] | GREEK | MYTHS | ROBERT | GRAVES | CASSELL

Price: 30s. Number of copies: 2,999. Published on 6 March 1958 in white dust-jacket printed in yellow, chestnut and black.

Notes: Impressions: 2nd, 15 November 1958 (1,500 copies); 3rd, November 1962. The introduction has been revised for this edition; and note 4 of Chapter 104 is new.

e. Second English 'edition', Pelican impression ([1960]):

ROBERT GRAVES | THE GREEK MYTHS | VOLUME ONE [TWO] | PENGUIN BOOKS

Collation as A72a.
I: 2 pp., blank; p. [I] PELICAN BOOKS | A508 | THE GREEK MYTHS | VOLUME ONE | ROBERT GRAVES | [*series emblem*]; pp. [2]–[8] as A72a; pp. [9]–10 FOREWORD; pp. [11] 12–24 INTRODUCTION; pp. [25]–370, as A72a; p. [371] MAP OF THE GREEK WORLD; pp. [372–373] map; p. [374] blank; pp. [375]–[382] publisher's advertisements, with p. [376] being blank.
II: as A72a.

18·0 × 10·7 cm. Bulk: I: 1·8 cm.; II: 2·1 cm. White wove paper; all edges trimmed. Bound in white paper covers printed in blue and black.

Price: 5s. per volume. Number of copies: I: 25,000; II: 24,000. Published in 1960.

Note: The text is that of A72d.

Impressions: 2nd, 1962.

First edition:

COLLECTED POEMS | 1955 | by Robert Graves | 1955 | DOUBLEDAY & COMPANY, INC. | GARDEN CITY, NEW YORK

Collation: [1]–[10]¹⁶, 160 leaves.

p. [i] COLLECTED POEMS | 1955; p. [ii] blank; p. [iii] list of books by Graves; p. [iv] blank; p. [v] title-page; p. [vi] Library of Congress card, copyright, printer's and designer's notices; p. vii TO CALLIOPE; p. [viii] blank; p. [ix] ACKNOWLEDGEMENTS; p. [x] blank; pp. xi–xii FOREWORD; pp. xiii–xx CONTENTS; pp. [1]–291 text, with pp. [1, 37, 71, 97, 157, 175, 209, 241, 261] being section headings and pp. [2, 36, 38, 70, 72, 98, 156, 158, 176, 210, 242, 260, 262] being blank; p. [292] blank; pp. 293–298 INDEX; pp. [299–300] blank.

20·8 × 13·8 cm. Bulk: 2·2/2·8 cm. White wove paper; all edges trimmed; top edges stained blue. Bound in light blue cloth; front and back blank; spine stamped in blue: *Collected* | *Poems* | 1955 | [*decorative rule*] | ROBERT | GRAVES

Price: $4.50. Number of copies: 3,500 (in two printings). Published 30 June 1955 in white dust-jacket printed in light and dark blue.

Contents: To Calliope – Foreword – 1: In the Wilderness– The Haunted House – Reproach – The Finding of Love – 'The General Elliott' – Rocky Acres – Outlaws – One Hard Look – A Frosty Night – Allie – Unicorn and the White Doe – Henry and Mary – Love without Hope – What Did I Dream? – The Country Dance – The Troll's Nosegay – The Hills of May – Lost Love – Vain and Careless – An English Wood – The Bedpost – The Pier-Glass – Apples and Water – Angry Samson – Down – Mermaid, Dragon, Fiend – 11: In Procession – Warning to Children – Alice – Richard Roe and John Doe – The Witches' Cauldron – Ancestors – Children of Darkness – The Cool Web – Love in Barrenness – Song of Contrariety – The Presence – The Land of Whipperginny – In No Direction – The Castle – Return – The Bards – Nobody – The Progress – Full Moon – Vanity – Pure Death – Sick Love – It Was All Very Tidy – 111: Callow Captain – Thief – Saint – The Furious Voyage – Song: Lift-Boy – Traveller's Curse after Misdirection – The Last Day of Leave – The Next Time – Ulysses – The Succubus – The Reader over My Shoulder – The Legs – Gardener – Front Door Soliloquy – In Broken Images – The Devil at Berry Pomeroy – On Rising Early – Flying Crooked – Fragment of a Lost Poem – Brother – 1V: Galatea and Pygmalion – The Devil's Advice to Story-Tellers – Sergeant-Major Money – Sea Side –Wm. Brazier – Welsh Incident – Vision in the Repair-Shop – Interruption – Act V, Scene 5–

A74   ADAM'S RIB   [1955

a. First edition:

[in brown:] ADAM'S RIB | *and other anomalous elements in* | *the Hebrew Creation Myth* | *a new view by* | ROBERT GRAVES | *with wood engravings by James Metcalf* | TRIANON PRESS

Collation: [1]⁴ [2]⁸ [3]¹⁰ [4]–[5]⁸ [6]⁴, 42 leaves.

p. [i] ADAM'S RIB; p. [ii] blank; p. [iii] statement of edition, printer's, designer's and publisher's notices; p. [iv] blank; p. [v] title-page; p. [vi] publisher's, distributor's and printing notices; p. [vii] CONTENTS; p. [viii] blank; pp. 1–19 ARGUMENT; p. [20] blank; p. [21] THE GENESIS VERSION; p. [22] blank; pp. 23–35 text; p. [36] blank; p. [37] THE HEBRON ICONS; pp. 38–72 [73] text and illustrations, text on even-numbered pages, illustrations facing on unnumbered pages, this part of the book being printed in brown; pp. [74]–[76] blank.

27·4 × 19·0 cm. Bulk: 1·1/1·7 cm. White wove paper; all edges trimmed. White wove endpapers. Bound in brick red cloth; front and back blank; spine stamped in gold, top to bottom: ADAM'S RIB *by Robert Graves* TRIANON

Price: 31s. 6d. Number of copies: 1,750. Published 22 July 1955 in grey dust-jacket printed in black.

b. Limited issue ([1955]):

Title-page as A74*a*.

Collation as A74*a*.
Remainder as A72*a*, except p. [ii]: This is Number [*letter or number written in*] of the Signed Edition | [*signature of Graves*] | [*signature of Metcalf*].

Size, paper and binding as A74*a*.

Price: 52s. 6d. Number of copies: 250 numbered; 26 lettered A–Z (*hors commerce*). Published as A74*a*.

. First American edition ([1958]):

ın brown:] ADAM'S RIB | *and other anomalous elements in* | *the Hebrew Creation Myth* | *a new view by* | ROBERT GRAVES | *ith wood engravings by James Metcalf* | NEW YORK · THOMAS ʻOSELOFF

Collation: [1]⁶ [2]–[6]⁸, 46 leaves.
2 pp., blank, front pastedown endpaper; 2 pp., blank, front free endpaper; pp. [i]–[ii] as A74*a;* p. [iii] designer's and illustrator's notices; p. [iv] blank; p. [v] title-page; p. [vi] copyright, edition, publisher's, Library of Congress

card and publication notices; pp. [vii]–[76] as A74*a;* 2 pp., blank, rear free endpaper; 2 pp., blank, rear pastedown endpaper.

27·3 × 19·0 cm. Bulk: 0·7/1·2 cm. White wove paper; all edges trimmed. Bound in medium red cloth; front and back blank; spine stamped in gold, down spine: ADAM'S RIB *by Robert Graves* [to front:] THOMAS [to back, parallel to previous] YOSELOFF

Price: $6.00. Number of copies: 2,000. Published in September 1958.

Note: 1,000 English sheets of A74*a* were distributed by Yoseloff at the same price; A74*b* was also distributed by him at $7.50; A74*a–b* were issued in March 1958.

A75   THE CROWNING PRIVILEGE   [1955]

a. First edition:

THE CROWNING | PRIVILEGE | THE CLARK LECTURES | 1954–1955 | ALSO VARIOUS ESSAYS ON POETRY | AND | SIXTEEN NEW POEMS | *by* | *ROBERT GRAVES* | [*publisher's emblem*] | CASSELL & COMPANY LTD | LONDON

Collation: [A]⁸ B–P⁸, 120 leaves.
p. [i] THE CROWNING PRIVILEGE; p. [ii] list of books by Graves; p. [iii] title-page; p. [iv] publisher's, copyright, publication and printer's notices; p. [v] *To the Masters and Fellows of* | *Trinity College, Cambridge;* | *in gratitude;* p [vi] blank; pp. vii–viii CONTENTS; p. ix FOREWORD; p. [x] blank; p. [1 THE CLARK LECTURES | 1954–1955; p. [2] blank; pp. 3–135 text; p. [136 blank; p. [137] VARIOUS ESSAYS | ON POETRY; p. [138] blank; pp. 139–21 text; pp. 215–230 SIXTEEN NEW POEMS

21·3 × 15·7 cm. Bulk: 1·6/2·1 cm. White wove paper; all edges trimmed White wove endpapers. Bound in black cloth; front and back blank; spin stamped in gold: The | Crowning | Privilege | ROBERT | GRAVES | CASSEI

Price: 15s. Number of copies: 3,012. Published 22 September 1955 in crea dust-jacket printed in green and black.

Contents: Foreword – The Clark Lectures, 1954–1955: 1. The Crownir Privilege – 2. The Age of Obsequiousness – 3. The Road to Rydal Mount 4. Harp, Anvil, Oar – 5. Dame Ocupacyon – 6. These Be Your Gods, Israel! – Various Essays on Poetry: Mother Goose's Lost Goslings – T Old Black Cow – The Essential E. E. Cummings – Juana de Asbaje Poems by Juana de Asbaje, with translations – The Poet and His Public Best Man, Bore, Bamboozle, Etc. – Theft – Kynge Arthur is Nat Dedε

Dr Syntax and Mr Pound – Sixteen New Poems: The Clearing – A Lost
Jewel – The Three Pebbles – The Question – The Window Sill – The Sea
Horse – Spoils – Beauty in Trouble – Poets' Corner – End of the World –
Penthesileia – To a Pebble in My Shoe – The Tenants – Coronation Address
– My Moral Forces – Interview.

Note: Contents differ from those of A75*b–c*.

b. First American edition (*1956*):

[four lines flush right:] The | Crowning | Privilege | COLLECTED
ESSAYS ON POETRY | [two lines flush left:] by ROBERT GRAVES |
| DOUBLEDAY & COMPANY, INC., GARDEN CITY, NEW YORK, 1956

Collation: [1]–[10]¹⁶, 160 leaves.
pp. [i]–[iv] blank; p. [1] [flush right:] THE CROWNING PRIVILEGE; p. [2] blank;
p. [3] list of books by Graves; p. [4] blank; p. [5] title-page; p. [6] [flush right:]
publisher's, copyright, printer's, designer's and edition notices; p. [7]
[flush right:] *To the Masters and Fellows* | *of Trinity College, Cambridge; in
gratitude;* p. [8] blank; p. [9] [flush right:] FOREWORD; p. [10] blank; pp.
11–12 [flush right:] CONTENTS; p. [13] [flush right:] THE CLARK LECTURES |
1954–1955; p. [14] blank; pp. [15]–142 text, with pp. [15, 36, 55, 79, 100,
119] being unnumbered; p. [143] [flush right:] VARIOUS ESSAYS ON POETRY;
p. [144] blank; pp. [145]–218 text, with pp. [145, 160, 166, 171, 189, 196,
201, 210, 216] being unnumbered; p. [219] [flush right:] THE COMMON
ASPHODEL; p. [220] blank; pp. [221]–311 text, with pp. [221, 239, 280, 293,
296, 308] being unnumbered; pp. [312]–[316] blank.

20·9 × 13·9 cm. Bulk: 2·3/2·8 cm. White wove paper; all edges trimmed.
White wove endpapers. Bound in yellow cloth; front and back blank;
spine printed in blue: THE | CROWNING | PRIVILEGE | [*in red: device of thirteen
winged crowns about circle*] | Robert | Graves | DOUBLEDAY

Price: $5.00. Number of copies: 4,000 (in two printings). Published 5 July
1956.

Contents: Omits poems of A75*a* and adds the following essays from
A63: Loving Mad Tom – Nietzsche – Coleridge and Wordsworth – Keats
and Shelley – Lucretius and Jeans – How Poets See – 'Mad Mr. Swinburne'
– The Ghost of Milton – The Common Asphodel.

c. Second British edition ([*1959*]):

THE | CROWNING PRIVILEGE | *Collected Essays on Poetry by* |
ROBERT GRAVES | PENGUIN BOOKS

Collation: [1]⁸ 2–22⁸, 176 leaves.

p. [1] PELICAN BOOKS | A451 | THE CROWNING PRIVILEGE | ROBERT GRAVES | [*publisher's emblem*]; p. [2] blank; p. [3] title-page; p. [4] publisher's, publication, copyright and printer's notices; p. [5] TO THE MASTERS AND FELLOWS | OF TRINITY COLLEGE CAMBRIDGE | IN GRATITUDE; p. [6] blank; p. [7] CONTENTS; p. [8] blank; p. [9] FOREWORD; p. [10] blank; p. [11] THE CLARK LECTURES | 1954–1955; p. [12] blank; pp. 13–[158] text, with pp. [36, 58, 85, 109, 131, 158] being unnumbered; p. [159] VARIOUS ESSAYS ON POETRY; p. [160] blank; pp. 161–[244] text, with pp. [177, 183, 189, 201, 210, 218, 224, 234, 241, 244] being unnumbered; p. [245] THE COMMON ASPHODEL; p. [246] blank; pp. 247–[347] text, with pp. [266, 313, 327, 330, 343, 347] being unnumbered; p. [348] blank; p. [349] publisher's advertisement; p. [350] blank; pp. [351–352] publisher's advertisements.

18·0 × 11·0 cm. Bulk: 1·6 cm. White wove paper; all edges trimmed. Bound in white paper covers printed in blue and black.

Price: 4s. Number of copies: 25,000. Published 28 May 1959.

Contents: As A75*b*.

A76   THE INFANT WITH THE GLOBE   [1955]

a. First edition:

PEDRO ANTONIO DE ALARCON | THE INFANT | WITH THE | GLOBE | *translated* | *with an introduction by* | ROBERT GRAVES | TRIANON PRESS

Collation: [1]¹⁶ 2–7¹⁶ 8/8*¹⁶/², 130 leaves.

p. [i] THE INFANT WITH THE GLOBE; p. [ii] blank; p. [iii] title-page; p. [iv] publisher's and printer's notices; p. [v] *Contents;* p. [vi] blank; pp. [vii] viii–xviii *Introduction;* pp. [1]2–240 text, with pp. [4, 8, 15, 23, 27, 29, 33, 41, 45, 56, 63, 74, 86, 91, 99, 104, 111, 129, 148, 169, 189, 198, 208, 216, 227] being unnumbered; pp. [241–242] blank.

18·4 × 12·3 cm. Bulk: 1·6/1·9 cm. White wove paper; all edges trimmed. White wove endpapers. Bound in rust cloth; front and back blank; spine stamped in gold: ALARCON | ★ | THE | INFANT | WITH THE | GLOBE | ★ | GRAVES | TRIANON | PRESS

Price: 15s. Number of copies unknown. Published 11 November 1955 in white dust-jacket printed in red and black.

b. American issue ([1955]):

[nine lines flush left of centre:] ROBERT | GRAVES | THE | INFANT | WITH | THE | GLOBE | *From the Spanish of* | *Pedro Antonio de Alarcón* | [*publisher's emblem left of remaining*] | [two lines flush left:] NEW YORK · LONDON | THOMAS YOSELOFF

Collation as A76a.
Remainder as A76a, except p. [iv] edition, publisher's, Library of Congress card, copyright, publication and printing notices.

18·3 × 12·3 cm. Bulk: 1·6/2·2 cm. Paper as A76a. Bound in orange cloth; front and back blank; spine printed: [down spine to front:] ROBERT | [down spine to back:] GRAVES | [down spine, centred:] THE INFANT WITH THE GLOBE | [down spine, to back, beginning below 'B' of 'GLOBE':] *Alarcón* | [remainder upright:] [*publisher's emblem*] | THOMAS | YOSELOFF

Price: $4.25. Number of copies: 1,500 Trianon sheets. Published 29 October 1959 in white dust-jacket printed in blue, orange and black.

A77 WINTER IN MAJORCA [1956]

a. First edition:

WINTER | IN MAJORCA | by | GEORGE SAND | WITH | JOSÉ QUADRADO'S | *Refutation of George Sand* | TRANS-LATED AND ANNOTATED | BY | ROBERT GRAVES | [*publisher's emblem*] | *CASSELL & COMPANY LTD* | *LONDON*

Collation: [A]⁸ B–M⁸ N/*²/⁸, 106 leaves.
pp. [i–ii] blank; p. [iii] WINTER IN MAJORCA; p. [iv] list of books by Graves; p. [v] title-page; p. [vi] publisher's, printer's, copyright and publication notices; p. vii CONTENTS; p. [viii] blank; p. ix ILLUSTRATIONS; p. [x] blank; pp. xi–xii FOREWORD; p. [1] WINTER IN MAJORCA | *by* | GEORGE SAND; p. [2] blank; p. 3 *AUTHOR'S NOTE;* p. [4] blank; pp. 5–9 text; p. [10] map; pp. 11–52 text; [plate, printed both sides]; pp. 53–68 text; [plate, printed both sides]; pp. 69–174 text; pp. 175–185 *HISTORICAL SUM-MARY;* p. [186] blank; pp. 187–200 *TO GEORGE SAND: A REFUTA-TION.*

21·5 × 13·8 cm. Bulk: 1·5/2·0 cm. White laid paper; all edges trimmed. White wove endpapers. Bound in red cloth; front and back blank; spine stamped in gold: Winter | in Majorca | GEORGE | SAND | *Translated and* | *annotated by* | ROBERT | GRAVES | CASSELL

131

Price: 15s. Number of copies: 1,370. Published 9 February 1956 in white dust-jacket printed in red, black and olive-tan.

Note: Impressions: 2nd, April 1956. Number of copies: 1,003.

b. Majorcan issue ([1956]):

WINTER | IN MAJORCA | by | GEORGE SAND | WITH | JOSÉ QUADRADO'S | *Refutation of George Sand* | TRANSLATED AND ANNOTATED | BY | ROBERT GRAVES | *VALLDEMOSA EDITION* | *MALLORCA*

Collation: [A]⁸ B–M⁸ N/✱²/⁸, 106 leaves.
Remainder as A77a, except p. [vi] copyright, publication and printing notices.

21·8 × 14·2 cm. Bulk: 1·3 cm. White wove paper; all edges trimmed. Bound in yellow paper cover; back blank; front cover: [*four lines in red:*] WINTER | IN MAJORCA | by GEORGE SAND | with José Quadrado's *Refutation of George Sand* | [*cut of George Sand*] | [*in red:*] TRANSLATED & ANNOTATED BY | ROBERT GRAVES; spine: [at top of spine, from bottom to top, in red:] WINTER IN MAJORCA | [in lower third of spine, upright:] George | Sand | translated | and | annotated | by | Robert | Graves | Valldemosa | edition | Mallorca; inner sides of front and back covers blank.

Price: undetermined. Number of copies: 2,009. Published 9 February 1956.

A78   ¡CATACROK!   [1956]

First edition:

¡CATACROK! | Mostly Stories, Mostly Funny | by | ROBERT GRAVES | [*publisher's emblem*] | CASSELL & CO LTD | LONDON

Collation: [A]⁸ B–N⁸, 104 leaves.
p. [1] ¡CATACROK!; p. [2] blank; p. [3] title-page; p. [4] publisher's, publication, copyright and printer's notices; pp. 5–6 CONTENTS; pp. 7–8 FOREWORD; pp. 9–203 text; pp. [204]–[208] blank.

21·5 × 15·7 cm. Bulk: 1·9/2·4 cm. White wove paper; all edges trimmed. White wove endpapers. Bound in light blue cloth; front and back blank; spine stamped in gold: ROBERT | GRAVES | ¡CATACROK! | CASSELL; title run downward across spine.

Price: 15s. Number of copies: 4,015. Published 8 November 1956 in white dust-jacket printed in yellow, robin's egg and black.

132

Contents: Foreword – Varro's Four Hundred and Ninety Books – Treacle Tart – The Full Length – An Appointment for Candlemas – The Devil Is a Protestant – Trín-Trín-Trín – Earth to Earth – Epics Are Out of Fashion – School Life in Majorca – Bulletin of the College of St Francis of Assisi – New Light on Dream-Flight – Period Piece – Protocols of Kitsch – Touristic Circular K37 – They Say . . . They Say – Week-End at Cwm Tatws – 6 Valiant Bulls 6 – He Went Out to Buy a Rhine – A Man May Not Marry His . . . – God Grant Your Honour Many Years – The White Horse, or 'The Great Southern Ghost Story' – A Bomb under My Monument – Thy Servant and God's – Ever Had a Guinea Worm? – Sappy Blancmange – Cambridge Upstairs – The Five Godfathers – Kill Them! Kill Them! – The Abominable Mr Gunn – Harold Vesey at the Gates of Hell – Flesh-Coloured Net Tights – 'Ha, Ha!' Chort-led Nig-ger – Life of the Poet Gnaeus Robertulus Gravesa – Ditching in a Fishless Sea – The Whitaker Negroes – Bathunts at Bathurst

Note: This book has been translated into Swedish.

A79   PHARSALIA   [1956]

a. First edition:

LUCAN | PHARSALIA | DRAMATIC EPISODES OF THE | CIVIL WARS | [*star*] | TRANSLATED | BY ROBERT GRAVES | [*heavy rule*] | [*three successively shorter light rules*] | PENGUIN BOOKS

Collation: [1]^{16} 2–3^{16} 4–6^8 7–9^{16}, 120 leaves.
p. [1] THE PENGUIN CLASSICS | EDITED BY E. V. RIEU | L66 | [*publisher's emblem*]; p. [2] blank; p. [3] title-page; p. [4] publisher's, publication and printer's notices; p. [5] CONTENTS; p. [6] blank; pp. 7–23[24] INTRODUCTION; pp. 25–238[239] text, with pp. [46, 66, 86, 106, 128, 149, 173, 196, 224] being unnumbered; p. [240] blank.

18·0 × 11·1 cm. Bulk: 1·1 cm. White wove paper; all edges trimmed. Bound in paper covers; front cover: [*solid rectangular purple border, inside which:*] | [*rectangular decorative rule border, inside which:*] | LUCAN | PHARSALIA | DRAMATIC | EPISODES OF THE | CIVIL WARS | [*roundel*] | A NEW TRANSLATION BY | ROBERT GRAVES | [*swelled purple rule*] | THE PENGUIN | CLASSICS | [at right:] 2/6; back cover: solid and decorative borders as front, inside which are publisher's advertisements; spine: [*purple band*] | [*decorative band*] | [up spine:] PHARSALIA | [*publisher's emblem*] | [up spine:] LUCAN | L66 | [*decorative band*] | [*purple band*]; inner sides of both covers blank.

Price: 2s. 6d. Number of copies: 30,000. Published 29 November 1956.

b. First American issue([1957]):

Title-page as A79a.

Collation: [1]–[3]¹⁶ [4]–[5]¹² [6]–[8]¹⁶, 120 leaves.
Remainder as A79a.

20·3 × 13·6 cm. Bulk: 1·5/2·1 cm. White wove paper; all edges trimmed; top edges stained blue; other edges spattered. White wove endpapers. Bound in red cloth-simulated boards; back blank; front stamped in gold with facsimile signature of Graves; spine stamped in gold, top to bottom: LUCAN · PHARSALIA

Price: $4.00. Number of copies: 3,000. Published in June 1957 in white dust-jacket printed in pink and black.

Note: There is an American paper-bound issue, identical with A79a, except on better paper. 20,000 copies were printed in the United States at $0.95.

c. Second English edition ([1961]):

THE BELLE SAUVAGE LIBRARY | LUCAN | PHARSALIA | DRAMATIC EPISODES OF THE | CIVIL WARS | TRANS-LATED BY | ROBERT GRAVES | [*publisher's emblem*] | CASSELL · LONDON

Collation: [1]–[11]⁸ [12]⁹ [13]⁸ [14]² [15]⁴ [16]⁸, 119 leaves, the final leaf of [12] being tipped in and [14] being unsewn and pasted between [13] and [15].
p. [i] PHARSALIA; p. [ii] blank; p. [iii] title-page; p. [iv] publisher's, copyright, publication and printing notices; pp. vi–xii INTRODUCTION; pp 1–214[215] text, with pp. [22, 42, 62, 82, 104, 125, 149, 172, 200] being unnumbered; p. [216] blank.

20·6 × 14·7 cm. Bulk: 1·3/1·8 cm. White wove paper; all edges trimmed White wove endpapers. Bound in dark buff cloth; front and back blank spine stamped in copper: ★ | [*rule*] | LUCAN | *Pharsalia* | [*rule*] | ★ | *Translated by* | ROBERT | GRAVES | ★ | [*rule*] | *Cassell* | [*rule*] | ★

Price: 12s. 6d. Number of copies undisclosed. Published 12 October 196 in white dust-jacket printed in orange, brown and black.

a. First edition:

[*whole enclosed within oval of medallions of the twelve Caesars:*]
THE | TWELVE | CAESARS | – | *Gaius Suetonius* | *Tranquillus* |
– | TRANSLATED BY | ROBERT GRAVES | – | *Penguin*
Books

> *Collation:* [A]¹⁶ B–K¹⁶, 160 leaves.
> p. [1] THE PENGUIN CLASSICS | EDITED BY E. V. RIEU | L72 | [*publisher's emblem*];
> p. [2] blank; p. [3] title-page; p. [4] publisher's, publication and printer's
> notices; p. [5] CONTENTS; p. [6] description of cover design; pp. [7]–8
> FOREWORD; pp. [9]10–309 text, with pp. [50, 148, 180, 208, 242, 262, 294]
> being blank and pp. [9, 51, 109, 149, 181, 209, 243, 255, 263, 273, 287, 295]
> being unnumbered; pp. [310–311] genealogical tables; p. [312] blank; pp.
> [313]314–315 descriptions of the medallions on the title-page; p. [316]
> blank; p. [317] publisher's advertisement; p. [318] blank; pp. [319–320]
> publisher's advertisements.

> 18·1 × 11·1 cm. Bulk: 1·5 cm. White wove paper; all edges trimmed.
> Bound in paper covers; front cover: [*solid rectangular purple border, inside*
> *which:*] | [*rectangular decorative rule border, inside which:*] | SUETONIUS | THE |
> TWELVE | CAESARS | [*roundel*] | TRANSLATED BY | ROBERT GRAVES | [*swelled*
> *purple rule*] | THE PENGUIN | CLASSICS | [*at right:*] 3/6; back cover: solid and
> decorative borders as front, inside which are publisher's advertisements;
> spine: [*purple band*] | [*decorative band*] | [down spine:] SUETONIUS | [*pub-*
> *lisher's emblem*] | [down spine:] THE TWELVE CAESARS | L72 | [*decorative band*] |
> [*purple band*]; inner sides of covers blank.

> *Price:* 3s. 6d. Number of copies: 40,000. Published 28 March 1957.

b. First American issue ([1957]):

> Title-page as A80*a*.

> *Collation:* [1]–[10]¹⁶, 160 leaves.
> Remainder as A80*a*, except p. [4] publication, publisher's, copyright and
> printing notcies.

> 20·2 × 13·4 cm. Bulk: 1·9/2·5 cm. White wove paper; all edges trimmed;
> top edges stained blue. Bound in red cloth-simulated boards; back blank;
> front stamped in gold with facsimile signature of Graves; spine stamped in
> gold, top to bottom: SUETONIUS · THE TWELVE CAESARS

Price: $4.50. Number of copies: 3,000. Published 19 July 1957 in white dust-jacket printed in black and mustard-gold.

Note: There is an American paper-bound issue, identical with A80*a*, except on better paper. 20,000 copies were printed in the United States at $0·95.

c. Second English edition ([1962]):

THE BELLE SAUVAGE LIBRARY | THE TWELVE | CAESARS | *Gaius Suetonius* | *Tranquillus* | TRANSLATED BY | ROBERT GRAVES | [*publisher's emblem*] | CASSELL · LON- DON

Collation: [1]–[18]⁸ [19]⁶, 150 leaves.

p. [i] THE TWELVE CAESARS; p. [ii] blank; p. [iii] title-page; p. [iv] publisher's, copyright, edition and printing notices; p. [v] CONTENTS; p. [vi] blank; pp. vii–viii FOREWORD; pp. 1–285 text, with pp. [94, 160, 218, 230, 238, 262, 270] being blank and p. [269] being unnumbered; pp. 286–287 genealogi- cal tables; p. [288] blank; pp. 289–291 THE COIN PORTRAITS OF THE TWELVE CAESARS; p. [292] blank.

20·4 × 14·4 cm. Bulk: 1·8/2·2 cm. White wove paper; all edges trimmed. White wove endpapers. Bound in light blue cloth; front and back blank; spine stamped in gold: [*flower*] | [*rule*] | The | Twelve | Caesars | [*rule*] | [*flower*] | SUETONIUS | Translated by | Robert | Graves | [*flower*] | [*rule*] | Cassell | [*rule*] | [*flower*]

Price: 15s. Number of copies: 3,104. Published 22 February 1962 in white dust-jacket printed in pink, blue, purple and black.

d. Third English edition (1964):

GAIUS SUETONIUS | TRANQUILLUS | THE | TWELVE CAESARS | TRANSLATED BY ROBERT GRAVES WOOD-ENGRAVINGS BY RAYMOND HAWTHORN LONDON | THE FOLIO SOCIETY | MCMLXIV

Collation: [A]⁸ B–N⁸ [O]⁸ P–Q⁴ [R]⁸ S–U⁸, 160 leaves.

p. [1] THE TWELVE CAESARS; p. [2] blank; p. [3] title-page; p. [4] copyrigh printing, printer's, binder's and typographical notices; p. [5] CONTENTS p. [6] blank; pp. [7]–8 INTRODUCTION; pp. [9–11] 12–318 text, with p [9, 51, 109, 149, 181, 209, 243, 257, 267, 279, 295, 303] being sectio headings, pp. [10, 52, 110, 150, 182, 210, 244, 258, 268, 280, 296, 304] bei woodcuts and pp. [11, 53, 111, 151, 183, 211, 245, 259, 269, 281, 297, 305] being unnumbered and pp. [148, 256, 267, 294] being blank; pp. [319–320] blank.

24·6 × 15·6 cm. Bulk: 2·3/3·0 cm. White wove paper; all edges trimmed; top edges stained blue. Endpapers printed with map of Roman Empire in deep blue with white lines and lettering; inner sides of free endpapers blank. Bound in brown-rust cloth; front and back stamped in gold at fore-edge with twelve medallions, six front and six back; spine stamped in gold: Suetonius | [*solid rectangular blue box with triangles above and below, all bordered with gold, printed from bottom to top:*] THE TWELVE CAESARS | Folio

Price: 29s. 6d. Number of copies undisclosed. Published in March 1964 in grey-blue box without dust-jacket.

A81   JESUS IN ROME   [1957]

First edition:

JESUS IN ROME | A HISTORICAL CONJECTURE | by | ROBERT GRAVES | and | JOSHUA PODRO | [*publisher's emblem*] | CASSELL & COMPANY LTD | LONDON

Collation: [A]⁸ B–F⁸, 48 leaves.
p. [i] JESUS IN ROME; p. [ii] list of books by Graves; p. [iii] title-page; p. [iv] publisher's, copyright, publication and printer's notices; p. [v] *Contents;* p. [vi] blank; pp. [1]2–89 text, with pp. [16, 38, 54, 68, 88] being unnumbered; p. [90] blank.

18·4 × 12·5 cm. Bulk: 0·8/1·2 cm. White wove paper; all edges trimmed. White wove endpapers. Bound in black cloth; front and back blank; spine stamped in gold: Jesus | in | Rome | *Robert* | *Graves* | *and* | *Joshua* | *Podro* | *Cassell*

Price: 8s. 6d. Number of copies: 3,006. Published 11 April 1957 in grey dust-jacket printed in red and black.

A82   THEY HANGED MY SAINTLY BILLY   [1957]

a. First edition:

THEY HANGED | MY SAINTLY BILLY | by | ROBERT GRAVES | *With twenty-three illustrations* | *in the text* | [*publisher's emblem*] | CASSELL & COMPANY LTD | LONDON

Collation: [A]⁸ B–R⁸ S⁶, 142 leaves.

p. [i] THEY HANGED MY SAINTLY BILLY; p. [ii] list of books by Graves; p. [iii] title-page; p. [iv] publisher's, printer's, copyright and publication notices; p. v CONTENTS; p. [vi] blank; p. vii LIST OF ILLUSTRATIONS; p. [viii] blank; pp. ix–xi FOREWORD; p. [xii] blank; pp. 1–269 text; pp. [270]–[272] blank.

21·6 × 13·8 cm. Bulk: 2·2/2·8 cm. White wove paper; all edges trimmed. White wove endpapers. Bound in black cloth; front and back blank; spine stamped in gold: THEY | HANGED | MY | SAINTLY | BILLY | ROBERT | GRAVES | CASSELL

Price: 21s. Number of copies: 5,370. Published 23 May 1957 in white dust-jacket printed in canary and black.

Note: This book has been translated into Italian and Swedish.

b. First American edition (1957):

[all flush left:] THEY HANGED | MY | SAINTLY BILLY | *The Life and Death | of | Dr. William Palmer | by | Robert Graves |* GARDEN CITY, NEW YORK, 1957 | DOUBLEDAY & COMPANY, INC.

Collation: [1]–[13]¹², 156 leaves.

p. [1] [all flush left:] THEY HANGED | MY | SAINTLY BILLY; p. [2] list of books by Graves; p. [3] title-page; p. [4] Library of Congress card, copyright and printing notices; pp. [5]6–7 *FOREWORD;* pp. [8–9] *CONTENTS;* p. [10] blank; pp. [11]12–312 text, with pp. [19, 32, 45, 60, 69, 86, 99, 112, 123, 133, 146, 162, 173, 183, 198, 210, 223, 237, 254, 265, 274, 294, 305] being unnumbered.

20·8 × 13·8 cm. Bulk: 2·3/2·8 cm. White wove paper; top and bottom edges trimmed; top edges stained red. White wove endpapers. Bound in buff cloth; front and back blank; spine stamped in red: [*rule*] | [*rule*] | [*broad decorative rule of rectangles and dot-chains*] | [*rectangular solid box, in which flush left the remainder in silver:*] They | Hanged | My | Saintly | Billy | Robert | Graves | Doubleday

Price: $3.95. Number of copies: 11,500 (in two printings). Published 23 May 1957 in white dust-jacket printed in red, pink, blue-green and black.

c. Second American edition ([1959]):

ROBERT GRAVES | [*rule*] | They Hanged | My Saintly | Billy | *The Life and Death | of | Dr. William Palmer* | AVON BOOK DIVISION | The Hearst Corporation | 575 Madison Avenue – New York 22

Collation: 128 leaves, glued at spine.

p. [1] blurbs; p. [2] *Complete and Unabridged;* p. [3] title-page; p. [4] copyright, publication and printing notices; pp. 5–7 *FOREWORD;* p. [8] blank; pp. 9–253 text; p. [254] biographical note; pp. [255–256] blank.

17·9 × 10·5 cm. Bulk: 1·5 cm. White wove paper; all edges trimmed; all edges stained yellow. Bound in white paper covers printed in purple, cerise, yellow, blue and black.

Price: $0.50. Number of copies undisclosed. Published 15 October 1959.

Note: This book is Avon Book G1037.

d. Second English edition ([1962]):

THEY HANGED | MY SAINTLY BILLY | ROBERT GRAVES | [*publisher's emblem*] | ARROW BOOKS

Collation: [A]¹⁶ B–I¹⁶, 144 leaves.

p. [i] THEY HANGED MY SAINTLY BILLY; p. [ii] blank; p. [iii] title-page; p. [iv] publisher's, edition, copyright, printer's and binder's notices; p. [v] CONTENTS; p. [vi] blank; p. [vii] ILLUSTRATIONS; p. [viii] blank; pp. ix–xi FOREWORD; p. [xii] blank; p. [xiii] THEY HANGED MY SAINTLY BILLY; p. [xiv] blank; pp. 1–270 text; pp. [271]–[274] publisher's advertisements.

17·7 × 11·0 cm. Bulk: 1·9 cm. White wove paper; all edges trimmed. Bound in paper covers printed in black and cerise.

Price: 5s. Number of copies undetermined. Published 8 January 1962.

Note: This edition is Grey Arrow Book No. G104.

A83   POEMS SELECTED BY HIMSELF   [1957]

First edition:

ROBERT GRAVES | [*swelled rule*] | *Poems Selected by Himself* | PENGUIN BOOKS

Collation: [A]¹⁶ B¹⁶ C/C★–D/D★⁴/¹⁶E–F¹⁶, 104 leaves.

p. [1] THE PENGUIN POETS | D39 | ROBERT GRAVES | [*publisher's emblem*]; p. [2] blank; p. [3] title-page; p. [4] publisher's, publication and printer's notices; p. [5] *Foreword;* p. [6] blank; pp. 7–11 *Contents;* p. [12] blank; pp. 13–198 text; pp. 199–204 *Index of First Lines;* p. [205] publisher's advertisement; p. [206] blank; pp. [207–208]publisher's advertisements.

18·1 × 11·1 cm. Bulk: 1·0 cm. White wove paper; all edges trimmed. Bound in paper covers printed with over-all background of elongated diamonds and triangles in green and black; on front, as if label: [*rectangular box of green light-heavy-light rules enclosing all:*] Robert | Graves | [*six-pointed star in green*] | SELECTED BY HIMSELF | [*publisher's emblem in green*] | THE PENGUIN | POETS | [at right:] 3/6; back has the design and in small rectangular box near bottom: NOT FOR SALE IN THE U.S.A.; spine has design and white box simulating label near top, in which: [*light-heavy-light rules in green*] | D39 | [*light green rule*] | [down spine:] Robert Graves | [*light green rule*] | D39 | [*light-heavy-light rules in green*]; inner sides of covers blank.

Price: 3s. 6d. Number of copies: 24,660. Published 29 August 1957.

Contents: Foreword – In the Wilderness – The Haunted House – Reproach – The Finding of Love – 'The General Elliott' – Rocky Acres – Outlaws – One Hard Look – A Frosty Night – Allie – Henry and Mary – Love without Hope – What Did I Dream? – The Country Dance – The Troll's Nosegay – The Hills of May – Lost Love – Vain and Careless – An English Wood – The Bedpost – The Pier-Glass – Apples and Water – Angry Samson – Down – Mermaid, Dragon, Fiend – In Procession – Warning to Children – Alice – Ancestors – The Cool Web – Love in Barrenness – Song of Contrariety – The Presence – The Land of Whipperginny – In No Direction – The Castle – Return – The Bards – Nobody – Full Moon – Vanity – Pure Death – Sick Love – It Was All Very Tidy – Thief – The Furious Voyage – Song: Lift Boy – Ulysses – The Succubus – The Reader over My Shoulder – The Legs – Gardener – In Broken Images – On Rising Early – Flying Crooked – Fragment of a Lost Poem – The Devil's Advice to Story-Tellers – Sea Side – Wm. Brazier – Welsh Incident – Hell – Synthetic Such – The Florist Rose – Lost Acres – At First Sight – Recalling War – Down, Wanton, Down! – A Former Attachment – Nature's Lineaments – Time – The Philosopher – On Dwelling – Parent to Children – Ogres and Pygmies – To Walk on Hills – To Bring the Dead to Life – To Evoke Posterity – Any Honest Housewife – Defeat of the Rebels – Never Such Love – The China Plate – Certain Mercies – The Cuirassiers of the Frontier – The Laureate – A Jealous Man – The Cloak – The Foreboding – With Her Lips Only – The Halls of Bedlam – A Country Mansion – Lovers in Winter – Advocates – On Portents – The Terraced Valley – The Chink – The Ages of Oath – Like Snow – End of Play – The Fallen Tower of Siloam – The Great-Grandmother – No More Ghosts – A Love Story – Dawn Bombardment – The Shot – The Thieves – Lollocks – To Sleep – Despite and Still – The Suicide in the Copse – Frightened Men – Language of the Seasons – Mid-Winter Waking – The Beach – The Villagers and Death – The Door – Under the Pot – Through Nightmare – She Tells Her Love While Half Asleep – Theseus and Ariadne – The Death Room – To Juan at the Winter Solstice – To Be Called a Bear – My Name and I – 1805 – The Persian Version – The Weather of Olympus – Grotesques i–vi –

Conversation Piece – I'm Through with You For Ever – Beauty in Trouble – Sirocco at Deyá – From the Embassy – The White Goddess – The Song of Blodeuwedd – Instructions to the Orphic Adept – Lament for Pasiphaë – Intercession in Late October – Counting the Beats – Your Private Way – The Survivor – Questions in a Wood – Darien – The Portrait – Prometheus – The Straw – Dialogue on the Headland – The Mark – The Sea Horse – Dethronement – Cat-Goddesses – The Blue-Fly – A Lost Jewel – The Window Sill – Spoils – Rhea – Leaving the Rest Unsaid – Index of First Lines

A84   5 PENS IN HAND   1958

First edition:

5 | PENS | IN | HAND | by Robert Graves | DOUBLEDAY & COMPANY, INC. GARDEN CITY, NEW YORK | 1958

Collation: [1]–[15]¹², 180 leaves.

p. [1] 5 Pens in Hand; p. [2] blank; p. [3] list of books by Graves; p. [4] blank; p. [5] title-page; p. [6] acknowledgement, copyright, printing, edition and designer's notices; p. [7] FOREWORD; p. [8] blank; pp. [9]10–11 CONTENTS; p. [12] blank; pp. [13]–360 text, with pp. [13, 31, 91, 145, 287, 331] being section-headings, pp. [14, 30, 32, 92, 144, 146, 286, 288, 332] being blank and pp. [15, 33, 54, 73, 93, 100, 104, 107, 114, 118, 123, 129, 137, 147, 152, 157, 161, 165, 175, 179, 184, 189, 194, 197, 202, 206, 211, 215, 219, 223, 227, 232, 235, 239, 243, 248, 253, 257, 264, 275, 289, 299, 317, 333] being unnumbered.

20·7 × 13·8 cm. Bulk: 2·7/3·3 cm. White wove paper; top and bottom edges trimmed. White wove endpapers. Bound in red-brown cloth with buff quarter-cloth spine; back blank; front has blue rule one-third from bottom across entire cover; spine stamped in brown and printed in blue: [*two lines in brown:*] *Robert* | *Graves* | [*four lines in blue:*] *5* | *PENS* | *IN* | *HAND* | [*blue rule*] | [*in brown:*] *Doubleday*

Price: $4.50. Number of copies: 4,500. Published 20 March 1958.

Contents: I. FOREWORD: Why I Live in Majorca – II. AMERICAN LECTURES: Legitimate Criticism of Poetry – The White Goddess – Diseases of Scholarship, Clinically Considered – III. CRITICAL ESSAYS: Pandora's Box and Eve's Apple – The Gold Roofs of Sinadon – Numismatics for Student Christians – An Eminent Collaborationist – Answer to a Religious Questionnaire – Paul's Thorn – Don't Fidget, Young Man! – Religion: None; Conditioning: Protestant – Colonel Lawrence's *Odyssey* – IV. MOSTLY STORIES, MOSTLY FUNNY: Varro's Four Hundred and Ninety Books – Treacle Tart – The Full Length – An Appointment for Candlemas – The Devil Is a Protestant –

Trín-Trín-Trín – Earth to Earth – Epics Are Out of Fashion – New Light on Dream-Flight – Period Piece – They Say . . . They Say – Week-End at Cwm Tatws – 6 Valiant Bulls 6 – He Went out to Buy a Rhine – A Man May Not Marry His . . . – God Grant Your Honour Many Years – The White Horse or 'The Great Southern Ghost Story' – The Five Godfathers – Kill Them! Kill Them! – The Abominable Mr Gunn – Harold Vesey at the Gates of Hell – Life of the Poet Gnaeus Robertulus Gravesa – Ditching in a Fishless Sea – I Hate Poems – The French Thing – Evidence of Affluence – A Bicycle in Majorca – v. HISTORICAL ANOMALIES: The Fifth Column at Troy – The Whitaker Negroes – A Dead Branch on the Tree of Israel – vi. POEMS 1955–1957; Prologue to a Poetry Reading at the Massachusetts Institute of Technology, Boston – The Face in the Mirror – Forbidden Words – Song for New Year's Eve – A Ballad of Alexander and Queen Janet – The Coral Pool – Gratitude for a Nightmare – Friday Night – The Naked and the Nude – Woman and Tree – Destruction of Evidence – Hotel Bed at Lugano – The Clearing – The Second-Fated – End of the World – Bitter Thoughts on Receiving a Slice of Cordelia's Wedding Cake – The Question – A Plea to Boys and Girls – A Bouquet from a Fellow Roseman – Yes – The Outsider

A85   THE POEMS OF ROBERT GRAVES   1958

First edition:

THE POEMS | OF | ROBERT GRAVES | *Chosen by Himself* | Doubleday Anchor Books | Doubleday & Company, Inc. | Garden City, New York | 1958

Collation: 320 pp., glued at spine.

p. [i] THE POEMS OF ROBERT GRAVES | [*series emblem*]; p. [ii] blank; p. [iii] biographical note; p. [iv] blank; p. [v] title-page; p. [vi] designer's, typographer's, copyright, printing and acknowledgement notices; p. [vii] FOREWORD; p. [viii] blank; p. [ix] TO CALLIOPE; p. [x] blank; pp. xi–xviii CONTENTS; pp. [1]–289 text, with pp. [1, 35, 67, 93, 151, 169, 203, 235, 255] being section-headings and pp. [2, 36, 68, 94, 152, 168, 170, 204, 234, 236, 254, 256] being blank; p. [290] blank; pp. 291–296 INDEX OF TITLES; pp. 297–302 INDEX OF FIRST LINES.

18·1 × 10·5 cm. Bulk: 1·8 cm. White wove paper; all edges trimmed. Bound in paper covers; front has grey background with Hera of Samos overprinted with: [at left:] A 139 [at right:] $1.25 | THE | POEMS | OF | ROBERT | GRAVES | [*in red:*] *Chosen by himself* | A DOUBLEDAY [*series emblem*] ANCHOR BOOK; back printed in red and black with blurb; spine has grey background, printed top to bottom: THE POEMS OF ROBERT GRAVES [*three words in red:*] *Chosen by himself* | Anchor | A139; inner sides of front and back covers blank.

Price: $1.25. Number of copies: 25,000. Published 5 June 1958.

Conversation Piece – Queen-Mother to New Queen – General Blood-stock's Lament for England – 'i Welcome to the Caves of Artá!' – I'm Through with You Forever – The Sacred Mission – Poet's Corner – Coronation Address – Beauty in Trouble – Sirocco at Deyá – From the Embassy – VIII: The White Goddess – The Allansford Pursuit – Amergin's Charm – The Battle of the Trees – The Song of Blodeuwedd – Instructions to the Orphic Adept – Lament for Pasiphaë – The Sirens' Welcome to Cronos – Intercession in Late October – The Jackals' Address to Isis – The Destroyer – Return of the Goddess – IX: With the Gift of a Ring – Count-ing the Beats – The Young Cordwainer – Your Private Way – The Sur-vivor – Questions in a Wood – Darien – The Portrait – Prometheus – The Straw – Cry Faugh! – Hercules at Nemea – Dialogue on the Headland – The Mark – Liadan and Curithir – The Sea Horse – Reproach to Julia – Dethronement – Cat-Goddesses – The Blue-Fly – A Lost Jewel – The Window Sill – Spoils – The Coral Pool – The Naked and the Nude – Woman and Tree – Bitter Thoughts on Receiving a Slice of Cordelia's Wedding-Cake – A Bouquet from a Fellow Roseman – Rhea – Leaving the Rest Unsaid – Index of Titles – Index of First Lines

A86 STEPS [1958]

First edition:

STEPS | *Stories* | *Talks* | *Essays* | *Poems* | *Studies in History* | BY | ROBERT GRAVES | [*publisher's emblem*] | CASSELL · LON-DON

Collation: [A]⁸ B–W⁸ X/X⋆2/8 Y⁸, 178 leaves.
pp. [i–ii] blank; p. [iii] STEPS; p. [iv] blank; p. [v] title-page; p. [vi] pub-lisher's, copyright, publication and printer's notices; pp. vii–ix *Contents*; p. [x] blank; p. xi *Foreword;* p. [xii] blank; pp. [1]–343 text, with pp. [1, 61, 155, 229, 263] being section-headings and pp. [2, 60, 62, 154, 156, 228, 230, 264] being blank; p. [344] blank.

21·6 × 13·8 cm. Bulk: 2·8/3·4 cm. White wove paper; all edges trimmed. White wove endpapers. Bound in sea-green cloth; front and back blank; spine stamped in gold: [*light-heavy-light rules*] | STEPS | [*light rule*] | [*longe heavy rule*] | [*light rule*] | ROBERT | GRAVES | [*light-heavy-light rules*] | CASSEL

Price: 30s. Number of copies: 2,996. Published 13 November 159 in blue grey dust-jacket printed in green and black.

Contents: Foreword – STORIES: A Bicycle in Majorca – Evidence Affluence – The Viscountess and the Short-Haired Girl – A Toast to A Gardner – TALKS: Legitimate Criticism of Poetry – The White Goddess

Sweeney among the Blackbirds – The Making and Marketing of Poetry –
Pulling a Poem Apart – ESSAYS: Pandora's Box and Eve's Apple – The Gold
Roofs of Sinadon – An Eminent Collaborationist – Don't Fidget, Young
Man! – Colonel Lawrence's *Odyssey* – Maenads, Junkies and Others – The
Language as Spoken – It Ended with a Bang – Legends of the Bible – And
the Children's Teeth are Set on Edge – Progressive Puericulture – POEMS:
Preface to a Reading of New Poems at the University of Michigan – The
Face in the Mirror – Song for New Year's Eve – Alexander and Queen
Janet – The Coral Pool – Gratitude for a Nightmare – Friday Night – The
Naked and the Nude – Woman and Tree – Forbidden Words – Hotel Bed
at Lugano – The Enlisted Man – A Slice of Wedding Cake – A Plea to
Boys and Girls – Trudge, Body! – Mike and Mandy – The Christmas
Robin – Nothing – Call It a Good Marriage – Read Me, Please! – The
Second-Fated – The Twin of Sleep – Around the Mountain – STUDIES IN
HISTORY: The Fifth Column at Troy – A Dead Branch on the Tree of
Israel – Was Benedict Arnold a Traitor? – The Cultured Romans – New
Light on an Old Murder – What Food the Centaurs Ate

Note: p. 315, ll. 3/4, has 'Whole,/some' for 'Whole-/some'.

A87   COLLECTED POEMS 1959   [1959]

First edition:

ROBERT GRAVES | COLLECTED | POEMS | 1959 |
[*publisher's emblem*] | CASSELL · LONDON

Collation: [A]⁸ B–U⁸ X/X⋆²/⁸, 170 leaves.

pp. [i–ii] blank; p. [iii] COLLECTED POEMS | 1959; p. [iv] blank; [*frontispiece,
back blank*]; p. [v] title-page; p. [vi] publisher's, copyright, publication and
printer's notices; p. [vii] TO CALLIOPE; p. [viii] blank; p. [ix] FOREWORD;
p. [x] blank; pp. [xi]–[xix] CONTENTS; p. [xx] blank; pp. [1]–320 text, with
pp. [1, 41, 75, 101, 161, 181, 215, 247, 261, 299] being section-headings
and pp. [2, 40, 42, 76, 102, 162, 180, 182, 216, 246, 248, 262, 298, 300] being
blank.

21·5 × 15·0 cm. Bulk: 2·5/2·9 cm. White wove paper; all edges trimmed.
White wove endpapers. Bound in bright green cloth; back blank; front
stamped in gold: COLLECTED | POEMS | 1959; spine stamped in gold: ROBERT
| GRAVES | [*rule*] | COLLECTED | POEMS | 1959 | CASSELL

Price: 25s. Number of copies: 3,037. Published 23 April 1959 in white dust-
jacket printed in bright green and black.

Contents: To Calliope – Foreword – 1: In the Wilderness – The Haunted
House – Reproach – The Finding of Love – 'The General Elliott' – Rocky
Acres – Outlaws – One Hard Look – A Frosty Night – Allie – Unicorn

VIII: The White Goddess – Amergin's Charm – The Battle of the Trees –
The Song of Blodeuwedd – Instructions to the Orphic Adept – Lament for
Pasiphaë – The Sirens' Welcome to Cronos – Intercession in Late October –
The Jackals' Address to Isis – The Destroyer – Return of the Goddess – IX:
With the Gift of a Ring – Counting the Beats – The Young Cordwainer –
Your Private Way – The Survivor – Questions in a Wood – Darien – The
Portrait – Prometheus – The Straw – Cry Faugh! – Hercules at Nemea –
Dialogue on the Headland – The Mark – Liadan and Curithir – The Sea
Horse – Reproach to Julia – Dethronement – Cat-Goddesses – The Blue-
Fly – A Lost Jewel – The Window Sill – Spoils – Rhea – X: The Face in the
Mirror – The Coral Pool – Gratitude for a Nightmare – Friday Night – The
Naked and the Nude – Woman and Tree – Forbidden Words – The
Enlisted Man – A Slice of Wedding Cake – A Plea to Boys and Girls –
Nothing – Call It a Good Marriage – Read Me, Please! – The Second-
Fated – The Twin of Sleep – Around the Mountain – Leaving the Rest
Unsaid

Note: Impressions: 2nd, November 1961 (1,971 copies); 3rd, January
1962 (2,000 copies).

A88   FABLE OF THE HAWK AND THE   1959
NIGHTINGALE

First edition:

FABLE OF THE HAWK AND THE NIGHTINGALE |
TRANSLATED FROM HESIOD'S WORKS | AND DAYS
[*fourteen characters in red:*] (lines 202–212) BY ROBERT GRAVES
| PRINTED IN LEXINGTON KENTUCKY AT | THE
STAMPERIA DEL SANTUCCIO M · CM · LIX

Collation: 4 leaves, sewn at centre.
p. [1] title-page; pp. [2]–[4] blank; p. [5] text, printed in blue, red and
black; p. [6] blank; p. [7] biographical note about Hesiod, statement of
edition and typographical notice; p. [8] blank.

26·7 × 19·8 cm. Bulk: 0·2/0·7 cm. White wove paper; all edges untrimmed. Bound in grey or brown boards with a label running from front
to back across spine; on front, in red: STAMPERIA DEL SANTUCCIO | BROAD-
SIDE NUMBER I | M · CM · LIX; label on back blank; on spine, bottom to
top, first word and virgule in red: HESIOD/GRAVES

Price: $6.00. Number of copies: 100, plus at least 10 gratis out of series.
Published midsummer 1959.

a. First edition:

[four lines flush left:] The | Anger | of | Achilles | [slightly right of centre:] HOMER'S *ILIAD* | [remainder flush left:] *Translated by* ROBERT GRAVES | *Illustrations by* RONALD SEARLE | *Doubleday & Company, Inc., Garden City, New York, 1959*

Collation: [1]¹² 2¹² [3]¹² 4–6¹² [7]–[8]¹² 9–16¹², 192 leaves.

p. [1] THE ANGER OF ACHILLES; pp. [2–3] list of books by Graves; p. [4] blank; p. [5] title-page; p. [6] copyright, printing and designer's notices; p. [7] To Kenneth Gay | in gratitude for twenty-five years | of patient critical help.; p. [8] blank; pp. [9]–10 Contents; pp. [11]–12 Illustrations; pp. [13] 14–35 Introduction; p. [36] blank; p. [37] THE ANGER OF ACHILLES; p. [38] blank; pp. [39]40–383 text, with pp. [54, 86, 100, 120, 144, 188, 234, 246, 308, 340, 384] being blank and pp. [55, 75, 87, 101, 121, 133, 145, 159, 175, 189, 207, 217, 235, 247, 263, 281, 295, 309, 317, 327, 341, 351, 367] being unnumbered; p. [384] blank; illustrations, all backs blank, face pp. 24, 48, 73, 97, [120], [144], 168, 216, 240, 264, 288, 313, 336, 361.

23·2 × 15·2 cm. Bulk: 3·1/3·9 cm. White wove paper; all edges trimmed. White wove endpapers. Bound in black cloth; back blank; front stamped in gold with figure of Achilles; spine stamped in gold, top to bottom: The Anger of Achilles | [three lines upright:] HOMER'S *ILIAD* | *Translated by* | ROBERT GRAVES | [down spine:] *Doubleday*

Price: $4.95. Number of copies: 11,000 (in two printings). Published 5 November 1959 in white dust-jacket printed in black, brown, yellow, brick-red, green, violet and blue.

Note: Signatures appear quite close to the gutter opposite the final line of text; others than shown may therefore show in other copies. This book has been translated into Swedish.

b. First English edition ([1960]):

[entire enclosed within rectangular decorative band box:] THE ANGER | OF | ACHILLES | *Homer's Iliad* | *translated by* | ROBERT GRAVES | CASSELL · LONDON

Collation: [A]¹⁶ B–K¹⁶ L⁴ M–N¹⁶, 196 leaves.

p. [i] THE ANGER | OF | ACHILLES; p. [ii] blank; p. [iii] title-page; p. [iv] publisher's, copyright, publication and printer's notices; pp. [v–v.

CONTENTS; p. [vii] To Kenneth Gay | in gratitude for twenty-five years | of patient critical help; pp. [viii–ix] map; p. [x] blank; pp. xi–xxxiv INTRODUCTION; pp. 1–357 text; p. [358] blank.

21·4 × 13·8 cm. Bulk: 2·7/3·3 cm. White wove paper; all edges trimmed. White wove endpapers. Bound in brown cloth; front and back blank; spine stamped in gold: ROBERT | GRAVES | [decorative band] | THE ANGER | OF | ACHILLES | [decorative band] | CASSELL

Price: 30s. Number of copies: 3,967. Published 10 March 1960 in cream dust-jacket printed in brown and black.

Note: Impression: 2nd, April 1960. Number of copies: 2,507.

c. Readers Union issue (1961):

[entire enclosed within rectangular decorative band box] | THE ANGER | OF | ACHILLES | Homer's Iliad | translated by | ROBERT GRAVES | READERS UNION · CASSELL | London 1961

Collation: as A89a.
Remainder as A89a, except p. [iv] has copyright and edition notices and p. [357] unnumbered.

21·2 × 13·6 cm. Bulk: 2·6/3·1 cm. White wove paper; all edges trimmed. White wove endpapers. Bound in light grey cloth; front and back blank; spine stamped in gold: The | Anger | of | Achilles | [light rule] | [broad rule] | [light rule] | HOMER'S ILIAD | TRANSLATED BY | ROBERT | GRAVES | [Readers Union emblem]

Price: 16s. Number of copies: 2,500. Published in October 1961.

d. Second English edition ([1962])

HOMER | [swelled rule] | THE ANGER OF ACHILLES | ILIAD) | TRANSLATED FROM THE GREEK BY | ROBERT GRAVES | [publisher's emblem] | A FOUR SQUARE CLASSIC

Collation: [A]¹⁶ B–L¹⁶, 176 leaves.
p. [i] FOUR SQUARE CLASSICS | GENERAL EDITOR: ILSA BAREA; p. [ii] list of works in the series; p. [iii] title-page; p. [iv] publication, copyright, edition, conditions of sale and printer's notices; p. [v] To Kenneth Gay | in gratitude for twenty-five years | of patient critical help; pp. vi–[vii] CONTENTS; pp. [viii–ix] map; p. [x] blank; pp. xi–xxx INTRODUCTION; pp. 1–322 text.

18·0 × 10·8 cm. Bulk: 1·8 cm. White wove paper; all edges trimmed. Bound in paper covers.

Price: 6s. Number of copies undisclosed. Published 15 November 1962.

A90   FOOD FOR CENTAURS   1960

First edition:

Food for Centaurs: | *Stories, Talks, Critical* | *Studies, Poems by* | *Robert Graves* | *[cut of centaur]* | DOUBLEDAY & COMPANY, INC. | GARDEN CITY, NEW YORK | 1960

Collation: [1]¹² 2–16¹², 192 leaves.
p. [1] *Food for Centaurs;* p. [2] blank; p. [3] list of books by Graves; p. [4] blank; p. [5] title-page; p. [6] copyright, printing and edition notices; p. [7] FOREWORD; p. [8] To Mildred Lockwood Lacey | in gratitude for her | generous heart; pp. [9–10] CONTENTS; pp. [11]–382 text, with pp. [11, 95, 147, 295, 351] being section-headings and pp. [12, 96, 146, 148, 294, 296, 350, 352] being blank; pp. [383–384] blank.

20·8 × 13·7 cm. Bulk: 2·8/3·4 cm. White wove paper; top and bottom edges trimmed. White wove endpapers. Bound in black cloth with green quarter-cloth spine; front and back blank; spine stamped in silver, printed in purple: *Robert* | *Graves* | *[purple enclosing device facing down]* | *[purple rectangular solid box, inside which, top to bottom:]* FOOD *for* CENTAURS | *[purple enclosing device, facing up]* | *Doubleday*

Price: $4.95. Number of copies: 5,500 (in two printings). Published 6 May 1960 in white dust-jacket printed in black, green, pink and blue.

Contents: Foreword – *Stories:* The Viscountess and the Short-Haired Girl – A Toast to Ava Gardner – She Landed Yesterday – The Lost Chinese – You Win, Houdini! – *Talks on Poetry:* Sweeney among the Blackbirds – The Making and Marketing of Poetry – Pulling a Poem Apart – *Studies in History:* To be a Goy – A Dead Branch on the Tree of Israel – Was Benedict Arnold a Traitor? – The Cultured Romans – New Light on an Old Murder – To Minorca! – The Dour Man – Praise Me and I Will Whistle to You! – What Was That War Like, Sir? – Centaur Food – The Fifth Column at Troy – *Critiques of New Books:* Maenad Junkies and Others – It Ended with a Bang – Legends of the Bible – Puck, Mab, the Billy Blin – The Pirates Who Captured Caesar – The Butcher and the Cur – Two Studies in Scientific Atheism – The Archetypal Wise Old Man – *Poems:* Preface to a Reading of Poems – Trudge, Body! – The Christmas Robin – Twice of the Same Fever – Nothing – Call It a Good Marriage – Read Me, Please! – The Twin of Sleep – Established Lovers

The Quiet Glades of Eden – Heroes in Their Prime – Catkind – The Young Goddess – Here Live Your Life Out – Joan and Darby – Superman on the Riviera – The Picture Nail – Old World Dialogue – The Were-Man – The Person from Porlock – Around the Mountain

A91   GREEK GODS AND HEROES   1960

a. First edition:

ROBERT GRAVES | [*three lines in brown:*] GREEK GODS | AND | HEROES | ILLUSTRATED BY DIMITRIS DAVIS | 1960 | DOUBLEDAY & COMPANY, INC. | GARDEN CITY, NEW YORK

Collation: [1]–[10]⁸, 80 leaves.

p. [1] GREEK GODS AND HEROES; p. [2] illustration of Pan in brown and black; p. [3] title-page; p. [4] copyright, printing and designer's notices; pp. 5–6 INTRODUCTION; pp. [7–8] CONTENTS; p. [9] GREEK GODS AND HEROES; p. [10] blank; p. [11] THE PALACE OF OLYMPUS and illustration in brown and black; p. [12] blank; pp. 13–155 text, with pp. [15, 24, 27, 31, 33, 35, 39, 41, 46, 49, 52, 55, 58, 62, 66, 69, 71, 73, 77, 81, 85, 90, 99, 104, 106, 110, 114, 121, 126, 131, 137, 142, 147, 152] being illustrations in black and brown; pp. 156–160 INDEX.

23·3 × 15·3 cm. Bulk: 1·0/1·5 cm. White wove paper; all edges trimmed. White wove endpapers; both front and back have illustration in brown o centaur, nymph, satyr, mermaid and offspring; inner free sides blank Bound in brownish grey cloth; back blank; front stamped in brown at upper right with vase; spine stamped in brown: Robert | Graves | [down spine:] GREEK GODS AND HEROES | Doubleday

Price: $2.95. Number of copies: 37,500 (in five printings). Published 9 November 1960 in white dust-jacket printed in yellow, orange, brown and green.

Note: This book has been translated into Dutch.

*. First English edition ([*1961*]):*

ROBERT GRAVES | MYTHS OF | ANCIENT | GREECE | ILLUSTRATED BY JOAN KIDDELL-MONROE | CAS-ELL · LONDON

Collation: [A]⁸ B–K⁸, 80 leaves.

p. [1] MYTHS OF ANCIENT GREECE; p. [2] illustration; p. [3] title-page; p. [4] publisher's, copyright, publication and printer's notices; pp. 5–6 INTRO-

DUCTION; pp. [7–8] CONTENTS; p. [9] MYTHS OF ANCIENT GREECE; p. [10] blank; p. [11] THE PALACE OF OLYMPUS and illustration; p. [12] blank; pp. 13–155 text, with pp. [15, 19, 25, 28, 32, 35, 40, 45, 48, 51, 54, 57, 61, 65 68, 71, 75, 79, 83, 88, 93, 98, 104, 108, 112, 117, 121, 125, 130, 134, 137, 142, 147, 152] being illustrations; pp. [156]–[160] INDEX.

21·5 × 14·0 cm. Bulk: 1·4/2·0 cm. White wove paper; all edges trimmed. White wove endpapers. Bound in grey cloth-textured boards; front and back blank; spine stamped in silver: Robert | Graves | [up spine:] Myths of Ancient Greece | Cassell

Price: 13s. 6d. Number of copies: 5,946. Published 9 November 1961 in white dust-jacket printed in brown and purple.

Note: Impressions: 2nd, January 1962 (3,011 copies); 3rd, December 1962 (2,931 copies); 4th, August 1964 (5,000 copies).

c. Second American edition ([1965]):

GREEK GODS | AND HEROES | [*concave rule*] | ROBERT GRAVES | [at right:] [*series emblem*]

Collation: 64 leaves, glued at spine.
p. [1] publisher's advertisement and blurb; p. [2] list of books in this series; p. [3] title-page; p. [4] publisher's, copyright, series, rights reservation, arrangement, edition and printing notices; pp. [5–6] CONTENTS; pp. [7]8–9 Introduction; p. [10] blank; pp. [11]12–116 text, with pp. [22, 32, 43, 94, 98, 103, 114,] being unnumbered; pp. [117] 118–127 Index; p. [128[publisher's advertisement.

16·1 × 10·6 cm. Bulk: 0·6 cm. White wove paper; all edges trimmed; all edges stained blue. Bound in white paper covers printed in gold, pink, yellow, and black; inner sides blank.

Price: $0.45. Number of copies: 75,000. Published 11 November 1965.

Note: This book is Dell Laurel-Leaf Library 3221.

A92   THE PENNY FIDDLE   [1960

a. First edition:

[*whole has four children, dog and cat in pink and black, one chil holding bow across bass viol, inside which nine lines:*] THE | PENNY

FIDDLE | *Poems for* | *Children* | *by* | *Robert Graves* | *Illustrated*
by | *Edward Ardizzone* | *[remainder below viol:]* Cassell — London

Collation: [A]⁸ B–D⁸, 32 leaves.
p. [1] *The Penny Fiddle;* p. [2] blank; p. [3] title-page; p. [4] publisher's,
copyright, publication and printer's notices; p. [5] *To* | TOMÁS | *on his*
eighth birthday; p. [6] blank; p. [7] *Contents;* pp. 8–[64] text and illustrations,
with pp. [9–10, 12, 14–15, 17–18, 21–22, 24–26, 28, 30, 32, 34–35, 39, 41–42,
46, 49, 53–54, 56–58, 61, 63–64] unnumbered.

21·5 × 16·3 cm. Bulk: 0·6/1·0 cm. White wove paper; all edges trimmed.
White wove endpapers. Bound in green cloth-simulated boards; front and
back blank; spine stamped in gold, bottom to top: CASSELL *[decorative*
device] The Penny Fiddle *[decorative device]* ROBERT GRAVES

Price: 12s. 6d. Number of copies: 6,238. Published 10 November 1960 in
white dust-jacket printed in black, green, pink and light blue.

Contents: The Penny Fiddle – Allie – Robinson Crusoe – The Six Badgers –
One Hard Look – Jock o'Binnorie – What Did I Dream? – Lift-Boy –
Henry and Mary – Dicky – Love without Hope – The Hills of May – In
the Wilderness – 'The General Elliott' – Vain and Careless – The Forbidden
Play – The Bedpost – The Well-Dressed Children – The Magical Picture –
The *Alice Jean* – A Boy in Church – How and Why – Warning to Children

Note: Impressions: 2nd, September 1961. Number of copies: 3,067.

Printed in Great Britain.

b. American issue ([1961]):

Title-page as A92a, except below viol: *DOUBLEDAY &*
COMPANY, INC. | *Garden City, New York*

Collation: [1]–[4]⁸, 32 leaves.
Remainder as A92a, except p. [4] publisher's emblem and copyright,
printing and edition notices.

23·3 × 15·5 cm. Bulk: 0·5/1·1 cm. Paper as A92a. Bound in green cloth;
front blank; back stamped with white publisher's emblem in lower right
corner; spine stamped in white, top to bottom: ROBERT GRAVES THE PENNY
FIDDLE DOUBLEDAY

Price: $2.50. Number of copies: 9,000 (including 3,000 institutional).
Published 8 September 1961 in dust-jacket as A92a.

Note: This issue uses slightly brighter colours and darker inking than A92*a.*

Printed in the U.S.

A93   MORE POEMS 1961   [1961]

First edition:

ROBERT GRAVES | MORE POEMS | 1961 | [*publisher's emblem*] | CASSELL · LONDON

Collation: [A]⁴ B–D⁸, 28 leaves.

pp. [i–ii] blank; p. [iii] MORE POEMS | 1961; p. [iv] blank; p. [v] title-page; p. [vi] publisher's, copyright, publication and printer's notices; p. [vii] FOREWORD; p. [viii] blank; pp. [ix–x] CONTENTS; p. [1] XI; p. [2] blank; pp. 3–26 text; p. [27] XII; p. [28] blank; pp. 29–45 text; p. [46] blank.

21·6 × 15·0 cm. Bulk: 0·5/1·1 cm. White wove paper; all edges trimmed. White wove endpapers. Bound in maroon cloth; front and back blank; spine stamped in gold, bottom to top: *Cassell Robert Graves* MORE POEMS 1961

Price: 10s. 6d. Number of copies: 3,913. Published 11 May 1961 in white dust-jacket printed black and brick-cherry.

Contents: Foreword – XI: Lyceia – Symptoms of Love – The Sharp Ridge – Under the Olives – The Visitation – Fragment – Apple Island – The Falcon Woman – Troughs of Sea – The Laugh – The Death Grapple – In Single Syllables – The Starred Coverlet – The Intrusion – Patience – The Cure – Hag-Ridden – Turn of the Moon – The Secret Land – Seldom Yet Now – To Myrto of Myrtles – Anchises to Aphrodite – XII: Two Children – A Lost World – The Dangerous Gift – Twice of the Same Fever – Surgical Ward: Men – Nightfall at Twenty Thousand Feet – The Simpleton – The Were-Man – Two Rhymes about Fate and Money – The Two Witches – The Person from Porlock – Established Lovers – The Quiet Glades of Eden – Here Live Your Life Out! – Burn It! – Joan and Darby – Song: Come, Enjoy Your Sunday!

A94   SELECTED POETRY AND PROSE   [1961]

First edition:

Selected Poetry and Prose of | ROBERT GRAVES | *Chosen, introduced and* | *annotated by* | JAMES REEVES | [*publisher's emblem*] | HUTCHINSON EDUCATIONAL

Collation: [A]¹⁶ B–F¹⁶ G–I⁸, 120 leaves.

p. [1] HUTCHINSON ENGLISH TEXTS | Selected Poetry and Prose of | ROBERT GRAVES; p. [2] list of books in this series; p. [3] title-page; p. [4] publisher's, publication, copyright and printer's notices; p. [5] HANC OLGAM GRAVEM | OLGAE MINIME GRAVI | D. D. ROBERTUS GRAVES; p. [6] ACKNOWLEDGEMENTS; pp. [7]–[10] Contents; pp. 11–20 Robert Graves: His Life and Writings; p. [21] Selected Poetry and Prose of | ROBERT GRAVES; p. [22] blank; pp. 23–215 text, with pp. [76, 130, 184] being blank; p. [216] blank; p. [217] NOTES; p. [218] blank; pp. 219–240 notes.

18·5 × 12·3 cm. Bulk: 1·5/1·8 cm. White wove paper; all edges trimmed. White wove endpapers. Bound in green cloth; back blank; front blind-stamped with publisher's emblem; spine stamped in silver: Edited by | JAMES | REEVES | [*decorative rule*] | [top to bottom, near front:] Selected Poetry and Prose | [top to bottom, parallel with preceding line, near back:] of Robert Graves | [*decorative rule*] | [*publisher's emblem interlocked with oval inside which is script HEJ*]

Price: 9s. 6d. Number of copies: 6,000. Published 15 May 1961 without dust-jacket.

Contents: Acknowledgements – Robert Graves: His Life and Writings – Pollux Boxes with King Amycus (*Golden Fleece*) – The Passage of the Bosphorus (*Golden Fleece*) – A Gladiatorial Combat (*I, Claudius*) – Public Works by the Emperor Claudius (*Claudius the God*) – The Expedition against Carthage (*Count Belisarius*) – Poems I: The Alice Jean – Diplomatic Relations – Welsh Incident – The Discovery of the Marquesas Islands (*The Isles of Unwisdom*) – The Execution of Charles I (*Wife to Mr. Milton*) – A Troopship Sails for the American Colonies, 1776 (*Sergeant Lamb of the Ninth*) – Poems II: The Haunted House – Retrospect: Jests of the Clock – The Pier-Glass – Outlaws – An English Wood – Rocky Acres – Lost Acres – In No Direction – The Next Time – The Legs – On Dwelling – The Cloak – The Beach – Vanity – Nature's Lineaments – Old Papa Johnson (*Occupation: Writer*) – The Abominable Mr. Gunn (*Catacrok*) – War on the Western Front, 1915 (*Good-Bye to All That*) – On Leave, 1916 (*Good-Bye to All That*) – Poems III: Lost Love – Love without Hope – Love in Barrenness – At First Sight – Time – The Great-Grandmother – To Lucia at Birth – Under the Pot – John Skelton – The Twin of Sleep – The Cool Web – Gardener – Flying Crooked – My Name and I – Any Honest Housewife – The Laureate – A Plea to Boys and Girls – Brother and Sister (*Antigua, Penny, Puce*) – A Stamp Auction (*Antigua, Penny, Puce*) – Poems IV: 1805 – 'The General Elliott' – Nobody – Traveller's Curse after Misdirection – To Bring the Dead to Life – The China Plate – Lollocks – Act V, Scene 5 – Brother – A Village Conflict – A History of Peace – Warning to Children – To Evoke Posterity – Notes

First edition:

ROBERT GRAVES | COLLECTED | POEMS | DOUBLE-DAY & COMPANY, INC. | GARDEN CITY, NEW YORK | 1961

Collation: 1–2^{12} [3]–[5]^{12} 6–7^{12} [8]–[15]^{12}, 180 leaves.
p. [1] COLLECTED POEMS; p. [2] blank; p. [3] list of books by Graves; p. [4] blank; p. [5] title-page; p. [6] acknowledgement, copyright, printing and edition notices; p. [7] TO CALLIOPE; p. [8] blank; p. [9] FOREWORD; p. [10] blank; pp. 11–20 CONTENTS; pp. [21]–350 text, with pp. [21, 53, 87, 111, 167, 185, 219, 245, 263, 291, 307, 333] being section-headings and pp. [22, 54, 88, 112, 166, 168, 184, 186, 218, 220, 244, 246, 262, 264, 290, 292, 308, 332, 334] being blank; pp. 351–358 INDEX OF FIRST LINES; pp. [359–360] blank.

20·8 × 13·9 cm. Bulk: 2·6/3·2 cm. White wove paper; top and bottom edges trimmed. White wove endpapers. Bound in grey cloth; back blank; front stamped in silver: [*decorative rule*] | [*solid brown rectangular box, inside which two lines:*] COLLECTED | POEMS | [*decorative rule*]; spine stamped in silver: [*decorative rule*] | [*solid brown rectangular box, inside which four lines:*] COLLECTED | POEMS | *Robert* | *Graves* | [*decorative rule*] | DOUBLEDAY

Price: $5.95. Number of copies: 6,000 (in two printings). Published 21 July 1961 in white dust-jacket printed in grey, black, and light and dark brown.

Contents: To Calliope – Foreword – I: In the Wilderness – The Haunted House – Reproach – The Finding of Love – 'The General Elliott' – Rocky Acres – Outlaws – One Hard Look – A Frosty Night – Allie – Unicorn and the White Doe – Henry and Mary – Love without Hope – What Did I Dream? – The Country Dance – The Troll's Nosegay – The Hills of May – Lost Love – Vain and Careless – An English Wood – The Bedpost – The Pier-Glass – Apples and Water – Angry Samson – Down – Mermaid, Dragon, Fiend – II: In Procession – Warning to Children – Alice – Richard Roe and John Doe – The Witches' Cauldron – Ancestors – The Coronation Murder – Children of Darkness – The Cool Web – Love in Barrenness – Song of Contrariety – The Presence – The Land of Whipperginny – In No Direction – The Castle – Return – The Bards – A Lost World – Nobody – The Progress – Full Moon – Vanity – Pure Death – Sick Love – It Was All Very Tidy – III: Callow Captain – Thief – The Furious Voyage – Song: Lift-Boy – Traveller's Curse after Misdirection – The Last Day of Leave – The Next Time – Ulysses – The Succubus – The Reader over My Shoulder – The Legs – Gardener – Front Door Soliloquy – In Broken Images –

Second-Fated – The Twin of Sleep – Around the Mountain – xi: Lyceia –
Symptoms of Love – The Sharp Ridge – Under the Olives – The Visita-
tion – Fragment – Apple Island – The Falcon Woman – Troughs of Sea –
The Laugh – The Death Grapple – In Single Syllables – The Starred
Coverlet – The Intrusion – Patience – Hag-Ridden – The Cure – Turn of
the Moon – Seldom, Yet Now – Anchises to Aphrodite – The Secret
Land – To Myrto of Myrtles – xii: Two Children – The Dangerous Gift –
Twice of the Same Fever – Surgical Ward: Men – Nightfall at Twenty
Thousand Feet – The Simpleton – The Were-Man – The Person from
Porlock – Established Lovers – The Quiet Glades of Eden – Here Live
Your Life Out! – Burn It! – Joan and Darby – Ruby and Amethyst –
Song: Come, Enjoy Your Sunday! – Leaving the Rest Unsaid – Index of
First Lines

A96   THE MORE DESERVING CASES   1962

First edition:

THE MORE | DESERVING CASES | Eighteen Old Poems |
for | Reconsideration | by | ROBERT GRAVES | Marlborough
College Press | 1962

Collation: [1]–[5]⁴, 20 leaves.

pp. [1–2] blank; p. [3] THE MORE DESERVING CASES; p. [4] portrait of Graves;
p. [5] title-page; p. [6] blank; p. [7] FOREWORD; p. [8] blank; p. [9] CON-
TENTS; p. [10] blank; pp. [11]–[37] text; p. [38] colophon and signature of
Graves; pp. [39–40] blank.

24·7 × 15·2 cm. Bulk: 0·3/1·0 cm. Heavy white wove paper; all edges
trimmed; top edges gilt. Wove endpapers with watered design; inner sides
blank. Bound in red morocco; back and spine blank; front stamped in
gold: THE MORE | DESERVING CASES | ROBERT GRAVES

Price: 3 gns. Number of copies: 400. Published 1 February 1962 without
dust-jacket.

Contents: Foreword – 1. Sullen Moods 1922 – 2. The Dialecticians 1922 – 3
A Village Feud 1923 – 4. The Clipped Stater 1923 – 5. Epitaph on an Un-
fortunate Artist 1923 – 6. The Corner Knot 1924 – 7. Death of the Farmer
1924 – 8. Virgil the Sorcerer 1924 – 9. Pygmalion to Galatea 1925 – 10
Diplomatic Relations 1925 – 11. The Philatelist Royal 1929 – 12. To be Les
Philosophical 1931 – 13. Variables of Green 1931 – 14. Devilishly Provoked
1933–15. The Miller's Man 1934 – 16. July 24th 1942 – 17. Safe Receipt of
Censored Letter 1942 – 18. The Blotted Copy-Book 1952

Note: An issue in blue buckram has white wove endpapers without design
and the top edges are not gilt; price: 2 gns.; number of copies: 350.

a. First edition:

OXFORD ADDRESSES | ON POETRY | by | ROBERT GRAVES | *Professor of Poetry, Oxford University* | 1961 | [*publisher's emblem*] | CASSELL · LONDON

Collation: [A]⁸ B–H⁸ I/I★²/⁴, 70 leaves.

p. [i] OXFORD ADDRESSES ON POETRY; p. [ii] blank; p. [iii] title-page; p. [iv] publisher's, copyright, edition and printer's notices; p. [v] AD COLL. SANCT. JOH. BAPT. ALUMNO | CANO REDEUNTI BENIGNISSAM; p. [vi] blank; p. [vii] table of contents; p. [viii] blank; p. [ix–x] *Foreword;* pp. [1]–129 text, with pp. [1, 27, 55, 83, 97, 109] being section-headings and pp. [2, 26, 28, 54, 56, 82, 84, 98, 108, 110] being blank; p. [130] blank.

21·6 × 13·9 cm. Bulk: 1·2/1·7 cm. White wove paper; all edges trimmed. White wove endpapers. Bound in dark blue cloth; front and back blank; spine stamped in gold: [at bottom:] CASSELL | [up spine:] Robert Graves OXFORD ADDRESSES ON POETRY [*title enclosed in double-rule box with swirls and diamond top and bottom*].

Price: 18s. Number of copies: 2,951.   Published 26 April 1962 in grey-blue dust-jacket printed in black and medium blue.

Contents: Foreword – The Dedicated Poet – The Anti-Poet – The Personal Muse – Poetic Gold – The Word 'Báraka' – The Poet's Paradise

b. First American edition (1962):

[at right:] *Robert Graves* | (PROFESSOR OF POETRY, OX-FORD UNIVERSITY) 1961 | OXFORD | ADDRESSES | ON POETRY | [*decorative device*] | [three lines at right:] *Double-day & Company, Inc.* | *Garden City, New York* | *1962*

Collation: 1–3¹² [4]–[6]¹², 72 leaves, the first gathering being signed on p. 24. p. [1] OXFORD | ADDRESSES | ON POETRY; pp. [2–3] list of books by Graves; p. [4] blank; p. [5] title-page; p. [6] dedication (as A97a, p. [v]), Library of Congress card, copyright, printing and edition notices; pp. [7]–8 *Contents;* pp. [9]–10 *Foreword;* pp. [11]–141 text, with pp. [11, 37, 65, 95, 109, 121] being section-headings, pp. [12, 38, 66, 96, 110, 122] being unnumbered and pp. [94, 120] being blank; pp. [142]–[144] blank.

20·8 × 13·7 cm. Bulk: 1·1/1·5 cm. White wove paper; top and bottom edges trimmed. White wove endpapers; all edges trimmed. Bound in grey cloth with black quarter-cloth spine; front and back blank; spine stamped in silver, top to bottom: [near front:] OXFORD ADDRESSES ON POETRY [near back:] Robert Graves [near front:] Doubleday

Price: $3.95. Number of copies: 4,000 (in two printings). Published 21 September 1962 in white dust-jacket printed in grey, dark blue and black.

A98 THE COMEDIES OF TERENCE 1962

a. First edition:

THE COMEDIES OF | TERENCE | [*swelled rule*] | Edited, with a Foreword, by | ROBERT GRAVES | ANCHOR BOOKS | DOUBLEDAY & COMPANY, INC. | GARDEN CITY, NEW YORK | 1962

Collation: 180 leaves, glued at spine.
p. [i] THE COMEDIES OF | TERENCE | [*series emblem*]; p. [ii] blank; p. [iii] biographical note; p. [iv] blank; p. [v] title-page; p. [vi] Library of Congress card, copyright, printing and edition notices; p. [vii] CONTENTS; p. [viii] blank; pp. [ix]x–xiv FOREWORD; p. [xv] THE COMEDIES OF | TERENCE; p. [xvi] blank; pp. [1]–334 text, with pp. [1–3, 15, 25, 34, 46, 59–61, 67, 72, 84, 94, 103–105, 113, 123, 133, 148, 161–163, 170, 182, 194, 208, 223–225, 231, 240, 255, 266, 283–285, 290, 298, 309, 323] being unnumbered and pp. [58, 160] being blank; pp. [335]–[344] publisher's advertisements.

18·1 × 10·6 cm. Bulk: 1·9 cm. White wove paper; all edges trimmed. Bound in white paper covers printed in blue and black; front has a woman holding a large mask with series number, price, title and series credits; back has blurb; spine: [top to bottom:] THE COMEDIES OF TERENCE EDITED BY ROBERT GRAVES | ANCHOR | A305 | [*triangle*]; inner sides of front and back covers blank.

Price: $1.45. Number of copies: 10,000. Published 18 May 1962.

Contents: Foreword – The Fair Andrian – The Mother-in-Law – The Self Tormentor – The Eunuch – The Tricks of Phormio – The Brothers

Note: The cover design is by Eugene Berman.
This edition is Anchor Book A305.
The text is revised from the seventh edition of Echard's translation.

b. Second American issue ([1962]):

THE COMEDIES OF | TERENCE | [*swelled rule*] | Edited, wit a Foreword, by | ROBERT GRAVES | ALDINE PUBLISH ING COMPANY/CHICAGO

Collation: [1]–[11]¹⁶, 176 leaves.

p. [i] THE COMEDIES OF | TERENCE | AN ALDINE LIBRARY EDITION; pp. [ii]–[v] as A98*a*; p. [vi] copyright, Library of Congress card, publication, publisher's and printing notices; pp. [vii]–334 as A98*a*; pp. [335–336] blank.

20·9 × 13·9 cm. Bulk: 2·3/3·0 cm. White wove paper; all edges trimmed. White wove endpapers. Bound in maroon cloth; front and back blank; spine stamped in silver: [down spine, near front:] THE COMEDIES | [down spine, near back, parallel to preceding line:] OF TERENCE | [remainder upright:] GRAVES | ALDINE | [*publisher's emblem*]

Price: $5.95. Number of copies: 2,000. Published 26 July 1962 in white dust-jacket printed in black and mauve as cover of A98*a*.

c. First English edition [(*1963*)]:

THE BELLE SAUVAGE LIBRARY | THE COMEDIES OF | TERENCE | ECHARD'S TRANSLATION | EDITED, WITH A FOREWORD, BY | ROBERT GRAVES | [*publisher's emblem*] | CASSELL · LONDON

Collation: [1]⁸ 2–11⁸ 12⁶ 13–20⁸ 21/21*a*²/⁴ 22⁸, 174 leaves.

p. [i] THE COMEDIES OF TERENCE; p. [ii] blank; p. [iii] title-page; p. [iv] publisher's, copyright, publication and printing notices; p. [v] CONTENTS; p. [vi] blank; pp. [vii] viii–xii FOREWORD; pp. [1]–335 text, with pp. [1, 59, 103, 161, 223, 283] being title pages, pp. [2–3, 15, 25, 34, 46, 60–61, 67, 72, 84, 94, 104–105, 113, 123, 133, 148, 162–163, 170, 182, 194, 207, 224–225, 231, 240, 255, 266, 284–285, 291, 299, 310, 324] being unnumbered and pp. [58, 160, 222] being blank; p. [336] blank.

20·4 × 14·6 cm. Bulk: 2·6/3·3 cm. White wove paper; all edges trimmed. White wove endpapers. Bound in brownish-grey cloth; front and back blank; spine stamped in gold: ★ | [*light rule*] | *The* | *Comedies of* | *Terence* | [*light rule*] | ★ | *Edited by* | ROBERT | GRAVES | ★ | [*heavy rule*] | *Cassell* | [*heavy rule*] | ★

Price: 16s. Number of copies: 2,866. Published on 13 June 1963 in white dust-jacket printed in black and dark yellow-green.

A99   ORATIO CREWEIANA   1962

First edition:

ORATIO CREWEIANA | MDCCCCLXII

Collation: 6 leaves, stapled twice at centre.

p. [1] title-page; pp. 2, 4, 6, 8, 10 text of oration in Latin; pp. 3, 5, 7, 9, 11 paraphrase in English; p. [12] printer's notice.

21·5 × 14·0 cm. Bulk: 0·04 cm. White wove paper; all edges trimmed.

Not for sale; distributed gratis. Number of copies: 1,400. Published 27 June 1962 by Oxford University Press.

A100   THE BIG GREEN BOOK   [1962]

First edition:

Robert Graves | THE BIG GREEN BOOK | [*illustration of boy lying on bed reading with woolly dog observing*] | illustrated by Maurice Sendak | THE CROWELL-COLLIER PRESS

Collation: [1]–[4]⁸, 32 leaves.

p. [1] THE BIG GREEN BOOK | [*illustration of boy sitting on hassock reading*]; p. [2] publisher's advertisements; p. [3] title-page; p. [4] edition, copyright and printing notices; pp. [5]–[63] text and illustrations; p. [64] blank.

28·6 × 19·0 cm. Bulk: 0·8/1·3 cm. White wove paper; all edges trimmed. Green wove endpapers. Bound in slick green cloth; spine blank; front printed: [*in white:*] ROBERT GRAVES | THE BIG GREEN BOOK | [*white rectangular border, inside which, in black over chartreuse, is illustration of little old man, woolly dog, aunt and uncle*] | [*in white:*] illustrated by Maurice Sendak | A MODERN MASTERS BOOK FOR CHILDREN; back printed with blurb and publisher's advertisement.

Price: \$1.95. Number of copies undetermined. Published 15 October 1962 without dust-jacket.

Note: Most copies have a silver label reading \$1⁹⁵ stuck at upper right front corner of cover. The same book was issued in England on 2 October 1963 with an English price label (15s.).

A101   NEW POEMS 1962   [1962

a. First edition:

ROBERT GRAVES | NEW POEMS | 1962 | [*publisher'* *emblem*] | CASSELL · LONDON

Collation: [A]⁸ B⁸ C/C★²/⁸, 26 leaves.
pp. [i–ii] blank; p. [iii] NEW POEMS | 1962; p. [iv] blank; p. [v] title-page;
p. [vi] publisher's, publication and printer's notices; p. [vii] FOREWORD;
p. [viii] blank; pp. [ix–x] CONTENTS; p. [1] XIII; p. [2] blank; pp. 3–25 text;
p. [26] blank; p. [27] XIV; p. [28] blank; pp. 29–42 text.

21·4 × 14·8 cm. Bulk: 0·4/1·0 cm. White wove paper; all edges trimmed. White wove endpapers. Bound in orange-rust cloth; front and back
blank; spine stamped in gold, bottom to top: *Cassell Robert Graves* NEW
POEMS 1962

Price: 12s. 6d. Number of copies: 3,082. Published 18 October 1962 in
white dust-jacket printed in black and orange-brown.

Contents: Foreword – XIII: Ruby and Amethyst – Recognition – Vari-
ables of Green – The Watch – Name Day – Uncalendared Love – The
Meeting – Lack – Not at Home – Horizon – Golden Anchor – Lion
Lover – Ibycus in Samos – Possessed – The Winged Heart – In Trance at
a Distance – The Wreath – In Her Praise – The Alabaster Throne – A
Restless Ghost – Between Moon and Moon – XIV: Beware, Madam! –
The Cliff Edge – The Miller's Man – Acrobats – Ouzo Unclouded – The
Broken Girth – Inkidoo and the Queen of Babel – Three Songs for the
Lute: I. Truth Is Poor Physic – II. In Her Only Way – III. Hedges Freaked
with Snow – The Ambrosia of Dionysus and Semele – The Unnamed
Spell

Note: Impressions: 2nd, August 1963. Number of copies: 1,500.

b. First American edition (*1963*):

NEW POEMS | [*swelled decorative rule*] | ROBERT GRAVES |
DOUBLEDAY & COMPANY, INC., GARDEN CITY,
NEW YORK, 1963

Collation: [1]–[3]¹², 36 leaves.
p. [*i*] NEW POEMS; p. [*ii*] blank; p. [*iii*] title-page; p. [*iv*] acknowledgement,
Library of Congress card, copyright, printing and edition notices; p. [*v*]
FOREWORD; p. [*vi*] blank; pp. *vii–viii* CONTENTS; pp. 1–64 text, with pp.
[4, 6, 8, 10, 12, 14, 16, 20, 24, 28, 34, 36, 38, 40, 42, 46, 48, 50, 52, 58, 62]
blank.

20·8 × 13·7 cm. Bulk: 0·6/1·1 cm. White wove paper; all edges trimmed. White wove endpapers. Bound in black cloth; back blank; front
stamped with signature of Graves in gold; spine stamped in gold, top to
bottom: *NEW POEMS* Robert Graves *DOUBLEDAY*

Price: $2.95. Number of copies: 3,500. Published 21 June 1963 in white dust-jacket printed in black and green.

A102   THE SIEGE AND FALL OF TROY   [1962]

a. First edition:

THE SIEGE | AND FALL | OF TROY | *by* | ROBERT GRAVES | *Illustrated by* | WALTER HODGES | [*publisher's emblem*] | CASSELL · LONDON

Collation: [A]⁸ B–I⁸, 72 leaves.

p. [i] *The Siege and Fall of Troy*; p. [ii] list of children's books by Graves; p. [iii] blank; p. [iv] illustration; p. [v] title-page; p. [vi] publisher's, copyright, edition and printer's notices; p. vii CONTENTS; p. [viii] blank; pp. ix–x INTRODUCTION; p. [xi] blank; pp. [xii–xiii] map; p. [xiv] illustration; pp. 1–119 text, with pp. [4, 12, 22, 32, 42, 50, 60, 68, 80, 92, 100, 108] being illustrations and pp. [11, 21, 41, 59, 99] being blank; p. [120] blank; p. [121] *Index*; p. [122] blank; pp. 123–128 index; pp. [129–130] blank.

21·6 × 14·0 cm. Bulk: 1·4/2·0 cm. White wove paper; all edges trimmed. White wove endpapers. Bound in brown cloth-simulated boards; front and back blank; spine stamped in gold: ROBERT | GRAVES | [up spine:] The Siege and Fall of Troy | CASSELL

Price: 15s. Number of copies: 7,553. Published 8 November 1962 in white dust-jacket with multicolour Trojan horse scene and author and title in yellow.

Note: Impressions: 2nd, November 1964. Number of copies: 3,000. This book has been translated into Dutch.

b. First American edition ([1963]):

[first four lines in pseudo-Celtic type:] ROBERT GRAVES | THE | SIEGE AND FALL | OF TROY | ILLUSTRATED BY C. WALTER HODGES | DOUBLEDAY & COMPANY, INC. | GARDEN CITY, NEW YORK

Collation: 64 leaves, glued to tape at spine.

p. [1] THE SIEGE AND FALL OF TROY; p. [2] frontispiece; p. [3] title-page; p. [4] Library of Congress card, copyright, printing and edition notices with publisher's emblem to left of all; p. [5] list of books for children by Graves; p. [6] blank; p. [7] CONTENTS; p. [8] blank; pp. 9–10 INTRODUCTION; p. [11] THE SIEGE AND FALL OF TROY; pp. [12–13] map; p. [14] blank; p[

15–120 text, with pp. [17, 22, 31, 35, 47, 53, 62, 71, 83, 91, 99, 106, 117] being illustrations, and pp. [42, 58, 74, 96, 110] being blank; p. [121] INDEX; p. [122] blank; pp. 123–128 index. Illustrations, frontispiece and map are printed in red.

23·3 × 15·0 cm. Bulk: 0·9/1·4 cm. White wove paper; all edges trimmed. Cream wove endpapers. Bound in rust-brown cloth; front and back blank; spine stamped in gold, top to bottom: [near front:] Robert | [near back, parallel to preceding line:] Graves | [in pseudo-Celtic type:] THE SIEGE AND FALL OF TROY | [remainder upright:] [*publisher's emblem*] | Doubleday

Price: $3.50. Number of copies: 20,000 (including 5,000 institutional). Published 4 October 1963 in white dust-jacket printed in yellow, orange, brown and black.

c. Second American edition ([1965]):

THE SIEGE AND | FALL OF TROY | [*concave rule*] | ROBERT GRAVES | [at right:] [*series emblem*]

> *Collation:* 64 leaves, glued at spine.
> p. [1] publisher's advertisements and blurb; p. [2] list of books in this series; p. [3] title-page; p. [4] publisher's, copyright, series, rights reservation, arrangement, edition and printing notices; p. [5] CONTENTS; p. [6] blank; pp. [7] 8–9 Introduction; p. [10] blank; p. [11] THE SIEGE AND FALL OF TROY; p. [12] blank; pp. [13] 14–112 text, with pp. [16, 22, 30, 39, 47, 54, 61, 68, 78, 89, 95, 102] unnumbered; pp. [113] 114–124 Index; pp. [125]–[128] publisher's advertisements.
> 16·1 × 10·5 cm. Bulk: 0·6 cm. White wove paper; all edges trimmed; all edges stained blue. Bound in white paper covers printed in blue, yellow, red, brown and black.
> *Price:* $0.45. Number of copies: 75,000. Published 11 November 1965.
> *Note:* This book is Dell Laurel-Leaf Library 7885.

A103   NINE HUNDRED IRON CHARIOTS   [1963]

First edition:

[*first two words in grey:*] Robert Graves Nine Hundred Iron Chariots | The Twelfth Arthur Dehon Little Memorial Lecture, Massachusetts Institute of Technology | Delivered in Kresge Auditorium, Cambridge, Massachusetts, on Wednesday, May 14, 1963 | [*rule*]

Collation: 12 leaves, stapled twice in centre.

p. [1] title-page; p. [2] copyright notice; pp. [3]–[21] text; p. [22] photograph of Graves and biographical note; p. [23] history of the lectures and list of lecturers; p. [24] blank.

22·9 × 15·3 cm. Bulk: 0·25 cm. White wove paper; all edges trimmed. Stiff white paper wrapper printed black; back black only; front as title-page in white, with author's name in red and in the centre an eclipse with white corona with the sun being Zeus in green; inner sides of both covers blank.

Not for sale; distribution gratis. Number of copies: 4,500; 3,000 issued 7 October 1963; 1,500 issued 30 October 1963 by Massachusetts Institute of Technology Press.

Note: The design is by W. John Lees.

A104　　　　　MAMMON　　　　　1964

First edition:

MAMMON | ORATION DELIVERED AT THE | LONDON SCHOOL OF ECONOMICS | AND POLITICAL SCIENCE | ON FRIDAY, 6 DECEMBER 1963 | BY | ROBERT GRAVES | THE LONDON SCHOOL OF ECONOMICS | AND POLITICAL SCIENCE | 1964

Collation: 14 leaves, sewn at centre with cover.

p. [1] title-page; p. [2] copyright notice; pp. 3–25 text; p. [26] printer's notice; pp. [27–28] blank.

21·0 × 13·8 cm. Bulk: 0·2 cm. White wove paper; all edges trimmed. Bound in light blue paper covers; front printed as title-page; all other sides blank.

Not for sale; supplied only to those present at the oration. Number of copies: 500. Published in March 1964.

A105　　　THE HEBREW MYTHS　　　1964

a. First edition:

HEBREW MYTHS | THE BOOK OF GENESIS | *by* | ROBERT GRAVES | *and* | RAPHAEL PATAI | MCMLXIV | DOUBLEDAY & COMPANY, INC. | GARDEN CITY, NEW YORK

Collation: 1–13¹², 156 leaves.

p. [1] HEBREW MYTHS | THE BOOK OF GENESIS; p. [2] blank; pp. 3–4 lists of books by Graves and Patai; p. [5] title-page; p. [6] Library of Congress card, copyright, printing and edition notices; pp. 7–8 CONTENTS; p. [9] HEBREW MYTHS | THE BOOK OF GENESIS; p. [10] blank; pp. 11–19 INTRODUC-TION; p. [20] blank; pp. 21–279 text, with pp. [123, 131, 239] being maps; p. [280] blank; pp. 281–294 ABBREVIATIONS, SOURCES AND ANNOTATED BIBLIOGRAPHY; pp. 295–311 INDEX; p. [312] blank.

23·4 × 15·3 cm. Bulk: 2·4/3·1 cm. White wove paper; top and bottom edges trimmed. White wove endpapers printed deep mustard with de-signs of facing dragons; inner sides of both blank. Bound in light grey cloth; back blank; front stamped with a scroll in blue, the unrolled portion forming a box inside which is stamped in gold: HEBREW MYTHS | The Book of Genesis; *spine stamped with solid blue rectangular box stamped in gold:* HEBREW | MYTHS | · | *Robert* | *Graves* | *&* | *Raphael* | *Patai* | [at bottom, outside of box:] DOUBLEDAY

Price: $4.95. Number of copies: 6,500. Published 20 March 1964 in white dust-jacket printed in grey, blue and mustard-gold.

Note: Printed in the U.S.

b. English issue ([1964]):

HEBREW MYTHS | THE BOOK OF GENESIS | *by* | ROBERT GRAVES | *and* | RAPHAEL PATAI | [*publisher's emblem*] | CASSELL · LONDON

Collation: [A]⁴ B–U⁸, 156 leaves.
Remainder as A105a except p. [6] publisher's, copyright, publication and printer's notices.

24·6 × 15·3 cm. Bulk: 2·8/3·6 cm. White wove paper; all edges trim-med. White wove endpapers. Bound in bright blue cloth; front blank; back blind-stamped with a script *L* near spine at bottom; spine stamped in gold: [*heavy rule*] | [*light rule*] | Hebrew | Myths | ROBERT | GRAVES & | RAPHAEL | PATAI | [*light rule*] | [*heavy rule*] | CASSELL

Price: 36s. Number of copies: 4,022. Published 8 October 1964 in slick white dust-jacket printed in black and blue with multicoloured illustration of Adam and Eve on front.

Note: Impressions: 2nd, 17 March 1965. Number of copies: 3,150.

Printed in Great Britain.

a. First edition:

Robert Graves | *[swelled rule]* | COLLECTED | SHORT | STORIES | DOUBLEDAY & COMPANY, INC. | GARDEN CITY, NEW YORK | 1964

Collation: [1]¹² 2–7¹² [8]–[14]¹², 168 leaves.
p. [i] COLLECTED SHORT STORIES; p. [ii] blank; pp. [iii]–iv list of books by Graves; p. [v] title-page; p. [vi] acknowledgement, Library of Congress card, copyright, rights reservation, printing and edition notices; pp. [vii]–viii CONTENTS; pp. [ix]–x [flush left:] *INTRODUCTION;* p. [xi] COLLECTED SHORT STORIES; p. [xii] blank; pp. 1–323 text, with pp. [1, 133, 175] being section headings, pp. [2, 132, 134, 176] being blank and pp. [3, 25, 37, 43, 48, 54, 58, 63, 68, 71, 80, 85, 90, 95, 100, 119, 135, 141, 154, 177, 183, 189, 202, 208, 221, 226, 250, 265, 286, 302] being unnumbered; p. [324] blank.

20·7 × 13·6 cm. Bulk: 2·4/2·9 cm. White wove paper; top and bottom edges trimmed. White wove endpapers. Bound in grey cloth; front and back blank; spine printed top to bottom: [near front:] ROBERT | [near back, parallel to preceding line:] GRAVES | [*in blue, near front:*] COLLECTED | [near back, parallel to preceding line:] SHORT STORIES | [upright:] DOUBLE-DAY

Price: $4.95. Number of copies: 7,000 (in two printings). Published 17 April 1964 in white dust-jacket printed in grey, black, blue and chartreuse.

Contents: Introduction – ENGLISH STORIES: The Shout – Old Papa Johnson – Treacle Tart – The Full Length – Earth to Earth – Period Piece – Week-End at Cwm Tatws [in title-page: Cwn] – He Went Out to Buy a Rhine – Kill Them! Kill Them! – The French Thing – A Man May Not Marry His . . . – An Appointment for Candlemas – The Abominable Mr Gunn – Harold Vesey at the Gates of Hell – Christmas Truce – You Win, Houdini! – ROMAN STORIES: Epics Are Out of Fashion – The Apartment House – The Myconian – MAJORCAN STORIES: They Say . . . They Say – 6 Valiant Bulls 6 – A Bicycle in Majorca – The Five Godfathers – Evidence of Affluence – God Grant Your Honour Many Years – The Viscountess and the Short-Haired Girl – A Toast to Ava Gardner – The Lost Chinese – She Landed Yesterday – The Whitaker Negroes

Note: Printed in the U.S.

b. English issue ([1965]):

Robert Graves | *[swelled rule]* | COLLECTED | SHORT | STORIES | *[publisher's emblem]* | CASSELL · LONDON

Collation: [1]–[9]^{16} [10]^8 [11]^{16}, 168 leaves.

p. [*i*] COLLECTED SHORT STORIES | [blurb (14 ll.)] ; p. [*ii*] blank; pp. [*iii–iv*] list of books by Graves; p. [*v*] title-page; p. [*vi*] acknowledgement, copyright, rights reservation, publication and printer's notices; remainder as A106*a*.

19·5 × 13·2 cm. Bulk: 2·4/3·0 cm. White wove paper; all edges trimmed. White wove endpapers. Bound in medium blue cloth-simulated boards; front and back blank; spine stamped in gold: [*heavy rule*] | [*light rule*] | Collected | Short | Stories | ROBERT | GRAVES | [*light rule*] | [*heavy rule*] | CASSELL

Price: 25s. Number of copies: 3,000. Published 18 November 1965 in white dust-jacket printed in slate blue, drab gold and black.

Note: Impressions: 2nd, November 1965 (2,000 copies); 3rd, 1966 (2,000 copies).
'The Apartment House' of A106*a* is here called 'The Tenement: A Vision of Imperial Rome'.

Printed in Great Britain.

A107   MAN DOES, WOMAN IS   1964

a. First edition:

ROBERT GRAVES | [*light rule*] | MAN DOES, | WOMAN IS | 1964 | [*publisher's emblem*] | CASSELL · LONDON

Collation: [A]^{10} B–D^8 E/E$^{\star2/8}$, 44 leaves.

pp. [i–ii] blank; p. [iii] MAN DOES, WOMAN IS | 1964; p. [iv] blank; p. [v] title-page; p. [vi] publisher's, copyright, publication and printer's notices; p. [vii] FOREWORD; p. [viii] blank; pp. [ix]–[xi] CONTENTS; p. [xii] blank; p. [1] xv; p. [2] blank; pp. 3–26 text; p. [27] xvi; p. [28] blank; pp. 29–53 text; p. [54] blank; p. [55] xvii; p. [56] blank; pp. 57–74 text; pp. [75–76] blank.

21·5 × 15·0 cm. Bulk: 0·8/1·4.cm. White wove paper; all edges trimmed. White wove endpapers. Bound in ultramarine cloth; front and back blank; spine stamped in gold, bottom to top: *Cassell Robert Graves* MAN DOES, WOMAN IS

Price: 16s. Number of copies: 4,010. Published 17 April 1964 in white dust-jacket printed in black and French blue.

Contents: Foreword – xv: A Time of Waiting – Expect Nothing – No Letter – The Why of the Weather – In Time – Fire Walker – Deed of Gift – At Best, Poets – She is No Liar – A Last Poem – The Pearl –The Leap – Bank Account – Judgement of Paris – Man Does, Woman Is –

The Ample Garden – To Myrto About Herself – The Three-Faced – Dazzle of Darkness – Myrrhina – Food of the Dead – Eurydice – To Beguile and Betray – I Will Write – XVI : Bird of Paradise – The Metaphor – Song: A Phoenix Flame – Secrecy – Joseph and Mary – An East Wind – Dance of Words – A Blind Arrow – The Oleaster – The Septuagenarian – *Non Cogunt Astra* – Song: Sword and Rose – Endless Pavement – In Disguise – A Measure of Casualness – In Time of Absence – The Green Castle – Not to Sleep – The Hearth – That Other World – The Beds of Grainne and Diarmuid – Rain of Brimstone – Consortium of Stones – The Black Goddess – XVII: Broken Neck – O – Woman of Greece – The Colours of Night – Between Trains – To the Teumessian Vixen – The Hung Wu Vase – *La Mejicana* – Lamia in Love – After the Flood – A Late Arrival – Song: With No Return – All I Tell You From My Heart – The Undead

b. Limited issue ([*1964*]):

Title-page as A107a.

Collation as A107a.

Remainder as A107a except p. [i] *Of this edition | there have been printed | 175 copies for sale, numbered 1–175 | and 26 copies not for sale, lettered A–Z | all signed by the author | This is No. [number written in] | [signature of Graves]* 21·6 × 14·7 cm. Bulk: 0·8/1·4 cm. Buff laid paper; all edges trimmed; watermarked with a crown and a script Glastonbury. Buff laid endpapers. Bound in buff linen with ultramarine quarter cloth spine with gold rules front and back near buff cloth; front and back otherwise blank; spine stamped in gold, bottom to top: *Cassell Robert Graves* MAN DOES, WOMAN IS

Price: 50s. Number of copies: 201. Published 18 June 1964 in transparent glassine wrapper.

c. American issue ([*1964*]):

ROBERT GRAVES | [*light rule*] | MAN DOES, | WOMAN IS | 1964 | Doubleday & Company, Inc. | Garden City, New York

Collation: 48 leaves, glued at spine.

pp. [i]–[iv] blank; p. [v] MAN DOES, WOMAN IS | 1964; p. [vi] blank; pp. [vii–viii] list of books by Graves; p. [ix] title-page; p. [x] *ACKNOW LEDGMENTS* and Library of Congress card, copyright, rights reser vation, printing and edition notices; p. [xi] FOREWORD; p. [xii] blank pp. [xiii]–[xv] CONTENTS; p. [xvi] blank; pp. [1]–74 as A107a; pp. [75] [80] blank.

20·7 × 14·0 cm. Bulk: 0·6/1·2 cm. White wove paper; top and bottom edges trimmed. Cream wove endpapers. Bound in black cloth with slick black quarter-cloth spine; front and back blank; spine stamped in silver, top to bottom: Man Does, Woman Is *by Robert Graves* Doubleday

Price: $3.95. Number of copies: 4,500. Published 20 November 1964 in white dust-jacket printed in black, scarlet and lake.

A108 EL FENOMENO DEL TURISMO 1964

ROBERT GRAVES | EL FENOMENO | DEL TURISMO | ATENEO | MADRID | 1 9 6 4 | XXV Aniversario | de la Paz Española

Collation: [1]⁸ [2]⁴ [3]⁸, 20 leaves.

2 pp., blank; p. [i] EL FENOMENO DEL TURISMO; p. [ii] blank; p. [iii] title-page; p. [iv] [entire flush right:] Conferencia pronunciada en el Ate- | neo de Madrid el 3 de marzo de 1964.; pp. 1–31 text; p. [32] blank; p. [33] ACABÓSE DE IMPRIMIR EN MADRID, | EN LOS TALLERES GRÁFICOS DE | BOLAÑOS Y AGUILAR, S. L., EL | DÍA 18 DE JUNIO DE 1964.; p. [34] blank.

19·3 × 11·5 cm. Bulk: 0·3 cm. White wove paper; all edges trimmed. Bound in white paper covers printed in medium cobalt blue and black.

Price: 20 ptas. Number of copies: undetermined. Published 3 March 1964. *Notes:* This book is no. 21 of the Coleccion Ateneo.

'Postscript, 1965' in *Majorca Observed* is largely a translation of this speech.

A109 ORATIO CREWEIANA 1964

First edition:

ORATIO | CREWEIANA | [*ornament*] | MDCCCCLXIV

Collation: 8 leaves, stapled twice at centre.

p. [1] title-page; pp. 2, 4, 6, 8, 10, 12 text of oration in Latin; pp. 3, 5, 7, 9, 11, 13 paraphrase in English; p. [14] printer's notice; pp. [15–16] blank.

21·5 × 13·8 cm. Bulk: 0·08 cm. Cream-white wove paper; all edges trimmed.

Not for sale; distributed gratis. Number of copies: 1,400. Published 24 June 1964 by Oxford University Press.

A110 ANN AT HIGHWOOD HALL [1946]

First edition:

entire related to cut in green and black of Ann having her portrait painted] | [*three lines in rectangular white box:*] ANN AT HIGH-WOOD | HALL | *Poems for Children* | [*remainder in rectangular white box:*] [*broken rule*] | *by* | [*broken rule*] | *Robert Graves* | *Illustrated by* | *Edward Ardizzone* | [*broken rule*] | *Cassell – London*

Collation: [A]⁸ B–C⁸, 24 leaves.

p. [i] *Ann at Highwood Hall*; p. [ii] blank; p. [iii] title-page; p. [iv] publisher's, copyright, publication and printer's notices; p. [v] *Contents*; p. [vi] blank; p. [vii] *To my grandchildren* | Georgina and David Graves | *with love*; p. [viii] blank; pp. 1–38 [39] text, with pp. [2–3, 4, 6–7, 9–12, 15–16, 19–20, 22, 24, 26, 28–33, 35, 37, 39] being unnumbered; p. [40] illustration.

21·6 × 16·2 cm. Bulk: 0·4/1·1 cm. White wove paper; all edges trimmed. White wove endpapers. Bound in powder-blue cloth-simulated boards; front and back blank; spine stamped in gold, bottom to top: CASSELL Ann at Highwood Hall ROBERT GRAVES

Price: 13s. 6d. Number of copies: 5,000. Published 8 October 1964 in white dust-jacket printed in black, blue, green and orange-pink.

Contents: Ann at Highwood Hall – St Valentine's Day – George II and the Chinese Emperor – I Have a Little Cough, Sir – The Sewing Basket – Joseph and Jesus – Caroline and Charles

AIII MAMMON AND THE BLACK GODDESS [1965]

a. First edition:

MAMMON AND THE | BLACK GODDESS | by | ROBERT GRAVES | [*publisher's emblem*] | CASSELL · LONDON

Collation: [A]⁸ B–L⁸, 88 leaves.

p. [i] MAMMON AND THE BLACK GODDESS; p. [ii] blank; p. [iii] title-page; p. [iv] publisher's, copyright, publication, acknowledgement and printer's notices; p. [v] table of contents; p. [vi] blank; p. [vii] *Foreword*; p. [viii] blank; pp. [1]–165 text, with pp. [1, 27, 53, 99, 115, 141] being section-headings and pp. [2, 26, 28, 52, 54, 100, 114, 116, 140, 142] being blank; pp. [166]–[168] blank.

21·4 × 13·9 cm. Bulk: 1·8/2·4 cm. White wove paper; all edges trimmed. White wove endpapers. Bound in slick grey cloth; front and back blank; spine stamped in gold, bottom to top: [at bottom, upright:] CASSELL | Robert Graves [*ornament*] [*inside double rule rectangular box:* MAMMON AND THE BLACK GODDESS [*ornament*]

Price: 21s. Number of copies: 3,000. Published on 8 March 1965 in grey dust-jacket printed in black and sea-green.

Contents: Foreword – Mammon – Nine Hundred Iron Chariots – Three Oxford Lectures on Poetry (Some Instances of Poetic Vulgarity; Technique in Poetry; The Poet in a Valley of Dry Bones) – Real Women – Moral Principles in Translation – Intimations of the Black Goddess

Note: Printed in Great Britain.

b. American issue (1965):

MAMMON AND THE | BLACK GODDESS | by | ROBERT
GRAVES | Doubleday & Company, Inc., Garden City, New
York | 1965

Collation: [1]–[11]⁸, 88 leaves.
Remainder as A111*a*, except p. [iv] Library of Congress card, copyright,
printing and edition notices.

20·8 × 13·8 cm. Bulk: 1·1/1·6 cm. White wove paper; top and bottom
edges trimmed. Blue wove endpapers, inner sides white. Bound in black
cloth with light blue quarter-cloth spine; front and back blank; spine
stamped, top to bottom: [in blue:] ROBERT GRAVES [in black:] MAMMON
AND THE BLACK GODDESS [in blue:] DOUBLEDAY

Price: $3.95. Number of copies: 4,000. Published 18 June 1965 in white
dust-jacket printed in light blue and black.

Note: Printed in the U.S.

A112   MAJORCA OBSERVED   [1965]

a. First edition:

[entire flush left of centre:] MAJORCA OBSERVED | by Robert
Graves | & Paul Hogarth | [*publisher's emblem*] | CASSELL –
LONDON

Collation: [1]–[10]⁸, 80 leaves.
2 pp., blank; p. [1] [flush right:] MAJORCA OBSERVED; p. [2] frontispiece;
p. [3] title-page; p. [4] publisher's, copyright, designer's and printer's
notices; p. [5] [flush left:] Contents; p. [6] illustration; pp. 7–150 text,
with pp. [55, 83, 91, 99, 109, 117, 125, 133] being section-headings, pp.
[25], 31, [40–41], 42, 45, [50], 59, 73, 79, [94, 123], 128, [131] containing
text and illustrations and pp. [10, 12, 15–16, 18–20, 24, 27–28, 30, 32,
35–38, 43–44, 46, 48, 52–54, 56, 63–64, 66, 69–70, 74, 76, 80–82, 84,
89–90, 92, 97–98, 100, 104, 106, 108, 110, 115–116, 118, 121, 124, 126,
132, 134, 136, 140, 143, 146, 148] being illustrations only; pp. [151–152]
illustrations; pp. [153]–[158] blank.

24·1 × 16·7 cm. Bulk: 1·3/2·1 cm. White laid paper; all edges trimmed.
White wove endpapers. Bound in rust cloth; front and back blank;
spine stamped in gold: Robert | Graves | & Paul | Hogarth | [up spine:]
MAJORCA OBSERVED | CASSELL

Price: 36s. Number of copies: 4,935. Published 13 May 1965 in white dust-jacket printed in black and light orange-buff.

Contents: Why I Live in Majorca 1953 – Postscript, 1965 – A Dead Branch on the Tree of Israel – Trín-Trín-Trín – School Life in Majorca 1955 – Bulletin of the College of St Modesto of Bobbio – God Grant Your Honour Many Years – Thy Servant and God's – Ditching in a Fishless Sea – George Sand in Majorca

Note: Both A112*a* and A112*b* were printed in England.

b. American issue ([1965]):

MAJORCA OBSERVED | by Robert Graves | & Paul Hogarth | DOUBLEDAY & COMPANY, INC. | GARDEN CITY NEW YORK

Collation as A112*a*.
Remainder as A112*a*, except p. [6] publisher's, copyright, designer's and printing notices.

Size, bulk, paper, endpapers and binding as A112*a*, except spine has DOUBLEDAY for CASSELL.

Price: $10.00. Number of copies: 1,624. Published 17 September 1965 in dust-jacket as A112*a*.

A113   LOVE RESPELT   [1965]

[*entire enclosed within abstract branch and circle design:*] | [flush left:] Love | [flush left:] Respelt | by | [flush left:] Robert Graves | [*rule*] | [flush left:] Cassell, London

Collation: [1]–[3]⁸, 24 leaves.
pp. [1–2] blank; p. [3] Of this book | there have been printed | 250 copies, numbered 1–250 | all signed by the author | This is No. [*number written in*] | [*signature of Graves*]; p. [4] blank; p. [5] [flush left:] Love | [flush left:] Respelt | by | [flush left:] Robert Graves | [*rule*]; p. [6] blank; p. [7] title-page; p. [8] publisher's, copyright, publication and printer's notices; p. [9] table of contents; p. [10] blank; pp. [11]–[42] text, with pp. [11, 14, 19, 34] having illustrations or designs as well as text; p. [43] design; p. [44] blank; p. [45] text; pp. [46]–[48] blank.

21·5 × 17·0 cm. Bulk: 0·4/1·1 cm. White laid paper; all edges trimmed. White laid endpapers. Bound quarter-cloth with grey pepper-and-salt cloth with slick black cloth spine; front and back blank; spine stamped in gold script, bottom to top: Cassell Love Respelt Robert Graves

Price: 50s. Number of copies: 250 plus 30 copies out of series. Published 16 July 1965 in white dust-jacket printed in black.

Contents: 1. The Red Shower – 2. Above the Edge of Doom – 3. Wild Cyclamen – 4. Gift of Sight – 5. Batxoca – 6. The Snap-Comb Wilderness – 7. Change – 8. A Court of Love – 9. Black – 10. Between Hyssop and Axe – 11. Gold and Malachite – 12. Ambience – 13. The Vow – 14. The Frog and the Golden Ball – 15. Those Who Came Short – 16. Whole Love – 17. This Holy Month – 18. The Blow – 19. The Impossible – 20. The Fetter – 21. Iron Palace – 22. True Joy – 23. Tomorrow's Envy of Today – 24. The Hidden Garden – 25. The Wedding – 26. What Will Be, Is – 27. Son Altesse – 28. Everywhere Is Here – 29. Song: The Far Side of Your Moon – 30. Deliverance – 31. Conjunction – 32. Nothing Now Astonishes – 33. Postscript

Notes: The printing throughout, except for pp. [3, 8], is a reproduction of Graves' MSS.

The illuminations are by Aemilia Laraçuen.

There is a reprint of 18 copies, lettered A–R, not for sale.

A114   COLLECTED POEMS 1965   1965

First edition:

ROBERT GRAVES | COLLECTED | POEMS | 1965 | [*publisher's emblem*] | CASSELL · LONDON

Collation: [A]⁸ B–Z⁸ AA–EE⁸ FF⁴ GG⁸, 236 leaves.
pp. [i–ii] blank; p. [iii] COLLECTED POEMS | 1965; p. [iv] blank; p. [v] title-page; p. [vi] publisher's, copyright, publication and printer's notices; pp. [vii–viii] FOREWORD; pp. [ix–xxii] CONTENTS; p. [1] 1; p. [2] blank; pp. 3–436 text with pp. [31, 67, 87, 135, 151, 181, 199, 209, 237, 255, 277, 287, 311, 327, 353, 379, 403] being section headings and pp. [30, 32, 66, 68, 88, 134, 136, 152, 180, 182, 200, 208, 210, 236, 238, 256, 278, 288, 312, 328, 354, 380, 404] being blank; pp. [437–438] blank; p. [439] INDEX TO FIRST LINES OF POEMS; p. [440] blank; pp. 441–449 [450] index.

21·5 × 14·8 cm. Bulk: 2·9/3·6 cm. White wove paper; all edges trimmed. White wove endpapers. Bound in bright ultramarine cloth; back blank; front stamped in gold: COLLECTED | POEMS | 1965; spine stamped in gold: ROBERT | GRAVES | [*rule*] | COLLECTED | POEMS | 1965 | CASSELL

Price: 42s. Number of copies: 5,135. Published 23 September 1965 in white dust-jacket printed in black and purplish ultramarine.

Contents: Foreword – 1: In the Wilderness – The Haunted House – Reproach – The Finding of Love – Rocky Acres – Outlaws – One Hard

B

BOOKS CONTAINING CONTRIBUTIONS BY ROBERT GRAVES

A complete listing of first book publications only is intended. No attempt has been made to include the many anthology reprintings of material already published by Graves in his own books.

B1   WELSH POETRY OLD AND NEW   1912

WELSH POETRY | OLD AND NEW | IN ENGLISH VERSE | BY | ALFRED PERCEVAL GRAVES, M.A. | ('CANWR CILARNÉ') | PRESIDENT OF THE IRISH LITERARY SOCIETY | LONDON REPRESENTATIVE OF THE COUNCIL OF THE CELTIC ASSOCIATION | MEMBER OF THE EXECUTIVE COMMITTEES OF THE FOLK SONG SOCIETY | AND OF THE WELSH AND IRISH FOLK SONG SOCIETIES | AND MEMBER OF THE HONOUR-ABLE SOCIETY OF CYMMRODORION | LONGMANS, GREEN, AND CO. | 39 PATERNOSTER ROW, LON-DON | NEW YORK, BOMBAY, AND CALCUTTA | 1912 | *All rights reserved*

Collation: [a]⁶ b–c⁸ B–L⁸ M⁶, 108 leaves.
2 pp., blank; p. [i] WELSH POETRY OLD AND NEW; p. [ii] blank; p. [iii] title-page; p. [iv] blank; p. [v] dedication; p. [vi] blank; p. [vii]–viii FOREWORD; p. [ix] x–xv PREFACE; p. [xvi] blank; pp. [xvii] xviii–xx CONTENTS; pp. [xxi] xxii–xlii INTRODUCTION; pp. [1] 2–134 text with pp. [13, 23, 42, 53, 64, 84, 97, 116] unnumbered; pp. [135] 136–144 A NOTE ON WELSH METRES; pp. [145] 146–170 BIOGRAPHICAL AND CRITICAL NOTES; pp. [171–172] blank.

18·5 × 12·4 cm. Bulk: 1·5/1·9 cm. White wove paper; all edges trimmed. White wove endpapers. Bound in medium dull green cloth; back blank; front stamped: WELSH POETRY | OLD AND NEW | IN ENGLISH VERSE | ALFRED PERCEVAL GRAVES | [near bottom, at right:] [*two concentric circles, inside which a solid circular black box, in which a red lion rampant*]; spine stamped: [*double rule*] | WELSH | POETRY | OLD AND NEW | IN ENGLISH | VERSE | A. P. | GRAVES | LONGMANS | [*double rule*]

Price: 2s. 6d. Number of copies: 2,000. Published 15 July 1912.

Note: Graves' contribution (p. 139) is an englyn called 'The Will O' the Wisp'.

[all flush left:] 'THE BRITISH SOLDIER' | AN EXHIBITION OF PICTURES | BY ERIC H. KENNINGTON | (An Official Artist on the Western Front) | WITH A PREFACE BY | ROBERT GRAVES | ERNEST BROWN & PHILLIPS | THE LEICESTER GALLERIES | LEICESTER SQUARE, LONDON | JUNE–JULY, 1918.

Collation: 8 leaves, unsigned, sewn three times in centre.

p. [1] title-page; p. [2] advertisement for artist's supplies; pp. 3–6 THE BRITISH SOLDIER; pp. 7–16 *Catalogue*

13·3 × 10·6 cm. Bulk: 0·2 cm. White wove paper; all edges trimmed. Bound in grey paper wrappers printed in black; front cover: ENTRANCE GALLERY AND REYNOLDS ROOM | [*rectangular single rule box enclosing all but final line:*] | [six lines flush left:] 'THE BRITISH SOLDIER' | AN EXHIBITION OF PICTURES | BY ERIC H. KENNINGTON | (An Official Artist on the Western Front) | WITH A PREFACE BY | ROBERT GRAVES | ERNEST BROWN & PHILLIPS | (W. L. PHILLIPS, C. L. PHILLIPS, O. F. BROWN) | THE LEICESTER GALLERIES | LEICESTER SQUARE, LONDON | EXHIBITION HO. 260. JUNE–JULY, 1918. PRICE THREEPENCE. | (*sic* [HO.]); inside front cover: advertisement for exhibit of watercolours by Capt. E. Handley-Read; inside back cover: advertisements for *Colour*; back cover: advertisement for official war publications.

Price: 3d. Number of copies: *c.* 1,200. Published in June 1918.

Note: Graves' contribution is 'The British Soldier' (pp. 3–6).

GEORGIAN | POETRY | 1918–1919 | [*three leaves*] | [*two leaves*] | [*leaf*] | THE POETRY BOOKSHOP | 35 Devonshire Street | Theobalds Road | W.C. | MCMXIX

Collation: [1]–[13]⁸, 104 leaves.

p. [i] GEORGIAN POETRY; p. [ii] publication notice; p. [iii] title-page; p. [iv] TO | THOMAS HARDY; p. [v] PREFATORY NOTE; p. [vi] blank; pp. [vii]–[x] CONTENTS; p. [1] section heading; p. [2] blank; pp. 3–191 text, with pp [9, 15, 27, 37, 47, 57, 71, 79, 91, 95, 105, 113, 123, 127, 139, 155, 163, 177] being section headings and pp. [8, 10, 14, 16, 28, 38, 48, 58, 72, 80, 92, 96, 106, 114, 124, 126, 128, 140, 156, 164, 178] being blank; p. [192] blank; pp. 193–196 BIBLIOGRAPHY; pp. [197–198] publisher's advertisements.

18·7 × 12·8 cm. Bulk: 1·4/1·9 cm. White laid paper watermarked with a crown and: Abbey Mills | Greenfield; top edges only trimmed and gilt; fore-edges unopened. White wove endpapers. Bound in goldis

yellow cloth; back blank; front stamped in gold: GEORGIAN POETRY |
1918–1919 | THE POETRY BOOKSHOP; spine stamped in gold: Georgian |
Poetry | 1918–1919 | [*inside a solid blue shield*:] P [*diamond*] B

Price: 6s. Number of copies undetermined. Published 15 November 1919.

Note: Graves' contribution is attributed in the index to *Country Sentiment*
(A5). But in fact that book was not published until March 1920. This is
therefore the first book publication of the following poems: 'A Ballad
of Nursery Rhyme' (pp. 81–83), 'A Frosty Night' (p. 84), 'True Johnny'
(pp. 85–86), 'The Cupboard' (p. 87), 'The Voice of Beauty Drowned'
(pp. 88–89) and 'Rocky Acres' (p. 90).
The title-page in some copies is a cancel.

B4   OXFORD POETRY 1921   1921

OXFORD POETRY | 1921 | EDITED BY | ALAN PORTER
RICHARD HUGHES | ROBERT GRAVES | OXFORD
BASIL BLACKWELL | MCMXXI

Collation: [A]⁴ B–E⁸, 36 leaves.
p. [i] OXFORD POETRY | 1921; p. [ii] publisher's advertisements; p. [iii]
title-page; p. [iv] printer's notice; p. [v] note; pp. [vi–vii] CONTENTS;
p. [viii] blank; pp. 1–64 text.

18·4 × 12·5 cm. Bulk: 0·6 cm. White wove paper; all edges trimmed.
Bound in dark blue paper wrapper; back blank; front has white paper
label at top left: [*rectangular single rule box enclosing all*:] Oxford | Poetry |
1921 | Oxford | Basil Blackwell

Price: 2s. Number of copies: 1,500. Published 21 November 1921.

Notes: Graves' contribution (pp. 21–29) is 'Cynics and Romantics',
'Unicorn and the White Doe', 'Sullen Moods', 'Henry and Mary', 'On
the Ridge' and 'A Lover Since Childhood'.
There was also a hardbound issue at 3s. 6d., slightly larger (19·0 × 12·7
cm.), the top edges unopened and the fore- and bottom edges untrimmed.

B5   A MISCELLANY OF POETRY   [1922]

A Miscellany of Poetry | 1920–1922 | *Edited by* | *William Kean*
Seymour | *London* | *JOHN G. WILSON* | 350 *Oxford Street,* |
W. 1

Collation: π^2 [*a*]^4 *b*–*o*^{8} *p*^{2}, 112 leaves.

2 pp., blank; p. [i] *A Miscellany of Poetry* | 1920–1922; p. [ii] publisher's advertisements; p. [iii] title-page; p. [iv] rights reservation notice and: Fifteen hundred copies of this book | were printed in December, 1922, | by the Westminster Press; pp. v–vi PREFATORY NOTE; pp. vii–x CONTENTS; pp. 1–203 text; p. [204] blank; p. [205] BIBLIOGRAPHY; pp. 206–210 bibliography; p. [211] printer's notice; p. [212] blank.

18·5 × 12·7 cm. Bulk: 1·3/1·7 cm. White laid paper; top edges trimmed; fore-edges unopened; bottom edges untrimmed. White wove endpapers. Bound in grey-blue boards with yellow cloth spine; white label on front: [*double-rule rectangular box enclosing all:*] *A Miscellany* | *of Poetry* | 1920–1922 | [*decorative swirl*] | *Edited by* | *William Kean Seymour;* back blank; spine stamped in gold: *A* | *Miscellany* | *of Poetry* | 1920–1922 | *William* | *Kean Seymour* | *J. G.* | *Wilson*

Price: 6s. Number of copies: 1,500. Published in December 1922.

Note: Graves' contribution is 'The Manifestation in the Temple' (pp. 67–68), 'The Avengers' (p. 69) and 'A False Report' (p. 70).

B6   CENOTAPH   [1923]

CENOTAPH | A BOOK OF REMEMBRANCE IN POETRY AND | PROSE FOR NOVEMBER THE ELEVENTH | COMPILED & EDITED BY | THOMAS MOULT | [*publisher's emblem*] | *The frontispiece from* | *a drawing by* | JOSEPH PIKE | JONATHAN CAPE | ELEVEN GOWER STREET LONDON

Collation: [A]^8 B–O^8, 112 leaves.

p. [1] CENOTAPH; p. [2] epigraphs from Euripides (3 ll.) and Shakespeare (7 ll.); [*plate, back blank, facing title-page, of cenotaph in Whitehall*]; p. [3] title-page; p. [4] publication, rights reservation and printer's notices; pp. 5–7 *Contents:* p. [8] blank; pp. 9–11 *Introductory Note;* p. [12] blank; p. [13] transcription of memorial to the unknown soldier; p. [14] blank; pp. 15–223 text; p. [224] blank.

17·9 × 10·3 cm. Bulk: 2·4/2·8 cm. Heavy white wove paper; top and fore-edges only trimmed. White wove endpapers. Bound in plum-brown cloth; back blind-stamped with publisher's emblem; front stamped in gold with a wreath; spine stamped in gold: [*broad decorative rule*] | CENOTAPH | JONATHAN CAPE | [*broad decorative rule*].

Price: 5s. Number of copies undisclosed. Published in November 1923.

Note: Graves' contribution is 'Peace' (p. 52); it is listed here as having appeared in *Fairies and Fusiliers* (A3); but it did not appear in that book

The | BEST POEMS | *of* 1923 | [*publisher's emblem*] | *Selected* |
by THOMAS MOULT & | *Decorated by* | PHILIP HAGREEN |
Jonathan Cape, Eleven Gower Street | LONDON

Collation: [A]⁸ B–I⁸, 72 leaves.
4 pp. as pastedown and free endpapers, second and third sides printed
with three designs of three leaves each, top and bottom, first and fourth
sides blank; p. [1] THE BEST POEMS OF 1923; p. [2] design of two nymphs
dancing; p. [3] title-page; p. [4] publication and printer's notices; p. [5]
To | THE MEMORY | *of* | MAURICE HEWLETT | *and* | HERBERT TRENCH; p. [6]
blank; pp. 7–12 *Contents*; pp. 13–14 *INTRODUCTION*; p. [15] THE
BEST POEMS OF 1923 | [*cut of fat baby in grass*]; p. [16] blank; pp. 17–135
text; pp. [136–137] blank; pp. [138–139] insides of free and pastedown
endpapers, as front; p. [140] blank and pasted down.

18·6 × 12·5 cm. Bulk: 1·1/1·5 cm. White laid paper; top edges only
trimmed; fore-edges unopened. Bound in royal blue cloth-textured
paper with 22 × 14 rows of circular gold designs overall; spine has white
label at top: *The* | BEST POEMS | *of* | 1923

Price: 6s. Number of copies undisclosed. Published in February 1924.

Note: Graves' contribution is 'Twin Souls' (pp. 68–69).

B8   GRACE AFTER MEAT   1924

GRACE AFTER MEAT | JOHN CROWE RANSOM |
With an Introduction by Robert Graves | Printed and published by
Leonard & Virginia | Woolf at the Hogarth Press 52 Tavistock |
Square London W.C. | 1924

Collation: [1]–[8]⁴, 32 leaves.
2 pp. blank, pasted to front cover; 2 pp. blank; p. [1] title-page; p. [2]
blank; p. [3] *To* | *ROBERT GRAVES*; p. [4] blank; p. [5] CONTENTS;
p. [6] blank; pp. 7–11 Introduction; p. [12] blank; pp. 13–57 text; p.
[58] blank; pp. [59–60] blank, pasted to back cover.

21·5 × 13·7 cm. Bulk: 0·5 cm. White wove paper; all edges trimmed.
Bound in gold-yellow boards with 24 × 16 designs of white and green
with red centres; back and spine blank; yellow label on front: [*rectangular
single-rule box enclosing all:*] GRACE | AFTER MEAT | JOHN CROWE RANSOM

Price: 4s. 6d. Number of copies: 400. Published on 30 October 1924.

Note: Graves' contribution is the introduction (pp. 7–11).

The | BEST POEMS | *of* 1924 | [*publisher's emblem* | Selected by |
THOMAS MOULT | & *decorated by* | PHILIP HAGREEN |
Jonathan Cape, Ltd., Thirty Bedford Square | LONDON

Collation: [A]⁸ B–I⁸, 72 leaves.
p. [i] THE BEST POEMS OF 1924 | [*interwoven J and C*]; p. [ii] cut of basket of
flowers; p. [iii] title-page; p. [iv] publication and printer's notices; p.
[v] *To* | THE MEMORY | *of* | ANATOLE FRANCE | *and* | JOSEPH CONRAD | *Poets*;
p. [vi] blank; pp. vii–xii *Contents*; pp. xiii–xv *INTRODUCTION*; p.
[xvi] blank; pp. 1–127 text; p. [128] blank.

18·8 × 12·6 cm. Bulk: 1·2/1·7 cm. White laid paper; top edges only
trimmed; fore-edges unopened. White laid endpapers; inner sides printed
with floral and vine design at each corner; first and fourth sides blank.
Bound in boards covered with rough green paper printed in dark blue
with design of splotches and spiderweb; spine has white paper label at
top: *The* | BEST | POEMS | *of* | 1924

Price: 6s. Number of copies undisclosed. Published in February 1925.

Note: Graves' contribution is 'Burrs and Brambles' (pp. 102–103).

B10 COLLINS' CHILDREN'S ANNUAL [1926]

[*first* 4 *ll. in red:*] COLLINS' | CHILDREN'S ANNUAL |
[*to right:*] TWELFTH YEAR | OF ISSUE | [14 *ll.* to left in
cream box, mainly rectangular:] [*in red:*] AUTHORS | ROB-
ERT | GRAVES | BARRY | PAIN | KATHARINE | TYNAN
| [*in red:*] ARTISTS | WINIFRED | ACKROYD | ANNE |
ANDERSON | DOROTHY | REES | [*in centre and to right of
cream box is red, yellow and blue picture of tot fishing for golliwog
doll*] | [*publisher's emblem*] | LONDON & GLASGOW | COL-
LINS' CLEAR-TYPE PRESS

Collation: π² [A]⁴ B–P⁶, 90 leaves.
p. [1] book-plate page; p. [2] coloured frontispiece; p. [3] title-page;
p. [4] cut of caravan; pp. 5–10 lists of contents; pp. 11–183 [184] text, with
pp. [15, 19, 22, 25, 31, 44, 49, 55, 62, 67, 71, 74, 79, 86, 91, 98, 103, 109,
110, 115, 122, 127, 134, 139, 146, 151, 158, 163, 170, 184] unnumbered
and pp. [27/28] and [37/38] being included in the pagination, though plates
(the first blank recto, the second verso) not included in the collation.

27·3 × 21·3 cm. Bulk: 3·5/4·3 cm. Heavy white wove paper; all edges
trimmed. White wove endpapers; inner sides printed with picture of a
boy and girl swinging in pink and grey; first and fourth sides blank.

Bound in cream boards; back blank; front has picture of boy and girl playing and in gold at top: COLLINS' | CHRISTMAS ANNUAL; light tan cloth spine printed in blue: *Collins'* | *Childrens'* | *Annual* | [*rectangular box with picture of two girls and a boy*] | COLLINS; *sic* [*Childrens'*]

Price: 5s. Number of copies unknown. Published in August 1926.

Note: Graves' contribution is 'The Story Teller' (p. 11) and 'The Penny Fiddle' (p. 12).

B11 MERCURY BOOK I 1926

. . THE . . | MERCURY BOOK | Being selections from Volumes I & II | of the *London Mercury,* made by | H. C. M. | LONDON: | WILLIAMS & NORGATE, LTD., | 14 HENRIETTA STREET, COVENT GARDEN, W.C.2 | [*rule*] | 1926

Collation: [A]⁸ B–U⁸, 160 leaves.
p. [i] THE MERCURY BOOK; p. [ii] blank; [*frontispiece, back blank*]; p. [iii] title-page; p. [iv] blank; p. [v] PREFATORY NOTE; pp. [vi–vii] EDITOR'S NOTE; pp. [viii–ix] CONTENTS; p. [x] blank; pp. 1–32 [33] 34–64 [65] 66–85 [86] 87–135 [136] 137–169 [170] 171–203 [204] 205–253 [254] 255–290 [291] 292–309; text; p. [310] blank.

21·3 × 16·8 cm. Bulk: 3·3/3·9 cm. Heavy white wove paper; top edges only trimmed. White wove endpapers. Bound in light orange cloth; back blind-stamped with publisher's emblem; front stamped in black: THE | MERCURY BOOK | [*head of Mercury*]; spine stamped in black: THE | MERCURY | BOOK | WILLIAMS & | NORGATE

Price: 7s. 6d. Number of copies unknown. Published in November 1926 in light orange dust-jacket printed in black.

Note: Graves' contribution is 'A Country Mood' (p. 205).

B12 THE BEST POEMS OF 1926 1927

The | BEST POEMS | *of* 1926 | [*publisher's emblem*] | *Selected by* | THOMAS MOULT | *& decorated by* | JOHN AUSTEN | LONDON | *Jonathan Cape, Thirty Bedford Square* | 1927

Collation: [A]⁸ B–H⁸ [I]⁴, 68 leaves.
p. [i] THE BEST POEMS OF 1926 | [*cut of cloud, moon, stars, dale with trees and house*]; p. [ii] [*cut of village in valley with two trees in foreground*]; p. [iii] title-page; p. [iv] printer's notice; p. [v] *To* | THE MEMORY | *of* | CHARLES

MONTAGU DOUGHTY | EVA GORE-BOOTH | ISRAEL ZANGWILL | *Poets* | [*design of rose with three large leaves*]; p. [vi] blank; pp. vii–xi *Contents:* p. [xii] stylized urban skyline; pp. xiii–xiv *INTRODUCTION*; pp. 1–120 text; p. [121] blank; p. [122] printer's notice.

18·6 × 12·6 cm. Bulk: 1·1/1·5 cm. White laid paper; top edges only trimmed; fore-edges unopened. White laid endpapers; inner sides printed with four masks, one at each corner, and piping child in centre; first and fourth sides blank. Bound in boards covered with pinkish brick-red paper printed with tree and flower modernistic design; white label at top of spine: *The* | BEST | POEMS | *of* | 1926

Price: 6s. Number of copies undisclosed. Published in January 1927.

Note: Graves' contribution is 'Four Children' (p. 1).

B13   LOVING MAD TOM   [1927]

LOVING MAD TOM | *Bedlamite Verses* | *Of the XVI and XVII Centuries* | With | FIVE ILLUSTRATIONS BY | NORMAN LINDSAY | [*double flower and leaf device*] | *Foreword By* ROBERT GRAVES | *The Texts Edited with Notes By* JACK LINDSAY | *Musical Transcriptions By* PETER WARLOCK | [*double flower and leaf device*] | THE FANFROLICO PRESS | FIVE BLOOMS-BURY SQUARE | LONDON

Collation: [1]⁶ [2]–[14]⁴, 58 leaves.
p. [i] blank; p. [ii] *This Edition is limited to* | 375 *copies, of which this is* | *No.* .... [*number written in over dots*]; p. [iii] LOVING MAD TOM; p. [iv] blank; p. [1] title-page; p. [2] blank; p. [3] illustration; p. [4] blank; pp. [5–6] CONTENTS; p. [7] THE REDISCOVERY OF | 'LOVING MAD TOM'; p. [8] blank; pp. 9–20 text; p. [21] THE POEMS; p. [22] blank; pp. 23–26 text; p. [27] illustration; pp. 28–30 text; p. [31] illustration; pp. 32–40 text; p. [41] illustration; pp. 42–54 text; p. [55] THE MUSICKS; p. [56] blank; pp. [57]–[60] music; p. [61] NOTES AND COMMENTARY; p. [62] blank; pp 63–110 text; p. [111] colophon; p. [112] blank.

28·2 × 22·0 cm. Bulk: 1·1/1·7 cm. White wove paper; top edges only trimmed and gilt. White wove endpapers. Both watermarked: 92 UNBLEACHED ARNOLD *and* MADE IN ENGLAND LINEN FIBRE. Bound quarter vellum; front and back in light olive-green laid paper; back blank; front stamped in gold with picture of Mad Tom derived from illustration on p. [41]; spine stamped in gold: LOVING | MAD | TOM

Price: 42s. Number of copies: 375. Published in December 1927.

Note: Graves' contribution is 'The Rediscovery of "Loving Mad Tom"' (pp. 9–20).

SCRUTINIES | By VARIOUS WRITERS | Collected by |
EDGELL RICKWORD | LONDON | WISHART & COM-
PANY | 1928

Collation: [1]⁸ 2–13⁸, 104 leaves.
p. [i] SCRUTINIES; p. [ii] blank; p. [iii] title-page; p. [iv] printer's and copyright notices; pp. v–vii FOREWORD; p. [viii] blank; p. ix CONTENTS; p.
[x] blank; pp. 1–196 [197] text, with pp. [15, 29, 41, 51, 73, 95, 109, 131,
145, 161, 181] being unnumbered section headings and pp. [14, 28, 94,
144, 180] being blank; p. [198] printer's notice.

19·0 × 13·2 cm. Bulk: 1·8/2·3 cm. White laid paper; top and fore-
edges trimmed; watermarked SAVORY Antique. White wove endpapers.
Bound in black cloth; front and back blank; spine stamped in gold:
[*broad rule*] | [*box in shape of squared-off shield, inside which 7 ll.:*] SCRUTINIES |
[*rule*] | *Critical Essays* | *by* | VARIOUS | WRITERS | [*dot*] | [*box inside which:*]
WISHART | [*broad rule*].

Price: 7s. 6d. Number of copies unknown. Published in March 1928.

Note: Graves' contribution is an essay on Kipling (pp. 74–93). Reprinted
A63.

B15 THE OXFORD BOOK OF CAROLS 1928

The | Oxford Book of | Carols | By | Percy Dearmer | R.
Vaughan Williams | Martin Shaw | Oxford University Press |
London: Humphrey Milford | 1928

Collation: [a]⁸ b/b2²/⁸ B/B2–Q/Q2²/⁶ R⁴, 142 leaves.
p. [i] The | Oxford Book of | Carols; p. [ii] blank; p. [iii] title-page; p.
[iv] edition and publisher's notices; pp. [v] vi–xxxiv PREFACE; pp. [xxxv]–
xxxvi ACKNOWLEDGEMENTS; pp. [1] 2–237 text; p. [238] blank; pp. [239]–
240 INDEX OF AUTHORS, SOURCES, &c.; pp. [241] 242–245 INDEX OF FIRST
LINES; pp. [246] 247–248 INDEX OF TITLES.

16·7 × 11·3 cm. Bulk: 1·7/2·1 cm. White wove paper; all edges trimmed. White wove endpapers. Bound in light cherry cloth; front and back
blind-stamped with design of five circles with bells and large cross;
spine stamped in gold: The | Oxford | Book of | Carols | Oxford

Price: 4s. 6d. Number of copies unknown. Published in April 1928.

Notes: Graves' contributions are No. 80 'Three Kings', translation of a
Flemish carol, and No. 84 'The Candle', translation of an Austrian carol.

The book exists in three editions: a complete music edition, a complete words edition and a cheap edition (words only, without notes). The complete words edition is described above; it precedes the others by some six months.

B16 THE ENORMOUS ROOM [1928]

THE | ENORMOUS ROOM | By | E. E. CUMMINGS | With an | Introduction | by | ROBERT GRAVES | [*publisher's emblem*] | JONATHAN CAPE 30 BEDFORD SQUARE | LONDON

Collation: [A]⁸ B–X⁸, 168 leaves.
p. [1] THE ENORMOUS ROOM; p. [2] blank; p. [3] title-page; p. [4] publication and printer's notices; p. 5 CONTENTS; p. [6] blank; pp. 7–15 INTRODUCTION; p. [16] blank; pp. 17–23 FOREWORD (1922); p. [24] blank; p. [25] THE ENORMOUS ROOM; p. [26] blank; pp. 27–332 text; pp. [333]–[336] blank.

20·2 × 12·9 cm. Bulk: 3·0/3·5 cm. White wove paper; top and fore-edges trimmed. White wove endpapers. Bound in dull plum cloth; front blank; back blind-stamped with publisher's emblem; spine stamped in gold: THE | ENORMOUS | ROOM | [*decorative leaf*] | E. E. CUMMINGS | JONATHAN CAPE

Price: 7s. 6d. Number of copies undisclosed. Published in July 1928.

Notes: Graves' contribution is the introduction (pp. 7–15).
This book was reprinted twice in 1928; in 1930 a Life and Letters Series impression was issued; the introduction has not appeared in American editions of this work.

B17 THE HOGARTH ESSAYS 1928

THE HOGARTH ESSAYS | [*publisher's emblem*] | DOUBLE-DAY, DORAN & COMPANY | INC. *GARDEN CITY,* *NEW YORK* 1928

Collation: [1]–[20]⁸ [21]⁴ [22]⁸, 172 leaves.
p. [i] THE HOGARTH ESSAYS; p. [ii] blank; p. [iii] title-page; p. [iv] right reservation, printer's and edition notices; pp. v–vi *Publisher's Note*; p. [vii] *Contents*; p. [viii] blank; p. [1] section heading; p. [2] blank; pp. 3–336 text, with pp. [31, 49, 67, 109, 133, 161, 195, 241, 277, 305] being unnumbered section headings and pp. [30, 48, 50, 110, 132, 134, 160, 162, 194, 196, 198, 240, 242, 278, 304, 306] being blank and pp. [32] and [68] being unnumbered with epigraphs.

20·4 × 13·8 cm. Bulk: 2·7/3·2 cm. White wove paper; top edges only trimmed. Cream wove endpapers; insides printed with watermark-like design in grey of waved chain and wire lines. Bound in cream boards with light gunmetal-blue cloth spine; back blank; front printed with basket of flowers in purple and green; spine has cream paper label: [*in purple:*] THE | [*in green:*] HOGARTH | [*in purple:*] ESSAYS

Price: $3.00. Number of copies unknown. Published 28 September 1928.

Note: Graves' contribution is 'The Future of the Art of Poetry' (pp. 163–193), a revision of *Another Future of Poetry* (A19).

B18 TO RETURN TO ALL THAT [1930]

TO RETURN TO ALL THAT | AN AUTOBIOGRAPHY | BY | ALFRED PERCEVAL GRAVES | LITT.D. DUBLIN, F.R.S.L. | [*publisher's emblem*] | London · Jonathan Cape · Toronto

Collation: [A]⁸ B–Y⁸, 176 leaves.

p. [1] TO RETURN TO ALL THAT; p. [2] blank; [plate, back blank]; p. [3] title-page; p. [4] publication, publisher's and printer's notices; p. 5 CONTENTS; p. [6] blank; p. 7 LIST OF ILLUSTRATIONS and acknowledgements; p. [8] blank; p. [9] TO RETURN TO ALL THAT; p. [10] blank; pp. 11–343 text; p. [344] blank; p. [345] BIBLIOGRAPHY; p. [346] blank; pp. 347–350 bibliography; pp. [351–352] blank.

20·1 × 13·4 cm. Bulk: 2·3/2·8 cm. White wove paper; top and fore-edges trimmed. White wove endpapers. Bound in maroon cloth; front blank; back blind-stamped with publisher's emblem; spine stamped in gold: TO RETURN | TO | ALL THAT | [*decorative floral divider*] | ALFRED | PERCEVAL | GRAVES | JONATHAN CAPE

Price: 7s. 6d. Number of copies undisclosed. Published in July 1930.

Note: Graves' contributions are 'The Hushu Bird' (p. 320), 'The Montrose Quagga' (pp. 320–21), 'Zachaeus Zerites' (p. 321) and the war letters printed in the *Spectator* in 1915 (C34).

B19 THE SECOND OMNIBUS BOOK [1930]

THE | SECOND | OMNIBUS BOOK | Containing three full-length Novels, | as well as Short Stories, Plays, | Parodies and Poems | by | J. B. PRIESTLEY | W. SOMERSET MAUGHAM | MAURICE BARING | ROBERT GRAVES | EDNA FERBER | J. C. SQUIRE | CHRISTOPHER BUSH |

and | AUGUSTUS CARP | Edited by | RUPERT HART-
DAVIS | [*publisher's emblem*] | LONDON | WILLIAM
HEINEMANN LIMITED

Collation: [A]⁶ B–T⁸ U⁴ W–Z¹⁶ AA–UU¹⁶, 538 leaves.

pp. [i–ii] blank; p. [iii] THE SECOND OMNIBUS BOOK; p. [iv] publisher's
advertisement; p. [v] title-page; p. [vi] reprinting, publication and printer's notices; p. [vii] EDITOR'S NOTE; p. [viii] blank; pp. [ix–x] CONTENTS;
pp. [xi–xii] half-title for Priestley contribution; pp. 1–292 [293] Priestley
text; pp. [294]–[296] blank; 2 pp., Maugham half-title; pp. 115–147
[148], 103–155 Maugham text; p. [156] blank; 2 pp., Baring half-title;
pp. 1–8, 49–59 [60], 149–155 [156] Baring text; pp. [1–2] Ferber half-title;
pp. 3–34 Ferber text; 2 pp., Squire half-title; pp. 77–82, 86–88, 100
Squire text; 2 pp., Carp half-title; pp. 1–274 Carp text; 2 pp., Graves
half-title; pp. 1–10 Graves text; 2 pp., Bush half-title; pp. 1–312 Bush
text.

18·7 × 12·5 cm. Bulk: 3·7/4·1 cm. White wove paper; all edges trimmed. White wove endpapers printed with map showing contributions
as locations; first and fourth sides blank. Bound in dark olive cloth; front
and back blank; spine stamped in gold: THE SECOND | OMNIBUS | BOOK |
[*star*] | [*two vertical parallel rules joined top and bottom*] | [*star*] | HEINEMANN

Price: 8s. 6d. Number of copies unknown. Published in August 1930.

Note: Graves' contribution consists of ten poems, six reprinted from
Poems 1914–1927, four new: 'To the Reader Over My Shoulder', 'The
Beast', 'The Terraced Valley' and 'Tail Piece: A Song to Make You and
Me Laugh'.

B20   THE YEAR'S POETRY   [1934]

THE YEAR'S POETRY | A REPRESENTATIVE SELEC-
TION | [*large solid dot*] | Compiled by | DENYS KILHAM
ROBERTS | GERALD GOULD · JOHN LEHMANN |
JOHN LANE THE BODLEY HEAD | LONDON

Collation: [a]⁸ b–i⁸, 72 leaves.

p. [1] THE YEAR'S POETRY; p. [2] blank; p. [3] title-page; p. [4] printer'
and publication notices; pp. 5–7 PREFACE; p. [8] blank; pp. 9–12 CONTENTS
p. [13] THE YEAR'S POETRY; p. [14] blank; pp. 15–144 text.

18·7 × 12·2 cm. Bulk: 1·1/1·5 cm. White wove paper; all edges trim
med; top edges stained red. White laid endpapers. Bound in tan cloth
front and back blank; spine stamped in red: THE | YEAR'S | POETRY | [*soli
dot*] | THE | BODLEY HEAD

Price: 6s. Number of copies unknown. Published on 4 December 1934.

Note: Contains 'Midsummer Duet, 1934' (pp. 139–144) by Laura Riding and Robert Graves; not reprinted by Graves, but in Riding's *Collected Poems*; the 'Second Voice' is Graves.

B21   LIVES OF THE ROMAN EMPRESSES   1935

LIVES OF THE | ROMAN EMPRESSES | THE HISTORY OF THE LIVES AND SECRET | INTRIGUES OF THE WIVES, SISTERS AND | MOTHERS OF THE CAESARS | By | JACQUES BOERGAS DE SERVIEZ | With An Introduction by | ROBERT GRAVES | *Author of 'I, Claudius', 'Claudius the God', etc.* | *Illustrated* | [*publisher's emblem*] | WM. H. WISE & CO. | 1935   [BOERGAS]

Collation: [1]–[27]¹⁶, 432 leaves.

2 pp., uncounted (recto: LIVES OF THE | ROMAN EMPRESSES; verso: blank); [*frontispiece, back blank, tipped to p.* (i)]; p. [i] title-page; p. [ii] copyright and printing notices; pp. iii–iv CONTENTS; p. vi LIST OF ILLUSTRATIONS; pp. vii–xiv INTRODUCTION TO THE | *LIVES OF THE ROMAN EMPRESSES* | By ROBERT GRAVES; pp. xv–xvi AUTHOR'S PREFACE; pp. xvii–xxiii historical note and chronological table; p. [xxiv] blank; p. [1] LIVES OF THE | ROMAN EMPRESSES; p. [2] blank; pp. 3–812 text; pp. 813–834 INDEX; pp. [835]–[838] blank; illustrations face pp. 6, 38, 166, 198, 294, 326, 486, 518, 678, 710.

21·1 × 13·9 cm. Bulk: 4·7/5·5 cm. White wove paper; all edges trimmed; top edges stained purple. White wove endpapers. Bound in purple cloth; back blank; front blind-stamped with fasci and a vertical band of dancing nymphs: spine has blind-stamping of fasci, circles, rules and solid rectangular boxes and is printed in silver: LIVES | of the | ROMAN | EMPRESSES | DE SERVIEZ | WISE & CO.

Price: $2.90. Number of copies unknown. Published in August 1935.

Note: Graves' contribution is the introduction (pp. vii–xiv).

322   EPILOGUE I   1935

EPILOGUE | A Critical Summary | *Volume I – Autumn* 1935 | [*swelled rule*] | *Editor:* | Laura Riding | *Assistant-Editor:* | Robert Graves | [*swelled rule*] | Contributors to this Issue: | [ten names in two columns:] MADELEINE VARA LAURA RIDING | JAMES REEVES   ROBERT GRAVES | THOMAS MATHEWS   HONOR WYATT | JOHN CULLEN JOHN

ALDRIDGE | LEN LYE WARD HUTCHINSON | [*swelled rule*] | THE SEIZIN PRESS · DEYA MAJORCA | AND | CONSTABLE & CO LTD | LONDON

Collation: [A]⁸ B–Q⁸, 128 leaves.

p. [i] EPILOGUE; p. [ii] blank; p. [iii] title-page; p. [iv] printer's notice; p. v CONTENTS; p. [vi] epigraph of 3 ll.; pp. 1–218 text; [*gathering of 4 leaves of coated paper, all versos blank*]; pp. 219–236 text; [*plate of photograph tipped in, verso blank*]; pp. 237–245 text; p. [246] Seizin Press advertisement; pp. [247–248] blank; pp. [249–250] blank as pastedown endpaper.

21·6 × 13·6 cm. Bulk: 1·7/2·1 cm. White laid paper; all edges trimmed. White laid front endpaper. Bound in buff boards printed in black; back blank; front: [at left:] Twice a Year [at right:] Volume I | EPILOGUE | A CRITICAL SUMMARY | [*cut of stage with temple prop, scroll, clouds*] | AUTUMN 1935 | Laura Riding [*turned rule*] Editor | Robert Graves [*turned rule*] Associate Editor | THE SEIZIN PRESS · DEYA MAJORCA | AND | CONSTABLE & CO. LTD. | LONDON | *Seven Shillings and Sixpence net*; spine: EPILOGUE | A | CRITICAL | SUMMARY | I | AUTUMN | 1935

Price: 7s. 6d. Number of copies unknown. Published in November 1935.

Note: Graves' contributions are 'A Poem Sequence: To the Sovereign Muse' ('The Challenge', 'Fiend, Dragon, Mermaid', 'To the Sovereign Muse', 'Green Loving', 'Like Snow') (pp. 87–92), 'Germany' (signed M[adeleine] V[ara], a house pseudonym, and reprinted as 'Nietzsche') (pp. 113–125), 'Coleridge and Wordsworth, Keats and Shelley' (pp. 157–174) and 'A Note on the Pastoral' (reprinted as 'The Pastoral') (pp. 200–207).

B23 THE FABER BOOK OF MODERN VERSE [1936]

THE FABER BOOK | OF MODERN VERSE | *edited by* MICHAEL | ROBERTS | *London* | FABER AND FABER *24 Russell Square*

Collation: π⁸ A–Y⁸, 184 leaves.

pp. [i–ii] blank; p. [iii] THE FABER BOOK | OF MODERN VERSE; p. [iv] blank p. [v] title-page; p. [vi] publication, publisher's, printer's and right notices; p. vii EDITOR'S NOTE; p. [viii] blank; pp. ix–xvi CONTENTS; pp 1–35 INTRODUCTION; p. [36] blank; p. [37] POETRY | [*rule*]; p. [38] blank pp. 39–342 text; p. [343] ACKNOWLEDGEMENTS | [*rule*] ; p. [344] blank pp. 345–350 ACKNOWLEDGMENTS; pp. 351–352 INDEX OF AUTHORS.

18·5 × 11·8 cm. Bulk: 2·0/2·5 cm. White wove paper; all edges trimmed; top edges stained rust-brown. White wove endpapers. Bound bright blue cloth; front and back blank; spine stamped in gold: THE | FABER | BOOK | OF | MODERN | VERSE | *edited by* | MICHAEL | ROBERTS | FABER AND | FABER

Price: 7s. 6d. Number of copies: 3,080. Published in February 1936.

Note: Contains thirteen poems by Graves (pp. 224–233) of which 'To Bring the Dead to Life' is first published here.

B24   EPILOGUE II   1936

EPILOGUE | A Critical Summary | *Volume II – Summer* 1936 | [*swelled rule*] | *Editor:* | Laura Riding | *Associate Editor:* | Robert Graves | [*swelled rule*] | Contributors to this Issue: | [ten names in two columns:] ALAN HODGE   HONOR WYATT | JAMES REEVES   KENNETH ALLOTT | MADELEINE VARA LAURA RIDING | WARD HUTCHINSON ROBERT GRAVES | KATHERINE BURDEKIN   GORDON GLOVER | [*swelled rule*] | THE SEIZIN PRESS · DEYA MAJORCA | AND | CONSTABLE & CO LTD | LONDON

Collation: [A]⁸ B–Q⁸ R¹, 129 leaves.

p. [i] EPILOGUE; p. [ii] publisher's advertisements; p. [iii] title-page; p. [iv] publisher's, publication and printer's notices; p. v CONTENTS; p. [vi] epigraph of 3 ll.; pp. 1–251 text; p. [252] text and printer's notice.

21·6 × 13·6 cm. Bulk: 1·8/2·2 cm. White laid paper; all edges trimmed. White laid endpapers. Bound in light green boards; back blank; front printed in black: [at left:] Twice a Year [ar right:] Volume II | EPILOGUE | A CRITICAL SUMMARY | [*cut of stage with temple prop, scroll, clouds*] | SUMMER 1936 | Laura Riding [*turned rule*] Editor | Robert Graves [*turned rule*] Associate Editor | THE SEIZIN PRESS . DEYA MAJORCA | AND | CONSTABLE & CO. LTD. | LONDON | *Seven Shillings and Sixpence net;* spine printed in black: EPILOGUE | A | CRITICAL | SUMMARY | II | SUMMER | 1936

Price: 7s. 6d. Number of copies unknown. Published in July 1936.

Note: Graves' contributions are 'Official and Unofficial Literature' (pp. 57–61), 'Stealing' (reprinted as 'Theft') (pp. 65–75), a note on a homiletic study 'Enthusiasm' (p. 89), 'The Exercise of English' (pp. 127–134), 'To Walk on Hills,' 'Never Such Love', 'The Climate of Thought' (pp. 145–147), 'Lucretius and Jeans' (pp. 208–220) and 'Neo-Georgian Eternity' (pp. 231–242).

B25   EPILOGUE III   1937

EPILOGUE | A Critical Summary | *Volume III – Spring* 1937 | swelled rule] | *Editor:* | Laura Riding | *Associate Editor:* | Robert

Graves | [*swelled rule*] | Contributors to this Issue: | [sixteen names in two columns:] MADELEINE VARA   ALAN HODGE | NORMAN CAMERON   HONOR WYATT | SALLY GRAVES   KARL GOLDSCHMIDT | BASIL TAYLOR ROBIN HALE | LUCIE BROWN   JOHN ALDRIDGE | WILLIAM ARCHER   HARRY KEMP | LAURA RIDING ROBERT GRAVES | WARD HUTCHINSON   THOMAS MATTHEWS | [centred:] JAMES REEVES | [*swelled rule*] | THE SEIZIN PRESS · DEYA MAJORCA | AND | CON-STABLE & CO LTD | LONDON

Collation: [A]⁸ B–L⁸ M–N¹⁰ O–Q⁸, 132 leaves.

p. [i] EPILOGUE; p. [ii] IN APOLOGY; p. [iii] title-page; p. [iv] publisher's, publication and printer's notices; p. v CONTENTS; p. [vi] epigraph in 3 ll.; pp. 1–190 text; [*gathering of 4 leaves of coated paper, versos blank*]; pp. 191–257 text; p. [258] text and printer's notice.

21·6 × 13·6 cm. Bulk: 2·0/2·4 cm. White laid paper; all edges trimmed. White laid endpapers. Bound in light red boards; back blank; front printed in black: [at left:] Twice a Year [at right:] Volume III | EPILOGUE | A CRITICAL SUMMARY | [*cut of stage with temple prop, scroll, clouds*] | SPRING 1937 | Laura Riding [*turned rule*] Editor | Robert Graves [*turned rule*] Associate Editor | THE SEIZIN PRESS . DEYA MAJORCA | AND | CON-STABLE & CO. LTD. | LONDON | *Seven Shillings and Sixpence net*; spine printed in black: EPILOGUE | A | CRITICAL | SUMMARY | III | SPRING | 1937

Price: 7s. 6d. Number of copies unknown. Published in April 1937.

Note: Graves' contributions are 'Politics and Poetry' (with Harry Kemp and Laura Riding, reprinted as 'Poetry and Politics') (pp. 6–53), 'The Theme of Fame' (with Laura Riding, as Madeleine Vara) (pp. 75–99), 'From a Private Correspondence on Reality' (with Laura Riding) (pp. 107–130), 'At the Marble Table', 'Parent to Children', 'The Exile', 'A Jealous Man', 'End of Play', 'The Halfpenny' (pp. 164–169), 'Drama' (with Alan Hodge and Laura Riding) (reprinted as 'Poetic Drama') and 'Book-Advertising' (pp. 239–246).

B26   T. E. LAWRENCE BY HIS FRIENDS   [1937]

T. E. LAWRENCE | BY HIS FRIENDS | EDITED BY | A. W. LAWRENCE | [*publisher's emblem*] | JONATHAN CAPE | THIRTY BEDFORD SQUARE | LONDON

Collation: [A]⁸ B–Z⁸ AA–NN⁸ OO/OO*²/⁸, 298 leaves.

p. [1] T. E. LAWRENCE BY HIS FRIENDS; p. [2] blank; [frontispiece, back blank]; p. [3] title-page; p. [4] publication, publisher's, printer's, paper-maker's and binder's notices; pp. 5–6 PREFACE; pp. 7–10 CONTENTS; p. 11 ILLUSTRATIONS; p. [12] blank; p. 13 DATES IN THE LIFE OF T. E. LAWRENCE

p. [14] blank; pp. [15]–[596] text, with pp. [15, 23, 39, 71, 109, 129, 151, 175, 203, 217, 239, 309, 323, 337, 359, 381, 393, 399, 421, 457, 511, 531, 563, 567, 583] unnumbered and pp. [16, 24, 38, 40, 70, 110, 128, 130, 152, 174, 176, 204, 216, 218, 238, 240, 308, 310, 322, 324, 338, 358, 360, 380, 382, 394, 400, 420, 422, 456, 458, 512, 530, 532, 564, 568, 582, 584, 596] blank; illustrations, all backs blank, face pp. 48, 154, 190, 234, 266, 376, 572.

21·6 × 14·5 cm. Bulk: 3·3/4·0 cm. White wove paper; top and fore-edges trimmed; top edges stained maroon. White wove endpapers. Bound in maroon cloth; front and back blank; spine stamped in gold: T. E. LAWRENCE | BY | HIS FRIENDS | [*publisher's emblem*]

Price: 15s. Number of copies undisclosed. Published 21 May 1937.

Note: Graves' contribution (pp. 325–331) is an essay largely adapted from *Lawrence and the Arabs* (A26). The abridged edition of B23 published by Cape in 1954 also contains the essay.

B27   THE MODERN POET   [1938]

The Modern Poet | an Anthology chosen and edited | by | GWENDOLEN MURPHY | London: Sidgwick & Jackson, Ltd. | 44 Museum Street, W. C. 1

Collation: π^{10} 1–13^8, 114 leaves.
p. [i] The Modern Poet; p. [ii] blank; p. [iii] title-page; p. [iv] publication and printer's notice; p. v PREFACE; p. [vi] blank; pp. vii–x INDEX OF AUTHORS; pp. xi–xiv ACKNOWLEDGEMENTS; pp. xv–xx THE MODERN POET; pp. [1] 2–143 text; p. [144] blank; pp. 145–203 COMMENTARY; p. [204] blank; pp. 205–208 INDEX OF FIRST LINES.

18·4 × 12·3 cm. Bulk: 1·4/1·9 cm. White wove paper; all edges trimmed. White wove endpapers. Bound in medium blue cloth; back blank; front blind-stamped with heavy-rule rectangular box, inside light-rule rectangular box, inside which, stamped in white: THE | MODERN POET | an Anthology | Gwendolen Murphy; spine stamped in white: [*heavy rule*] | [*light rule*] | THE | MODERN | POET | [*four dots*] | Gwendolen | Murphy Sidgwick | & Jackson | [*light rule*] | [*heavy rule*]

Price: 3s. 6d. Number of copies: 30,000 (in many printings). Published 25 May 1938.

Note: Graves' contribution (pp. 78–84) includes the first appearance of 'The Wretch' (p. 81), later 'The Laureate'; there are also notes on 'The Wretch' (pp. 182–83).

THE WORLD | AND OURSELVES | Laura Riding | [*epi-graph of 9 ll.*] | CHATTO & WINDUS | LONDON

Collation: [A]⁶ B–Z⁸ AA–KK⁸ LL/LL★²ᐟ⁸, 272 leaves.
p. [i] THE WORLD AND OURSELVES; p. [ii] note; p. [iii] title-page; p. [iv] publisher's, printing and rights reservation notices; p. v–viii *Contents;* pp. ix–xi *Foreword;* p. [xii] blank; pp. [1]–529 text, with pp. [1, 45, 131, 221, 369] being section headings and pp. [2, 46, 130, 132, 222, 368, 370] being blank; p. [530] blank; p. [531] printer's notice; p. [532] blank.

21·8 × 13·7 cm. Bulk: 3·8/4·4 cm. White laid paper; top and fore-edges trimmed; top edges stained maroon. White wove endpapers. Bound in maroon cloth; front and back blank; spine stamped in gold: THE | WORLD AND | OURSELVES | [*swirl*] | Laura Riding | CHATTO | AND WINDUS

Price: 15s. Number of copies undetermined. Published in November 1938.

Note: Graves' contribution is a letter (pp. 120–126).

B29   THE LEFT HERESY IN LITERATURE   [1939]
AND LIFE

THE LEFT HERESY IN | LITERATURE AND LIFE | BY | HARRY KEMP, LAURA RIDING | AND OTHERS | [*publisher's emblem*] | METHUEN PUBLISHERS LONDON | ESSEX STREET STRAND W.C.2

Collation: π⁴ [1]⁸ 2–17⁸, 140 leaves.
p. [i] THE LEFT HERESY IN | LITERATURE AND LIFE; p. [ii] blank; p. [iii] title-page; p. [iv] publication and printing notices; p. v FOREWORD; p. [vi] blank; pp. vii–viii CONTENTS; p. [1] section heading; p. [2] blank; pp. 3–270 text, with pp. [63, 121, 177, 213, 255] being section headings, pp. [65, 257] being unnumbered and pp. [64, 122, 178, 214, 256] being blank; p. [271] blank; p. [272] printer's notice.

18·5 × 12·0 cm. Bulk: 2·3/2·8 cm. White wove paper; all edges trimmed. White wove endpapers. Bound in dull orange cloth; front and back blank; spine stamped in red: *THE LEFT* | *HERESY* | *In Literature* | *and Life* | *HARRY KEMP,* | *LAURA RIDING* | *and others* | *METHUEN*

Price: 7s. 6d. Number of copies undetermined. Published in May 1939 in white dust-jacket printed in black and red.

Note: Sections V and VI of this book are a revised reprint of 'Politics and Poetry' from *Epilogue* III (B25).

WORK IN HAND | ALAN HODGE | NORMAN CAM-
ERON | ROBERT GRAVES | *The New Hogarth Library* |
Vol. VI | THE HOGARTH PRESS | 37 MECKLENBURGH
SQUARE | LONDON, W.C.1

Collation: [A]⁸ B–D⁸, 32 leaves.

p. [1] ALAN HODGE, NORMAN CAMERON, ROBERT | GRAVES: WORK IN HAND;
p. [2] list of books by three authors, publication and distribution notices;
p. [3] title-page; p. [4] AUTHORS' NOTE and printer's notice; p. 5 contents
page for Hodge; p. [6] blank; pp. 7–25 text of Hodge; p. [26] blank; p.
27 contents page for Cameron; p. [28] blank; pp. 29–41 text of Cameron;
p. [42] blank; p. 43 contents page for Graves; p. [44] blank; pp. 45–64
text of Graves.

18·1 × 11·9 cm. Bulk: 0·5/0·8 cm. White wove paper; all edges trimmed. White wove endpapers. Bound in seagreen cloth; front and back
blank; spine printed in red, bottom to top: HODGE, CAMERON, GRAVES
[*star*] Work in Hand

Price: 2s. 6d. Number of copies undetermined. Published in March 1942 in
sand-orange dust-jacket printed in blue-green.

Note: The Graves contents are: A Love Story – Dawn Bombardment –
The Worms of History – The Beast – A Withering Herb – The Shot –
Dream of a Climber – The Thieves – Lollocks – To Sleep – Despite and
Still – The Suicide in the Copse – Frightened Men – A Stranger at the
Party – The Oath – Language of the Seasons – Mid-Winter Waking –
The Rock at the Corner.

B31 LONDON CALLING 1942

[flush left:] LONDON | [flush right:] CALLING | EDITED BY |
Storm Jameson | [*publisher's emblem*] | HARPER & BRO-
THERS · PUBLISHERS | New York and London | 1942

Collation: [1]–[21]⁸, 168 leaves.

p. [i] *London Calling*; p. [ii] title and list of authors; p. [iii] title-page;
p. [iv] copyright, printing, rights reservation and edition notices; pp.
v–vi *Contents*; p. [vii] *London Calling*; p. [viii] blank; pp. 1–308 text;
pp. 309–322 biographical notes; p. [323] designer's, manufacturer's and
publisher's notices; pp. [324]–[328] blank.

20·6 × 13·8 cm. Bulk: 2·7/3·2 cm. White wove paper; top edges only
trimmed. White wove endpapers. Bound in chestnut cloth; back blank;
front blind-stamped at lower right with publisher's emblem; spine

stamped in gold, printed in grey: [*solid grey rectangular box, inside which five lines:*] | [*rectangular gold single-rule box enclosing solid chestnut box, inside which two lines:*] | London | Calling | [*2 ll. in gold:*] Edited by | STORM JAMESON | [*in grey:*] HARPER

Price: $2.50. Number of copies: 2,000. Published on 13 November 1942 in white dust-jacket printed in green, tan and black.

Note: Graves' contribution (pp. 177–198) is *Horses: A Play Chiefly for Children.*

B32   AN OLD SAYING   1945

AN OLD SAYING | *BY* | ALGERNON CHARLES SWIN-
BURNE | [*decorative swirl*] | *With a Foreword by* | ROBERT
GRAVES | [*decorative swirl*] | JOHN S. MAYFIELD | 1945

Collation: 6 leaves, stapled twice at centre.
pp. [1–2] blank; p. [3] title-page; p. [4] copyright and printer's notices;
p. [5] NOTE; p. [6] blank; pp. [7–8] FOREWORD; p. [9] AN OLD SAYING |
[*decorative swirl*]; p. [10] blank; p. [11] text of poem; p. [12] blank.

19·7 × 11·7 cm. Bulk: 0·1 cm. White laid paper; all edges trimmed.
Bound in cream laid wrappers; back blank; front: AN OLD SAYING | *BY* |
ALGERNON CHARLES SWINBURNE

Not for sale. Number of copies: 35. Published in late summer 1945.

Notes: Graves' contribution is the foreword, pp. [7–8]; reprinted A63.
According to John S. Mayfield, in his note to the 1947 edition of this
same work, the true first edition is a mimeographed one, done in spring
1945 on Saipan for interim copyright purposes only; but I have not seen
that edition.

B33   HA! HA! AMONG THE TRUMPETS   [1945]

HA! HA! AMONG THE | TRUMPETS | *Poems in Transit* |
by | ALUN LEWIS | *Foreword by* | ROBERT GRAVES |
London | *George Allen & Unwin Ltd*

Collation: [1]–[5]⁸, 40 leaves.
2 pp., blank; p. [1] HA! HA! AMONG THE TRUMPETS | *Poems in Transit*
p. [2] publisher's advertisements; [*frontispiece, back blank*]; p. [3] title-page
p. [4] publication and rights notices, epigraph (3 ll.), edition notice (Edi-
tion limited to 50 copies of which | this is No. [*number written in*]), wa
economy and printer's notices; pp. [5–6] Contents; pp. [7]–[12] Foreword
pp. 13–75 text; p. [76] publisher's notice.

18·4 × 12·4 cm. Bulk: 0·7/1·0 cm. Heavy white wove paper; top edges trimmed and gilt; fore-edge trimmed; watermarked with a shell with a lion and: HANDMADE. Bound in dark blue cloth; front and back blank; spine stamped in gold, bottom to top: Ha! Ha! *among the Trumpets* ALUN LEWIS; at bottom of spine, upright: G | A | & | U; the book is fitted with a dark blue ribbon bookmark.

Price: 10s. 6d. Number of copies: 50. Published 19 July 1945.

Note: Graves' contribution is the foreword (pp. [7]–[12]). An ordinary edition of this book (5,000 copies) was published at the same time, price 5s. 6d.

B34   BRITISH THOUGHT 1947   1947

[*whole enclosed within single-rule rectangular box:*] BRITISH | THOUGHT | 1947 | *With an introduction by* IVOR BROWN | [*publisher's emblem*] | *THE GRESHAM PRESS* | PUBLISHERS | NEW YORK · 1947

Collation: [1]–[14]¹⁶ [15]⁸, 232 leaves.

p. [i] BRITISH THOUGHT 1947; p. [ii] blank; p. [iii] title-page; p. [iv] copyright, manufacturing and rights reservation notices; pp. v–vii *TABLE OF CONTENTS*; p. [viii] blank; pp. 9–17 INTRODUCTION; pp. 18–22 *PUBLISHER'S NOTE*; p. [23] BRITISH THOUGHT 1947; p. [24] blank; pp. 25–456 text; pp. 457–461 *NOTES ON AUTHORS*; pp. [462]–[464] blank.

21·6 × 15·2 cm. Bulk: 2·9/3·7 cm. White wove paper; all edges trimmed. White wove endpapers. Bound in scarlet cloth; front and back blank; spine stamped in silver: [*broad rule*] | [*light rule*] | BRITISH | THOUGHT | 1947 | [*swelled rule*] | INTRODUCTION | BY | IVOR BROWN | THE | GRESHAM | PRESS | [*light rule*] | [*broad rule*].

Price: $3.75. Number of copies unknown. Published summer 1947.

Note: Graves' contribution is 'It Was a Stable World' (pp. 226–235).

B35   EXPOSICIÓN GRUPO DE LOS SIETE   1948

EXPOSICIÓN | [*2 ll. in red:*] GRUPO DE LOS | SIETE | [*seven circles with a top hat in each*] | GALERIAS QUÌNT | 12 a 25 de Junio | Palma, 1948

Collation: 4 leaves, stapled twice at centre.

pp. 1–3 PRESENTACIÓN Y JUSTIFICACIÓN | DEL GRUPO DE LOS SIETE; p. 4 PRISMA; pp. 5–7 LOS SIETE DEL GRUPO EN | EL « GRUPO DE LOS SIETE »; p. [8] blank.

21·3 × 15·5 cm. Bulk: 0·1 cm. White wove paper; all edges trimmed. Bound in green wrapper transcribed as title-page; inside front cover blank; inside back cover: CATÁLOGO; outside back cover: printer's notice.

Price and number of copies: undetermined. Published 12 June 1948.

Note: Graves' contribution (pp. 1–3) is the presentation.

B36 SATURDAY BOOK 8 [1948]

[flush left:] *The Saturday* | [left of centre:] *Book* | [*7 ll. in mirror on stand:*] *being* | *the eighth annual* | *issue of this celebrated* | *cabinet of curiosities* | *and looking-glass of* | *past and* | *present* | [remainder flush left:] *edited by* | LEONARD RUSSELL | *the book designed by* | *LAURENCE SCARFE* | HUTCHINSON *are the publishers*

Collation: [A]⁸ [B]⁴ [C]⁴ χ⁸ D–M⁸ [N]⁴ O⁸ [P]⁴ Q–T⁸, 144 leaves.
p. [1] *The Saturday Book 8th Year*; p. [2] calligraphic portrait; p. [3] title-page; p. [4] epigraph, table of contents, publication, printer's and engraver's notices; pp. 5–128 text, with pp. [15–48] and [97–112] being unnumbered; [foldout four-colour plate wrapped around H]; pp. 129–288 text, with pp. [217–225, 233] being unnumbered.

22·9 × 14·9 cm. Bulk: 1·7/2·2 cm. White wove paper; all edges trimmed; signatures [A, B, C, χ, G, N, P] on coated paper. Bound in bright orange cloth; front and back blank; spine stamped in gold: edited | by | Leonard | Russell | [down spine:] The Saturday Book—8 | [upright:] HUTCHINSON

Price: 21s. Number of copies: 20,000. Published in October 1948.

Note: Graves' contribution is 'The Place for a Holiday' (pp. 90–94), about Deyá.

B37 ROBERT ROSS [1952]

Robert Ross | Friend of Friends | Letters to Robert Ross, Art Critic | and Writer, together with extracts | from his published articles | *Edited by* | MARGERY ROSS | [*publisher's emblem*] | JONATHAN CAPE | THIRTY BEDFORD SQUARE | LONDON

Collation: [A]⁸ B–Z⁸, 184 leaves.
p. [1] ROBERT ROSS: FRIEND OF FRIENDS; p. [2] blank; [*frontispiece, back blank*]; p. [3] title-page; p. [4] publication, Dewey decimal, printer's and

binder's notices; p. [5] ILLUSTRATIONS; p. [6] *To | William, and the Friends of | Robert Ross*; p. [7] twelve-line poem, 'To Robert Ross' by Siegfried Sassoon; p. [8] blank; pp. 9–14 INTRODUCTION; pp. 15–16 ACKNOWLEDG-MENTS; p. [17] ROBERT ROSS: FRIEND OF FRIENDS; p. [18] blank; pp. 19–345 text; pp. 346–360 appendixes; pp. 361–367 INDEX; p. [368] blank; illustrations face pp. 20, 22, 24/25, 35, 47, 80, 125, 180, 224, 276, 284.

21·8 × 14·0 cm. Bulk: 2·3/2·8 cm. White wove paper; top and fore-edges trimmed; top edges stained green. White wove endpapers. Bound in sea-green cloth; front and back blank; spine stamped in gold: ROBERT | ROSS | ★ | FRIEND | OF | FRIENDS | [*curled decorative rule*] | MARGERY | ROSS | [*publisher's emblem*]

Price: 30s. Number of copies undisclosed. Published in March 1952 in grey dust-jacket printed in red and black.

Note: Graves' contribution is letters *passim.*

B38   EDDIE MARSH   [1953]

Eddie Marsh | SKETCHES FOR A COMPOSITE LITERARY PORTRAIT OF | SIR EDWARD MARSH, K.C.V.O., C.B., C.M.G. | *Compiled by* | CHRISTOPHER HASSALL | *and* | DENIS MATHEWS | *Published by* LUND HUMPHRIES *for the* | CONTEMPORARY ART SOCIETY | *The Tate Gallery, London SW 1*

Collation: [1]–[2]⁸ [3]¹⁰, 26 leaves.
p. [1] EDDIE MARSH; p. [2] facsimile of MS; p. [3] title-page; p. [4] publication and printer's notices; p. 5 CONTENTS; p. 6 ILLUSTRATIONS; pp. 7–8 NOTE; p. 9 FOREWORD; pp. 10–11 Introduction; p. [12] blank; pp. 13–51 text; p. [52] blank; plates as follows: one leaf, printed both sides, tipped between pp. 16/17; two leaves, printed four sides, sewn between pp. 24/25; one leaf, printed both sides, tipped between pp. 32/33; two leaves, printed four sides, sewn between pp. 42/43.

22·8 × 15·1 cm. Bulk: 0·6 cm. Cream wove paper watermarked: BASINGWERK PARCHMENT; all edges trimmed. Issued in white paper covers with white wrapper printed in black and light yellow-green; front printed with a photo of Marsh, below which in a green band: [*in white:*] Eddie Marsh | SKETCHES FOR A COMPOSITE LITERARY PORTRAIT OF | SIR EDWARD MARSH, K.C.V.O., C.B., C.M.G. | [*bar*] | *Lund Humphries*; back blank; spine reads, top to bottom: [*in white to dot:*] EDDIE MARSH · *Sketches for a Composite Literary Portrait*

Price: 7s. 6d. Number of copies: 2,500. Published 5 May 1953.

Note: Graves' contribution is a biographical memoir (pp. 25–26).

New Poems | [*swelled rule, at centre of which is a fancy circular device, inside which*:] 1953 | *A P.E.N. Anthology* | *Edited by* | ROBERT CONQUEST | MICHAEL HAMBURGER | HOWARD SERGEANT | *Introduction by* | C. V. WEDG-WOOD | PRESIDENT OF THE P.E.N. | [*publisher's emblem*] | London | MICHAEL JOSEPH

Collation: [A]⁸ B–K⁸ L⁶, 86 leaves.

p. [1] NEW POEMS | [*fancy circular device, inside which*:] 1953; p. [2] publisher's advertisement; p. [3] title-page; p. [4] publisher's and printer's notices; pp. [5]–[12] *Contents*; pp. [13] 14–16 *Introduction*; pp. [17]–18 *Foreword*; pp. [19] section heading; p. [20] blank; pp. 21–160 text, with pp. [41, 59, 79, 103, 121, 141] being section headings and pp. [40, 42, 60, 80, 104, 122, 140, 142] being blank; pp. 161–172 *The Contributors*.

20·2 × 13·0 cm. Bulk: 1·0/1·4 cm. White wove paper; all edges trimmed. White wove endpapers. Bound in white boards with red and black designs (11 × 6); black cloth spine stamped in silver: *New* | *Poems* | [*swelled decorative rule*] | *1953* | [*swelled decorative rule*] | *a* | *P. E. N.* | *Anthology* | [*publisher's emblem*] | MICHAEL | JOSEPH

Price: 10s. 6d. Number of copies: 3,000. Published 18 May 1953.

Note: Graves' contributions are 'Dialogue on the Headland' (pp. 25–26), 'The Straw' (p. 26), 'The Foreboding' (p. 27) and 'The Survivor' (pp. 27–28).

WILLIAM SARGANT | ★ | *Battle for the Mind* | A PHYSIO-LOGY OF CONVERSION | AND BRAIN-WASHING | [*publisher's emblem*] | HEINEMANN | MELBOURNE LONDON TORONTO

Collation: [A]⁸ B–R⁸, 136 leaves.

p. [i] *Battle for the Mind* | A PHYSIOLOGY OF CONVERSION | AND BRAIN-WASHING; p. [ii] blank; [*frontispiece, back blank*]; p. [iii] title-page; p. [iv] publisher's, publication and printer's notices; p. [v] *Contents*; p. [vi] blank; pp. vii–viii *List of Illustrations*; p. [ix] *Acknowledgements*; p. [x] epigraph (20 ll.) from George Salmon; pp. xi–xii [xiii] *Foreword*; p. [xiv] blank; pp. xv–xxiv *Introduction*; pp. 1–236 text; pp. 237–240 *Bibliography*; pp. 241–248 *Index*; illustrations are two gatherings, sewn between I and K.

21·4 × 13·8 cm. Bulk: 2·3/3·0 cm. White laid paper; all edges trimmed. White wove endpapers. Bound in salt-and-pepper cloth; fron blank; back stamped in lower right with a maroon publisher's emblem; spine stamped with a solid maroon rectangular box at top printed in silver: *Battle* | *for the* | *Mind* | ★ | WILLIAM | SARGANT; solid maroon rectangular box at bottom printed in silver: HEINEMANN

Price: 25s. Number of copies undetermined. Published 15 April 1957 in white dust-jacket printed in red and black.

Note: Chapter 8, 'Brain-Washing in Ancient Times', pp. 166–176, is by Graves.

B41 COLLECTED POEMS OF 1957
NORMAN CAMERON

THE | COLLECTED POEMS | OF | NORMAN CAMERON | 1905–1953 | ★ | With an Introduction by | ROBERT GRAVES | LONDON | THE HOGARTH PRESS | 1957

Collation: [A]⁴ B–E⁸, 36 leaves.
p. [1] COLLECTED POEMS; p. [2] blank; [*frontispiece, back blank*]; p. [3] title-page; p. [4] publisher's, printer's and rights notices; pp. [5]–[7] CONTENTS; p. [8] NOTE; pp. 9–24 *Introduction*; pp. 25–72 text.

21·4 × 13·8 cm. Bulk: 0·5/1·0 cm. White laid paper; all edges trimmed. White wove endpapers. Bound in boards covered with dusty mauve paper; back blank; front reads: [*broad decorative rule rectangular box enclosing all:*] | *The* | *Collected Poems of* | NORMAN | CAMERON | [*decorative rule*] 1905–1953 | [*decorative rule*] | *With* | *an Introduction by* | ROBERT GRAVES *The Hogarth Press*; spine reads, top to bottom: COLLECTED POEMS [*star*] Norman Cameron *The Hogarth Press*; cover printing is blue.

Price: 15s. Number of copies: 750. Published 11 June 1957 in mauve laid dust-jacket printed in blue, as cover.

Note: Graves' contribution is the introduction (pp. 9–24).

B42 MEMORY AND HER NINE DAUGHTERS 1957

MEMORY AND HER NINE DAUGHTERS, THE MUSES, | a pretext for printing cast into the mould | of a dialogue in four chapters, by victor hammer. | GEORGE WITTEN-BORN, INC. | 1018 madison avenue, new york city, 21— new york. | MDCCCCLVII

Collation: π^4 a–i⁶, 58 leaves.

2 pp., blank; 1 p., title-page; 1 p., rights reservation notice; p. i half-title; pp. ij–iij translation of vv. 53–84 of Hesiod's *Theogony* by Graves; p. iv diagram; pp. 1–103 text; pp. 104–107 NOTES AND REMARKS; p. [108] colophon: two-hundred and fifty-two copies | have been printed at the hand press by | carolyn r. hammer | victor hammer has set the pages | number [*square bracket*] [*number written in*] [*square bracket*] | A + M + D + G

24·7 × 15·5 cm. Bulk: 1·4/2·1 cm. White laid paper; top edges only trimmed. Endpapers are a blank four-leaf sheet, top unopened, sewn in separately. Bound in paper-covered boards; front printed in black, blue and rust with 34 ll. of text and catchword; back printed with 35 ll. of text in rust and black with catchword; spine printed in rust, up spine: hammer: 4 dialogues.

Price: $9.50. Number of copies: 252. Published in midsummer 1957 in light tan laid dust-jacket printed in black.

Note: Graves' contribution is the translation from Hesiod (pp. ij–iij).

B43 NEW POEMS 1957 [1957]

New Poems | [*swelled rule with fancy circular device in centre, inside which*:] 1957 | *Edited by* | KATHLEEN NOTT | C. DAY LEWIS | THOMAS BLACKBURN | [*publisher's emblem*] | *London* | MICHAEL JOSEPH

Collation: [A]⁸ B–H⁸ I⁶, 70 leaves.

p. [1] NEW POEMS | [*fancy circular device, inside which*:] 1957; p. [2] blank; p. [3] title-page; p. [4] publisher's, printer's, papermaker's and binder's notices; pp. [5]–[7] *Contents*; p. [8] blank; pp. [9]–10 *Introduction*; p. [11] *The Poems*; p. [12] blank; pp. 13–132 text; pp. [133] 134–140 *The Contributors*.

20·1 × 13·0 cm. Bulk: 1·0/1·4 cm. White wove paper; all edges trimmed. White wove endpapers. Bound in boards covered with paper in 5½ × 3 floral design; yellow cloth spine stamped in black: *New Poems* | [*swelled decorative rule*] | 1957 | [*swelled decorative rule*] | *a* | *P. E. N. Anthology* | [*publisher's emblem*] | MICHAEL | JOSEPH

Price: 15s. Number of copies: 2,000. Published 21 October 1957.

Note: Graves' contribution is 'The Coral Pool' (p. 56).

piero heliczer | [*row of 19 solid circular spots*] | YOU COUL
HEAR THE SNOW MELTING & | DRIPPING INTO
THE DEERS MOUTH   [COUL] [DEERS]

Collation: 12 leaves, unsigned, stapled twice in the centre.
p. [1] blank; p. [2] letter from Graves, dated 7 March 1958; pp. [3]–[23]
text; p. [24] blank, with photograph of Heliczer pasted in upper left
corner.

15·9 × 15·7 cm. Bulk: 0·2 cm. Grey laid paper; top and bottom edges
trimmed. Issued in yellow paper wrapper; across back: you coul hear
the snow dripping | [on front, continuous:] and falling into the deers
mouth; front has splotchy orange overprinting; inside of front cover is
title-page, flush right; inside back cover: *by piero heliczer* | GIRL BODY |
available through the dead language | [*row of 13 solid circular spots*] | title by
siggy wessberg | photograph by harold chapman | press work by the dead
language paris | dixhuit rue descartes

Price: undetermined. Number of copies undetermined. Published in 1958.

Note: Graves' contribution is the letter (p. [2]).

A | GOLDEN LAND | *Stories, Poems, Songs* | *New and Old* |
[*cut of woman cradling child in arms*] | *Edited by* JAMES REEVES |
Illustrated by GILLIAN CONWAY | *and others* | CONSTABLE
AND COMPANY LTD | *London*

Collation: π⁸ A–Z⁸ 2A–2H⁸, 256 leaves.
p. [i] A GOLDEN LAND; p. [ii] blank; p. [iii] title-page; p. [iv] copyright,
acknowledgement, publisher's and printer's notices; p. [v] TO THE MEMORY
OF | WALTER DE LA MARE | 1873–1956 | '*The best in this kind are but shadows*';
p. [vi] blank; pp. vii–x CONTENTS; pp. xi–xiv INTRODUCTION; pp. xv–
xvi ACKNOWLEDGMENTS; pp. 1–489 text; pp. 490–496 indexes.

23·5 × 15·6 cm. Bulk: 3·2/3·9 cm. White wove paper; all edges trimmed; top edges stained light orange. Mustard-orange wove endpapers.
Bound in medium blue cloth; front and back blank; spine stamped in
gold: A | Golden | Land | [*swelled rule*] | JAMES | REEVES | *Constable*

Price: 25s. Number of copies undetermined. Published 9 October 1958 in
white dust-jacket printed in black, orange, blue and green.

Notes: Graves' contributions are 'The Six Badgers' (p. 260) and 'The
Pumpkin' (p. 286).
The jacket-design is by Jane Paton.

[all but cut flush left:] Lover Man | by Alston Anderson | [*cut of boy and girl holding hands*] | Cassell · London

Collation: [A]⁸ B–M⁸, 96 leaves.
p. [i] [flush left:] Lover Man; p. [ii] blank; p. [iii] title-page; p. [iv] publisher's copyright, edition and printer's notices; p. [v] For Marshall, with thanks; p. [vi] blank; pp. vii–xi [flush left:] Foreword by | Robert Graves; p. [xii] [flush left:] Illustrations by | Denys and Judith Valentine; p. [xiii] [flush left:] Contents; p. [xiv] blank; pp. [1] 2–177 [178] text, with pp. [5, 16, 17, 20, 28, 29, 46, 49, 56, 57, 65, 72, 73, 77, 89, 105, 115, 128, 140, 141, 170, 171, 178] unnumbered.

20·0 × 12·5 cm. Bulk: 1·1/1·5 cm. White wove paper; all edges trimmed. White wove endpapers; inner sides black; Bound in black cloth; front and back blank; spine stamped in white: ANDERSON | [*solid rectangular box, inside which, up spine, black showing through:*] LOVER MAN | CASSELL

Price: 16s. Number of copies undetermined. Published 9 April 1959.

Note: Graves' contribution is the foreword (pp. vii–xi).

B47 THE LAST PHARISEE [1959]

THE LAST | PHARISEE | THE LIFE AND TIMES OF | RABBI JOSHUA BEN HANANYAH | A FIRST-CENTURY IDEALIST | *By* | JOSHUA PODRO | *Foreword by* | ROBERT GRAVES | [*publisher's emblem*] | VALLENTINE, MITCHELL | 37 Furnival Street, London, EC4

Collation: [A]¹⁶ B–D¹⁶, 64 leaves.
p. [1] THE LAST PHARISEE; p. [2] blank; p. [3] title-page; p. [4] copyright notice, author's advertisement and printer's and binder's notices; p. 5 CONTENTS; p. [6] blank; pp. 7–10 FOREWORD; pp. 11–117 text; pp. 118–119 APPENDIX; pp. 120–124 A SELECT BIBLIOGRAPHY; pp. 125–128 INDEX.

21·5 × 13·9 cm. Bulk: 0·9/1·4 cm. White wove paper; all edges trimmed. White wove endpapers. Bound in dull red cloth; front and back blank; spine stamped in gold: [*rule*] | [*swelled decorative rule*] | [*rule*] | The Last | Pharisee | [*rule*] | JOSHUA | PODRO | Vallentine | Mitchell

Price: 16s. Number of copies: 2,000 (not all bound up). Published 1 Jun 1959 in yellow-brown dust-jacket printed dark brown.

Note: Graves' contribution is the foreword (pp. 7–10).

EDWARD MARSH | PATRON OF THE ARTS | *A Biography* | BY | CHRISTOPHER HASSALL | [*publisher's emblem*] | LONGMANS

Collation: π^8 1 + /1*–22 + /2$^{2\star8/8}$ 23 + /*/$^{\star\star2/4/8}$, 374 leaves.

p. [i] EDWARD MARSH | PATRON OF THE ARTS; p. [ii] blank; [frontispiece, back blank]; p. [iii] title-page; p. [iv] publisher's, copyright, publication, manufacturing and printer's notices; p. v CONTENTS; p. [vi] blank; pp. vii–viii ILLUSTRATIONS; pp. ix–xvi PREFACE; pp. 1–680 text; pp. 681–703 appendixes; pp. 704–707 ACKNOWLEDGEMENTS; p. [708] blank; pp. 709–732 INDEX; illustrations appear between pp. 64/65, 96/97, 224/225, 256/257, 416/417, 448/449, 626/627.

22·2 × 14·5 cm. Bulk: 4·0/4·8 cm. White wove paper; all edges trimmed; top edges stained light blue. White wove endpapers. Bound in navy-blue cloth; back blank; front stamped in gold with facsimile autograph of Marsh; spine has light grey solid rectangular box near top, inside which: [*rectangular decorative rule box enclosing 6 ll.*] | EDWARD | MARSH | *A Biography* | [*three diamonds*] | CHRISTOPHER | HASSALL | LONGMANS

Price: 42s. Number of copies: 9,870. Published 8 June 1959 in white dust-jacket printed in light blue and black.

Note: Graves' contribution is letters, *passim*.

B49   LAROUSSE ENCYCLOPEDIA   [1959]
                OF MYTHOLOGY

LAROUSSE | ENCYCLOPEDIA OF | [*in red-brown:*] MYTH-OLOGY | [*cut of frieze*] | *With an Introduction by* | ROBERT GRAVES | LONDON | BATCHWORTH PRESS LIMITED

Collation: [1]–[31]^8 [32]–[33]^4, 256 leaves.

p. [i] LAROUSSE | ENCYCLOPEDIA OF | MYTHOLOGY; p. [ii] blank; p. [iii] title-page; p. [iv] series, translator's, publication, publisher's and copyright notices; pp. v–viii INTRODUCTION; pp. [ix–x] CONTENTS; p. [xi] LIST OF COLOUR PLATES; p. [xii] cut; pp. [1] 2–492 text, with pp. [8–9, 12–13, 15, 18, 20–23, 29, 33, 38–39, 44–45, 49, 61, 64–65, 73, 87, 89–90, 93–95, 97, 101, 108, 110, 112, 114, 116, 127, 134, 143, 145, 147, 152–53, 156–57, 161–63, 166–68, 176–77, 179, 185, 188, 192–95, 202–205, 208–209, 213, 223–24, 228–30, 234–35, 251, 253, 256–57, 262–63, 280–81, 293, 295, 306–308, 311–14, 321–23, 334–35, 339–41, 344, 356–57, 369–75, 382, 385, 387–91, 393, 406–407, 412–13, 432–33, 441, 448–49, 456–59, 466–67, 470–71, 473, 480, 483, 490, 493, 495] being unnumbered and with colour plates facing pp. 36, 100, 212, 244, [356], 404, 420, 452; pp. [493]–494 A SELECTED LIST FOR FURTHER READING; pp. [495] 496–500 INDEX OF NAMES.

28·7 × 20·2 cm. Bulk: 2·8/3·5 cm. White wove paper; all edges trimmed. Photographic white wove endpapers; inner sides of free endpapers
blank. Bound in mustard cloth; back black; front stamped with bull and
with black band at right, mustard spelling out MYTHOLOGY from top to
bottom; spine stamped in black: M | Y | T | H | O | L | O | G | Y | BATCH- |
WORTH | PRESS

Price: 63s. Number of copies: unknown. Published 4 September 1959
in white dust-jacket printed in red, black and yellow.

Note: Graves' contribution is the introduction (pp. v–viii).

B50   THE ST. TRINIAN'S STORY   [1959]

[*in wiggly Searle letters:*] The St Trinian's Story | The whole
ghastly dossier compiled by | Kaye Webb | with contributions
by | SIRIOL HUGH-JONES | MALCOLM ARNOLD
BERTOLT BRECHT | JOHNNY DANKWORTH MI-
CHAEL FLANDERS | SIDNEY GILLIAT ROBERT GRAVES |
JAMES LAVER C. DAY LEWIS | G. W. STONIER DON-
ALD SWANN | D. B. WYNDHAM LEWIS | and | Ronald
Searle | [*publisher's emblem*] | PERPETUA BOOKS

Collation: [1]–[7]⁸ [8]⁴, 60 leaves.
p. [1] Searle drawing; p. [2] Searle cartoon; p. [3] title-page; p. [4] edition,
publisher's, distributor's, copyright and printer's notices; p. [5] dedication; p. [6] acknowledgements and sketch; p. [7] sketch and *Contents*;
p. [8] reproduction of newspaper clipping; pp. [9] 10–117 [118] text with
pp. [12, 16, 20, 25, 26, 30, 31, 36, 37, 38, 40, 41, 42, 43, 47, 48, 52, 56, 59,
61, 63, 69, 71, 73, 77, 79, 85, 88, 93, 102, 105, 107, 109, 111, 113, 114]
unnumbered; pp. [119–120] blank.

24·6 × 18·4 cm. Bulk: 1·2/1·8 cm. White wove paper; all edges trimmed. Yellow wove endpapers printed in black; first and fourth sides blank.
Bound in black cloth; back blank; front stamped in gold: The St Trinian's
Story and a trumpeting angel; spine stamped in gold, top to bottom
[to front:] *Compiled by* | [parallel to previous line, to back:] *Kaye Webb*
[in single column:] THE ST. TRINIAN'S STORY *Perpetua*

Price: 21s. Number of copies: 16,500. Published 23 November 1959.

Note: Graves' contribution is 'School Hymn for St. Trinian's' (p. 49
with music by Johnny Dankworth facing; the introduction says the
poem was 'originally composed as a flamenco for the Deya Girls' Choir

HODGKINSON

Collation: 4 leaves, unnumbered, stapled twice at centre.
front cover: title-page; inside front-cover: 'The Intruders' by Graves;
p. [1] biographical sketch of Hodgkinson by Alan Bowness; p. [2] list
of paintings; p. [3] biographical data; p. [4] reproduction of painting;
inside back cover, near bottom: 20th April–7th May 1960 | Daily 10 am–
6 pm Except Sunday | Private View on Tuesday 19th April 1960 | 7–9 pm
Cocktails; back cover: [flush left:] drian gallery | 7 porchester place marble
arch london w2 pad9473

22·8 × 17·7 cm. White laid paper; all edges trimmed; pp. [1]–[4] coated.

Price undetermined. Number of copies: 1,000. Published in April 1960.

Note: Graves' contribution is 'The Intruders' (inside front cover).

B52   EXPLORATIONS IN COMMUNICATION   1960

[entire flush left:] EXPLORATIONS | IN COMMUNICA-
TION | *An Anthology* | Edited by Edmund Carpenter and Mar-
shall McLuhan | Beacon Press Beacon Hill Boston

Collation: [1]–[3]¹⁶ [4]–[5]⁸ [6]–[8]¹⁶, 112 leaves.
p. [i] [flush left:] EXPLORATIONS IN COMMUNICATION; p. [ii] list of contributors; p. [iii] title-page; p. [iv] copyright, Library of Congress card and
printing notices; pp. v–vi [at left:] ACKNOWLEDGMENTS; pp. vii–viii CON-
TENTS; pp. ix–xii [at left:] INTRODUCTION; p. [xiii] [flush left:] EXPLORA-
TIONS IN COMMUNICATION; p. [xiv] blank; pp. 1–208 text; pp. 209–10
[at left:] NOTES ON CONTRIBUTORS.

20·2 × 13·7 cm. Bulk: 1·5/2·0 cm. White wove paper; all edges trimmed. White wove endpapers. Bound in dark brown cloth; back blank;
front blind-stamped with publisher's emblem; spine stamped in white,
down spine, in two lines and three ranks: [near front:] CARPENTER EX-
PLORATIONS IN BEACON [near back:] MCLUHAN COMMUNICATION PRESS

Price: $4.00. Number of copies undisclosed. Published in May 1960 in
white dust-jacket printed in red and black.

Note: Graves' contribution (pp. 155–161) is 'Comments on "Lineal and
Non-Lineal Codifications of Reality" ', reprinted from C541.

VIVA | CAMENA | LATINA HVIVS AETATIS CARMINA |
COLLECTA ET EDITA AB | IOSEPHO EBERLE | CVM
COMMENTARIOLO | IOSEPHI ET LINAE IJSEWIJN-
JACOBS | DE LITTERIS LATINIS RECENTIORIBVS | IN
AEDIBVS ARTEMIDOS | TVRICI ET STVTTGARDIAE |
MCMLXI

Collation: [1]–[2]⁸ 3–14⁸ 15⁴, 116 leaves.

p. [1] VIVA CAMENA; p. [2] blank; p. [3] title-page; p. [4] copyright notice;
pp. 5–14 PRAEFATIO; p. 15 AD LIBRVM; p. [16] blank; p. [17] METRA; p. [18]
blank; pp. 19–140 text; p. [141] RHYTHMI; p. [142] blank; pp. 143–182
text; p. [183] COMMENTARIOLVS | AVCTORES ET ANNOTATIONES | TITVLI ET
INITIA CARMINVM | INDEX; p. [184] blank; pp. 185–199 text; p. [200]
blank; pp. 201–221 text; p. [222] blank; pp. 223–229 index of first lines
and titles; p. [230] blank; p. [231] INDEX; p. [232] rights reservation,
printer's and printing notices.

20·8 × 12·0 cm. Bulk: 1·5/2·0 cm. White wove paper; all edges trimmed. Tan laid endpapers watermarked with a crown and, in Gothic:
Abbey Mills | Greenfield. Bound in boards covered with very light Vene-
tian red wove paper; front and back blank; spine stamped in gold, up
spine, near top: VIVA CAMENA

Price: 18.50 marks. Number of copies: 2,550. Published 7 September
1961 in brownish grey dust-jacket printed in black and reddish brown.

Note: Graves' contribution is a two-line Latin poem, 'Turdo Merula',
on p. 59; it contains the misprint 'tarde' for 'turde' in l. 2.

B54   THE ARTISTS' AND WRITERS'   [1961]
COOKBOOK

[*3 ll. in the centre of a swelled braided rug and doily design:*] THE |
ARTISTS' & WRITERS' | COOKBOOK | EDITED BY |
BERYL BARR | AND | BARBARA TURNER SACHS |
DESIGNED BY | NICOLAS SIDJAKOV | [*swelled decorative
rule*] | CONTACT | EDITIONS | SAUSALITO, CALIFOR-
NIA | [*swelled decorative rule*] [*All text and decorative rules in purple;
upper design only black*]

Collation: [1]¹⁰ [2]–[19]⁸ [20]¹⁰, 328 leaves.

p. [i] cut of quills and printing press; p. [ii] Library of Congress card, typographer's, printer's, publisher's, copyright and printing notices; p. [iii]
title-page; p. [iv] blank; p. [v] [*device*] | dedicated | to the art of imper-
fection | in the kitchen | [*device*]; p. [vi] blank; pp. [vii]–[xiv] TABLE OF

CONTENTS; p. [xv] FOREWORD; pp. [xvi]–[xx] foreword; pp. 1–288 text; pp. [289]–[294] FROM THE EDITORS; pp. [295]–[307] CONTRIBUTORS; p. [308] blank.

24·3 × 18·5 cm. Bulk: 2·6/3·3. White wove paper; all edges trimmed. White wove endpapers. Bound in white cloth printed overall with names of the contributors in purple and olive.

Price: $10.00. Number of copies: at least 20,000. Published 1 November 1961 in grey box with arrangement of old cuts (3 × 4) and title on one side and title, authors, designer, introducer, publisher and price on other; spine blank.

Note: Graves' contribution is a recipe for Sevillian yellow plum conserve (p. 284).

B55   X   [1961]

[*in red:*] X | VOLUME ONE 1960–61 | EDITED BY DAVID WRIGHT | AND PATRICK SWIFT | [*publisher's emblem*] | BARRIE AND ROCKLIFF | LONDON

Collation: π^4 [1]^8 2–5^8 [6]^8 7–10^8 [11]^8 12–14^8 15^4 16^8 [17]^8 18^8 19$^{\star 4}$ 20^4 21–22^8, 168 leaves.

p. [i] [*in red:*] x | VOLUME ONE; p. [ii] blank; p. [iii] title-page; p. [iv] copyright, publisher's, printer's and edition notices; pp. [v–vi] PREFACE; pp. [vii–viii] CONTENTS; pp. [1]–328 text, with pp. [2, 45, 76, 81, 82, 83, 84, 143, 161, 162, 163, 164, 247, 249, 250, 251, 252, 325, 327] unnumbered; plate of 1 leaf between pp. 32/33, 34/35, 62/63, 200/201, 280/281, 288/289 and of 2 leaves between pp. 136/137, 184/185.

26·0 × 16·4 cm. Bulk: 3·1/3·8 cm. White wove paper; all edges trimmed; top edge stained brick-red. White wove endpapers. Bound in cream boards; back blank; front stamped with large gold x; spine stamped in gold: x | VOLUME | ONE | BARRIE | & | ROCKLIFF

Price: 32s. 6d. Number of copies: 800. Published 10 November 1961.

Note: Graves' contribution is 'November 5th Address' (pp. 171–176).

B56   THE VIOLENT SEASON   1962

[first 7 ll. flush left:] THE | VIOLENT | SEASON | A NOVEL BY | ROBERT GOULET | W. H. ALLEN | LONDON 1962 | [to right:] [*publisher's emblem*]

Collation: [A]^8 B–S^8, 144 leaves.
p. [1] blurb and quote from Graves; p. [2] blank; p. [3] title-page; p. [4] copyright, edition and printer's notices; pp. 5–288 text.

19·7 × 13·0 cm. Bulk: 2·6/3·3 cm. White wove paper; all edges trimmed. White wove endpapers. Bound in slick red cloth; front and back blank; spine stamped in gold: [*heavy rule*] | The | *Violent* | *Season* | *ROB-ERT* | *GOULET* | [*heavy rule*] | [*publisher's emblem*] | W · H · | ALLEN

Price: 18s. Number of copies unknown. Published on 14 January 1962 in white dust-jacket printed in red and black.

Notes: Graves' contribution is the advertisement on p. [1]. The dust-jacket, designed by M. M. Carder, has a letter from Graves on the back.

B57   LE MORTE D'ARTHUR   [1962]

Sir Thomas Malory's | [*in white, in a black band, in mock-Celtic type:*] LE MORTE D'ARTHUR | King Arthur and the | Legends of the Round Table | *A RENDITION IN MODERN IDIOM BY* | [*in Gothic:*] Keith Baines | *WITH AN INTRO-DUCTION BY* | [*in Gothic:*] Robert Graves | *DECORATIVE ILLUSTRATIONS BY ENRICO ARNO* | *BRAMHALL HOUSE* | *NEW YORK*

Collation: [1]–[16]^{16}, 256 leaves.
p. [*i*] [in Gothic:] Le Morte d'Arthur; p. [*ii*] cut of castle, ladies and two knights jousting; p. [*iii*] title-page; p. [*iv*] edition, copyright, rights reservation, Library of Congress card and printing notices; p. [*v*] [in Gothic:] For Anna; p. [*vi*] cut of knight with raised sword; pp. *vii–viii* preface; pp. *ix–x* [in Gothic:] Contents; pp. *xi–xx* [in Gothic:] Introduction; pp. *21–507* text and illustrations; pp. *508–512* [in Gothic:] Appendix.

23·5 × 15·5 cm. Bulk: 2·3/2·9 cm. White wove paper; all edges trimmed. White wove endpapers. Bound in brown-grey cloth; front and back blank; spine printed in brown: [down spine, in Gothic:] Sir Thomas Malory Le Morte d'Arthur | [remainder upright:] [*publisher's emblem*] | BRAMHALL | HOUSE

Price: $6.00. Number of copies undisclosed. Published in May 1962 in tan cream wove dust-jacket printed in black and brown.

Note: Graves' contribution is the introduction (pp. *xi–xx*).

B58   LETTERS TO T. E. LAWRENCE   [1962]

LETTERS | to | [*in red:*] T. E. LAWRENCE | Edited by | A. W LAWRENCE | [*publisher's emblem*] | LONDON | JONATHAN CAPE 30 BEDFORD SQUARE

Collation: [A]⁸ B–O⁸, 112 leaves.

p. [1] LETTERS TO T. E. LAWRENCE; p. [2] blank; p. [3] title-page; p. [4] edition, copyright, printer's, papermaker's and binder's notices; pp. [5–6] CONTENTS; pp. [7–8] PREFACE; p. [9] LETTERS TO T. E. LAWRENCE; p. [10] NOTE; pp. 11–24 text; 2 pp. reproductions of MS, part of the signature, but not included in the enumeration; pp. 25–120 text; 2 pp. reproductions of MS; pp. 121–160 text; 2 pp. reproductions of MS; pp. 161–214 text; pp. 215–216 INDEX; pp. [217–218] blank.

22·8 × 15·4 cm. Bulk: 1·7/2·2 cm. White wove paper; all edges trimmed; top edge stained brown. White wove endpapers printed with grey background for facsimile signatures of contributors; first and fourth sides blank. Bound in dark mustard cloth; front and back blank; spine stamped in gold: LETTERS | TO | T. E. | LAWRENCE | [*4 diamonds in diamond shape*] | [*publisher's emblem*]

Price: 35s. Number of copies undisclosed. Published 16 July 1962.

Note: Graves' contribution is letters (pp. 107–115). There are references to him *passim*.

B59   IN THE CLEARING   [1962]

IN THE | CLEARING | BY | ROBERT | FROST | [*publisher's emblem*] | [*swelled rule*] | HOLT, RINEHART AND WINSTON | LONDON

Collation: [1]⁸ 2⁸ [3]⁸ 4–5⁸ 6⁴ 7⁸, 52 leaves.

p. [1] IN THE CLEARING BY ROBERT FROST; p. [2] blank; p. [3] title-page; p. [4] publication, copyright and printer's notices; pp. [5–6] CONTENTS; pp. 7–10 INTRODUCTION | by | ROBERT GRAVES; p. [11] IN THE CLEARING | 'And wait to watch the water clear, I may'; p. [12] blank; pp. 13–31 text; p. [32] blank; p. [33] CLUSTER OF FAITH; pp. 34–39 text; p. [40] blank; pp. 41–90 text; p. [91] QUANDARY; pp. 92–101 text; pp. [102]–[104] blank.

22·9 × 15·3 cm. Bulk: 0·9/1·4 cm. White wove paper; all edges trimmed. Cream-white textured wove endpapers. Bound in grey cloth; front and back blank; spine stamped in silver, top to bottom: ROBERT FROST / IN THE CLEARING *Holt · Rinehart · Winston*

Price: 21s. Number of copies: 5,000. Published on 28 September 1962 in white dust-jacket printed in black and red.

Note: Graves' contribution is the introduction (pp. 7–10).

B60   POET'S CHOICE   1962

POET'S | CHOICE | [*fancy swelled rule*] | EDITED BY | Paul

Engle and Joseph Langland | [*publisher's emblem* | THE DIAL
PRESS NEW YORK 1962

Collation: [1]–[8]¹⁶ [9]⁴ [10]–[11]¹⁶, 164 leaves.
[2 pp., blank]; p. [i] POET's | CHOICE | [*fancy swelled rule*]; p. [ii] blank;
p. [iii] title-page; p. [iv] copyright, rights reservation, Library of Congress
card, designer's and manufacturer's notices and acknowledgements; pp.
v–vii acknowledgements; p. [viii] blank; pp. ix–xi table of contents; p.
[xii] blank; pp. xiii–xvii [flush left:] THE POET ON HIS POEM; p. [xviii]
blank; p. [xix] POET's | CHOICE | [*fancy swelled rule*]; pp. 1–291 text; p.
[292] blank; pp. 293–303 BRIEF BIOGRAPHIES; pp. [304]–[306] blank.

23·1 × 15·5 cm. Bulk: 2·0/2·7 cm. White wove paper; top edges only
trimmed. Rust wove endpapers. Bound in maroon cloth; front and back
blank; spine stamped in gold: [*decorative device*] | [down spine:] POET's
CHOICE | [*decorative device*] | EDITED BY | ENGLE | AND | LANGLAND [with a
fancy G] | [*publisher's emblem*] | DIAL

Price: $6.95. Number of copies: 10,000. Published 29 October 1962 in
cream dust-jacket printed in rust, gold and black.

Note: Graves' contribution is a comment (pp. 29–30) on 'The Troll's
Nosegay', also printed here.

B61   THE SUFIS   1964

[flush left:] THE | [flush right:] SUFIS | *Idries Shah* | [flush left:]
Introduction by | [flush right:] *Robert Graves* | DOUBLEDAY
& COMPANY, INC. | GARDEN CITY, NEW YORK, 1964

Collation: [1]¹² 2–9¹² [10]–[18]¹², 216 leaves.
p. [*i*] [flush left:] THE | [flush right:] SUFIS; p. [*ii*] example of 'Sufi illus-
trative calligraphy'; p. [*iii*] title-page; p. [*iv*] Library of Congress card,
copyright, rights reservation, printing and edition notices; pp. [*v*]–*vi*
CONTENTS; p. [*vii*] THE SITUATION; p. [*viii*] blank; pp. [*ix*] x–
xxii INTRODUCTION; pp. [*xxiii*] xxiv–xxvi AUTHOR'S PREFACE;
pp. [1] 2–365 text, with pp. [11, 34, 56, 98, 104, 115, 137, 147, 164, 172,
182, 192, 206, 217, 225, 228, 235, 249, 261, 286, 308, 317, 326, 345, 356]
being unnumbered; pp. [366] 367–400 ANNOTATIONS; pp. [401]
402–403 [404] appendixes; pp. [405–406] blank.

20·8 × 13·7 cm. Bulk: 3·1/3·7 cm. White wove paper; top and bottom
edges trimmed. White wove endpapers. Bound in grey cloth; back blank;
front blind-stamped with calligraphic emblem; spine stamped: THE
SUFIS | *Idries* | *Shah* | DOUBLEDAY

Price: $5.95. Number of copies: 4,000 (in two printings). Published 17 January 1964 in white dust-jacket printed in black, yellow, red and magenta.

Note: Graves' contribution is the introduction, pp. [*ix*] *x–xxii.*

B62   GOLDENSHEEP   [1964]

[entire flush left:] KEITH BAINES | Goldensheep | *A Sequence of Poems to Judith* | [*publisher's emblem*] Longmans

Collation: [A]⁸ B–C⁸, 24 leaves.
p. [1] [flush left:] title and blurb; p. [2] blank; p. [3] title-page; p. [4] [flush right:] publisher's, edition, copyright and printer's notices; p. [5] [flush left:] CONTENTS; p. [6] blank; p. [7] [flush left:] PROLOGUE; p. [8] blank; pp. 9–48 text.

$21 \cdot 7 \times 13 \cdot 9$ cm. Bulk: $0 \cdot 3/0 \cdot 9$ cm. White wove paper; all edges trimmed. Grey laid endpapers watermarked with a crown, below which a Gothic: Glastonbury. Bound in mustard canary cloth; back blank; front stamped: [*heavy orange rule*] | [*in gold:*] GOLDEN-SHEEP | [*heavier orange rule*]; spine stamped in gold, top to bottom: GOLDENSHEEP · KEITH BAINES LONGMANS

Price: 18s. Number of copies: 750. Published 7 September 1964 in white dust-jacket printed in black and yellow.

Note: Graves' contributions are the blurb on p. [1], which is repeated on the front flap of the dust-jacket and the prologue (p. 7).

B63   AS IT WAS   [1964]

AS IT WAS | *Terence Hards* | *with an Introduction by Robert Graves* | The Seizin Press, Deyá, Mallorca | distributed by | HEINEMANN: LONDON

Collation: [1]–[6]⁴, 24 leaves.
p. [1] AS IT WAS; p. [2] blank; p. [3] title-page; p. [4] publisher's, distributor's, publication, copyright and printer's notices; p. [5] Contents; p. [6] blank; pp. 7–8 FOREWORD; pp. 9–48 text.

$21 \cdot 5 \times 13 \cdot 4$ cm. Bulk: $0 \cdot 4/0 \cdot 9$ cm. White laid paper; top and fore-edges only trimmed; watermarked with a crown and: Abbey Mills | Greenfield [in Gothic]. White wove endpapers. Bound in black cloth; front and back blank; spine stamped in gold, top to bottom: Hards AS IT WAS Seizin – Heinemann

Price: 12s. 6d. Number of copies undetermined. Published 21 September 1964 in grey-blue dust-jacket printed in black.

Note: Graves' contribution is the foreword (pp. 7–8).

B64   THE COLLECTED POEMS OF   [1964]
                      FRANK PREWETT

THE | COLLECTED | POEMS OF | FRANK | PREWETT | [*publisher's emblem*] | CASSELL · LONDON

Collation: [A]⁸ B–C⁸ D⁴ E⁸, 36 leaves.

p. [i] THE COLLECTED POEMS | OF FRANK PREWETT; p. [ii] blank; [*frontispiece, back blank*]; p. [iii] title-page; p. [iv] publisher's, copyright, edition, rights reservation and printer's notices; pp. v–vi CONTENTS; pp. vii–[viii] INTRO-DUCTION; pp. 1–46 text of poems; p. [47] *Three Broadcast Talks (1954)* | FARM LIFE IN ONTARIO | FIFTY YEARS AGO; p. [48] blank; pp. 49–63 text; p. [64] blank.

21·6 × 14·9 cm. Bulk: 0·6/1·1 cm. White wove paper; all edges trimmed. White wove endpapers. Bound in deep blue cloth; front and back blank; spine stamped in gold, bottom to top: CASSELL THE COLLECTED POEMS OF FRANK PREWETT

Price: 21s. Number of copies: 500. Published in November 1964 in white dust-jacket printed in blue, olive and black.

Notes: Graves' contribution is the introduction (pp. vii–[viii]). Graves is also quoted on the front of the dust-jacket and inside the front flap. The dust-jacket was designed by Edward Ripley.

B65   OPINIONS AND PERSPECTIVES   1964

OPINIONS | AND PERSPECTIVES | from | The New York Times Book Review | EDITED AND WITH AN INTRO-DUCTION | BY FRANCIS BROWN | [*publisher's emblem*] | HOUGHTON MIFFLIN COMPANY BOSTON | [in Gothic:] The Riverside Press Cambridge | 1964

Collation: [1]–[12]¹⁶ [13]⁴ [14]–[15]¹⁶, 228 leaves.

p. [i] OPINIONS AND PERSPECTIVES | from | The New York Times Book Review; p. [ii] blank; p. [iii] title-page; p. [iv] printing, copyright, permission, rights reservation, Library of Congress card and printing notices; pp. [v] vi–viii Contents; pp. [ix] x–xiii Introduction; p. [xiv] blank; pp. [1]–247 text, with pp. [1, 61, 111, 205, 255, 305, 375] being section-headings, pp. [2, 62, 112, 206, 256, 306, 376] being blank and 62 pp. being unnumbered; p. [428] blank; p. [429] INDEX; p. [430] blank; pp. [431] 432–441 index; p. [442] blank.

21·4 × 14·6 cm. Bulk: 2·9/3·4 cm. White wove paper; top and bottom edges trimmed. White wove endpapers. Bound in forest green cloth; back blank; front stamped in gold: OPINIONS | AND PERSPECTIVES | from | The New York Times Book Review; spine stamped in gold: OPINIONS | AND | PERSPEC- | TIVES | BROWN | HMCO

Price: $ 6.95. Number of copies undetermined. Published 18 November 1964 in white dust-jacket printed in bright green and black.

Note: Graves' contribution (pp. [257] 258–62) is 'Mostly It's Money That Makes a Writer Go, Go, Go.'

B66   THE VALLEY OF THE LATIN BEAR   1965

[p. 2:] *The Valley of the* | [*part of cut of village and hills*] | [flush left:] *Foreword by Robert Graves* | NEW YORK [*turned rule*] 1965

[p. 3:] *Latin Bear* | [*remainder of cut*] | *by* ALEXANDER LENARD | [flush right:] *with pen-and-ink sketches by the author* | E. P. DUTTON & CO., INC.

Collation: [1]–[7]¹⁶, 112 leaves.

p. [i] blank; p. [ii] author's advertisement; p. [1] [flush right:] The Valley of the Latin Bear; pp. [2–3] title-page; p. [4] author's disclaimer, copyright, rights reservation, publication, Library of Congress card and edition notices and publisher's emblem; pp. 5–7 FOREWORD; p. [8] blank; p. [9] [flush right:] The Valley of the Latin Bear; p. [10] blank; pp. 11–219 text, with pp. [30–31, 66, 118–19, 138, 194–95] being unnumbered; pp. [220]–[222] blank.

20·2 × 13·6 cm. Bulk: 1·7/2·2 cm. White wove paper; all edges trimmed. White wove endpapers. Bound in orange boards with blue-green cloth spine; back blank; front printed in black with sketch of house; spine printed: *The* | *Valley* | *of* | *the* | *Latin* | *Bear* | LENARD | DUTTON

Price: $4.95. Number of copies: 7,000. Published 19 May 1965 in white dust-jacket printed in turquoise-green, black, red, yellow and blue.

Note: Graves' contribution is the foreword (pp. 5–7).

C

CONTRIBUTIONS TO PRESS AND PERIODICALS

Poems are starred.

An indication of content is given when a title is not self-explanatory and the
  article has not been reprinted.

'Reprinted' often means 'reprinted with revisions'.

Articles, letters and reviews to which Graves' contributions are replies are
  listed here in conjunction with relevant entries.

1911

C1 ★Mountain Side at Evening. *Carthusian* 10 : 425 June.

1912

C2 Why Jigsaws Went out of Fashion. [With Rosaleen
  Graves.] *Westminster Gazette*, 21 December, p. 2; *Saturday*
  Westminster Gazette, 21 December, p. 9.

  A short story.

1913

C3 Ragtime. *The Greyfriar* 6 : 86–88 April.
  Not signed; acknowledged.

C4 One Hundred Years Ago. *The Green Chartreuse*, July, p. 2.
  Not signed; acknowledged.

C5 ★The King's Son. *The Green Chartreuse*, July, p. 3.

C6 My New-Bug's Exam. *The Green Chartreuse*, July, p. 4.

C7 How to Do Things. *The Green Chartreuse*, July, p. 11.
  Not signed; acknowledged.

C8 ★The Miser of Shenham Heath. *The Green Chartreuse*,
  July, p. 13.

C9   ★Jolly Yellow Moon. *Carthusian* 11 : 173–74 October.

C10   ★Rondeau: The Clouds. *Carthusian* 11 : 174 October.

C11   ★Love and Black Magic. *Carthusian* 11 : 187 November.

C12   ★'Am and Advance: A Cockney Study. *Carthusian* 11 : 188 November.

C13   ★Peeping Tom. *Spectator* 111 : 758, 8 November.

C14   ★Ballad of the White Monster. *Carthusian* 11 : 205 December.
Signed 'Z'; in the Lockwood notebook.

C15   ★Alcaics Addressed to My Study Fauna. *Carthusian* 11 : 206 December.
Signed 'Z'; in the Lockwood notebook.

C16   ★The Future. *Carthusian* 11 : 206 December.

C17   ★Pan Set at Nought. *Carthusian* 11 : 207 December.

C18   ★The Cyclone. *Carthusian* 11 : 207 December.

1914

C19   ★The Ape God. *Carthusian* 11 : 229 February.

C20   ★Lament in December. *Carthusian* 11 : 231 February.

C21   ★Ghost Music. *Carthusian* 11 : 232 February.

C22   ★Merlin the Diviner. *Carthusian* 11 : 233 February.
Signed 'Z'; in the Lockwood and Berg notebooks.

C23   ★A Day in February. *Carthusian* 11 : 247 March.

C24   ★The Wasp. *Carthusian* 11 : 248 March.

C25   ★Five Rhymes: My Hazel Twig – After the Rain – Envy – Triolet: The King's Highway – The Glorious Harshness of the Parrot's Voice. *Carthusian* 11 : 252 March.

C26 [Letter about the General Library Committee.] [With others.] *Carthusian* 11 : 263 March.

C27 *Two Moods. *Carthusian* 11 : 267–68 April.
Signed 'Z'; in the Lockwood notebook.

C28 *Youth and Folly. *Carthusian* 11 : 268–69 April.
Signed 'Peccavi'.

C29 [Letter about triolets.] *Carthusian* 11 : 284 April.
Signed 'X'.

C30 The Druid's Club. *The Greyfriar* 6 : 127–29 April.
About the Charterhouse club of this name.

C31 *The Briar Burners. *Carthusian* 11 : 286 June.
Unsigned; acknowledged.

C32 *The Tyranny of Books. *Carthusian* 11 : 311 July.
Unsigned; in the Lockwood notebook.

C33 *The Organ Grinder. *The Greyfriar* 6 : 149 July.

1915

C34 Some Trench Scenes. *Spectator* 115 : 329–31, 11 September.
Reprinted in A. P. Graves' *To Return to All That* (B18); see also references in A32.

1916

C35 *Between La Bassée and Bethune. *Westminster Gazette*, 6 March, p. 2.

C36 *The Morning before the Battle. *Westminster Gazette*, 13 March, p. 2.

C37 *The Dead Fox-Hunter. *Westminster Gazette*, 20 September, p. 2; *Saturday Westminster Gazette*, 23 September, p. 7

C38 *The Cottage. *Carthusian* 12 : 14 November.

C39 *The Dead Boche. *Cambridge Magazine* 6 : 302, 10 February.

C40 *The Last Post (June, 1916). *Nation* (London) 20 : 735, 3 March.
With 'Died of Wounds' by Siegfried Sassoon with the title 'Two Poems by Soldiers.'

C41 *Not Dead. *Carthusian* 12 : 69 April.

C42 *The Lady Visitor in the Pauper's Ward. *Carthusian* 12 : 69 April.

C43 *The Last Post. *Living Age* 293 : 130, 21 April.

1918

C44 *Country at War. *Colour* 8 : 39 March.

C45 *The Two Brothers: An Allegory. *Colour* 8 : 80 May.

C46 *Jonah. *Literary Digest* 57 : 40, 4 May.

C47 *The Picture Book. *New Statesman* 11 : 213, 15 June.

C48 *Peace. *New Statesman* 11 : 493, 21 September.

C49 *A Pinch of Salt – The Lady Visitor in the Pauper Ward – When I'm Killed – To Lucasta on Going to the Wars – for the Fourth Time – The Shivering Beggar – Escape – The Last Post. *Literary Digest* 59 : 36–38, 16 November.

C50 *True Johnny. *Land and Water* 2955 : 11, 26 December.

1919

C51 *The Leveller. *New Statesman* 12 : 302, 11 January.

C52 *Neglectful Edward. *Land and Water* 2958 : 14, 16 January.

C53 *Sospan Fach. *Reveille* 1 : 473–4 February.

C54 *Bazentin, 1916. *Land and Water* 2961 : 31, 6 February.

C55 *Country at War. *Land and Water* 2963 : 15, 20 February.

C56 *The Leveller. *Literary Digest* 60 : 39, 8 March.

C57 *Hate Not, Fear Not. *New Statesman* 12 : 552, 22 March.

C58 *True Johnny. *Living Age* 300 : 768, 22 March.

C59 Parodies and Prisoners. *Daily Herald*, 12 April, p. 8.
Review of E. de Stein's *The Poets in Picardy* and Alec Waugh's *The Prisoners of Mainz*.

C60 Foreword. *The Owl* 1 : [3] May.
Probably by Graves, the literary editor.

C61 *Ghost Raddled. *The Owl* 1 : 8 May.

C62 *A Frosty Night. *The Owl* 1 : 9 May.

C63 *Sospan Fach. *Living Age* 301 : 335, 10 May.

C64 *Loving Henry. *Land and Water* 2976 : 36, 22 May.

C65 A Nine-Year-Old Looks at the World. *Daily Herald*, 28 May, pp. 8–9.
Review of Daisy Ashford's *The Young Visiters*.

C66 *The Boy out of Church. *Land and Water* 2979 : 25, 12 June.

C67 *The Kiss. *Century* 98 : 417 July.

C68 An Old Friend. *Daily Herald*, 16 July, p. 8.
Review of Samuel Butler's *The Way of All Flesh*.

C69 *Dicky – Hawk and Buckle – The Cupboard. *Poetry* 14 : 252–55, August.

C70 A Master Singer of Joy and Pity. *Daily Herald*, 3 September, p. 2.
Review of *Collected Poems of W. H. Davies*.

C71 *Ghost Raddled. *Living Age* 302 : 640, 6 September.

C72 *A Frosty Night. *Living Age* 302 : 768, 20 September.

C73 ★Advice to Lovers. *The Owl* 2 : 8 October.

C74 ★One Hard Look. *The Owl* 2 : 9 October.

C75 ★Becker's Ghost. *Nation* (London) 26 : 392, 13 December.

1920

C76 ★Country Mood. *London Mercury* 1 : 272 January.

C77 ★The Treasure Box. *New Statesman* 14 : 436, 17 January.

C78 ★Catherine Drury. *Land and Water* 3011 : 13, 22 January.

C79 ★The Personal Touch. *Spectator* 124 : 110, 24 January.
Signed 'Tom Fool'; reprinted A7.

C80 ★Song: The Ring and Chain. *Voices* 3 : 16 February.

C81 ★The Treasure Box. *Living Age* 304 : 473, 21 February.

C82 ★Country Mood. *Living Age* 304 : 496, 21 February.

C83 ★The Troll's Nosegay. *To-Day* 7 : 2 March.

C84 ★Words to the Tune of 'Black Horse Lane'. *Spectator* 124 : 308, 8 March.

C85 Books at Random. *Woman's Leader and the Common Cause* 12 : 159, 19 March.
Signed 'FUZE'; acknowledged. About the dropping of compulsory Greek at Oxford, Hardy's honorary degree and John Masefield.

C86 ★The Hills of May. *Woman's Leader* 12 : 176, 26 March.

C87 ★Lost Love. *The Apple of Beauty and Discord* 1 : 86 2nd Quarter.

C88 Books at Random. *Woman's Leader* 12 : 209, 1 April.
Signed 'FUZE'. See C83. Review of Aldous Huxley's *Limbo* and speculations about who buys books.

C89 Books at Random. *Woman's Leader* 12 : 230, 9 April.
Signed 'FUZE'. See C83. On the 'holiness' of books, the bad effect of booksellers on publishers and E. B. Browning.

C90 ★Reproach. *Athenaeum* 94 : 508, 16 April.

C91 Books at Random. *Woman's Leader* 12 : 252, 16 April.
Signed 'FUZE'. See C83. On literary back-scratching.

C92 Books at Random. *Woman's Leader* 12 : 300, 30 April.
Signed 'FUZE'. See C83. About his library and reorganizing his bookshelves.

C93 Books at Random. *Woman's Leader* 12 : 348, 14 May.
Signed 'FUZE'. See C83. About Mabel Nicholson and referring to women artists by their married names.

C94 Books at Random. *Woman's Leader* 12 : 373, 21 May.
Signed 'FUZE'. See C83. About children's literature.

C95 Words to the Tune of 'Black Horse Lane'. *Living Age* 305 : 496, 22 May.

C96 ★The Troll's Nosegay. *Literary Digest* 65 : 46, 22 May.

C97 Books at Random. *Woman's Leader* 12 : 393, 28 May.
Signed 'FUZE'. See C83. About slang.

C98 ★Kit Logan and Lady Helen. *Oxford and Cambridge Miscellany* (June 1920), p. 1.

C99 ★The Stake. *London Mercury* 2 : 138 June.

C100 [Review of Robert Nichols' *Aurelia*.] *Isis* 563 : 11, 9 June.
Signed 'R. G.' Possibly by Graves.

C101 Books at Random. *Woman's Leader* 12 : 439, 11 June.
Signed 'FUZE'. See C83. About *Irene Iddesleigh*.

C102 Books at Random. *Woman's Leader* 12 : 462, 18 June.
Signed 'FUZE'. See C83. About Traherne, Campion, Donne, Douglas, Henryson, Darley, Clare and Skelton: 'neglected and recently rescued' poets.

C103 ★Storm: At the Farm Window. *Spectator* 124 : 828, 19 June.

C104 ★The Pier-Glass. *Athenaeum* 94 : 823, 25 June.

C105 Books at Random. *Woman's Leader* 12 : 486, 25 June.
Signed 'FUZE'. See C83. On blasphemy in art.

C106 Books at Random. *Woman's Leader* 12 : 585, 30 July.
Signed 'FUZE'. See C83. A 'holiday letter' from Hwch Goch.

C107 *Lady Student: A Study in Norman Influences. *Anglo-French Review* 4 : 52–53 August.

C108 *Incubus. *Spectator* 125 : 336, 11 September.

C109 *Lady Student: A Study in Norman Influences. *Living Age* 306 : 682, 11 September.

C110 *The Traveller's Curse after Misdirection (from the Welsh). *Saturday Review of Literature* 1 : 121, 20 September.

C111 *Delilah's Parrot: From the *Coronation Murder* Cycle. *Carthusian* 13 : 32 October.

C112 Isis Idol: Mr. T. E. Lawrence (Arabia and All Souls). *Isis* 567 : 5, 27 October.
Unsigned; acknowledged.

1921

C113 *The Finding of Love. *London Mercury* 3 : 254–55 January.

C114 *Raising the Monolith. *Athenaeum*, 7 January, p. 8.

C115 *The Magical Picture. *Saturday Westminster Gazette*, 22 January, p. 10.

C116 *The Magical Picture. *Living Age* 309 : 124, 9 April.

C117 *'The General Elliott'. *Spectator* 126 : 491, 16 April.

C118 *Song of Contrariety. *Outlook* 47 : 393, 7 May.

C119 *Cynics and Romantics. *To-Day* 8 : 154 June.

C120 *Records for Wonder. *Saturday Westminster Gazette*, 4 June, p. 10.

C121 *Raising the Monolith. *Living Age* 309 : 586, 4 June.

C122 *Song of Contrariety. *Living Age* 309 : 794, 25 June.

C123 *On the Ridge. *Nation* (London) 29 : 613, 23 July.

C124 *The Lands of Whipperginny. *Voices* 5 : 110 Autumn.

C125 *Sullen Moods – A Lover Since Childhood – The Bedpost – Old Wives' Tales. *London Mercury* 4 : 455–58 September.

C126 *Lawyer's Tale. *New Republic* 28 : 103, 21 September.

C127 A Parable. *Form* 1 : 17–20 October.
Reprinted A7, Sec. VIII.

C128 *Old Wives' Tales. *Literary Digest* 71 : 32, 22 October.

C129 *A Lover Since Childhood. *Literary Digest* 71 : 134, 29 October.

C130 The Dangers of Definition. *SPE Tract* 6, pp. 23–26.

C131 *Philosophers. *Form* 1 : 56 November–December.

C132 *The Sewing Basket (A Wedding Present from Jenny Nicholson to Winifred Roberts). *Spectator* 127 : 595–96, 5 November.

C133 Poets and anthologies. *Times Literary Supplement*, 1 December, p. 789.
Letter commending T. S. Eliot's complaint about anthologies.

C134 How English Is Taught. *Daily Herald*, 14 December, p. 7.
Review of *The Teaching of English in England* by a committee of the President of the Board of Education.

C135 *Christmas Eve. *New Republic* 29 : 125, 28 December.

1922

C136 Inspiration and the Pattern. *Form* 1 : 103 January.

C137 *Old Lob-Lie-by-the-Fire. *Spectator* 128 : 15, 7 January.

C138 *On Preserving a Poetical Formula – Epitaph on an Unfortunate Artist. *Spectator* 128 : 175, 11 February.

C139 *The Red Ribbon Dream. *New Republic* 30 : 43, 8 March.

C140 *Philosophers. *Harpers* 144 : 722 May.

C141 *The Rock Below. *London Mercury* 6 : 17 May.

C142 *Whipperginny (as 'Wipperginny'). *London Mercury* 6 : 129 June.

C143 Answers to a Questionnaire. *Chapbook* 27 : 11–14 July.

C144 *On D – A Lover Who Died in an Accident. *Spectator* 129 : 16, 1 July.

C145 The Illogic of Stoney Stratford and of Poetry. *Spectator* 129 : 87, 15 July.

C146 *Whipperginny. *Literary Digest* 74 : 36, 15 July.

C147 Poetic Catharsis and Modern Psychology. *Spectator* 129 : 151–52, 29 July.

C148 Alexander Pope. *Daily Herald*, 30 August, p. 7.
Short biographical and critical note.

C149 *A Forced Music. *Spectator* 129 : 305, 2 September.

C150 *Return. *Saturday Review* 134 : 420, 16 September.

C151 Mr Graves Replies. *Literary Review* [of *New York Evening Post*], 7 October, p. 98.
Review by Joseph Wood Krutch, 12 August, p. 868.

C152 *A Forced Music. *Living Age* 315 : 56, 7 October.

C153 *Return. *Independent* 109 : 236, 28 October.

C154 *An English Wood. *New Republic* 32 : 248, 1 November.

C155 *Children of Darkness. *New Republic* 33 : 11, 29 November.

C156 *Mirror, Mirror – Return. *Bookman* (New York) 56 . 448 December.

C157 *On the Poet's Birth. *Fugitive* 1 : 103 December.

C158 *A Valentine. *Fugitive* 1 : 112 December.

1923

C159 *The Avengers. *The Observer*, 14 January, p. 13.

C160 *Children of Darkness. *Bookman* (New York) 56 : 718 February.

C161 *The Lord Chamberlain Tells of a Famous Meeting. *Poetry* 21 : 257–61 February.

C162 *The Snake and the Bull. *Chapbook* 35 : 19–21 March.

C163 *A Dewdrop. *Harpers* 146 : 526 March.

C164 *A Dewdrop. *Spectator* 130 : 406, 10 March.

C165 *Lost Love. *Living Age* 317 : 116, 14 April.

C166 The Eagle and the Wren. *Nation and Athenaeum* 33 : 272–73, 26 May.

Review of Edith Sitwell's *Bucolic Comedies* and C. M. Doughtys' *Mansoul*.

C167 *Twin Souls. *Saturday Review* 135 : 733, 2 June.

C168 *Misgivings, on Reading a Popular 'Outline of Science'. *Lyric* 3 : 1 July.

C169 Mr. Hardy and the Pleated Skirt. *Nation and Athenaeum* 33 : 451–52, 7 July.

C170 *Twin Souls. *Living Age* 318 : 330, 18 August.

C171 What Is Bad Poetry? *North American Review* 218 : 353–68 September.

C172 *The Safe, or Erewhon Redivivus. *Winter Owl* [November], pp. 18–19.

Signed 'John Doyle'.

C173 Interchange of Selves. [As by B. K. Mallik.] *Winter Owl* [November], pp. 28–43.

C174 *Full Moon. *Winter Owl* [November], pp. 44–45.

C175 *The Knowledge of God. *Winter Owl* [November], p. 59.

C176 British or English. *SPE Tract* 15, p. 22.
About usage of the two words.

C177 A Poetess and Five Poets. *Nation and Athenaeum* 34 : 278–79, 17 November.
Review of *Trentaremi and Other Moods* by Sir Rennell Rodd, *Poems* by W. S. Blunt, *Autumn Midnight* by Frances Cornford, *The Day's Delight* by Geoffrey Dearmer, *A Devonshire Garden* by R. H. Foster and *Plummets* by Henry Allsopp.

C178 *Henry and Mary. *Current Opinion* 75 : 736 December.

C179 A 'Galileo of mares' nests.' *Spectator* 131 : 949–50, 15 December.
On Samuel Butler.

C180 'The Victorian Pageant.' *Nation and Athenaeum* 34 : 492–93, 29 December.
Review of John Drinkwater's *Victorian Poetry* and Frances M. Sim's *Robert Browning: Poet and Philosopher*.

1924

C181 *Northwards from Oxford: An Architectural Progress. *Nation and Athenaeum* 34 : 516, 5 January.

C182 *The Kingfisher's Return from Being Stuffed. [With Molly Adams.] *Spectator* 132 : 52, 12 January.

C183 A 'Galileo of mares' nests.' *Living Age* 321 : 180–83, 26 January.

C184 *The Cost. *Oxford Outlook* 6 : 76–77 February.

C185 Ejaculations before Reviewing. *Nation and Athenaeum* 34 : 670–71, 9 February.
Review of *At Dawn* by Hon. Evan Morgan, *An Offering of Swans* by Oliver Gogarty, *The Death of Itylus* by Edward Glyn-Jones, *The Wise Men Come to Town* by William Jeffrey and *Frogs at Twilight* by Helen Nicholson.

C186 Mr. Hardy and the Pleated Skirt. *New Republic* 38 : 77–79, 12 March.

C187 'The Freeing of Ariel.' *Nation and Athenaeum* 34 : 891–92, 22 March.

Review of *Ariel: A Shelley Romance* by André Maurois.

C188 Wanted: Poetic Value Charts. *Nation and Athenaeum* 35 : 20, 5 April.

Review of *The Chilswell Book of English Poetry*, ed. Robert Bridges.

C189 Kensington Gardens to Looking Glass Land. *Nation and Athenaeum* 35 : 88, 19 April.

Review of *Kensington Gardens* by Humbert Wolfe, *The Pilgrim of Festus* by Conrad Aiken and *The Sleeping Beauty* by Edith Sitwell.

C190 ★At the Games. *English Life* 2 : 348–50 May.

C191 The Cup Final. *Nation and Athenaeum* 35 : 144, 3 May.

Aston Villa v. Newcastle.

C192 Eleven Plays. *Nation and Athenaeum* 35 : 250, 252, 24 May.

Review of *Tunnel Trench* by Hubert Griffith, *Krishna Kumari* by Edward Thompson, *First Blood* by Allan Monkhouse, *The Fanatics* by Miles Malleson, *The Three Barrows* by Charles McEvoy, *The Forest* by John Galsworthy, *Far above Rubies* by Alfred Sutro, *Taffy* by Caradoc Evans, *Beyond the Horizon* and *Gold* by Eugene O'Neill and *Punchinello* by Alfred Rosenberg.

C193 Critical Limitations. *Nation and Athenaeum* 35 : 542, 544, 6 July.

Review of *The Awakening and Other Poems* by Don Marquis, *Selected Poems* and *New Hampshire* by Robert Frost, *The White Stallion* by F. V. Branford, *Tally Ho! and Other Hunting Noises* by J. B. Morton, *Visiting Winds* by Eric N. Batterham, and *Wayfaring* by William Force Stead.

C194 ★Sergeant-Major Money: An Economic Allegory. *Nation and Athenaeum* 35 : 476, 12 July.

C195 ★A Vehicle, to Wit, a Bicycle. *New Statesman* 17 : 414, 16 July.

C196 ★Modern Poetry: 'That This House Approves the Trend of Modern Poetry.' *Adelphi* 2 : 288–90 September.

C197 ★Allie – Burrs and Brambles. *London Mercury* 10 : 459–61 September.

C198 Gold and Iron. *Nation and Athenaeum* 35 : 723, 13 September.

Review of H. J. Massingham's *In Praise of England*.

C199 Anthologies Private and Public. *Nation and Athenaeum* 35 : 751, 20 September.

Review of N. G. Royde-Smith's *A Private Anthology* and John Buchan's *The Northern Muse*.

C200 *A History. *Decachord* 1 : 146 November–December.

C201 Poets in War and Peace. *Saturday Review of Literature* I: 250, 1 November.

About Hardy, Doughty and the young 'War-poets'.

C202 *The Presence. *Nation and Athenaeum* 36 : 266, 15 November.

C203 Eleven Pounds Weight of Verse. *Nation and Athenaeum* 36 : 333–34, 29 November.

Review of *Flame and Shadow* by Sara Teasdale, *April Twilights* by Willa Cather, *The Wayland-Dietrich Saga* by Katherine M. Buck, *Collected Works* and *Selected Poems* by Herbert Trench, *The Magic Grape* by Reginald Cripps, *Poems* by Henry Derozio, *The Well of Memory* by E. E. Speight and *Miss Bedell* by C. C. Abbott.

C204 *From Our Ghostly Enemy. *London Mercury* 11 : 128–29 December.

C205 Muscular Poetry. *Saturday Review of Literature* I : 412, 27 December.

Review of John Crowe Ransom's *Chills and Fever*.

1925

C206 *From Our Ghostly Enemy. *Literary Digest* 84 : 31, 3 January.

C207 'Beastly' Skelton. *Nation and Athenaeum* 36 : 614–15, 31 January.

Review of Richard Hughes' edition of Skelton.

C208 Such Stuff As Dreams. *Saturday Review* 139 : 80, 24 January.

Letter in reply to review of A11, 139 : 32–33, 10 January.

C209 Sensory Vehicles of Poetic Thought. *Saturday Review of Literature* 1 : 489–90, 31 January.

C210 *The Clipped Stater – Essay on Knowledge – A Letter from Wales. *Calendar* 1 : 23–31 March.

C211 Mr. Santayana, Mr. Freeman and Others. *Nation and Athenaeum* 36 : 815–16, 14 March.

Review of Santayana's *Lucifer*, John Freeman's *The Grove* and Thomas Moult's *Best Poems of 1924*.

C212 Poetic 'Control' by Spirits. *Southwest Review* 10 : 55–62 April.

C213 *Ballad of Tilly Kettle. *Nation and Athenaeum* 37 : 16, 4 April.

C214 *Passing of the Farmer. *London Mercury* 12 : 8–9 May.

C215 Tarantula barbipes and Some Poets. *Nation and Athenaeum* 37 : 140, 142, 2 May.

Review of *Poems and Fables* by R. C. Trevelyan, *An Essex Harvest* by H. H. Abbott, *Collected Poems* by Maurice Baring, *The Spirit of Happiness* by Lord Gorell, *Parallax* by Nancy Cunard, *Complete Poems* by Emily Dickinson, *First Poems* by Edwin Muir and *Adriatica* by Ferenc Békássy.

C216 *A Letter: Richard Rolls to His Friend, Captain Abel Wright. *Southwest Review* 10 : 87–91 July.

C217 *The Marmosite's Miscellany. *Calendar* 2 : 1–14 September.

Signed 'John Doyle'.

C218 An Oxford Guide Book. *Nation and Athenaeum* 37 : 735–36, 19 September.

Review of L. Rice-Oxley's *Oxford Renowned*.

C219 Keats and Mr. Murry. *Calendar* 2 : 131–35 October.

Review of John Middleton Murry's *Keats and Shakespeare*.

C220 *Ovid in Defeat. *London Mercury* 12 : 568–69 October.

C221 *An Occasion. *Nation and Athenaeum* 38 : 150, 24 October.

C222 Mr. George Pontifex and More Recent Travellers. *Nation and Athenaeum* 38 : 184, 31 October.

Review of *The Little World* by Stella Benson.

C223 *Ancestors. *Chapbook* 40 : 51 [November].

C224 *Four Children. *Spectator* 135 : 972, 28 November.

C225 On Foul and Blasphemous Tongues. *Calendar* 2 : 248–57 December.

C226 *The Corner Knot. *Fugitive* 4 : 124 December.

C227 Donnybrook Fair and Seven Poets. *Nation and Athenaeum* 38 : 442, 444, 19 December.

Review of *Poems* by Barrington Gates, *The Old Gods and Other Poems* by Richard Rowley, *The Cattle Drive in Connaught* by Austin Clarke, *I Heard a Sailor* by Wilfrid Gibson, *Selected Poems* by Aldous Huxley, *Songs of Salvation, Sin and Satire* by Herbert E. Palmer and *Poems, Brief and New* by William Watson.

C228 *The Hobby Horse.

An extempore poem included in C227.

C229 *Bargain. *Spectator* 135 : 1143, 19 December.

1926

C230 [Review of Edward Thompson's *The Other Side of the Medal.*] *Calendar* 2 : 364–66 January.

C231 *Four Children. *Literary Digest* 88 : 28, 2 January.

C232 *Bargain. *Literary Digest* 88 : 34, 23 January.

C233 *Virgil the Sorcerer. *Calendar* 2 : 376–78 February.

C234 The Future of English Poetry. *Fortnightly Review* 125 : 289–302 March; 125 : 443–53 April.

C235 *Pygmalion to Galatea. *London Mercury* 14 : 10–11 May.

C236 *Toads. *London Mercury* 14 : 232–33 July.

C237 *Pygmalion to Galatea. *Living Age* 330 : 27–28, 3 July.

C238 *The Corner Knot. *Literary Digest* 90 : 34, 14 August.

C239 Piping Peter and Others. *Nation and Athenaeum* 39 : 617, 28 August.

> Review of *The Green Bough* by Ann Allnutt Knox, *The Laburnum Branch* by Naomi Mitchison, *Martha-Wish-You-Ill* by Ruth Manning-Sanders, *Collected Poems* by A.E., *Poems 1902–1925* by Edward Thompson and *Chorus of the Newly Dead* by Edwin Muir.

C240 *The Taint. *Harpers* 153 : 502 September.

C241 The State of Poetry. *Saturday Review of Literature* 3 : 129–30, 25 September.

> Shortened version of C234.

C242 Mothering Poetry. *Nation and Athenaeum* 40 : 30–31, 9 October.

> Review of *Poets and Their Art* by Harriet Monroe.

C243 *Dumpling's Address to Gourmets. *Nation and Athenaeum* 40 : 113, 23 October.

C244 *Boots and Bed. *Harpers* 153 : 758 November.

C245 *Pure Death. *Nation* (New York) 123 : 509, 17 November.

C246 Impenetrability I. *Fortnightly Review* 126 : 781–92 December.

C247 *The Cool Web. *London Mercury* 15 : 127 December.

C248 *A Dedication of Three Hats. *Saturday Review of Literature* 3 : 445, 18 December.

1927

C249 Impenetrability II. *Fortnightly Review* 127 : 59–73 January.

C250 The Anthologist in Our Midst. [With Laura Riding.] *Calendar* 4 : 22–36 April.

C251 *In the Beginning Was a Word – The Cool Web – The Bait. *Poetry* 30 : 16–18 April.

C252 [Review of Malinowski's *Crime and Custom in Savage Society* and *Myth in Primitive Psychology* and W. H. R. Rivers' *Ethnology*.] *Criterion* 5 : 247–52 May.

C253 *An Independent. *Saturday Review of Literature* 3 : 939, 2 July.

C254 [Note on Poe.] *Bookman* (London) 72 : 258 August.

C255 Mallory of Everest. *Nation and Athenaeum* 41 : 723, 3 September.

Review of *George Leigh Mallory: A Memoir* by David Pye.

C256 [Letter in answer to a review of Laura Riding's *The Close Chaplet*.] *Criterion* 6 : 357–59 October.

Review by John Gould Fletcher, 6 : 168–72 August; rejoinder by Fletcher 6 : 546–47 December.

C257 *O Jorrocks I Have Promised. *transition* 7 : 133 October.

C258 *The Dead Ship. *London Mercury* 17 : 14 November.

1928

C259 Thomas Hardy. *Sphere* 112 : 129, 28 January.

C260 New Tales about Lawrence of Arabia. *World's Work* 55 : 389–98 February.

C261 Lawrence of Arabia as a Buck Private. *World's Work* 55 : 508–16 March.

C262 The Real Col. Lawrence. *World's Work* 55 : 663–70 April.

C263 The Making of a Conqueror. *World's Work* 56 : 100–11 May.

C264 A Letter from William Wordsworth. *Life and Letters* 1 : 208–11 August.

C265 Patronage and the English Poets. *Fortnightly Review* 130 : 400–08 September.

C266 'The Enormous Room': A Note by Robert Graves *Now and Then* 29 : 25–26 Autumn.

C267 Trench History. *Nation and Athenaeum* 44 : 420, 15 December.

Review of *Ten Years Ago* by R. H. Mottram and *Undertones of War* by Edmund Blunden.

C268 The Future of Humour. *Nation and Athenaeum* 44 : 441, 22 December.

Letter in reply to E. V. Knox's review of A30 at 44 : [379], 8 December.

1929

C269 Romantic Criticism. [With Laura Riding.] *Times Literary Supplement*, 3 January, p. 12.

Letter supporting the *TLS* review of Humbert Wolfe's *Dialogues and Monologues*.

C270 By a Thames Window. *Evening News*, 26 February, p. 11.

Reprinted as 'Thames-Side Reverie'.

C271 On Charity. *Manchester Guardian*, 8 February, p. 20.

Reprinted as 'Charity Appeals'.

C272 I Solve Man's Dress Problem for Myself, At Least – and Nobody Jeers! *Evening News*, 24 July, p. 11.

C273 More War Books. *Nation and Athenaeum* 45 : 629–30, 10 August.

Review of *A Subaltern's War* by Charles Edmonds and *The Wet Flanders Plain* by Henry Williamson.

C274 Robert Graves Replies. *Daily Mail*, 16 December, p. 10.

C275 Troops Who Stuck It Out. *Daily Mail*, 17 December, p. 10.

C276 Soldier-Poet Hits Back at Critics. *Daily Herald*, 23 December, pp. 1, 6.

1930

C277 The Jocks. *Daily Mail*, 2 January, p. 8.

Letter in answer to a letter signed 'Black Watch' (*Daily Mail*, 19 December, p. 10) about a supposed German rating of British divisions.

C278 The Cheshire Regiment. *Morning Post*, 23 January, p. 9.

Letter in answer to Sir Hastings Anderson, *Morning Post*, 3 January, p. 4, about the Royal Welch Fusiliers' rivalry with the Cheshire.

C279 What It Feels Like to be Famous. *Daily Herald*, 7 February, p. 4.

C280 A Brass Hat in No Man's Land. *Now and Then* 36 : 7–9 Summer.

Review of book of same title by Brig. Gen. F. P. Crozier.

C281 The Garlands Wither. *Times Literary Supplement*, 26 June, p. 534.

Letter about war novels.

1931

C282 Modern Riddles. [With Laura Riding.] *Times Literary Supplement*, 26 February, p. 154.

Letter in answer to review of A34, *TLS*, 1 January, p. 8.

C283 Salute of Guns. *Now and Then* 38 : 36–37 Spring.

Review of war book of same title by Donald Boyd.

C284 An Incomplete Complete Skelton. *Adelphi* n.s. 3 : [146] 147–58 December.

Review of Philip Henderson's edition of Skelton.

1933

C285 'Old Soldiers Never Die.' *Times Literary Supplement*, 14 September, p. 611.

Letter about review of A41, *TLS*, 31 August, p. 571; rejoinder *TLS*, 28 September, p. 651.

1934

C286 'I, Claudius.' *Bookman* (London) 86 : 201 July.

Reply to review by Jack Lindsay, *Bookman* 86 : 166 June.

C287 English Epigrams. *Times Literary Supplement*, 19 July, p. 511.

Letter ascribing an epigram to Skelton, not Herrick. Rejoinder, *TLS*, 2 August, p. 541.

C288 [Answers to a questionnaire on poetry.] *New Verse* 11 : 5–6 October.

C289 Mr. Lindsay's Rome. *Bookman* (London) 87 : 123 November.

Review of Jack Lindsay's *Caesar Is Dead*.

C290 Mr. Graves and Mr. Lindsay. *Bookman* (London) 87 : 197 December.

Reply to Lindsay, *Bookman* 87 : 66 October. See C289.

1935

C291 A Letter from Robert Graves. *Left Review* 2 : [128]–29 December.

Reply to Montagu Slater, 'The Turning Point', *Left Review* 2 : 15–23 October.

1936

C292 [Letter about the Lawrence-Feisal letters in reply to front-page article of 16 June.] *News Chronicle*, 29 June, p. 15.

1938

C293 Powerless in the Matter. *Spectator* 160 : 510–11, 25 March.
About trouble with ministries.

C294 English Humorists. *Times Literary Supplement*, 28 May, p. 369.

Letter about neglect of Skelton.

1939

C295 Ubu Empereur: La Mort de Caligula. *Les Annales politiques et littéraires* 113 : 446–53, 25 April.
Reprinted from the French translation of *I, Claudius*.

C296 The Mad Caligula Humors Himself. *Reader's Digest* 35 : 68–70 September.
Condensed from A42.

C297 *On Rising Early – One Hard Look. *Scholastic* 35 : 25–26E, 30 October.

1941

C298 Leave, 1915. *Lilliput* 8 : 278–79 April.
Memoirs.

C299 Thursday Morning and Our Long Week-End. [With Alan Hodge.] *Readers News*, October.
[Seen only as extracted clipping.]

C300 War Poetry in This War. *Listener* 26 : 566–67, 23 October.
Reprinted as 'The Poets of World War II'.

1942

C301 Common Sense about Ghosts. *Atlantic* 169 : 752–55 June.

C302 [Letter on patience.] *The Times*, 18 August, p. 5.

C303 *The Eugenist. *English Review* 34 : 84 October.

C304 *1805. *Listener* 28 : 494, 15 October.

C305 [Letter on Scipio and Belisarius.] *The Times*, 29 October, p. 5.

1943

C306 'Wife to Mr. Milton.' *Times Literary Supplement*, 2 February, p. 67.
Reply to review, *TLS*, 30 January, p. 53.

C307 [Letter about fourth terms for U. S. Presidents.] *The Times*, 12 March, p. 5.

C308 *The Persian Version – Apollo of the Physiologists – The Beach – The Villagers and Death – The Oldest Soldier – Grotesques (i–v). *New Writing and Daylight* (Summer), pp. 74–77.

C309 Eyes on the Reader. *Times Literary Supplement*, 19 June p. 295.
Reply to review of A55, *TLS*, 12 June, p. 283. Rejoinder, 3 July p. 319. Further reply by Graves, 3 July, p. 319.

C310 It Happened in 537 A.D. *Lilliput* 13 : 424–26 December.
About Belisarius.

1944

C311 *The Door – Death by Drums – Under the Pot – To Lucia at Birth – Through Nightmare. *Wales* 4 : 32–33 January.

C312 It Happened in 513 B.C. *Lilliput* 14 : 122–34 February.
About Darius and Herodotus.

C313 Dog, Lapwing and Roebuck. *Wales* 4 : 34–51 Summer.

C314 Bards and Gleemen. *Wales* 4 : 95–97 Summer.
Review of *Other Men's Flowers* by Field-Marshall Viscount Wavell.

C315 [Letter on Independence Day broadcast.] *The Times*, 7 July, p. 5.

C316 [Letter on the unicorn's beard.] *The Times*, 7 August, p. 5.

C317 [Letters on the teaching of English.] *The Times*, 29 August, p. 5; 8 September, p. 8; 13 September, p. 8; 20 September, p. 8.

C318 Dog, Lapwing and Roebuck (2). *Wales* 4 : 36–50 Autumn.

C319 [Letter about Thomas Atkins.] *The Times*, 23 October, p. 5.

C320 [Letter on usage of 'from' and 'to'.] *The Times*, 17 November, p. 5.

1945

C321 Dog, Lapwing and Roebuck (3). *Wales* 4 : 57–67 Winter.

C322 The Search for Thomas Atkins. *Lilliput* 16 : 99–103 February.

C323 *The Shot. *Tomorrow* 5 : 40 October.

C324 *A Stranger at the Party. *Tomorrow* 5 : 27 December.

C325 *The Blodeuwedd of Gwion ap Gwreang – Battle of the Trees. *Wales* 5 : 22–25 December.

1946

C326 A Conversation at Paphos, A.D. 43. *Windmill* 1 : 143–54 [Winter].

C327 *The Persian Version. *Atlantic* 177 : 146 March.

C328 The Scholar in the Scullery. *The Times*, 2 March, p. 5.
Manual work necessary for scholars.

C329 *To Juan at the Winter Solstice. *Nation* 163 : 19, 6 July.

C330 It Was a Stable World. *Cornhill* 162 : 113–20 Autumn.

C331 'King Jesus.' *Times Literary Supplement*, 21 December, p. 629.
Reply to review, 7 December, p. 601. See C332.

1947

C332 'King Jesus.' *Times Literary Supplement*, 25 January, p. 51.
Further reply to review (see C331). Further reply by Graves, 29 March, p. 141. Rejoinders, 4 January, p. 9; 15 February, p. 91; 8 March, p. 103.

C333 [Reply to review of A59.] *Tablet* 189 : 122, 8 March.

C334 *Gulls and Men. *Tomorrow* 7 : 42 May.

C335 'King Jesus.' *Commentary* 4 : 84–86 July.
Reply to review by Mordecai S. Chertoff, 3 : 391–93 April.

C336 The Feud of St. Peter and St. Paul. *Tomorrow* 6 : 19–26 August.
Reprinted as 'Está en su casa'.

C337 *The Sirens' Welcome to Red-Faced Cronos. *Tomorrow* 7 : 49 September.

C338 Historic Logic of 'King Jesus'. *Cornhill* 162 : 433–39 Autumn.

C339 Folk Dance in Majorca. *Dance Index* 6 : 149 October.

C340 *Return of the Goddess Artemis – Intercession in Late October. *Poetry* 71 : 22–23 October.

C341 *To Be Named a Bear. *Tomorrow* 7 : 31 October.

C342 *The Last Day of Leave. *Tomorrow* 7 : 16 November.

1948

C343 *Return of the Goddess – Intercession in Late October. *New Statesman* 35 : 29, 10 January.

C344 *The Sirens' Welcome to Red-Faced Cronos. *New Statesman* 35 : 69, 24 January.

C345 What Is Asphodel? *Fortnightly Review* 169 : 214–15 March.
Reprinted as 'The Common Asphodel'.

C346 [Analysis of 'The Return of the Goddess Artemis.'] *Poetry: A Crtical Supplement* (April), pp. 18–21.
Reply to John Frederick Nims' analysis, October 1947, pp. 14–16.

C347 The Song the Sirens Sang. *Times Literary Supplement*, 24 April, p. 233.
Mentions the forthcoming A61.

C348 'Digested Classics.' *Times Literary Supplement*, 12 June, p. 331.
About A39. Part of a lengthy correspondence.

C349 The White Goddess. *Spectator* 180 : 767, 25 June.
Reply to review of A61 by G. E. Daniel, 180 : 680, 4 June.

C350 The White Goddess. *Nation* 167 : 634, 4 December.

1949

C351 Wordsworth and Annette. *Times Literary Supplement*, 23 April, p. 265.
About Wordsworth's guilt: reply to letter by John Eglinton, 19 March, p. 185.

C352 *The Chink. *Poetry Review* 40 : 172 June–July.

C353 *The Chink. *Poetry Review* 40 : 298 August–September.
Corrected text of C352 and letter.

C354 *Conversation Piece. *Tomorrow* 8 : 48 August.

C355 The Future of Western Religion. *Tomorrow* 9 : 5–10 September.

C356 Parable of the Talents: A Suggested Emendation. *Listener* 42 : 445, 448, 15 September.

C357 'The Common Asphodel.' *Times Literary Supplement*, 4 November, p. 715.
Letter in reply to review, 30 September, p. 632, and to letter, 14 October, p. 665. Rejoinder 11 November, p. 733.

1950

C358 [Answer to a religious questionnaire.] *Partisan Review* 17 : 133–37 February.

C359 *The Jackals' Address to Isis. *Poetry* 75 : 257 February.

C360 *The Death Room. *New Yorker* 25 : 35, 4 February.

C361 How Mad Are Hatters? *Lilliput* 26 : 31–33 March.

C362 *Counting the Beats. *Good Housekeeping* 130 : 42 April.

C363 *Conversation Piece. *New Statesman* 39 : 518, 6 May.

C364 'The Golden Ass.' *Times Literary Supplement*, 30 June, p. 405.
Reply to review, 2 June, p. 336.

C365 My Favorite Forgotten Book. *Tomorrow* 9 : 59–6(August.
Reprinted in 'The Age of Obsequiousness'.

C366 *Homage to Texas. *New Yorker* 26 : 28, 2 September.

C367 *Advice to Lovers. *New Yorker* 26 : 28, 16 September.

C368 A Mantleful of Northwind. *Nine* 5 : 291–97 Autumn.

The first half is a review of Joseph Campbell's *The Hero with a Thousand Faces*; the second half is C365.

C369 'Wellcome to the Caves of Arta.' *New Yorker* 26 : 42, 9 December.

1951

C370 *My Name and I. *New Yorker* 26 : 38, 6 January.

C371 *For the Rain It Raineth Every Day. *New Yorker* 27 : 28, 24 March.

C372 The Language of Myth. *Hudson Review* 4 : 1–21 Spring.

C373 *The Survivor. *Tomorrow* 10 : 41 May.

C374 Bunyan at the Siege of Leicester. *Times Literary Supplement*, 11 May, p. 293.

C375 *The Young Cordwainer. *New Statesman* 41 : 685, 16 June.

C376 *Primrose and Periwinkle – Prometheus – Darien. *Hudson Review* 4 : 204–07 Summer.

C377 *The Ghost and the Clock. *Tomorrow* 10 : 49 July.

C378 *The Survivor. *New Statesman* 42 : 160, 11 August.

C379 *Questions in a Wood. *Listener* 46 : 787, 8 November.

C380 *Prometheus. *Listener* 46 : 829, 15 November.

C381 *With the Gift of a Ring – Cry Faugh! – The Foreboding – The Straw – Hercules at Nemea. *Poetry* 79 : 125–29 December.

C382 *Damocles. *New Yorker* 27 : 54, 1 December.

1952

C383 Mother Goose's Lost Goslings. *Hudson Review* 4 : 586–97 Winter.

C384 *Lovers in Winter. *New Yorker* 27 : 82, 19 January.

C385 *The Foreboding – Cry Faugh! – The Straw – With the Gift of a Ring. *New Statesman* 43 : 101, 26 January.

C386 Mr. Alexander Clifford. *The Times*, 28 March, p. 8.
Obituary.

C387 *I'm Through with You Forever. *New Yorker* 28 : 89, 29 March.

C388 The Future of Western Religion. *Nine* 8 : 209–19 Spring.

C389 The Shout. *Fantasy and Science Fiction* 3 : 75–91 April.

C390 *I'm Through with You Forever. *Spectator* 188 : 543, 25 April.

C391 *A Pinch of Salt. *Saturday Review of Literature* 35 : 8, 3 May.

C392 *Dialogue on the Headland. *New Statesman* 43 : 746, 21 June.

C393 Jungian Mythology. *Hudson Review* 5 : 245–57 Summer.
Discussion of Jungian response to mythology.

C394 *Rhea. *New Statesman* 44 : 109, 26 July.

C395 The Seventh Man: Tributes to Sir Max Beerbohm on His Eightieth Birthday. *Listener* 48 : 338, 28 August.
Part IV is by Graves.

C396 *The Sacred Mission. *Poetry* 81 : 39 October.

C397 *Dethronement. *Atlantic* 190 : 75 December.

C398 *Advice to Col. Valentine. *New Yorker* 28 : 26, 27 December.

1953

C399 The Devil is a Protestant. *Botteghe Oscure* 12 : 114–23.

C400 *The Devil at Berry Pomeroy – Hippopotamus's Address to the Freudians – The Portrait – Twin to Twin – Leaving the Rest Unsaid. *Hudson Review* 5 : 517–20 Winter.

C401 *The Devil at Berry Pomeroy. *New Statesman* 45 : 43, 10 January.

C402 The Old Black Cow. *New Statesman* 45 : 299, 14 March.

C403 *Cat-Goddesses. *New Yorker* 29 : 38, 14 March.

C404 *From the Embassy. *Poetry* 82 : 14 April.

C405 *With Her Lips Only. *Times Literary Supplement*, 10 April, p. 232.

C406 *Dethronement. *Listener* 49 : 726, 30 April.

C407 *To the Queen. *Time and Tide* 34 : 747, 6 June.

C408 The Marriage of Hercules and Eve. *New Statesman* 45 : 781–82, 27 June.
Review of Levy's *The Sword from the Rock.*

C409 *Sirocco at Deyá. *New Statesman* 45 : 738, 20 June.

C410 *The Mark. *Listener* 50 : 12, 2 July.

C411 *The Blue-Fly. *New Yorker* 29 : 28, 11 July.

C412 *Leaving the Rest Unsaid. *Times Literary Supplement*, 31 July, p. 490.

C413 *The Sea Horse. *Atlantic* 192 : 96 August.

C414 *The Encounter. *New Statesman* 46 : 211, 22 August.

C415 The Lower Criticism. *New Statesman* 46 : 237–38, 29 August.
Review of Rupert Furneaux's *The Other Side of the Story.*

C416 *Cat-Goddesses. *New Statesman* 46 : 291, 12 September.

C417 *Liadan and Curithir. *Time and Tide* 34 : 1210, 19 September.

C418 Progressive Puericulture. *Hudson Review* 6 : 476–80 Autumn.

Review of Meigs, Eaton, Nesbitt and Vigners' *A Critical History of Children's Literature*.

C419 What Happened to Atlantis? *Atlantic* 192 : 71–74 October.

C420 *Considine. *Punch* 225 : 457, 14 October.

C421 *Juggler. *Saturday Review of Literature* 36 : 12, 17 October.

C422 Dr. Syntax and Mr. Pound. *Punch* 225 : 498, 21 October.

C423 *To the Queen. *Atlantic* 192 : 47 November.

C424 *Hippopotamus's Address to the Freudians. *Punch* 225 : 568, 11 November.

C425 Juana Inés de la Cruz. *Encounter* 1 : 5–13 December.
Reprinted as 'Juana de Asbaje'.

C426 *The Juggler. *Time and Tide* 34 : 1575, 5 December.

C427 Gospel Truth. [With Joshua Podro.] *New Statesman* 46 : 762, 12 December.
Letter in reply to review of A69 by H. L. Short, 46 : 692, 694, 28 November; see C431.

C428 *Esau and Judith. *New Statesman* 46 : 765, 12 December.

1954

C429 Paul's Thorn. *Literary Guide* 69 : 3–4 January.

C430 School Life in Majorca. *Punch* 226 : 56–57, 6 January.
Reprinted with the addition of the *Bulletin*.

C431 Gospel Truth. [With Joshua Podro.] *New Statesman* 47 : 70, 16 January.
Reply to review of A69; see C427.

C432 [Letter.] [With Joshua Podro.] *Listener* 51 : 142–43, 21 January.
Reply to review of A69, 50 : 1136, 31 December 1953.

C433 Royal Victims. *Spectator* 192 : 103–04, 22 January.
Review of Margaret Alice Murray's *The Divine King in England*.

C434 *Young Witch. *Atlantic* 193 : 49 February.

C435 *Advice to Col. Valentine. *New Statesman* 47 : 196, 13 February.

C436 Treacle Tart. *Punch* 226 : 236–38, 17 February.

C437 'The Nazarene Gospel Restored.' *Times Literary Supplement,* 5 March, p. 153.
Reply to review, 19 February, p. 125. Further reply by Graves and Podro, 26 March, p. 201. Rejoinders 12 March, p. 169 and 2 April, p. 217. See also the editorial apology, 22 July, 1955, p. 413.

C438 Week-End at Cwm-Tatws. *Punch* 226 : 404–05, 31 March.

C439 The Language as Spoken. *Hudson Review* 7 : 155–60 Spring.
Review of *The Oxford Book of English Talk.*

C440 *Birth of a Great Man. *New Yorker* 30 : 30, 10 April.

C441 [Reply to review of A69.] [With Joshua Podro.] *Twentieth Century* 155 : 431–35 May.
Reply to review by E. L. Allen, 155 : 256–62 March; rejoinder 155 : 435–36 May.

C442 The Full Length. *Punch* 226 : 546–47, 5 May.

C443 *Spoils of Love. *New Yorker* 30 : 36, 22 May.

C444 From 'The Uneconomist.' *Punch* 226 : 640–41, 26 May.
Reprinted as 'Sappy Blancmange'.

C445 God Grant Your Honour Many Years. *Punch* 227 : 10–11 31 May.

C446 Books in General. *New Statesman* 47 : 761, 12 June.
Reprinted as 'The Essential E. E. Cummings'.

C447 *Spoils of Love. *New Statesman* 47 : 792, 19 June.

C448 Six Valiant Bulls. *Punch* 226 : 752–54, 23 June.
Reprinted as '6 Valiant Bulls 6'.

C449 Discoveries in Greek Mythology. *Hudson Review* 7 : 167–81 Summer.

C450 Books in General. *New Statesman* 48 : 17–18, 3 July.
Review of John Clare's *Poems*, ed. James Reeves.

C451 No. 2 Polstead Road. *New Statesman* 48 : 105–06, 24 July.
Review of T. E. Lawrence's *Home Letters*.

C452 Flesh-Coloured Net Tights. *Punch* 227 : 176, 4 August.

C453 Freud and Gotthilf von Schubert. *Times Literary Supplement*, 6 August, p. 501.
Letter suggesting anticipation of Freud in von Schubert (Graves' great-grandfather).

C454 Thy Servant and God's. *Punch* 227 : 232–33, 18 August.

C455 Majorca, the Fortunate Island. *Harper's Bazaar* 88 : 184–89, 272–73 September.
Reprinted as 'Why I Live in Majorca'.

C456 ★Birth of a Great Man. *New Statesman* 48 : 269, 4 September.

C457 Varro's 400 and 90 Books. *Punch* 227 : 320–22, 8 September.

C458 How the Gospels Were Written. [With Joshua Podro.] *Literary Guide* 69 : 18–22 October.
Material of A69.

C459 Working Models for Young Poets? *Times Literary Supplement*, 1 October, p. 625.
Letter in reply to suggestion that he and Empson might serve as such. Further replies by Graves, 29 October, p. 689, and 19 November, p. 739. Rejoinders, 15 October, p. 657, and 12 November, p. 721. Initiated by a review of Richard Aldington's *Ezra Pound and T. S. Eliot*, 10 September, p. 574.

C460 'A Man May Not Marry His ...' *New Statesman* 48 : 386–87, 2 October.

C461 *The Window Sill. *New Statesman* 48 : 476, 16 October.

C462 *Beauty in Trouble. *New Yorker* 30 : 34, 16 October.

C463 A Poet and His Public. *Listener* 52 : 711–12, 28 October.

C464 The Nativity – I. [With Joshua Podro.] *Literary Guide* 69 : 21–23 November.
Material of A69.

C465 The Nativity – II. [With Joshua Podro.] *Literary Guide* 69 : 17–20 December.
Material of A69.

C466 An Appointment for Candlemas. *Punch* 227 : 680–82, 1 December.

C467 Kynge Arthur is Nat Dede. *New Statesman* 48 : 745–46, 4 December.
See C473.

C468 *Beauty in Trouble. *New Statesman* 48 : 746, 4 December.

C469 *A Lost Jewel. *New Yorker* 30 : 22, 25 December.

C470 The Five Godfathers. *Punch* 227 : 824–26, 29 December.

1955

C471 The Nativity – III. [With Joshua Podro.] *Literary Guide* 70 : 17–21 January.
Material of A69.

C472 The White Horse. *Punch* 228 : 95–97, 12 January.

C473 Malory's Arthur. *New Statesman* 49 : 107, 22 January.
Letter in reply to Hugh Vaudrey, 49 : 45, 8 January, which is a reply to C467.

C474 Epics are out of Fashion. *Punch* 228 : 234–36, 16 February.

C475 Earth to Earth. *New Statesman* 49 : 240–41, 19 February.

C476 'The Greek Myths.' *Times Literary Supplement*, 25 March, p. 181.

Reply to review, 4 March, p. 137. Rejoinder 29 April, p. 209.

C477 The Integrity of the Poet. *Listener* 53 : 579–80, 31 March.

Letters in reply 53 : 623,7 April and 53 : 669, 14 April.

C478 Peasant Poet. *Hudson Review* 8 : 99–105 Spring.

Review of John Clare's *Poems*.

C479 These be Your Gods, O Israel! *Essays in Criticism* 5 : 129–50 April.

Replies 5 : 293–98 July.

C480 The Terror of History. *Spectator* 194 : 399–401, 1 April.

Review of Mircea Eliade's *The Myth of the Eternal Return*.

C481 *A Lost Jewel. *New Statesman* 49 : 476, 2 April.

C482 Numismatics for Student Christians. *New Statesman* 49 : 546, 16 April.

C483 They Say ... They Say. *Punch* 228 : 491–93, 20 April.

C484 Gerard Manley Hopkins. *Times Literary Supplement*, 29 April, p. 209.

Letter of apology for siring the new critical approach to Hopkins.

C485 *The Clearing. *New Yorker* 31 : 33, 30 April.

C486 The Oedipus Myth. *Atlantic* 195 : 56–59 May.

Version of A72.

C487 Christ and Caesar. *New Statesman* 49 : 650, 7 May.

Letter in reply to letter by W. A. Wordsworth 49 : 580, 23 April, which is reply to C482.

C488 *(Say) – The Three Pebbles – Penthesilea. *London Magazine* 2 : 35–36 June.

C489 The Abominable Mr. Gunn. *Punch* 228 : 782–84, 29 June.

C490 Greek Myths and Pseudo-Myths. *Hudson Review* 8 : 212–30 Summer.

About the Trojan War and myths surrounding it; material of A72.

C491 The Whitaker Negroes. *Encounter* 5 : 21–29 July.

C492 ★The Clearing. *New Statesman* 50 : 19, 2 July.

C493 ★Question. *New Yorker* 31 : 24, 30 July.

C494 New Light on Dream-Flight. *New Republic* 133 : 18–19, 8 August.

C495 Under the Shadow of Yggdrasil. *New Statesman* 50 : 219–20, 20 August.

Review of Brian Branston's *Gods of the North* and Walter Otto's *Homeric Gods.*

C496 ★The Tenants. *New Yorker* 31 : 28, 3 September.

C497 ★To a Spiteful Critic. *Punch* 229 : 327, 21 September.

C498 [Letter about review of A69.] *Shenandoah* 7 : [65]–66 Autumn.

Review by Hugh Kenner, 6 : 44–53 Spring 1955; rejoinder by Kenner, 7 : 66–67 Autumn.

C499 An Appointment for Candlemas. *Fantasy and Science Fiction* 9 : 124–28 October.

C500 Graves, Gods and Psychoanalysts. *New Statesman* 50 : 398, 1 October.

Reply to Jacquetta Hawkes, 50 : 243, 27 August, which is a reply to C495.

C501 Trín-Trín-Trín. *Punch* 229 : 394–95, 5 October.

C502 Spoiled Honeymoon. *Atlantic* 196 : 72, 74, 76, 78, 80 December.

On George Sand and Chopin. See A77.

C503 ★The Tenants. *New Statesman* 50 : 800, 10 December.

1956

C504 The Etruscans. *Art News Annual* 25 : 100–20, 180, 183.

Reprinted as 'The Cultured Romans'.

C505 English Nursery Rhymes. *Listener* 55 : 99–101, 19 January.
Review of *The Oxford Nursery Rhyme Book*, ed. Peter and Iona Opie.

C506 These Be Thy Gods, O Israel! *New Republic* 134 : 16–18, 27 February; 134 : 17–18, 5 March.

C507 *End of the World. *Poetry London–New York* 1 : 16 March–April.

C508 Cambridge Upstairs. *Punch* 230 : 216–17, 14 March.

C509 'Ha, Ha!' Chort-led Nig-ger. *Punch* 230 : 331–33, 21 March.

C510 *The Coral Pool. *Punch* 320 : 424, 11 April.

C511 Edmund Wilson: A Protestant Abroad. *New Republic* 134 : 13–16, 30 April.
Reprinted as 'Religion: None; Conditioning: Protestant'.

C512 Culture Creep. *Commentary* 21 : 573–77 June.
Review of Richard Dorson's *The Negro Folktale in Michigan*.

C513 *Gratitude for a Nightmare. *New Statesman* 51 : 631, 2 June.

C514 *Woman and Tree. *New Yorker* 32 : 38, 9 June.

C515 *Max Beerbohm at Rapallo. *Punch* 230 : 755, 27 June.

C516 *A Bouquet from a Fellow Roseman. *New Yorker* 32 : 30, 30 June.

C517 *The Grandfather's Complaint. *Punch* 231 : 155, 8 August.

C518 Pandora's Box and Eve's Apple. *New Republic* 135 : 16–18, 13 August.

C519 *Song: A Beach in Spain. *Punch* 231 : 251, 29 August.

C520 Ditching in a Fishless Sea. *Punch* 231 : 276–78, 5 September.

C521 Pandora's Box and Eve's Apple. *Spectator* 197 : 324, 7 September.

C522 Soldier's Homer. *New Republic* 135 : 17–19, 24 September.
Reprinted as 'Colonel Lawrence's *Odyssey*'.

C523 *The Demon. *Poetry London–New York* 1 : 13 Winter.

C524 Jewish Jesus, Gentile Christ. *New Republic* 135 : 25–27, 15 October.
Reprinted as 'Don't Fidget, Young Man!'

C525 *To a Caricaturist, Who Got Me Wrong. *New Republic* 135 : 27, 17 October.

C526 Robert Graves Demurs. *Commentary* 22 : 471–72 November.
Reply to Arnold Sherman, 'A Talk with Robert Graves', 22 : 364–66 October. Rejoinder by Sherman, 22 : 472.

C527 I Hate Poems. *Punch* 231 : 612–14, 21 November.

C528 *A Ballad of Alexander and Queen Janet – Destruction of Evidence. *London Magazine* 3 : 17–19 December.

C529 *A Plea to Boys and Girls. *Time and Tide* 37 : 1460, 1 December.

C530 Roots of Arthurian Mythology. *Times Literary Supplement*, 21 December, p. 766.
Reprinted as 'The Gold Roofs of Sinadon'.

C531 Criticism of Sir Herbert Read. *New Republic* 135 : 17–19, 24 December.
Reprinted as 'An Eminent Collaborationist'.

C532 Two Celtic Anthologies. *New Statesman* 52 : 848, 29 December.
Review of *Early Irish Lyrics*, ed. Gerard Murphy, and *The Burning Tree*, ed. Gwyn Williams.

1957

C533 *The Second-Fated. *New Republic* 136 : 17, 7 January.

C534 *The Face in the Mirror. *New Yorker* 32 : 34, 12 January.

C535 Majorca Xuetas. *Jewish Chronicle*, 18 January, p. 17; 25 January, pp. 17, 27; 1 February, pp. 17, 22.
Reprinted as 'A Dead Branch on the Tree of Israel'.

C536 *A Plea to Boys and Girls. *Atlantic* 199 : 59 February.

C537 A Dead Branch on the Tree of Israel. *Commentary* 23 139–46 February.

C538 *The Naked and the Nude. *New Yorker* 32 : 105, 1 February.

C539 *Yes. *New Yorker* 33 : 82, 23 February.

C540 The Cultured Romans. *Listener* 57 : 341–42, 28 February.

C541 Comments on 'Lineal and Non-Lineal Codifications'. *Explorations* 7 : [46] 47–51 March.

C542 Comments on 'Symbolization and Value'. *Explorations* 7 : [67] 68–73 March.

C543 *In Jorrocks's Warehouse. *London Magazine* 4 : 13 March.

C544 The Diseases of Scholarship Clinically Considered. *New Republic* 136 : 13–15, 6 March; 136 : 17–19, 20 May.

C545 The Most Cultured of All Romans. *Listener* 57 : 379–80, 7 March.
About Nero. See C617.

C546 Caesar: When Comes Such Another? *New York Times Magazine*, 10 March, pp. 17, 28, 31.

C547 [Letter about C540.] *Listener* 57 : 428, 14 March.

C548 *The Naked and the Nude. *New Statesman* 53 : 350, 16 March.

C549 An Even More Cultured Roman. *Listener* 57 : 471–72, 21 March.
About Lucan.

C550 [Letter about C545.] *Listener* 57 : 643, 18 April.

C551 *The Face in the Mirror. *New Statesman* 53 : 517, 20 April.

C552 *Fever. *Atlantic* 199 : 35 May.

C553 *The Outsider. *Harpers* 241 : 72 May.

C554 How to Avoid Mycophobia. *Saturday Review* 40 : 21–22' 47, 11 May.

Review of the Wassons' *Mushrooms, Russia and History*.

C555 John Milton Muddles Through. *New Republic* 136 : 17–19, 27 May.

Reprinted in 'Legitimate Criticism of Poetry'.

C556 Legends of the Jews. *Commentary* 23 : 583–86 June.

Reprinted as 'Legends of the Bible'.

C557 *The Outsider. *New Statesman* 53 : 784, 15 June.

C558 *To a Caricaturist Who Got Me Wrong. *Time and Tide* 38 : 736, 15 June.

C559 A Bicycle in Majorca. *New Yorker* 33 : 28–32, 22 June.

C560 The White Goddess. *New Republic* 136 : 9–15, 24 June.

C561 *Fever. *New Statesman* 54 : 24, 6 July.

C562 All Child's Children Got Itch. *Times Literary Supplement*, 19 July, p. 441.

Reply to review of A20b, 5 July, p. 414.

C563 *Bitter Thoughts on Receiving a Slice of Cordelia's Wedding Cake. *New Yorker* 33 : 34, 27 July.

C564 Mushrooms, Food of the Gods. *Atlantic* 200 : 73–77 August.

Reprinted as 'What Food the Centaurs Ate' and 'Centaur's Food'.

C565 Imaginary Museums. *Times Literary Supplement*, 9 August, p. 483.

Reply to a quotation in a leader of 19 July, p. 441. Further reply by Graves, 15 November, p. 689.

C566 Jesus in Rome. [With Joshua Podro.] *Times Literary Supplement*, 16 August, p. 495.

Reply to review, 26 July, p. 461. Rejoinder 30 August, p. 519. Further letter by Graves and Podro, 20 September, p. 561.

C567 After a Century, Will Anyone Care Whodunit? *New York Times Book Review*, 25 August, pp. 5, 24.

About detective stories.

C568 Wordsworth by Cable. *New Republic* 137 : 10–13, 9 September.

Reprinted in 'Legitimate Criticism of Poetry'.

C569 *Augeias and I. *New Statesman* 54 : 321, 14 September.

C570 [Letter on Thomas Atkins.] *The Times*, 24 September, p. 9.

C571 Evidence of Affluence. *New Yorker* 33 : 38–42, 12 October.

C572 And the Children's Teeth Are Set on Edge. *New Republic* 137 : 15–18, 28 October.

C573 *The Second-Fated. *Encounter* 9 : 13 November.

C574 *Friday Night. *Punch* 233 : 535, 6 November.

C575 *Bitter Thoughts. *Time and Tide* 38 : 1530, 7 December.

C576 Maenads, Junkies and Others. *New Republic* 137 : 16–18, 23 December.

1958

C577 A Life Bang-Full of Kicks and Shocks. *New York Times Book Review*, 5 January, p. 6.

Reprinted as 'It Ended with a Bang'. Rejoinders 16 February, p. 36, and 9 March, p. 36.

C578 The Glass Castle and the Grail. *Time and Tide* 39 : 45–46, 11 January.

Review of Geoffrey Ashe's *King Arthur's Avalon*. Reply by Ashe 39 : 70, 18 January.

C579 *Fingers in the Nesting Box. *New Yorker* 34 : 104, 29 March.

C580 Sweeney among the Blackbirds. *Texas Quarterly* 1 : 83–102 Spring.

C581 *Nothing. *Saturday Review* 41 : 69, 12 April.

C582 Archetypal Wise Old Man. *New Statesman* 55 : 538, 26 April.

C583 A Toast to Ava Gardner. *New Yorker* 34 : 34–38, 26 April.

C584 Two Studies in Scientific Atheism. *New Republic* 138 : 13–17, 28 April.
Review of Bertrand Russell's *Why I Am an Atheist* and Julian Huxley's *Religion without Revaluation*.

C585 *The Stable Door. *New Statesman* 55 : 640, 17 May.

C586 New Light on an Old Murder. *Sunday Times*, 18 May, p. 9.
Letter in reply, 25 May, p. 4. Graves' reply, 15 June, p. 4.

C587 *The Enlisted Man. *New Yorker* 34 : 115, 24 May.

C588 Caesar and the Pirates. *New Republic* 138 : 17–18, 26 May.
Reprinted as 'The Pirates Who Captured Caesar'.

C589 *Augeias and I. *Harpers* 216 : 35 June.

C590 *Woman and Tree. *Time and Tide* 39 : 704, 7 June.

C591 *Around the Mountain. *New Yorker* 34 : 26, 5 July.

C592 Doctor Paccard of Mont Blanc. *New Republic* 139 : 21–22, 7 July.
Review of *The First Ascent of Mont Blanc* by Graham Brown and Sir Gavin de Beer.

C593 Mostly It's Money That Makes a Writer Go, Go, Go. *New York Times Book Review*, 13 July, p. 5.

C594 *Flight Report. *Saturday Review* 41 : 30, 9 August.

C595 The Wall. *Times Literary Supplement,* 15 August, p. x.
About bad books and the difficulties of publishing.

C596 Praise Me, and I Will Whistle to You. *New Republic* 139 : 10–15, 1 September.

C597 ★The Twin of Sleep. *New Yorker* 34 : 107, 27 September.

C598 The American Poet as a Businessman. *Esquire* 50 : 47, 51, 56, 58 October.
Reprinted as 'The Making and Marketing of Poetry'.

C599 The Viscountess and the Short-Haired Girl. *Gentleman's Quarterly* 27 : 82–83, 124, 126, 128, 130, 132, 138, 140, 141 October.

C600 ★Call It a Good Marriage. *New Statesman* 56 : 534, 18 October.

C601 ★Read Me, Please! *New Yorker* 34 : 44, 18 October.

C602 What Was That War Like, Sir? *Observer,* 9 November, pp. 3–4.
About World War I. Letters of reply, 16 November, p. 6; 23 November, p. 6; 30 November, p. 20.

C603 The Sinking of Sea Venture. *The Times,* 20 November, p. 13.

C604 Seven Poets. *New World Writing* 14 : 7–10 [December].
Introduction to a small anthology of poems by T. S. Matthews, James Reeves, Sally Chilver, Alastair Reid, Terence Hards, Martin Seymour-Smith and Marnie Pomeroy.

1959

C605 How to Pull a Poem Apart. *Harpers* 218 : 78–80 January.
Reprinted as 'Pulling a Poem Apart'.

C606 ★Superman on the Riviera. *Spectator* 202 : 19, 2 January.

C607 ★Old World Dialogue. *Harpers* 218 : 58 March.

C608 She Landed Yesterday. *New Yorker* 35 : 31–37, 7 March.

C609 *Here Live Your Life Out! *New Yorker* 35 : 34, 28 March.

C610 She Landed Yesterday. *Lilliput* 44 : 31–35 April.

C611 What It Feels Like to be a Goy. *Commentary* 27 : 413–19 May.
Reprinted as 'To be a Goy'.

C612 The Shout. *Fantasy and Science Fiction* 16 : 51–67 May.

C613 *Picture Nail. *Spectator* 202 : 667, 8 May.

C614 *Heroes in Their Prime. *New Yorker* 35 : 42, 23 May.

C615 *The Enlisted Man. *Times Literary Supplement*, 5 June, p. 338.

C616 *Heroes in Their Prime. *New Statesman* 57 : 832, 13 June.

C617 Ignoblest Roman of Them All. *New York Times Magazine*, 14 June, pp. 22, 26, 28, 30, 32.
About Nero. See C545.

C618 Dour Man. *New Republic* 141 : 16–17, 14 July.

C619 Puck, Mab and the Billy Blin. *New Statesman* 58 : 83, 18 July.

C620 *Established Lovers. *Spectator* 203 : 107, 24 July.

C621 *Catkind. *Spectator* 203 : 115, 24 July.

C622 *Here Live Your Life Out! *New Statesman* 58 : 250, 29 August.

C623 Dour Man. *Encounter* 13 : 66–69 September.

C624 Interview with a Dead Man. *Fantasy and Science Fiction* 17 : 87–89 September.

C625 Enter, the Leaden Age of Bullfighting. *New York Times Magazine,* 13 September, pp. 28–29, 51–52, 54.

See C635.

C626 And What Would We Do without 'Etc.'? *New York Times Magazine,* 20 September, pp. 47, 50.

C627 Would-Be Jews. *New Republic* 141 : 24–25, 28 September.

Review of *San Nicandro: The Story of a Religious Phenomenon* by Elena Cassin. Letter in reply by Solomon H. Green 141 : 30–31, 9 November; reply by Graves 141 : 31, 9 November.

C628 *Established Lovers. *Atlantic* 204 : 44 October.

C629 *Catkind. *Harpers* 219 : 77 October.

C630 *The Person from Porlock. *Papeles de son Armadans* 15 : 50 October.

C631 *The Quiet Glades of Eden. *Spectator* 203 : 479, 9 October.

C632 Pen and Gown. *The Times,* 22 October, p. 15.

Why modern literature should not be in the curriculum.

C633 Homer's Winks and Nods. *Atlantic* 204 : 101–07 November.

Reprinted as part of introduction to A89.

C634 [Quotes from *The Anger of Achilles* as captions to illustrations from the book by Ronald Searle.] *Harper's Bazaar* 93 : 136–137 November.

C635 Bullfighting. *Lilliput* 45 : 35–37 November.

See C625.

C636 I Discover Israel. *Holiday* 26 : 66–77, 234, 239–43 December.

C637 The Lost Chinese. *Lilliput* 45 : 46–52 December.

C638 *Joan and Darby. *New Yorker* 35 : 54, 12 December.

C639 *Joan and Darby. *Spectator* 203 : 911, 18 December.

C640 *The Young Goddess. *New Yorker* 35 : 58, 26 December

C641 [Letter in reply to review of A89.] *The Fat Abbot* 1 : 54–55 Winter.

Review by Adam Parry, 1 : 52–59 Fall; rejoinder by Parry 1 : 55–56 Winter.

C642 Isle of Tranquillity: Minorca. *Holiday* 27 : 50–55, 154–57 January.

Reprinted as 'To Minorca!'

C643 The Case of the Difficult Husband. *Playboy* 7 : 51–52, 54, 85–87 January.

Reprinted as 'The Lost Chinese'.

C644 *Surgical Ward: Men. *Spectator* 204 : 113, 22 January.

C645 *Twice of the Same Fever. *New Yorker* 35 : 32, 23 January.

C646 Hebrew and Greek. *Commentary* 29 : 173–75 February.

Review of Moses Hadas' *Hellenistic Culture.*

C647 You Win, Houdini! *London Magazine* 7 : 28–37 February.

C648 *The Were-Man. *Saturday Review* 43 : 20, 6 February.

C649 *Twice of the Same Fever. *Spectator* 204 : 438, 25 March.

C650 *Surgical Ward: Men. *Atlantic* 205 : 50 April.

C651 An Imperial Tale. *Holiday* 27 : 74–79, 151–154 April.

Reprinted as 'The Apartment House'.

C652 *Song: A Month of Sundays. *London Magazine* 7 : 29 April.

C653 *The Mysteries of the Toadstool God. *London Magazine* 7 : 11–12 May.

C654 November 5th Address. *X* 1 : 171–176 June.

C655 *The Intruders. *Saturday Review* 43 : 31, 2 July.

C656 The Gaudy Games. *Sports Illustrated* 13 : 56–64, 1 August.

Reprinted as 'The Myconian'.

C657 ★Teiresias. *New Statesman* 60 : 191, 6 August.

C658 ★The Intruders – Lyceia. *Listener* 63 : 299, 25 August.

C659 ★Two Rhymes about Fate and Money. *Spectator* 205 : 344, 2 September.

C660 ★Burn It. *New Statesman* 60 : 392, 17 September.

C661 The Case for Xanthippe. *Kenyon Review* 22 : 597–605 Fall.
Reason and philosophy vs. poetry.

C662 Party of one. *Holiday* 28 : 8, 10–13 October.
About hexing.

C663 ★Song: The Smile of Eve. *New Statesman* 60 : 532, 8 October.

C664 What Bird for Britain? *The Times*, 28 October, p. 13.
About a national bird.

C665 ★Jock o' Binnorie – Robinson Crusoe. *New Statesman* 60 : 654, 29 October.

C666 ★The Person from Porlock. *Atlantic* 206 : 170 November.

C667 ★Fate and Money. *Good Housekeeping* 151 : 234 November.

C668 ★How and Why. *Saturday Review* 43 : 34, 5 November.

C669 ★Lyceia. *Saturday Review* 43 : 108, 12 November.

C670 ★Nightfall at Twenty Thousand Feet. *New Yorker* 36 : 50, 19 November.

C671 ★Conversaciones Poeticas de Formentor. *Papeles de Son Armadans* 57 : 14 December.

C672 ★Song: A Month of Sundays. *Saturday Review* 43 : 39, 24 December.

C673 *The Quiet Glades of Eden. *Saturday Review* 43 : 25, 31 December.

1961

C674 *Symptoms of Love – The Sharp Ridge – Under the Olives – The Visitation – Fragment – Apple Island – The Falcon Woman – Troughs of Sea – The Laugh – The Death Grapple – In Single Syllables – The Starred Coverlet – The Intrusion – Patience – Hag-Ridden – The Cure – Turn of the Moon – Seldom, Yet Now – The Secret Land – To the Muse Goddess – Anchises to Aphrodite. *Observer*, 22 January, p. 21.

C675 An Uneasy Compromise. *Observer*, 19 March, pp. 21–22.
Review of the *New English Bible*. Letters of reply 26 March, p. 22.

C676 Dead Man's Bottles. *Fantasy and Science Fiction* 20 : 52–64 April.

C677 *A Lost World. *New Yorker* 37 : 39, 1 April.

C678 *Piebald's Tail. *Ladies Home Journal* 78 : 112 May.

C679 Before the Ceiling Falls In. *Daily Express*, 31 May, p. 6.
Interview with many quotations.

C680 Service to the Muse. *Atlantic* 207 : 43–44 June.
Introductory comments to C681.

C681 *Symptoms of Love – The Sharp Ridge – Under the Olives – The Visitation – Fragment – Apple Island – The Falcon Woman – Troughs of Sea – The Laugh – The Death Grapple – The Starred Coverlet – The Intrusion – In Single Syllables – Patience – Hag-Ridden – The Cure – To the Muse Goddess – The Secret Land – Seldom Yet Now – Turn of the Moon – Anchises to Aphrodite. *Atlantic* 207 : 45–48 June.
See C680.

C682 *Sullen Moods. *New Yorker* 37 : 44, 9 September.

C683 *The Cool Web. *Times Literary Supplement*, 13 October, p. 695.
A translation into German by Erich Fried.

C684 ★The Dialecticians. *Atlantic* 208 : 157 November.

C685 ★Two Witches. *Good Housekeeping* 153 : 218 November.

C686 ★Matador Gored. *Saturday Evening Post* 234 : 53, 4 November.

C687 ★Four New Love Poems: Horizon – In Her Praise – Trance – Variables of Green. *Saturday Evening Post* 234 : 93, 11 November.

C688 The Dedicated Poet: The Oxford Inaugural Lecture. *Encounter* 17 : 11–18 December.

C689 ★Burn It! *Harpers* 233 : 49 December.

1962

C690 The Word Báraka. *Proceedings of the American Academy of Arts and Letters and the National Institute of Arts and Letters*, Series 2, Number 12, pp. 105–115.

C691 Virgil Cult. *Virginia Quarterly Review* 38 : 13–35 Winter.
Reprinted as 'The Anti-Poet'.

C692 ★The Ambrosia of Dionysus and Semele. *New Yorker* 37 : 30, 13 January.

C693 ★Golden Anchor – In Trance at a Distance – Possessed – A Restless Ghost – Uncalendared Love – Vicissitudes of Love. *New Yorker* 37 : 30, 27 January.

C694 ★Beware, Madam! *Atlantic* 209 : 48 February.

C695 [Answer to a questionnaire about poetry.] *London Magazine* n.s. 1 : 27 February.

C696 Criticizing Poetry. *Times Literary Supplement*, 2 February, p. 73.
Reply to editorial of same title, 12 January, p. 25; further reply by Ken Geering, 9 February, p. 89; rejoinder by Graves, 23 February, p. 121.

C697 The Tenement: A Vision of Imperial Rome. *New Strand* 1 : 331–336, March.
Reprinted as 'The Apartment House'.

C698 *Two New Poems: Confiteor Ut Fas – O. *Oxford Magazine* n. s. 2 : 255, 15 March.

C699 Ignore the Poet. *The Times*, 30 March, p. 15.
Letter advising this attitude.

C700 *Golden Anchor – Horizon – In Her Praise – Uncalendared Love – The Ambrosia of Dionysus and Semele – Trance. *New Statesman* 63 : 644, 4 May.

C701 *Three New Poems: The Lion Lover – The Recognition – Not at Home. *Saturday Evening Post* 235 : 66, 5 May.

C702 The Virgil Tradition. *The Times*, 22 May, p. 13.
Letter in reply to report of public lecture.

C703 *Between Moon and Moon – Ibycus in Samos – The Meeting – Name Day – The Wreath. *Encounter* 18 : 36–37 June.

C704 The Toughest Battle of All: When a Regiment is Fighting for Its Life. *Daily Express*, 9 June, p. 8.
About maintenance of regiments, regimental names and regimental traditions.

C705 *Lion Lover. *New Statesman* 63 : 914, 22 June.

C706 Poetic Gold. *Georgia Review* 16 : 122–130 Summer.

C707 Journey to Paradise. *Holiday* 32 : 36–37, 110–111 August.
Reprinted as 'The Poet's Paradise'.

C708 *Not at Home – A Restless Ghost – The Recognition. *New Statesman* 64 : 364, 21 September.

C709 *The Cliff Edge. *Atlantic* 201 : 86 October.

C710 *Ouzo Unclouded. *Poetry* 101 : 43 October.

C711 Nummick. *The Times*, 14 November, p. 13.
Etymological speculation.

C712 *The Passing of Oisín. *Atlantic* 210 : 64 December.

C713 *Judgement of Paris. *Georgia Review* 16 : 445 Winter.

C714 Robert Graves Writes ... *Poetry Book Society Bulletin*, no. 35, pp. 1–2, December.

C715 *The Meeting. *Poetry Book Society Bulletin*, no. 35, p. 2, December.

C716 Wave No Banners. *Saturday Evening Post* 235 : 34–35, 38, 40–41, 15 December.
Reprinted as 'Christmas Truce'.

C717 [Blurb for Tucci's *Before My Time*.] *Daily Mail*, 20 December, p. 10.

1963

C718 *After the Flood. *Atlantic* 211 : 60 January.

C719 Some Hebrew Myths and Legends. [With Raphael Patai.] *Encounter* 20 : 3–18 February.
Reprinted A105 as the introduction and sections 5–7, 9–10.

C720 The Truest Poet. *Sunday Times*, 3 February, p. 26.
On the death of Frost.

C721 The Fight to the Finish in 1914–1918. *Sunday Times*, 24 February, p. 25.

C722 Hebrew Myths and Legends. [With Raphael Patai.] *Encounter* 20 : 12–18 March.
Reprinted A105 as sections 11, 13–15.

C723 The Poet in a Valley of Dry Bones. *Horizon* 5 : 84–88 March.

C724 *The Corner Knot. *New Yorker* 39 : 44, 23 March.

C725 *The Why of the Weather. *Saturday Review* 46 : 36, 13 April.

C726 *After the Flood – Endless Pavement – A Late Arrival – The Septuagenarian. *New Statesman* 65 : 600, 19 April.

C727 Pretense on Parnassus. *Horizon* 5 : 81–85 May.
Reprinted as 'Some Instances of Poetic Vulgarity'.

C728 T. E. Lawrence and the Riddle of 'S.A.' *Saturday Review* 46 : 16–17, 15 June.

C729 *The Why of the Weather. *New Statesman* 65 : 934, 21 June.

C730 Redbook Dialogue. *Redbook* 121 : 58–59, 112, 114–15, 117 September.

See C737.

C731 The Golden Age. *Times Literary Supplement*, 6 September, p. 677.

About Virgil.

C732 *Herself to Herself. *Saturday Review* 46 : 28, 28 September.

C733 *To Beguile and Betray – Vixen Goddess – Dance. *Virginia Quarterly Review* 39 : 597 Autumn.

C734 *The Apple [*i.e.*, Ample] Garden – At Best, Poets – A Measure of Casualness – A Time of Waiting – Expect Nothing – She is No Liar – The Pearl – New Moon through Glass. *Atlantic* 212 : 66–67 October.

C735 *Between Trains. *Harper's Bazaar* 97 : 191 November.

C736 Poetry's False Face. *Horizon* 5 : 42–47 November.

Reprinted as 'Technique in Poetry'.

C737 The Trouble with Men. *Weekend*, 6 November, pp. 16–18.

A duologue with Gina Lollobrigida. See C730.

C738 *Myrrhina. *Poetry* 103 : 182 December.

C739 A Poet's Investigation of Science. *Saturday Review* 46 : 82–88, 7 December.

Partial reprint of A103.

1964

C740 *All I Tell You from My Heart – To Myrto about Herself – In Time – Man Does, Woman Is – The Leap – In Disguise. *Kenyon Review* 26 : 80–82 Winter.

C741 Real Women. *Ladies Home Journal* 81 : 151–155 January.

C742 *Joseph and Jesus. *Sunday Times*, 5 January, p. 28.

C743 *St. Valentine's Day. *Atlantic* 213 : 94 February.

C744 Why Read Poetry? *Holiday* 35 : 10, 16–18 February.

C745 *A Time of Waiting – Expect Nothing – The Pearl. *New Statesman* 672 : 212, 7 February.

C746 Poet and Public School. *Sunday Times*, 29 March, p. 38.
Review of *Charterhouse: An Open Examination Written by the Boys*. Replies 5 April, p. 19. Reply by Graves, 12 April, p. 19.

C747 *Occasions of Love: The Ample Garden – She is No Liar – A Measure of Casualness – At Best, Poets. *Critical Quarterly* 6 : 8–9 Spring.

C748 *The Encounter. *Georgia Review* 18 : 49. Spring.

C749 Insulation. *Times Literary Supplement*, 9 April, p. 291.
Letter about an accusation of insularity. See also the leader of 27 February, a letter by Christopher Middleton, 5 March, p. 195, and letters of 19 March, p. 235.

C750 *Non cogunt stellae* – Rain of Brimstone – Song: Sword and Rose. *New Republic* 150 : 21, 11 April.

C751 The Lasting Echoes of the Kaiser's War. *New York Times Magazine*, 17 May, pp. 16–17, 86, 88, 90.

C752 Mammon. *Encounter* 22 : 21–29 June.

C753 *Bank Account. *McCalls* 91 : 151 June.

C754 *A Last Poem. *New Yorker* 40 : 39, 6 June.

C755 *Rain of Brimstone. *Times Literary Supplement*, 11 June, p. 504.

C756 *Vixen Goddess – New Moon through Glass – Dance. *New Statesman* 67 : 914, 12 June.

C757 *In Time. *Sunday Times*, 28 June, p. 35.

C758 *All I Tell You from My Heart. *Spectator* 213 : 52, 10 July.

C759 Witches in 1964. *Virginia Quarterly Review* 40 : 550–559 Autumn.

C760 *The Fire Walker – That Other World. *Harper's Bazaar* 98 : 261 October.

C761 *Hearth. *New Republic* 151 : 20, 3 October.

C762 *The Clipped Stater. *Mt. Adams Review* 1 : 26–28 November–December.

Includes a quotation from A49.

D

MISCELLANEA

(The discontinuous numbering in this section is intentional.)

MANUSCRIPTS

D1   The Lockwood Memorial Library, Buffalo, New York.

This collection consists mainly of the working manuscripts of the poetry, from earliest drafts to finished poems. Many of the early drafts are written on versos of discarded manuscripts of the prose works. The collection also includes a copy of *Good-Bye to All That* (A32 *f*) corrected for the revised edition, the Claudius script (*The Fool of Rome*) done for Alexander Korda and two notebooks of drafts and fair copies of early poems.

D2   The Berg Collection, New York Public Library.

The Graves items in this collection include business and personal letters (many to Sir Edward Marsh), fair copies of poems, a corrected typescript of *King Jesus* and a notebook of early poems.

D3   Humanities Research Center, University of Texas, Austin.

This collection includes business and personal letters and some fair copies of poetry.

D4   Prose manuscripts.

A collection, privately owned, includes the manuscripts, typescripts and working papers for *John Kemp's Wager, My Head! My Head!, Contemporary Techniques of Poetry, Another Future of Poetry, The English Ballad, John Skelton, But It Still Goes On, Old Soldiers Never Die, Old Soldier Sahib, Almost Forgotten Germany, Antigua, Penny, Puce, Sergeant Lamb of the Ninth, Wife to Mr. Milton, The Golden Fleece, The Common Asphodel, The Infant with the Globe, They Hanged My Saintly Billy,* and *The Anger of Achilles*, as well as manuscripts of stories, essays and reviews, plus some unpublished material. As in D1, much material exists on versos.

GRAMOPHONE RECORDS

D10   Caedmon TC–1066. Recorded in London 3 November 1954. Read by Graves.

Contents: Side 1: The White Goddess, Chapter I (in part) – The Haunted House – Outlaws – Allie – Love without Hope – What

Did I Dream? – The Hills of May – Angry Samson – In Procession – Warning to Children – The Cool Web – Song of Contrariety – The Presence – Side 2: Flying Crooked – Any Honest Housewife – A Jealous Man – The Cloak – Time – Ogres and Pygmies – To Bring the Dead to Life – Like Snow – The Fallen Tower of Siloam – A Love Story – Theseus and Ariadne – To Juan at the Winter Solstice – The Death Room – My Name and I – The Survivor – The Foreboding – Cat-Goddesses – The Blue-Fly – Sirocco at Deyá – Leaving the Rest Unsaid.

D11   Argo RG 191. Read by Graves.

Contents: Side 1: The Bards – Full Moon – It Was All Very Tidy – Thief – Trudge, Body! – Christmas Robin – The Devil's Advice to Storytellers – William Brazier – Welsh Incident – On Dwelling – To Walk on Hills – The Cuirassiers of the Frontier – The Halls of Bedlam – On Portents – Dawn Bombardment – Side 2: Frightened Men – Language of the Seasons – The Beach – The Villagers and Death – The Persian Version – Two Grotesques: The Lion-Faced Boy – Dr. Newman with the Crooked Pince-Nez – Beauty in Trouble – Your Private Way – Darien – Prometheus – The Face in the Mirror – The Coral Pool – Gratitude for a Nightmare – Friday Night – The Naked and the Nude – Forbidden Words – A Slice of Wedding Cake – Around the Mountain.

D12   Folkways FL9888. Contemporary English Literature. Side 1, bands 1–6, are read by Graves.

Contents: I'm Through with You Forever – In the Wilderness – The Troll's Nosegay – Mike and Mandy – Traveller's Curse – Song: Lift-Boy

D13   Jupiter jep OOC2 (45 rpm). Contents as D12.

D14   Listen LPV2. Recorded in London 28 April 1959. Read by Graves.

Contents: Side 1: Rocky Acres – Lost Love – An English Wood – The Pier-Glass – Mermaid, Dragon, Fiend – Ulysses – The Succubus – Gardener – Front Door Soliloquy – In Broken Images – On Rising Early – Sea Side – Hell – Down, Wanton, Down! – Nature's Lineaments – The Philosopher – To Evoke Posterity – Certain Mercies – With Her Lips Only – The Reader over My Shoulder – Side 11: Advocates – The Terraced Valley – The Ages of Oath – End of Play – The Great-Grandmother – No More Ghosts – The Shot – The Thieves – To Sleep – Despite and Still – The Oath – Mid-Winter Waking – The Door – From the Embassy – Cry Faugh! – The Mark – The Sea Horse – The Lost Jewel – The Window Sill – Spoils – Call It a Good Marriage – To Calliope.

D15 Colpix PS1002. A Little Treasury of Twentieth Century British Poetry, ed. Oscar Williams.

Contents: An English Wood – Ogres and Pygmies – Nature's Lineaments – A Love Story.

D16 Gryphon GR902. An Album of Modern Poetry, ed. Oscar Williams. Read by Graves.

Contents: The Legs – The Naked and the Nude.

D17 Caedmon TC0995. Recorded in 1954. Read by Graves.

Contents: Poem for My Son (To Juan at the Winter Solstice).

EPHEMERA

D20 The poem 'To Juan at the Winter Solstice' was privately printed as a folder:

To Juan | at the Winter Solstice | [*device*]

Collation: 2 leaves, folded at centre.

p. [1] title-page; pp. [2–3] text of poem, dated 22 December 1944; p. [4] [rule] | Printed for the Author by | Stuart G. Goad, 12, Fore Street, Brixham.

17·9 × 13·1 cm. White laid paper; all edges trimmed.

D21 The poem 'The Person from Porlock' was issued as an offprint from C630, as follows:

ROBERT GRAVES | THE PERSON FROM POR-LOCK | (*Versión castellana por C. J.C. autorizada por R.G.*) | [*in green:* man in wide hat and cape, holding up his right hand] | Madrid – Palma de Mallorca | MCMLIX

Collation: 2 leaves, sewn at centre.

p. 48 text; p. 49 reproduction of MS of poem; p. 50 translation by Camilo José Cela; p. [51] blank.

19·6 × 13·9 cm. White wove paper; all edges trimmed. Bound in stiff paper covers; front cover transcribed as title; back cover blank; inside front cover: De PAPELES DE SON ARMADANS, n.º XLIII. Octubre de 1959 | *Tirada aparte de cincuenta* | *ejemplares numerados.* | *Ej.* n.º [*number*] | [*signature of Graves*] | [*holograph date*].

D22 The poem 'Conversaciones poéticas de Formentor' was issued as an offprint from C671, as follows:

ROBERT GRAVES | CONVERSACIONES POÉTI-CAS DE FORMENTOR | [*in red:* flower and leaf] | Madrid – Palma de Mallorca | MCMLX

Collation: 2 leaves, sewn at centre.
p. 14 text; p. 15 translation by Camilo José Cela; pp. [16–17] blank.

19·7 × 13·9 cm. White wove paper; all edges trimmed. Bound in stiff cream paper covers; front cover transcribed as title; back cover blank; inside front cover: De PAPELES DE SON ARMADANS, nº LVII bis. Diciembre de 1960. | *Tirada aparte de cincuenta* | *ejemplares numerados.* | Ej. nº [*number*].

D23   The poem 'Cat-Goddesses' was issued as a Christmas greeting as a stiff card, folded in the centre.

D24   The poem 'Between Dark and Dark' was printed as part of a Seizin Press throwaway dated 1929.

D25   The poem 'To Magdalena Mulet, Margita Mora and Lucia Graves, May 4, 1954' was printed as a card of 4 pp., with Spanish translation.

COMMENTARY

D30   The film 'My Majorca' has a narrative read by Graves. The American agent for this film is Film Images, New York.

D31   Graves wrote his own part in the Esso World Theatre television production of 'Greece: The Inner World'. The first telecast was on 19 April 1964. Reprinted as 'The Inner World'.

SCRIPT

D35   The Anger of Achilles: An Epic for Radio. A radio script for the British Broadcasting Corporation. Presented on the Home Service 17/31 May 1964 and on the Third Programme 10 June 1965.

D40 Homer's Daughter. Read by Athena Lorde. New York: American Foundation for the Blind. 9 Talking Book records.

D41 I, Claudius. Los Angeles: Braille Institute of America, 1938. 5v. Press-Braille.

D42 Sergeant Lamb's America. Cincinnati: Clovernook Printing House for the Blind, 1941. 4v. Press-Braille.

D43 Proceed, Sergeant Lamb. Louisville: American Printing House for the Blind, 1942. 4v. Press-Braille.

D44 Wife to Mr. Milton. Read by Sheila Wildheimer. 5 7"-reels of magnetic tape. Library of Congress no. 1455.

D45 Poems 1938–1945. Free Library of Philadelphia. Hand-copied Braille.

D46 Wife to Mr. Milton. Library of Congress; Wayne County Library, Detroit. Hand-copied Braille.

D47 Lawrence and the Arabian Adventure. Multnomah County Library, Portland, Oregon. Hand-copied Braille.

D48 Count Belisarius. London: National Library for the Blind.

D49 Homer's Daughter. *Ibid.*

D50 I, Claudius. *Ibid.*

D51 Claudius the God. *Ibid.*

D52 The Isles of Unwisdom. *Ibid.*

D53 Sergeant Lamb of the Ninth. *Ibid.*

D54 Proceed, Sergeant Lamb. *Ibid.*

D55 Wife to Mr. Milton. *Ibid.*

D56 The Crowning Privilege. *Ibid.*

D58 Good-Bye to All That. *Ibid.*

D58 Lars Porsena. *Ibid.*

D59 Lawrence and the Arabs. *Ibid.*

D60 The Long Week-End. *Ibid.*

MUSIC

D70 Ivor Gurney: Star-Talk. London: Stainer and Bell, 1927.

D71 Ivor Gurney: Hawk and Buckle.
Apparently unpublished.

D72 Ivor Gurney: Nine of the Clock. [As by 'John Doyle'.] In *Twenty Songs*, Vol. 1: 1–10, pp. 19–20. London: Oxford University Press, 1938.

D73 Ivor Gurney: Goodnight to the Meadow. In *A Third Volume of Ten Songs*. London: Oxford University Press, 1953.
A setting of 'Nine O'Clock'.

D74 Peter Wishart: *Half Way to Sleep*. Song cycle with words by Graves.
Apparently unpublished.

D75 Peter Wishart: *Songs and Satires: A Suite of 6 Madrigals*. London: Stainer and Bell, 1961.
Includes a setting of 'Philatelist Royal'.

D76 Peggy Glanville-Hicks: *Nausicaa*. An opera based on *Homer's Daughter*.
Apparently unpublished. The libretto is by Graves.

RADIO BROADCASTS

The British Broadcasting Corporation has furnished the following list of broadcasts in which Graves has taken part. HS stands for

Home Service, LP for Light Programme, TP for Third Programme, M for Midland.

D80	9 September 1949	TP	Parable of the Talents. See C356.
D81	21 March 1950	TP	Poetry reading.
D82	4 September 1951	TP	Review of Jung and Kerényi's *Introduction to a Science of Mythology*.
D83	12 November 1951	TP	Poetry reading.
D84	24 August 1952	TP	The Seventh Man. See C395.
D85	28 November 1952	TP	The Geography of the Golden Fleece Legend.
D86	19 January 1953	TP	Poetry reading.
D87	17 August 1953	TP	The Whitaker Negroes. See C491.
D88	27 September 1953	TP	Poetry reading.
D89	25 October 1953	LP	Poetry reading
D90	29 November 1953	TP	Poems by Norman Cameron. See B41.
D91	20 October 1954	HS	A Poet and His Public. See C463.
D92	12 January 1955	TP	Poetry reading.
D93	20 February 1955	HS	Thomas Hardy – by His Friends.
D94	27 March 1955	TP	The Integrity of the Poet. See C477.
D95	25 December 1955	TP	The Great Bag Pudding. Review of *The Oxford Nursery Rhyme Book*. See C505.

D96	6 June 1956	TP	A Poet's Reading Compared with an Actor's.
D97	7 June 1956	TP	Poetry reading.
D98	3 October 1956	TP	Poetry reading.
D99	20 February 1957	TP	The Cultured Romans. See C540.
D100	3 March 1957	TP	The Most Cultured Roman of Them All. See C545.
D101	17 March 1957	TP	An Even More Cultured Roman. See C549.
D102	19 May 1957	HS	Frankly Speaking.
D103	15 June 1957	TP	Nero: Forgetting the Fiddler. See C617.
D104	5 October 1958	TP	Folk Song Morality.
D105	3 December 1958	TP	Lawrence of Cloud's Hill.
D106	10 December 1958	HS	Review of James Reeves' *Collected Poems*.
D107	4 March 1960	HS	Interviewed.
D108	5 August 1960	TP	Conversation with Robert Graves I.
D109	9 August 1960	TP	Conversation with Robert Graves II.
D110	23 October 1960	HS	Panelist on 'The Brains Trust',
D111	14 January 1961	HS	Review on 'The World of Books'.
D112	12 February 1961	HS	Poetry reading.
D113	4 April 1961	HS	In the South-East: Oxford.

D114 20 June 1961   HS   In Our Time: Field-Marshal Haig.

D115 22 August 1961   HS   Poetry reading.

D116 6 December 1961   LP   Woman's Hour: interviewed.

D117 14 October 1962   TP   Poetry reading.

D118 31 October 1962   M   Witchcraft.

D119 29 June 1964   HS   Before My Time.

E

A SELECTIVE BIBLIOGRAPHY OF
WORKS ABOUT ROBERT GRAVES

(The discontinuous numbering in this section is intentional.)

BOOKS AND PAMPHLETS

E1 Cohen, J. M.: *Robert Graves*. Edinburgh: Oliver and Boyd, 1960.

E2 Day, Douglas: *Swifter Than Reason: The Poetry and Criticism of Robert Graves*. Chapel Hill: University of North Carolina Press, 1963; London: Oxford University Press, 1964.

E3 Enright, D. J.: *Robert Graves and the Decline of Modernism*. Singapore: University of Malaya, n.d. [c. 1960]. Reprinted in *Essays in Criticism* 11:319–336 July 1961.

E4 Musgrove, Sydney: *The Ancestry of 'The White Goddess.'* Auckland: University of Auckland, 1962. Bulletin No. 62, English Series No. 11.

E5 Seymour-Smith, Martin: *Robert Graves*. London: British Council and National Book League, 1956. Writers and Their Work No. 78.

ARTICLES, DISSERTATIONS AND PARTS OF BOOKS

E10 Adams, Hazard: 'Criticism: Whence and Whither.' *American Scholar* 28:226–38 Spring 1959.

E11 Adcock, A. St. John: Poets in Khaki. *Bookman* (London) 55: [83]84–100 December 1918.

E12 Aiken, Conrad: *Scepticisms*. New York: Alfred A.Knopf, 1919. Pp. 193–98.

E13 Algren, Nelson: Sentiment with Terror. *Poetry* 55:157–59, December 1939.

E14 Anon: [Letter of apology from reviewer of A26.] *Times Literary Supplement*, 8 December 1927, p. 934.

E15 Anon: A Poet's Journey. *Times Literary Supplement*, 7 December 1951, p. 784.

E16 Anon: The Reward. *Spirit* 22:3–4 March 1955. Comment on C463.

E17 Anon: The Goddess and the Poet. *Time* 66:100–102, 18 July 1955.

E18 Anon: Obscurity in Poetry. *Times Literary Supplement*, 16 January 1959, p. 33.

E19 Anon: A Personal Mythology. *Times Literary Supplement*, 5 June 1959, p. 336.

E20 Anon: Signs of an All Too Correct Compassion. *Times Literary Supplement*, 9 September 1960, supp. p. xiii.

E21 Anon: The Poet and the Juke-Box. *Times Literary Supplement*, 9 December 1960, p. 797.

E22 Anon: Professing Poetry. *Times Literary Supplement*, 10 February 1961, p. 89.

E23 Anon: Profile of the Week. *Observer*, 26 February 1961, p. 9.

E24 Anon: Swearing on the Bible. *America* 105:415, 10 June 1961.

E25 Anon: Prodigious Old Lion of Letters. *Life* 54:57–58, 63, 28 June 1963.

E26 Atkins, John: *Tomorrow Revealed*. London: Neville Spearman, 1955. Chapter 7 and *passim*.

E27 Auden, W. H.: A Poet of Honor. *Shenandoah* 13:[5]6–11 Winter 1962. Reprinted from *Mid-Century* 28:3–9 July 1961.

E28 Blackburn, Thomas: *The Price of an Eye*. London: Longmans, 1961. Chapter 5 and *passim*.

E29 Blissett, William: Robert Graves. *Canadian Forum* 34:59, 61 June 1954.

E30 Blunden, Edmund: Convention and Misrule. *Times Literary Supplement*, 2 December 1955, p. 723.

E31 Blunden, Edmund: *War Poets, 1914–1918*. London: Longmans Green, 1958. No. 100 of supplements to British Book News.

E32 Bogan, Louise: *Selected Criticism*. New York: Noonday Press, 1955. Pp. 316–18.

E33 Boutell, H. S.: Modern English First Editions: Robert (Von Ranke) Graves, 1895–. *Publishers Weekly* 117:2140–42, 19 April 1930. Corrected by Graves.

E34 Bullough, Geoffrey: *The Trend of Modern Poetry*. London: Oliver and Boyd, 1949.

E35 Campbell, Roy: Contemporary Poetry. In *Scrutinies*, ed. Edgell Rickword, pp. 161–80. London: Wishart and Company, 1928.

E36 Campbell, Roy: *The Georgiad*. London: Boriswood, 1931.

E37 Church, Richard: *British Authors*. London: Longmans, 1948.

E38 Church, Richard: *Eight for Immortality*. London: J. M. Dent, 1941.

Contains 'Robert Graves: A Traveller in the Desert', reprinted from *Fortnightly Review* 155:384–91 April 1941.

E39 Connolly, Cyril: The Professor and the Others. *Sunday Times*, 29 April 1962, p. 31.

E40 Cooper, Roger: Graves in Public. *New Statesman* 62:626, 27 October 1961.

E41 Cowan, Louise: *The Fugitive Group*. Baton Rouge: Louisiana State University Press, 1959.

E42 Creeley, Robert: Her Service is Perfect Freedom. *Poetry* 93:395–98 May 1959.

E43 Cruttwell, Robert W.: Irish Imagery. *Times Literary Supplement*, 19 December 1929, p. 1082.

E44 Cutler, Frances Wentworth: Soldier-Poets of England. *Sewanee Review* 28:85–92 January 1920

E45 Davie, Donald: Impersonal and Emblematic. *Shenandoah* 13:[38] 39–44 Winter 1962.
Reprinted from *Listen* 3:31–36 Spring 1960.

E46 Davie, Donald: The Toneless Voice of Robert Graves. *Listener* 62:11–13, 2 July 1959.

E47 Dudek, Louis: The Case of Robert Graves. *Canadian Forum* 40:199–201 December 1960.

E48 Dudek, Louis: Julian Huxley, Robert Graves and the Mythologies. *Delta* 4:8–9 July 1958.

E49 Enright, D. J.: The Example of Robert Graves. *Shenandoah* 13:[13]14–15 Winter 1962.

E50 Fabes, Gilbert H. and William A. Foyle: *Modern First Editions: Points and Values (Second Series)*. London: W. and G. Foyle Ltd., 1931. Pp. 34–36.

E51 Fairchild, Hoxie Neal: Georgians. In *Religious Trends in English Poetry*, Vol. V, pp. 347–91. New York: Columbia University Press, 1962.

E52 Fraser, G. S.: *The Modern Writer and His World*. London: Derek Verschoyle, 1953.

E53 Fraser, G. S.: The Poet and His Medium. In *The Craft of Letters in England*, ed. John Lehmann, pp. 98–121. London: Cresset Press, 1956.

E54 Fraser, G. S.: The Reputation of Robert Graves. *Shenandoah* 13:[19]20–32 Winter 1962.

E55 Fraser, G. S.: A Universal Man. *Literary Guide* 70:6–8 May 1955.

E56 Fraser, G. S.: *Vision and Rhetoric*. London: Faber and Faber 1959. Pp. 135–48.

E57 Fuller, Roy: Poetry: Tradition and Belief. In *The Craf* *of Letters in England*, ed. John Lehmann, pp. 74–79. London: Cresset Press, 1956.

E58   Fuller, Roy: Some Vintages of Graves. *London Magazine* 5: 56–59 February 1958.

E59   Gaskell, Ronald: The Poetry of Robert Graves. *Critical Quarterly* 3:213–22 Autumn 1961.

E60   Gosse, Edmund: Some Soldier Poets. *Edinburgh Review* 226: 296–316 October 1917.

E61   Graves, Charles: *The Bad Old Days 1899–1929*. London: Faber and Faber, 1951.

E62   Green, Peter: Robert Graves as a Historical Novelist. *Critic* 20:46–50 January 1962.

E63   Gregory, Horace: Faithful to a Goddess and a Queen. *New York Times Book Review*, 16 July 1961, pp. 1, 20.

E64   Gregory, Horace: Robert Graves: A Parable for Writers. *Partisan Review* 20:44–54 January–February 1953.

E65   Gunn, Thom: In Nobody's Pantheon. *Shenandoah* 13:[34]–35 Winter 1962.

E66   Haller, John: Conversations with Robert Graves. *Southwest Review* 42:237–41 Summer 1957.

E67   Haller, John: Robert Graves in Lecture and Talk. *Arizona Quarterly* 15:[150]151–56 Summer 1959.

E68   Harling, Robert: Robert Graves in Majorca. *Sunday Times*, 30 October 1955, p. 8.

E69   Hassall, Christopher: *Edward Marsh*. London: Longmans, 1959.

E70   Haylett, Brian: *A Critical Study of the Poetry of Robert Graves*. Unpublished London University thesis, 1963.

E71   Hayman, Ronald: Robert Graves. *Essays in Criticism* 5:32–43 January 1955.

E72 Hoffman, Daniel G.: The Unquiet Graves. *Sewanee Review* 67: 305–316 Spring 1959.

E73 Hough, Graham: *Image and Experience: Reflections on a Literary Revolution.* London: Duckworth, 1960.

E74 Howarth, Patrick: *Squire: 'Most Generous of Men.'* London: Hutchinson, 1963.

E75 Janeway, Elizabeth: An Evaluation of Robert Graves, a Neglected Writer. *Nrw York Times Book Review,* 18 September 1949, p. 5.

E76 Jarrell, Randall: Graves and the White Goddess. *Yale Review* 65:302–14 Winter 1956; 65:467–78 Spring 1956.

E77 Jarrell, Randall: *Poetry and the Age.* New York: Alfred A. Knopf, 1955. Pp. 200–14.

E78 Jennings, Elizabeth: Robert Graves. *Spectator* 213:17, 3 July 1964.

E79 Johnston, John H.: *English Poetry of the First World War.* Princeton: Princeton University Press, 1964.

E80 Jones, Ernest: [Review of A11]. *Imago* 11:203–204 1925.

E81 Jones, R. Gerallt: The Poetry of Robert Graves. Unpublished University of Wales (Bangor) thesis, 1957.

E82 Lawrence, T. E.: *The Letters of T. E. Lawrence.* London: Jonathan Cape, 1938.

E83 Lindsay, Jack: *Franfolico and After.* London: Bodley Head, 1962.

E84 Lucas, F. L.: *Authors Dead and Living.* London: Chatto and Windus, 1926.

E85 Mais, S. P. B.: *Books and Their Writers.* New York: Dodd, Mead and Co., 1920.

E86 Matthews, T. S.: Robert Graves. *Book of the Month Club News,* March 1935, p. [3].

E87 Monro, Harold: *Some Contemporary Poets (1920)*. London: Leonard Parsons, 1920. Pp. 172–74.

E88 Moore, Geoffrey: *Poetry Today*. London: British Council, 1958.

E89 Moran, James: The Seizin Press of Laura Riding and Robert Graves. *Black Art* 2:34–39 Summer 1963. V. E124.

E90 Muir, Edwin: Contemporary Writers: VI: Mr. Robert Graves. *Nation* (London) 39:554–55, 14 August 1926; *Nation* (New York) 123:217–19, 8 September 1926.

E91 Muir, Edwin: *Transition*. London: Hogarth Press, 1926. Pp. 163–76.

E92 Nemerov, Howard: The Poetry of Robert Graves. In *Poetry and Fiction*, pp. 112–17. New Brunswick, N.J.: Rutgers University Press, 1963.

E93 Nicholson, Jenny: My Father, Robert Graves. *Lilliput* 10: 283–86 April 1942.

E94 Parise, Anthony Giuseppe: *The Private Myth in the Poetry of Robert Graves*. Unpublished University of Wisconsin dissertation, 1963.

E95 Peschmann, H.: Salute to Robert Graves. *English* 14 : 2–8 Spring 1962.

E96 Pettet, E. C.: The Poetry of Robert Graves. *English* 3:216–20 1941.

E97 Pick, J. B.: The Poet as Cynic: A Discussion of Robert Graves' Poetry. *Outposts* 14:23–25 Summer 1949.

E98 Press, John: *The Fire and the Fountain*. Oxford: Oxford University Press, 1955.

E99 Quennell, Peter: The Multiple Robert Graves. *Horizon* 4: 50–55 January 1962.

E100 Quennell, Peter: *The Sign of the Fish*. London: Collins, 1960.

E101 Ransom, Will: *Private Presses and Their Books*. New York: R. R. Bowker Co., 1929.

E102 Read, Herbert and Edward Dahlberg: Robert Graves and T. S. Eliot. *Twentieth Century* 166:54–62 August 1959.

E103 Reeves, James: *A Short History of English Poetry*. London: Heinemann, 1961.

E104 Riding, Laura: [Letter in defence of A33]. *Times Literary Supplement*, 26 December 1929, p. 1097.

E105 Rosenberg, Bruce A.: Graves' 'To Juan at the Winter Solstice.' *Explicator* 21: item 3 September 1962.

E106 Schwartz, Delmore: Graves in Dock: The Case for Modern Poetry. *New Republic* 134:20–21, 19 March 1956.

E107 Sidgwick, Frank: Tom of Bedlam's Song. *London Mercury* 7: 518–24 March 1923. See correspondence 7:638 April; 8:79–80 May; 8:188–89 June; 8:303 July; 8:414 August.

E108 Sillitoe, Alan: I Reminded Him of Muggleton. *Shenandoah* 13:[47]48–50 Winter 1962.

E109 Simon, Irène: A Note on Two Recent English Novels. *Revue des Langues Vivantes* 13:45–48 1947.

E110 Simon, John: Nowhere is Washing So Well Done. *Mid-Century* 16:11–18 September 1960.

E111 Skelton, Robin, *The Poetic Pattern*. London: Routledge and Kegan Paul, 1956.

E112 Smith, Stevie: [Review of A59]. *Times Literary Supplement*, 6 August 1954, p. xlvi.

E113 Spender, Stephen: How Much Should a Biographer Tell? *Saturday Review* 47:16–19, 25 January 1964.

E114 Spender, Stephen: Poetry for Poetry's Sake and Poetry Beyond Poetry. *Horizon* 76:221–38 April 1946.

E115 Steen, Marguerite: *William Nicholson*. London: Collins, 1943.

E116 Steiner, George: The Genius of Robert Graves. *Kenyon Review* 22:340–65 Summer 1960. Reply by G. Stade 22:[674] 675–77 Fall 1960 with rejoinder by Steiner 22:677–79.

E117 Sturge Moore, T.: *Some Soldier Poets*. London: Grant Richards, 1919. Pp. 27–44.

E118 Swanson, Roy Arthur: Graves' 'Hercules at Nemea'. *Explicator* 15:56 June 1957.

E119 Swanson, Roy Arthur: *Heart of Reason*. Minneapolis: T. S. Denison, 1963. Chapter 11.

E120 Swinnerton, Frank: *The Georgian Literary Scene*. London: William Heinemann, 1935.

E121 Symons, Julian: *The Thirties: A Dream Resolved*. London: Cresset Press, 1960.

E122 Thwaite, Anthony: *Contemporary English Poetry*. London: Heinemann, 1959. Pp. 125–39.

E123 Trilling, Lionel: *A Gathering of Fugitives*. Boston: Beacon Press, 1956. Pp. 20–30. Reprinted from *The Griffin*, 1955.

E124 Turner, Michael L.: The Seizin Press: An Additional Note. *Black Art* 2:84–86 Autumn 1963. V. E89.

E125 Ure, Peter: Yeats and Mr Graves. *Times Literary Supplement*, 12 June 1959, p. 353.

E126 Ussher, Arland: Robert Graves: The Philoctetes of Majorca. *Dublin Magazine* 32:18–21 July–September 1957.

E127 Vickery, John B.: Three Modes and a Myth. *Western Humanities Review* 12:371–78 Autumn 1958.

E128 Ward, A. C.: *Twentieth Century Literature 1901–1950*. London: Methuen, 1956.

E129 Waugh, Arthur: *Tradition and Change*. New York: E. P. Dutton, 1919.

E130 Weisinger, Herbert: *The Agony and the Triumph*. East Lansing: Michigan State University Press, 1964. Pp. 146–158.

E131 West, Herbert F., Jr.: Here's a Miltonic Discovery. *Renaissance Papers*, pp. 69–75, 1961 (for 1958–60).

E132 Wilkinson, Marguerite: *New Voices*. New York: Macmillan, 1928.

E133 Williams, Charles: *Poetry at Present*. Oxford: Oxford Univeristy Press, 1930. Pp. 194–206.

E134 Williams-Ellis, Amabel: *An Anatomy of Poetry*. Oxford: Basil Blackwell, n.d. [c. 1922].

E135 Wilson, Colin: Some Notes on Graves's Prose. *Shenandoah* 13:[55] 56–62 Winter 1962.

SELECTED REVIEWS

E136 A1: *Voices* 3:167 May 1920 (Louis Golding).

E137 A3: *Carthusian* 12:181 March 1918 (? G[eorge] M[allory]); *Dial* 65:214–15, 19 September 1918 (Conrad Aiken).

E138 A5: *Athenaeum* 94:472, 9 April 1920 (John Middleton Murry); *Crescent* [literary supplement to *Carthusian*] 1:29 June 1920; *Bookman* (New York) 52:57–66 September 1920 (Raymond M. Weaver); *Nation* (New York) 111:414–15, 13 October 1920 (Mark Van Doren).

E139 A6: *Nation* (New York) 114:48–49, 11 January 1922 (Mark Van Doren); *Voices* 5:91 Summer 1921 (Louis Golding); *New Republic* 28:196–97, 12 October 1921.

E140 A7: *Nation* (New York) 115:214, 30 August 1922 (Mark Van Doren); *Nation and Athenaeum* 31:797–98, 16 September 1922 (J. Middleton Murry); *Freeman* 6:187–88, 1 November 1922 (John Gould Fletcher); *New Republic* 32:340–41, 22 November 1922 (Conrad Aiken); *Carthusian* 13:410 December 1922.

E141 A8: *New Statesman and Nation* 20:779–80, 7 April 1923 (F. L. Lucas); *Bookman* (London) 64:163–64 June 1923 (John Freeman); *London Mercury* 8:206 June 1923 (J. C. Squire); *Saturday Review* 135:726, 2 June 1923 (Lord David Cecil); *Literary Review* (of the New York *Evening Post*), 22 September 1923, pp. 61–62 (William Rose Benet); *Nation* 117: 401–402, 10 October 1923 (Mark Van Doren).

E142 A9: *Nation and Athenaeum* 33:749–50, 15 September 1923 (F. L. Lucas).

E143 A12: *Nation and Athenaeum* 37:50, 11 April 1925 (Bamyon Dobree).

E144 A15: *Nation and Athenaeum* 37:546, 1 August 1925 (Victoria Sackville-West).

E145 A20: *Nation and Athenaeum* 40:595–96, 29 January 1928 (Barrington Gates); letter, 40:657–58, 12 February (Herbert E. Palmer); [1957 ed.:] *Western Folklore* 17:300–301 October 1958 (James N. Tidwell); *Midwest Folklore* 8:106–107 Summer 1958 (Tristram P. Coffin).

E146 A21: *Books*, 2 October 1927, p. 15 (G. P. Krapp).

E147 A23: *New Republic* 60:277–78, 23 October 1929 (Babette Deutsch).

E148 A26: *New Republic* 54:399, 16 May 1928 (Van Wyck Brooks); *Yale Review* 18:176–77 September 1928 (D. B. Macdonald).

E149 A28: *Saturday Review of Literature* 6:85–87, 31 August 1929 (Horace M. Kallen); *Saturday Review* 144:822–23, 10 December 1927 (Edward Shanks).

E150 A29: *American Bookman* 69:104–105 March 1929 (Herbert Gorman).

E151 A32: *Criterion* 9:763–69 July 1930 (Herbert Read); *Fortnightly Review* 133: 281–82 February 1930 (Gerald Bullett); *Nation and Athenaeum* 46:462–63, 28 December 1929 (Bonamy Dobree); *Bookman* (London) 77:237–38 January 1930 (St. John Adcock); *Nation* 130:186–87, 12 February 1930 (Clifton Fadiman); *New Republic* 62:23–24, 19 February 1930 (T. S. Matthews); [rev. ed.:] *Commentary* 25:360–61 April 1958 (Dan Jacobson).

E152 A33: *New Republic* 62:23–24, 19 February 1930 (T. S. Matthews).

E153 A35: *Fortnightly Review* 134:856 December 1930 (V. S. Pritchett); *Nation* 132:301–303, 18 March 1931 (Horace Gregory).

E154 A36: *Fortnightly Review* 135:419–20 March 1931 (Richard Church).

E155 A39: *Virginia Quarterly Review* 10:455–59 July 1934 (Edward Wagenknecht); *New Statesman* 5:389, 25 March 1933 (G. W. Stonier); *Fortnightly Review* 139:676–77 May 1933 (Arthur Waugh).

E156 A42: *New Statesman* 7:733–34, 12 May 1934 (Peter Quennell); *Nation* 138:679–80, 13 June 1934 (Mary McCarthy); *Spectator* 152:714, 4 May 1934 (Graham Greene); *Fortnightly Review* 142: 127–28 July 1934 (L. A. G. Strong); *New Republic* 79:245, 11 July 1934 (Rolfe Humphries); *Classical Journal* 30:366–69 March 1935 (D. C. Woodworth).

E157 A43: *Spectator* 153:732, 9 November 1934 (William Plomer); *New Statesman* 8:690, 692, 10 November 1934 (Peter Quennell); *Saturday Review of Literature* 11:601, 6 April 1935 (Elmer Davis); *Nation* 140:424, 10 April 1935 (Mary McCarthy); *New Republic* 82:250, 10 April 1935 (T. S. Matthews); *London Mercury* 31:181–82 December 1934 (Richard Church); *American Mercury* 35:116–17 May 1935 (Laurence Stallings); *Classical Journal* 30:366–69 March 1935 (D. C. Woodworth).

E158 A44: *New Republic* 87:80, 27 May 1936 (T. S. Matthews).

E159 A46: *London Mercury* 35:84 November 1936 (Richard Church).

E160 A47: *New Statesman* 15:659–60, 16 April 1938 (V. S. Pritchett); *Nation* 147:698, 24 December 1938 (Mary McCarthy); *Classical Review* 52:198 November 1938 (J. M. Hussey).

E161 A48: *London Mercury* 39:215–16 December 1938 (Edwin Muir); *Cambridge Review* 60:332–33, 21 April 1939 (J. Bronowski); *Kenyon Review* 2:100–103 Winter 1940 (John Gould Fletcher).

E162 A51: *New Statesman* 20:290–91, 21 September 1940 (George Orwell); *Saturday Review of Literature* 23:5, 2 November 1940 (Stephen Vincent Benet); *Catholic World* 152:523–30 February 1941 (Charles Willis Thompson).

E163 A52: *Times Literary Supplement*, 16 November 1940, pp. 578, 584; *Spectator* 165:644, 13 December 1940 (D. W. Brogan); *Saturday Review of Literature* 24:5, 18,31 May 1941 (Crane Brinton); *American Sociological Review* 6:923 December 1941 (A. M. Lee); *American Historical Review* 47:413 January 1942 (G. T. Hankin); *Foreign Affairs* 20:384 January 1942 (R. G. Woolbert).

E164 A55: *Times Literary Supplement*, 12 June 1943, p. 283.

E165 A57: *Classical Review* 59:78–79 December 1945 (J. R. Bacon).

E166 A58: *Poetry* 70:98–102 May 1947 (Robert Liddell Lowe).

E167 A61: *Nation* 167:438–39, 16 October 1948 (Robert Fitzgerald); *Hudson Review* 2:133–38 Spring 1949 (Joseph Bennett); *Poetry* 73:362–64 March 1949 (Stanley Edgar Hyman); *Archaeology* 2:56 Spring 1949 (George E. Mylonas).

E168 A63: *Listener* 42:637, 13 October 1949 (Geoffrey Grigson).

E169 A69: *Interpretation* 9:102–105 January 1955 (C. F. Nesbitt).

E170 A71: *Spectator*, 11 March 1955, p. 298 (Kingsley Amis); *Classical Journal* 53:248–49 1958 (Kevin Herbert).

E171 A72: *Twentieth Century* 157:454–61 May 1955 (M. J. C. Hodgart and S. J. Papastavrou); *Classical Review* n.s. 5:208–09 June 1955 (H. J. Rose); *Classical Journal* 51:191–92 January 1956 (Kevin Herbert); *Gnomon* 28:553–55 1956 (Karl Kerényi); *Sewanee Review* 64:498–507 Summer 1956 (C. M. Bowra); *Phoenix* 12:15–25 Spring 1958 (Jay Macpherson).

E172 A73: *New York Times Book Review*, 10 July 1955, p. 3 (Horace Gregory); *New Yorker* 31:67, 30 July 1955 (Louise

Bogan); *Poetry* 87:175–79 December 1955 (Richard Wilbur); *Nation* 181:516, 10 December 1955 (John Ciardi).

E173 A75: *Saturday Review of Literature* 39:9–10, 28 July 1956 (Horace Gregory); *Virginia Quarterly Review* 32:635–37 Autumn 1956 (Douglas Bush).

E174 A79: *Phoenix* 11:183 Winter 1957 (D. M. Shepherd); *Latomus* 16:714 October 1957 (F. Duysinx); *Classical Review* 8:83–84 March 1958 (E. J. Kenney); *Classical Journal* 53:285–87 1958 (Roy A. Swanson); *ClassicalWorld* 51:244 May 1958 (M. V. T. Wallace).

E175 A80: *Latomus* 16:714 October 1957 (F. Duysinx); *English Historical Review* 73:340–41 April 1958 (A. R. Burn); *Classical Review* 8:286–87 December 1958 (G. B. Townend); *Classical Journal* 53:285–87 1958 (Roy A. Swanson); *Classical World* 51:243–44 May 1958 (Arthur Stanley Pease).

E176 A81: *Church Quarterly Review* 159:123–25 January–March 1958 (H. H. Hoskins).

E177 A83: *Encounter* 9:83–84 November 1957 (Graham Hough).

E178 A84: *New York Times Book Review*, 23 March 1958, p. 26 (T. S. Matthews); *Saturday Review* 41:28, 29 March 1958 (Moses Hadas).

E179 A87: *Times Literary Supplement*, 5 June 1959, p. 336.

E180 A89: *New York Times Book Review*, 8 November 1959 p. 50 (Dudley Fitts); *Nation* 189:424, 5 December 1959 (George Steiner); *New Republic* 142:16, 25 January 1960 (Richmond Lattimore); *Guardian*, 11 March 1960, p. 7 (Louis MacNeice); *Spectator*, 18 March 1960, p. 399 (Matthew Hodgart); *New Statesman* 59:409, 19 March 1960 (W. B. Stanford); *London Magazine* 7:66 June 1960 (Rex Warner); *Classical World* 53:157–62 February 1960 (P. C. Wilson); *Classical Journal* 57:281–82 March 1962 (John E. Rexine).

E181 A93: *New Statesman* 61:958, 16 June 1961 (Donald Davie); *Poetry* 100:104–20 May 1962 (Charles Tomlinson).

E182 A95: *New Republic* 145:24, 7 August 1961 (Richmond Lattimore); *Poetry* 100:305–309 August 1962 (Ernest Sandeen).

E183 A98: *Classical World* 56:22 October 1962 (Frank O. Copley).

E184 A101: *Poetry* 103:318–19 February 1964 (James Dickey).

E185 A105: *Reporter* 30:45, 9 April 1964 (Moses Hadas).

APPENDIX I

THE AUSTRALIAN SCHOOL EDITION OF
LAWRENCE AND THE ARABS

The Australian National Bibliography for 1942 contains the following entry:

> Graves, Robert von Ranke. Lawrence and the Arabs: concise ed. prepared by W. T. Hutchins: portrait sketches by Evelyn Faulds, and a map. (Longmans, 3s.) pp. x, 154 sm. 80. Lond., [Melb.], 1942.

This book is obviously not the same as A26e, pp. xii, 180, London, 1940; if it exists, it should be A26f. The National Library of Australia, which is a copyright depository library, has no copy of it. The publishers confirm its existence; but so far efforts to locate a copy have failed.

APPENDIX II

EUROPEAN EDITIONS IN ENGLISH

A42   *I, Claudius.* Hamburg: Albatross, 1935. Albatross Modern Continental Library no. 266. 1938[4]; 1941[5].

A43   *Claudius the God.* Hamburg: Albatross, 1935. Albatross Modern Continental Library no. 290. 1936[2]; 1939[3].

A46   *Antigua, Penny, Puce.* Leipzig: Albatross, 1937. Albatross Modern Continental Library no. 335.

A47   *Count Belisarius.* Leipzig: Albatross, 1939. Albatross Modern Continental Library no. 393.

A62   *Seven Days in New Crete.* Stuttgart: Tauchnitz, 1952. Tauchnitz Edition, n.s. 110.

C285A [Letter in reply to review of *The Gold Falcon.*] *New York Times Book Review*, 5 November, p. 24. Review by Edith H. Walton, 3 September, p. 6.

C290A [Letter from Deyá.] *Focus I*, January 1935, pp. 4–5.

C290B [Letter from Deyá.] *Focus II*, February–March 1935, pp. 12–15.

C290C [Letter from Deyá.] *Focus III*, April–May 1935, pp. 23–28.

C290D [Letter from Deyá.] *Focus IV*, December 1935, pp. 29–3

C290E *Majorcan Letter, 1935. [With Laura Riding.] *Focus IV*, December 1935, pp. 1–9.

C290F *Christmas. *Focus IV*, December 1935, pp. 18–19.

C290G Robert's 'Likes'. *Focus IV*, December 1935, pp. 40–42.

C727A The Sacred Mushroom-Trance. *Story* 140 : 6–13 May–June 1963.

Reprinted from A97.

C748A The Inner World. *Greek Heritage* 1 : 46–47 Spring 1964.

Reprinted from D31.

D4 This collection has been pur chased by Southern Illinois University, Carbondale.

Titles of books are in italics; poems are starred; prose appears in quotation marks; other entries are conventional. Section E is not indexed.

Kenner, Hugh, C498
Kennington, Eric, A26a–b, d; B2
'Kensington Gardens to Looking Glass Land', C189
Kenyon Review, C661, 740
Kerenyi, Karl, D82
Kiddell-Monroe, Joan, A91b
'Kill Them! Kill Them!' A78, 84, 106
King Jesus, A59; D2
' "King Jesus",' C331–32, 335
★The Kingfisher's Return, A16; C182
★The King's Son, C5
Kipling, Rudyard, A63; B14
★The Kiss, A4, 6, (48); C67. V. ★Fragment
★Kit Logan and Lady Helen, A6; C98
Knopf, Alfred A., A3b–c, 5b, 6b, 7a, 8b, 14b
★The Knowledge of God, A10, 23, 24, (48); C175
Knox, Ann Allnutt, C239
Knox, E. V., C268
Korda, Alexander, D1
Krutch, Joseph Wood, C151
'Kynge Arthur Is Nat Dede', A75; C467
'La Belle Dame Sans Merci', A7
★La Mejicana, A107, 114
Lacey, Mildred Lockwood, A90
★Lack, A101, 114
Ladies Home Journal, C678, 741
★Lady Student: A Study in Norman Influences, C107, 109
★The Lady Visitor in the Pauper Ward, A2, 3; C42, 49
★Lament for Pasiphaë, A57, 58, 60, 73, 83, 85, 87, 95, 114
★Lament in December, C20
★Lamia in Love, A107, 114
Land and Water, C50, 52, 54–55, 64, 78
★The Land[s] of Whipperginny, A8, 23, 24, 48, 56, 60, 73, 83, 84, 87, 95, 114; C124
★Landscape, A33, 36. V. ★Nature's Lineaments
Lane, Allen, A42f
Lane, John, B20
Langland, Joseph, B60
'The Language as Spoken', A86; C439
'The Language of Myth', C372
★Language of the Seasons, A58, 60, 73, 83, 85, 87, 95, 114; B30; D11
Laraçuen, Aemilia, A113
★Largesse to the Poor, A37, 40, 48, 60
Larousse Encyclopedia of Mythology, B49
Lars Porsena, A21, 65; C225; D58

'L'Arte della Pittura', A7
★The Last Day of Leave, A60, 73, 85, 87, 95; C342
The Last Pharisee, B47
★A Last Poem, A107, 114; C754
★The Last Post, A2, 3, 23, 24; C40, 43, 49
'The Lasting Echoes of the Kaiser's War', C751
★A Late Arrival, A107; C726
★The Laugh, A93, 95, 114; C674, 681
★The Laureate, A48, 50, 60, 73, 83, 85, 87, 94, 95, 114; B27. V. ★The Wretch
Laurel-Leaf Library, A91c, 102c
Lawrence, A. W., B26, 58
Lawrence, T. E., A7, 14, 26, 49; B26, 58; C112, 260–63, 292, 451, 728; D105
Lawrence and the Arabian Adventure, A26; D47, 59; App. I
Lawrence and the Arabs, A26; D47, 59; App. I
'Lawrence of Arabia as a Buck Private', A26; C261
'Lawyer's Tale, C126. V. ★Richard Roe and John Doe
'The Laying-On of Hands', A7
Le Morte d'Arthur, B57
'The Leaden Age of Bullfighting', C625
★The Leap, A107, 114; C740
'Leave, 1915', C298
★Leaving the Rest Unsaid, A48, 68, 73, 83, 85, 87, 95, 114; C400, 412; D10
★Leda, A48, 60, 73, 85, 87, 95, 114
Lee, Dorothy, C541–42
Lees, W. John, A103
The Left Heresy in Literature and Life, B29
Left Review, C291
'Legends of the Bible', A86, 90; C556
'Legends of the Jews', C556
★The Legion, A23, 24, 48
'Legitimate Criticism of Poetry', A84, 86
★The Legs, A37, 40, 48, 50, 60, 73, 83, 85, 87, 94, 95, 114; D16
Lehmann, John, B20
Leicester Galleries, B2
Lenard, Alexander, B66
Les Annales politiques et littéraires, C295
The Less Familiar Nursery Rhymes, A27
★A Letter: Richard Rolls to His Friend, Captain Abel Wright, C216. V. ★A Letter from Wales

326